OTHER TITLES BY SAM M. INTRATOR

Teaching with Fire: Poetry That Sustains the Courage to Teach

Stories of the Courage to Teach: Honoring the Teacher's Heart

*Tuned In and Fired Up: How Teaching Can Inspire
Real Learning in the Classroom*

LIVING THE QUESTIONS

LIVING THE QUESTIONS

*Essays Inspired by
the Work and Life of
Parker J. Palmer*

Sam M. Intrator, Editor

JOSSEY-BASS
A Wiley Imprint
www.josseybass.com

Published by Jossey-Bass
A Wiley Imprint
989 Market Street, San Francisco, CA 94103-1741
www.josseybass.com

Jossey-Bass books and products are available through most bookstores. To contact Jossey-Bass directly call our Customer Care Department within the U.S. at 800-956-7739, outside the U.S. at 317-572-3986, or fax 317-572-4002.

Jossey-Bass also publishes its books in a variety of electronic formats. Some content that appears in print may not be available in electronic books.

Library of Congress Cataloging-in-Publication Data

Living the questions: essays inspired by the work and life of Parker J. Palmer / Sam M. Intrator, editor.—1st ed.
    p. cm.
  Includes bibliographical references.
  ISBN 0-7879-6554-5 (alk. paper)
  1. Palmer, Parker J. 2. Christian life. 3. Spiritual life—Christianity. I. Palmer, Parker J. II. Intrator, Sam M.
BV4501.3.L59 2005
230'.96'092—dc22   2004024485

Printed in the United States of America
FIRST EDITION
HB Printing   10 9 8 7 6 5 4 3 2 1

CONTENTS

Preface   xi
    Diana Chapman Walsh

Gratitudes   xv

A Journey of Questions: xvii
    The Life and Work of Parker J. Palmer

"THIS LIVE ENCOUNTER"   1

Chapter One   Now I Become Myself   5

Notions of Presence   8
    Chip Wood

Learning by Heart: An Ode to My Vocation as a Teacher   20
    Marianne Novak Houston

Insights on the Inner Life of Healers   30
    Henry Emmons, M.D.

Late Openings?   42
    David J. Maitland

What Sound Does the Soul Make?   52
    Mary Rose O'Reilley

Chapter Two   Be Not Afraid   57

Thinking Ourselves Home: The Cultivation of Wisdom   60
    Dawna Markova

Because of My Not Knowing   73
    Mark Nepo

The Courage to Learn   82
    Thomas F. Beech

Learning from the Workplace: Professional Life as an
Opportunity for Personal Growth   89
  Jane Tompkins

The True Professional   98
  Margaret J. Wheatley

MOVING THE HEART
TO THE CENTER   103

_____

Chapter Three   Learning in Community   107

Crossing the Great Divides: The Power of Radio to Connect
People Across Boundaries   110
  Jean Feraca

Integrating Life and Thought: As Teacher, Student,
Colleague, Friend   120
  Bardwell Smith

Wholeness in Science and Personal Life   131
  Ian G. Barbour

Living the Night into Day: A Response to Dark Times   146
  Joel Elkes, M.D.

Soul and Role, Politicians and Politics   152
  W. Douglas Tanner Jr.

Chapter Four   Opening Space for the Inner Life   163

"How Can I Keep from Singing?": Seeking the Wisdom of Sound 166
  Shirley H. Showalter

The Threads We Follow   183
  Marcy Jackson and Rick Jackson

The Lehrergarten: A Vision for Teacher Education   197
  Sally Z. Hare

The Inner and Outer Life in Medicine: Honoring Values,
Relationships, and the Human Element in Physicians' Lives   210
  Paul Batalden, M.D. and David C. Leach, M.D.

A Journey of the Heart: Seeking the Questions Worth Living 219
  Douglas Orr

TRUE SELF UNLEASHED 227

Chapter Five Leading from Within 231

Turning Toward a New Leadership 234
Jay Casbon

On Philanthropy and the Inner Life 243
Michael Lerner

It Also Takes Courage to Lead 256
Russ S. Moxley

If We Pay Attention 270
L. J. Rittenhouse

Inspiring Communities of Caring and Conscience 281
David Dodson

Chapter Six Rescuing the Sacred 289

Take This to Heart 292
Zalman M. Schachter-Shalomi

How Then Shall We Live? Suffering and Wonder in
the New Commons 298
Sharon Daloz Parks

On Beyond Revenge: Leadership for Peace 309
Diana Chapman Walsh

A World Shaped by Choice 322
Peter M. Senge

Parker J. Palmer Resources and Bibliography 331

The Editor 341

The Contributors 343

Credits 349

PREFACE

WHAT KIND OF WORLD COULD WE CREATE together on this earth if we were able to speak to and hear one another from our deepest yearnings and our most heartfelt concerns and dreams?

What if we could sit together in circles of honesty and trust, sit in stillness, welcome silence, be patient, discover wonder and mutual gratitude, learn together, and gradually build new confidence in our ability to create spaces in which to hear and speak our unique stories and find our common truths? What if we could learn to listen, and let our lives speak?

The contributors to this volume honoring Parker J. Palmer have, in his presence and through the remarkable corpus of his work, experienced firsthand the resilience of the human spirit (our own and others') and the deep reservoir of improbable hope that can emerge from the "circles of trust" into which he has invited us and taught us the disciplines to replicate.

Disciplines they are. Make no mistake about that. This work is anything but superficial New Age affirmation. Don't expect to find comfortable simplifications here. Parker's work is the culmination of years of rigorous intellectual labor through which he has now hacked his way into that rare and spacious clearing aspired to by the jurist Oliver Wendell Holmes: the "simplicity on the far side of complexity."

Parker speaks for himself far more eloquently than any of the rest of us could hope to speak for him; nor would we presume to try. Among other deterrents, we would be violating a cardinal rule of his. We'd be crashing through the woods, invading his sacred space. Specifically, the invitation to contribute an essay for this celebratory volume explicitly "entreated" prospective authors to "focus on ideas and perspectives central to your own stance and vocation," and thereby indirectly (rather than overtly) acknowledge the impact of Parker Palmer and his work. The editor, the publisher, and the honoree himself were united in this vision of the project, we were gently told, lest we be tempted to stray.

We *were* asked to orient around the central themes of Parker's work, and to reflect on how remaining attentive to our inner lives has been vital to sustaining and informing our creative work in the diverse worlds in which we serve. Although they are not a group generally given to defiance of authority, the authors found themselves in the awkward position of chafing against the instruction, so firm and elegant, that we speak only briefly of our debt to Parker Palmer. Hence the mini-essays at the head of each chapter in which the author is granted just a modicum of space to voice a personal debt to this man we so revere.

Parker's books have introduced hundreds of thousands of readers to his vision for a better world, beginning in the only place any of us has the power to begin (or end): with our own identity and integrity, our own evolving lives. His readers are captivated, as are we all, by the authenticity that shines through his writing and by his distinctive blend of pragmatism and poetry. He sees the world without illusion, appraises it analytically, penetrates its paradoxes, knows its dark underside, and understands the shadows all too well.

Yet, as a teacher at heart, he trusts that knowledge can set us free—but only a particular kind of knowledge, one that sustains connections and affirms life. "A knowledge that springs from love," he writes in *The Courage to Teach*,[1] "will implicate us in the web of life; it will wrap the knower and the known in compassion, in a bond of awesome responsibility as well as transforming joy; it will call us to involvement, mutuality, accountability."

Ultimately, then, this book is a study of involvement, mutuality, accountability. It is that, and a labor of love. It honors a person and a process, and it emanates from the process that the person has shaped, defined, refined, tested, and articulated. The book itself is a product of the circle of trust to which it bears witness.

Indeed, it emerged quite literally from a circle of trust, a retreat at the Fetzer Institute at which twenty-five of the authors gathered with Parker and Sharon Palmer and representatives of Jossey-Bass in July 2003 to share aspirations and struggles with writing essays for the book. In addition to a number of preexisting connections between members of the group, all were connected through Parker and ultimately through a powerful vocational thread we wove as we talked. We brought bulletins from the front about what it means to do this work of integrating head and heart, the work of leading from within. Finding appropriate words was the biggest part of the challenge we faced. "We really don't know that much about anything," Parker confessed at the outset. "So we might as well take off our masks and join others in our vulnerability." Someone else observed how "cruel" and competitive the world of academia can be, but adding that when it comes down to it "we haven't got time to be anything but tender to each other." Parker spoke of having as a college student been given "the grace and space to see something that I didn't fully understand then, but something, nonetheless, that I was able to take out into the world"—

and to take it out with "the gratitude for which there is no way to say thank you other than to pass it along."

He gave us the space and grace over that three-day period to incubate the stories that this book now takes out into the world and passes along. Each of us was allocated ten to twelve minutes with the full group to use however we wished. Members of the group were asked to listen with the noninvasive discipline Parker teaches for clearness committees, attending for sincere and deep questions that might be useful, simply jotting them down, and passing them along at the end for the writer to use or not, at his or her discretion.

This book, like the work, is rooted in the world of education even as it transcends that world. It is rooted in the American experience and the goal Jacob Needleman identifies as lying "at the heart of the idea of democracy in its uniquely American form . . . bringing people together under the guidance of conscience."[2] And yet, it transcends that world too and expands outward what is possible to conceive for humankind.

Closing the second afternoon of the writers' retreat, Parker expressed to a small group (a former investment banker, a business consultant, a publisher, and a political advisor) how proud he was to have their lives and their work represented in the book. "Each of you," he observed, "has redeemed a whole arena of work in my mind, areas which, if I didn't know you and a few others, I would find so alienating and frightening. I want to honor all of you for that, and I want to hold the mystery. I could never have imagined that what I write from the comfort of my home could help people stand tall in worlds that would mow me down. To know that I can be there through my words and vicariously through your lives is a writer's great privilege. I used to feel that it was a kind of hypocrisy, but that was before I understood the ecology of vocation."

As the poet Mary Oliver (one of Parker's favorites) watched creatures in nature going about their work—a grasshopper, an ant, a snake, a flock of wild geese—she composed a kind of elegy to the ecology of vocation, to the reality that each of us has a special place in the natural order and to the mystery that each of us, in our small way, is making a profound and indispensable contribution to the whole.[3] The contributors to this book are living that mystery, and with it a tension between darkness and light. On the one hand, many of us sense that we are entering a period of great danger. On the other, we still harbor an innate belief in the miracle of hope.

At the end of our time together, Parker read us the passage by Leonard Cohen with which he opens his latest book, *A Hidden Wholeness*: "The blizzard of the world / has crossed the threshold / and it has overturned / the order of the soul."[4] Our task now, Parker suggested, is no less than to "reestablish the threshold of our humanity," to hold the blizzard at bay so that others may rediscover their souls. "This is not a dream wish," he added, invoking our time together. "I've experienced it too often to believe that it is anything but real."

If there is a unitary message the writers in this volume seek to convey, it is the belief that we can find our way again. It is also the warning that time is short. We write at once with conviction, uncertainty, and urgency. We write with gratitude, humility, and love.

DIANA CHAPMAN WALSH
Wellesley, Massachusetts
February 2005

NOTES

1. Palmer, P. J. *The Courage to Teach*. San Francisco: Jossey-Bass, 1998, p. 32.

2. Needleman, J. *The American Soul: Rediscovering the Wisdom of the Founders*. New York: Tarcher, 2002, p. 25.

3. Oliver, M. "Song of the Builders." In *Why I Wake Early*. Boston: Beacon Press, 2004.

4. Cohen, L. "The Future." 1992 by Sony Music Entertainment.

GRATITUDES

ON THE LAST PAGE in the last chapter of Parker Palmer's *The Courage to Teach*, there is a line that I have highlighted with uncommon vigor: "Some of us may learn that conventional rewards pale as we experience the satisfaction of living by our best lights." As I knit the final strands of this project together—a volume that includes thirty-two authors drawn from far-flung disciplines, generations, and professions—I have come to believe that this line, more than any other, evokes the question woven through this volume: How do we live, both alone and together, by our best lights?

Our answers arc broadly across the disciplines, professions, and faiths. What should one expect? We are physicians, university presidents, physicists, teachers, clergy, and more; our contributions to this volume embody our diverse world. Yet we also gather in common cause, which is to pay tribute to Parker J. Palmer the teacher, the writer, and our cherished friend. On behalf of our authors: thank you, Parker, for moving us closer to understanding what it takes to live a life by "our best lights."

Elizabeth V. Spelman has written a book, *Repair: The Impulse to Restore in a Fragile World*, on our human impulse to mend, improve, repair, and minister to that which needs tending. *Living the Questions* owes so much to Megan Scribner, a gifted and expert editor whose capacity to fix, repair, and tend to writing and writers refines this human impulse to rare heights. For her insight, her friendship, and her unflagging good humor I am profoundly grateful. She is marvelous at what she does.

If Megan's gift is to hone and improve what has already been created, then her counterpart in my life and in this work is Rick Jackson, the codirector of the Center for Teacher Formation, whose uncanny ability to make things happen and put "wheels on ideas" guided this book from inception to production. Resourceful and gently tenacious, Rick is an extraordinary leader and a man I passionately admire. Marcy Jackson's grace and grounded, wise presence helped keep me and this project moving forward.

Anybody who has been in the Palmer home knows that Sharon Palmer is a quilter extraordinaire. The landscape quilts that hang throughout the house are breathtaking in their intricacy and beauty. I can also attest that her quilting skills carry *far* beyond these tapestries. She has worked tirelessly and with great love to help weave all the details together and to keep the project moving. Thank you, Sharon.

A special thanks to a loosely joined cadre of advisors to this project who participated in a number of critical conversations that helped coalesce the organization of the book: Becky van der Bogert, Jay Casbon, Rob Kunzman, Mark Nepo, Mike Poutiatine, and Diana Chapman Walsh. Your understanding of Parker and his work helped shape the contours of the volume. Also making important contributions to the ideas at the center of the book and providing indispensable support around the logistics of organizing the project were Tracey Denlinger and Robin Gaphni from the Center for Teacher Formation.

As with anything I've ever written (with the exception of those teenage years), I give thanks to my Mom, Anna Intrator, for her keen eye as a reader and her unfailing sense for what's real and what's not.

I also thank Tom Beech, Mickey Olivanti, David Sluyter, and the staff at the Fetzer Institute for their support. The commitment of the Institute has been instrumental in both advancing Parker's work and supporting this volume.

The Jossey-Bass team combines utter professionalism with passionate regard for the human dimensions of the project. Sheryl Fullerton, the executive editor of the Religion in Practice Series, worked with me at every stage of the process. She knows Parker's work as deeply as anybody I'm aware of, and her questions unflaggingly invited deeper clarity. A special thank you to Andrea Flint for guiding this complex book to press. Thank you to the rest of the skilled and thoughtful Jossey-Bass team: Catherine Craddock, Tom Finnegan, Chandrika Madhavan, Sandy Siegle, Karen Warner, and Danna West.

At Morgan Hall in Northampton, Massachusetts, much of this book was assembled. Thank you to Christine Barbuto and my colleagues for your questions and support. To Emily Freeman Daniels for her thoughtful help in compiling the bibliography.

Parker's book *Let Your Life Speak* has special meaning in my house. I belong to three "lives" who speak with uncommon energy. To Casey, Kaleigh, and Jake: I am so proud to be your father. To my wife, Jo-Anne, your support and steady strength make so much possible for all of us.

A Journey of Questions:
The Life and Work of
Parker J. Palmer

Sam M. Intrator

I AM A TEACHER, a father, a husband, a writer, a baseball coach, and much more. My life, like those of so many of my colleagues and fellow citizens, moves quickly and is full of demands, complexities, and expectations. And I get the sense that most people—mothers and fathers, lawyers and teachers, policemen and stockbrokers—are running hard, trying to provide for their families, keep on top of ever-increasing work demands, stay connected to their communities, maintain a semblance of physical vigor, and live up to their ideals of what constitutes a life lived with virtue and honor.

Now nudging forty, I find myself struggling to make everything fit together. In my impatient moments, I'm eager for a quick fix or silver-bullet special: a self-help handbook, a pill, and even some firm finger-wagging advice. In my more shameful times, I hunt around for others to blame. In my better moments, I seek fuller, wiser counsel. I aspire to be in companionship with those who can help me root down to the core of an issue, to shuck away the extraneous and catch clear sight of what really matters. In my own journey toward living a more integrated life, a life in which the gap between my deep beliefs and my actions in the world feels less gaping, I have no wiser teacher and important companion than Parker J. Palmer.

I am not alone in my genuine reverence for this stoop-shouldered, six-foot-three, former-Methodist-turned-Quaker. Parker's books have sold more than a half million copies, and his latest book, *A Hidden Wholeness*, was nominated for a 2005 Pulitzer Prize in the category "distinguished works of nonfiction."[1] In 1998, the Leadership Project, a national survey of ten thousand administrators and faculty, named Parker J. Palmer one of the thirty "most influential senior leaders" in higher education and one of the ten key "agenda setters" of the decade, noting that "he has inspired a generation of teachers and reformers with evocative visions of community, knowing, and

Parker J. Palmer, 2003

spiritual wholeness."[2] He has been the recipient of numerous awards including eight honorary doctorates and several lifetime achievement awards.

The breadth of his accomplishments and the reach of his influence is all the more remarkable because of his independent standing as a "traveling teacher" who, for nearly twenty years, has been unattached to any institution. A writer, lecturer, and workshop leader known early in his career primarily in a relatively small circle of campus ministers and progressive religious educators, Parker through his work has moved forcefully past boundaries and into the mainstream—evoking the imagination of people in an astonishing range of disciplines and professions including public school teachers, physicians, college administrators, lawyers, clergy, philanthropists, and corporate executives. In a typical year Parker gives at least one hundred talks, workshops, and retreats.

In honor of Parker's sixty-fifth year, the idea of this volume was born. Our intent is to celebrate Parker's remarkable achievements not by producing a classic *festschrift,* a book in which authors pay homage to the individual being honored, but by extending and advancing the conversation of the themes that have been at the heart of Parker's writing and teaching: the shape of an integral life; the meaning of community, teaching, and learning for transformation; and nonviolent social change. In this spirit, I have worked closely with Parker to assemble the roster of thirty-two authors who contributed to this project. The wide range of professions, disciplines, and generations represented in this roster is testament to the stunningly broad reach of Parker's work.

Here is a sampling of the wonderful diversity of our authors: college presidents, physicians, poets, clergy, scientists, public school teachers, philanthropic foundation presidents, business consultants, community organizers, and an elementary school principal. Three of the authors taught Parker when he was an undergraduate. Others know him from his decade-long service to a Quaker retreat center; from his work with public school teachers over the last ten years; or from his lectures, workshops, and writings. While drawn from far-flung fields, this circle of authors is held together by the belief that there is a critical intersection between the inner life and the external, active life of the world.

The questions these authors address focus on the concerns at the heart of Parker's work. Our hope is that their essays will illuminate Parker's long-time quest to understand how the journey of the spirit animates the questions we ask within our institutions and communities:

- How can we be who we truly are in settings that unceasingly pressure us to be something or somebody else?

- How can we create spaces and communities that welcome the soul?

- How, in a harried, often-violent world, do we advance change that honors the soul and nurtures community?

Every essay in *Living the Questions* is prefaced by a mini-essay written by the contributor briefly describing his or her relationship to Parker the teacher, the writer, the man. More than any single tribute to the wisdom, compassion, and compelling presence of Parker, these narratives evoke a fuller portrait: loving, accessible, wise, vulnerable, perceptive, honest, and heart-achingly funny. The following is just a taste.

From Shirley H. Showalter, president of Goshen College:

> I love to hear Parker laugh. When he does, for a split second the universe opens up and swallows all kinds of dichotomies. He is always

pointing us not to himself but to "the great thing," the subject. Behind everything he writes I hear inaudible music.

From Paul Batalden, a doctor of pediatrics at Dartmouth Medical School:

Parker has helped me make sense of what I do as a teacher and as a physician deeply committed to forming and developing health professionals at all stages of their lives. Parker and I have laughed together. We have struggled together as we searched for our truths. He has taught me to appreciate poetry and the artistry of careful words. He has helped me appreciate the value of stillness and silence in the midst of busyness and noise. I deeply respect him and value his friendship.

From Doug Orr, president of Warren Wilson College:

Parker's first intersection with my life's journey began when he was speaker at the Presidents' Institute of the 1993 Council of Independent Colleges and recipient of the CIC Outstanding Service Award. He was being recognized for his significant contributions to independent liberal arts colleges.

In the course of his address, Parker, in his vintage self-deprecating humor, recounted his earlier Outward Bound experience of being frozen in place as he was perched precariously on the side of a cliff during one of the program's challenging "rappelling" exercises—a metaphorical perch that college presidents know all too well. After interminable nervous frozen moments, Parker recalled being asked by staff members on the ground, "Is anything wrong?" and replying in a high, squeaky voice, "I don't want to talk about it." As a fellow Outward Bound graduate, and one who gained profound teaching and learning lessons through the experience, I was determined to get to know this kindred spirit.

In subsequent years, his writing, teaching, friendship, and gentle poetic spirit have repeatedly inspired my own life and work.

As I read through these impassioned personal tributes to Parker, I am struck by the consistent admiration for his courage and determination to live a life congruent with the ideas and principles he writes and talks about. He himself is fond of quoting the great jazz saxophonist Charlie Parker, "If it's not in your heart, it's not in your horn." The intertwining of "heart and horn" as they play out across Parker Palmer's life is the focus of this introduction.

In preparation for my writing this essay, Parker invited me to spend several days with him and his wife Sharon at their home in Madison, Wiscon-

Parker rappelling at Hurricane Island Outward Bound, 1979

sin. We were joined by our friends Rick and Marcy Jackson, the twosome who have worked so seamlessly with Parker in their role as codirectors of the Center for Teacher Formation. There were many moving and uproarious moments in the almost thirty hours of conversation I recorded.[3] But none was more poignant to me than when I asked Parker to describe the intersection of his life with the poem "The Woodcarver" by the fourth century B.C. Taoist teacher Chuang Tzu. Parker writes about this story in his first book, *The Promise of Paradox: A Celebration of Contradictions in the Christian Life,* and it appears in every one of his six other books. I have never been in a workshop with Parker when he has not used this poem to help create a space in which people can talk to each other about the issues at the center of their lives.

Parker responded to my request by saying, "For a long time, this poem has been a template for my life. It is a story I have tried to live into, though not always successfully, about a character with whom I've had many inner conversations." After a pause, Parker began reciting "The Woodcarver" by heart.

THE WOODCARVER

Khing, the master carver, made a bell stand
Of precious wood. When it was finished,
All who saw it were astounded. They said it must be
The work of spirits.
The Prince of Lu said to the master carver:
"What is your secret?"

Khing replied: "I am only a workman:
I have no secret. There is only this:
When I began to think about the work you commanded
I guarded my spirit, did not expend it
On trifles, that were not to the point.
I fasted in order to set
My heart at rest.
After three days fasting,
I had forgotten gain and success.
After five days
I had forgotten praise or criticism.
After seven days
I had forgotten my body
With all its limbs.

"By this time all thought of your Highness
And of the court had faded away.
All that might distract me from the work
Had vanished.
I was collected in the single thought
Of the bell stand.

"Then I went to the forest
To see the trees in their own natural state.
When the right tree appeared before my eyes,
The bell stand also appeared in it, clearly, beyond doubt.
All I had to do was to put forth my hand
and begin.

"If I had not met this particular tree
There would have been
No bell stand at all.

"What happened?
My own collected thought
Encountered the hidden potential in the wood;

From this live encounter came the work
Which you ascribe to the spirits."

—Chuang Tzu[4]

Stanza by stanza Parker sifted through this poem, using it as a kaleidoscope to refract portions of his life. The moment that left us all hushed occurred while Parker was thinking through the exchange between the Prince and the master carver: "What is your secret?" "I am only a workman. I have no secret." This moved Parker to describe his own vocation: "My work has taken many forms. But very simply, I am a teacher. I think that the most deeply true words I've ever written are the first few words in *The Courage to Teach*: 'I am a teacher at heart. . . .' I rewrote that opening line a hundred times, but I finally got it right."

That he did. As I combed through Parker's writings; interviewed a range of colleagues, friends, and students; and spoke to many others who knew Parker only through his writing and speaking, what emerged was a portrait of a teacher: a teacher at heart and of the heart—a traveling teacher whose "secret" has been and continues to be his ability to create hospitable space in his writing, his talking, and his teaching for those of us trying to ask questions about our life's journey and discover a little more about ourselves and our world.

Classically trained at the University of California at Berkeley to be a sociologist, Parker J. Palmer has been blown by the winds of his vocational journey far off the standard academic sailing lanes. After finishing his doctorate, Parker left the academy, and to this day jokingly calls himself a "recovering sociologist." For nearly four decades Parker has devoted himself to exploring issues of fundamental importance: what factors distort and wound our souls and how can we develop ways of living, teaching, and learning together so that we can bring more light and life to the world?

In Parker's latest book, *A Hidden Wholeness,* he begins with an image that evokes a powerful theme coursing through the breadth of his work. He describes how farmers on the Great Plains, at the first signs of a blizzard, would run a rope from the back door of the house out to the barn to serve as a guide for finding their way through the whiteout. As Parker tells us, these farmers all knew stories of people who had been lost in the storm. He then expands the metaphor to encompass the sense so many people have of being lost, disconnected, and afraid. Lost, as in deaf to the life-giving voice of the "inner teacher." Lost, as in lacking the capacity to discern or live out their callings in the world. Lost, as in deprived of the sustenance of community. And lost, as in belonging to a mass society that has degenerated into coarse and brittle ways of being together.

Delivered by a grimmer spokesperson, Parker's diagnosis might leave us quaking at the bleakness of it all. Yet somehow his analysis of the affliction feels more like the tender diagnosis of a healer who understands that healing depends, most of all, on a clear-sighted, precise understanding of the root cause of the affliction. It is an understanding woven together by a man who brings to bear cogent analytic skills honed by his training as a scholar and researcher and softened by the time spent in monasteries and other religious communities—all of which pass through the prism of his life experiences, including several harrowing bouts with clinical depression, which he calls "a school of the spirit in which I have learned more about who I am and who I'm not than at any other time I can think of."[5]

While it is folly to believe that one can precisely summarize the corpus of Parker's work, the three strands that emerge might be understood as follows:

- All human activity emerges from our inwardness, for better or worse. As we work and live, we project the condition of our souls onto our relationships. Sustaining good relationships among those with whom we work and live requires self-knowledge of our inner terrain.

- There are pedagogies and ways of knowing that can invite and welcome the soul and heal the person. For Parker, being a writer who honors the sacred and being a teacher whose practice invites the soul into circles of trust are important life callings.

- The route to enduring social change runs through individuals who join together after making a decision to live with integrity and wholeness. Despite his affection for the monastic life, Parker is a man of action who calls on us to understand the dynamics of social movements and participate in "right action."

These themes weave themselves through the many speeches, essays, poems, and books that Parker has written and are an intellectual project worthy of honor unto themselves. However, one of Parker's most admired gifts and, I believe, one of his most courageous attributes, is his ability to speak and write with great candor about his own struggle to live a life in conversation with his inner beliefs. And particularly appealing is his honesty about his own failures, inadequacies, and shadows. By writing and sharing these, he makes the inner journey less daunting and more inviting to his readers and students.

Henry Emmons, a physician and contributor to this volume, makes this point powerfully in his mini-essay on Parker:

I first encountered Parker Palmer when I read *Let Your Life Speak,* which touched me deeply. It was written with such wisdom, openness, and acceptance. Reading it was like sitting down with a close friend—a really *articulate* friend. He had faced his life, accepted it, and allowed himself to be transformed by it. He gently offered that same possibility to me.

It was refreshing to encounter an author who was so endearingly human. My internal "truth meter" shot way up as I read Parker's words. Later, when I heard him speak, I had the same experience—only more strongly. I felt enlivened as I listened, and I knew it was still possible to work with the soul. Here was someone who was doing it!

The Formative Years

Parker was born in Chicago in 1939 and raised in Wilmette, Illinois, one of the affluent suburbs that make up Chicago's North Shore. His father, Max J. Palmer—who came to Chicago from a blue-collar family in Waterloo, Iowa, seeking work during the Great Depression—taught Parker and his two sisters, Sharon and Susan, that they were "in, but not of, the North

Parker with his sisters, Sharon and Susan,
and their mother, LaVerne Palmer, 1945

Parker dancing in a high school stage play, 1957

Shore." Parker speaks of feeling a bit like an "outlander" in Wilmette, but
with a sense of pride that came from his father's insistence that kindness,
integrity, and a capacity for hard work were far more important than
wealth.

Parker attended public schools and graduated from New Trier High
School in 1957. Though he was an outgoing and popular young person—
chosen by his peers, for example, to be president of the Student Council—
Parker talks about his school years with some ambivalence. He describes
himself as an uninspired but dutiful student, whose desire for solitude, or
the company of one or two special friends, took him out of the social
swirl that was so central to life at New Trier. But several admiring classmates who knew him in high school described him as a special presence
and the "best and the brightest."

When he graduated from high school in 1957, Parker had his mind set
on a two-step career, as attested to by a senior-year interview with him in

the New Trier student newspaper. Having met a Naval Reserve pilot who worked in his father's office, Parker thought his first step after college would be a stint as a Navy aviator. Then—having been asked by his father to help craft language to market some of his company's products—Parker thought a career in advertising would be just right for him.

A voracious extracurricular reader who from a young age took delight in puns and other kinds of wordplay, Parker found advertising and its attention to language alluring. As he says, looking back, "Advertising is about rhetoric, the power of language, animating and motivating people, for better or for worse!" "Park loved language," remembers Charlie Glasser, Parker's best friend during his teenage years. "One of our favorite activities was to go to the movies and sit in the balcony and redo the dialogue ourselves," he told me. "The two of us would be sitting there chattering away making up the dialogue."[6]

According to Charlie, a frequent guest for dinner at the spacious three-story Victorian house, the Palmer home was alive with compelling and lively conversation. Presiding over the give-and-take was Parker's father, whom Parker and Charlie both admired, respected, and deeply enjoyed. "He was a wonderful listener and genuine source of wisdom," Charlie explained. "Even when we were teenagers and thought we knew it all, he was a powerful source of support."[7]

Parker with Charlie Glasser, 2003

Parker and Charlie are good friends to this day. Charlie became president of John F. Kennedy University in California, where he invited Parker to receive an honorary degree at a 1990 graduation ceremony attended by Parker's parents, Max and LaVerne Palmer, who were then in their early eighties. The occasion was especially meaningful according to Charlie because for the first time in the university's history a commencement address received a standing ovation.

Charlie says: "That moment, as much as any I remember across nearly fifty years of friendship, so fully embodies Park's life and gifts. Max and LaVerne were there in the audience; their son was receiving an honorary degree; and I, their 'second son,' was the presiding president. In twenty years of JFK commencements, there had never been a standing ovation. What makes it special is that the students of JFK University are secretaries, insurance salesmen, firefighters—a wonderful cross-section—and Park's great gift has always been finding a way to speak to people of many sorts. He brings wisdom to people's lives."[8]

Many of Parker's most important values find their taproot in his relationship with his father. In an interview with the poet Mark Nepo, Parker describes one dimension of that relationship:

> During the Depression, my Dad took work as a temporary bookkeeper for E.A. Hinrichs & Co., which supplied fine china and silverware to hotels, restaurants, railroads, and airlines. Fifty years later he was the owner and chairman of the board. As he rose in the leadership of that company, he would sit me down every now and then and say: "Now, Park, you've visited our office and our warehouse. You've seen the cartons of china, the delivery trucks, the office building, the desks, the calculating machines, and the typewriters. Someday, when I sell this company, all of that will be considered as our assets."
>
> Then he would say, "But there's going to be another item on our inventory of assets that isn't physical and tangible. The name of that other item is 'good will'—a technical accounting term that represents the reputation you have for doing your work with integrity, coming through on your promises, and treating people decently. And 'good will' is going to have a larger dollar value than all the tangible assets in this company. I've spent many years building up good will for E.A. Hinrichs & Co. because that's where the real value in our business is. I've seen too many people who didn't understand that, who did everything backwards, destroyed good will, and destroyed their company in the process."
>
> I've never forgotten what Dad said about generosity of spirit and the way the world responds to it. But even if "good will" had not helped

Parker's father, Max J. Palmer, 1985

the bottom line, it would still have been important to my father. It simply made him feel good to do business this way.[9]

After Parker graduated from New Trier in, as he says, "the undistinguished middle" of his class, he was accepted at Carleton College in Northfield, Minnesota, a place that he describes as the setting for a major turning in his life. His aspirations for a career in advertising faded as he came under the mentorship of a number of Carleton faculty members, three of whom—Ian Barbour, David Maitland, and Bardwell Smith—have essays in this volume.

Under the tutelage of his Carleton professors, Parker began to find his stride as a student. His grades improved and, demonstrating an adventurous intellectual vitality, he became the first person at Carleton to take on a double major (philosophy and sociology). In reflecting back on those years, Parker says, "As the first person in my family to go to college, it took me a long time to think of myself as having an academic vocation. I came from a business family and, farther back, from a family of skilled craftsmen. I had no sense of myself as an intellectual, and intellectuals scared me."

But at Carleton, encounters with certain faculty members and their spouses began to reshape Parker's horizons. Parker reflects on the dramatic effect these relationships had on him:

> I think the impact that these people of powerful integrity had on my life can be put very simply: I wanted to be like them. I wanted to be like David Maitland, like Ian Barbour, like Bard Smith—not in every detail, but in the essence of who they were. They seemed to me to be good people living good lives to good purpose. They were not trying to impose themselves on me, but they cared about me and they evoked my gifts and my dreams.

By the time Parker graduated, he had been elected to Phi Beta Kappa and awarded a prestigious Danforth Graduate Fellowship. Each year, the Danforth Foundation chose one hundred college seniors who demonstrated both academic excellence and strong religious-ethical convictions

Parker as a freshman at Carleton College, 1958

to receive a grant that would support them through both seminary and a doctoral program.

Receiving the Danforth Fellowship changed Parker's life in several ways. It allowed him to meet Robert Rankin, vice president of the Danforth Foundation, who became one of Parker's most vital mentors, colleagues, and friends. It inspired Parker's confidence in his own potential as a scholar. And it provided helpful financial support for two important decisions: in the summer of 1961, he married Sally Hartley, and in the fall of 1961, he enrolled at Union Theological Seminary in New York City.

First Encounters with Vocation

Parker has written about his time in New York City in *Let Your Life Speak:* "I went from college neither to the navy nor to Madison Avenue but to Union Theological Seminary in New York City, as certain that the ministry was now my calling as I had been a few years earlier about advertising and aviation. So it came as a great shock when, at the end of my first year, God spoke to me—in the form of mediocre grades and massive misery—and informed me that under no conditions was I to become an ordained leader in His or Her church. Always responsive to authority, as one was if raised in the fifties, I left Union and went west, to the University of California at Berkeley."[10]

In the fall of 1962, Parker entered Berkeley's doctoral program in sociology, having become intrigued with the sociology of religion as an undergraduate at Carleton under the guidance of yet another key mentor, William L. Kolb.

An important feature of Parker's Berkeley years was participation in a national project sponsored by the Danforth Foundation called "The Church, the University, and Social Policy," directed by Kenneth Underwood, a well-known sociologist of religion from Wesleyan University. After attending several gatherings of affiliated scholars, Parker was asked to play a key role in the Bay Area Colloquium of the project. Despite being in his mid-twenties, Parker found himself participating in a national network, writing papers, attending seminars, and feeling a sense of belonging that he did not feel within the academic community of Berkeley.

During this time a version of Parker's M.A. thesis was published in a two-volume collection of papers emerging from the Danforth project.[11] His essay "A Typology of World Views" introduced some original thinking about understanding the nature of religious commitment and garnered Parker some acclaim as a rising young scholar. In the introduction to the two-volume work, Kenneth Underwood singled out Parker's work for its imaginative conceptual model. Underwood commended Parker for the range of his intellectual insight and curiosity and then, remarkably, praised him not just for his promise as a writer, but for his contributions to the assembly of Danforth scholars, most of whom were well-established researchers in the field.

Underwood wrote of Parker, "He is as anxious to contribute to a model of the study of the self as he is to take on the past conceptual apparatus of sociology in defining religion. He wishes also to make sure that we see the church and the university not simply in official and operational terms, but as institutions with different missions and embodiments of purpose. Thus, throughout the study, he helped the staff to live in constant awareness of abstractions which are facile in conversation and of the ultimate necessity of locating them in the world of phenomena. He is convinced of the centrality of the study of religious phenomena as a key to all sorts of human behavior, for beliefs have to do with assumptions from which men proceed to live, face death, give meaning to work and leisure."[12]

Forty years later, when he showed me that quote, Parker was clearly energized by the memory of his days with the Danforth project. "Even then," he said, "I was fascinated by themes of self and society and of 'putting wheels on ideas.' " Then Parker read aloud part of the Underwood quote: "He [Parker] is . . . anxious to contribute to a model of the study of the self . . ."

Looking up with a smile of delight, he went on, "Get this! Underwood then quotes my definition of the self, written when I was twenty-five years old: 'An organic entity, constituted by its social and sub-social environments, and by its own creative decision-making faculties.' "[13] After a pause, Parker continued, "What strikes me is that, way back then, my interest in the interaction between self and world was right there—but the prose stinks! It was around that time that one of my professors pointed out just how contorted my writing was, which launched me on a life-long quest to figure out how to write well. And I'm still working on it!"

For Parker, having someone of Underwood's reputation and stature recognize his promise as a scholar was both gratifying and important. He remembers going to scholarly meetings after Underwood's public testimonial to his work and being singled out as "*the* Parker Palmer" that Underwood was always talking about in his travels around the country. In fact, as he recalled, with a twinkle in his eye, "I took a lot of guff about that! But Ken Underwood was a good guy and he very generously promoted my career."

Tagged as an emerging scholar, Parker nonetheless suffered in graduate school. One of the demoralizing features was the way some sociology of religion faculty at Berkeley adhered to what Parker calls a "reductionist, debunking orientation," an approach that clashed with Parker's own sensibilities. Parker decided that he had to leave Berkeley, at least for a while. In explaining the move, he said, "Occasionally, I found myself walking the streets of Berkeley at night, crying because I felt so out of place. I needed to find out if I liked teaching enough to put up with the misery of getting a Ph.D."

So, in 1965, Parker and Sally and their first child, Brent, whom they adopted before they left Berkeley, moved to Beloit College in Wisconsin, at the invitation of his Carleton mentor Bill Kolb, who had become dean of the faculty at Beloit. During two dynamic years at Beloit, Parker reveled in the experience of teaching and received the "Teacher of the Year" award at age twenty-eight.

Energized by a new sense of purpose, Parker became determined to finish his degree. But, while teaching at Beloit, he had encountered the work of Robert N. Bellah, future author of the now well-known *Habits of the Heart*, and already an admired and innovative scholar at Harvard who approached religion from a standpoint that was respectful, not reductionist. Parker decided that he wanted to study with Bellah and began inquiring into the possibility of transferring from Berkeley to Harvard. He soon learned, however, that Bellah had just accepted the Ford Professorship at Berkeley. Amazed by the coincidence, Parker decided to return to Berkeley in the fall of 1967—the same fall that son Todd was born—and soon began working with Bellah, who became chair of his dissertation committee.

In 1969, apparently on track to finish his dissertation on the role of religious symbolism in the political modernization of Colonial America, Meiji Japan, and Turkey under Ataturk, Parker started looking for a job. Given his ambivalence about research, he was eager to "do sociology" rather than intellectualize about it. At the invitation of Elden Jacobson, he took a job with the Washington, D.C., Center for Metropolitan Studies, intent on working with Jacobson in Silver Spring, Maryland, to establish a community-organizing institute focused on the creative potentials of racial diversity.

As the Palmers were packing to move, Parker was dealt a hard blow. He received a note from Robert Bellah saying that the dissertation he had submitted "wouldn't do" and needed substantial revision. But, with their move already in motion, the Palmers had no choice: Parker, Sally, Brent, and Todd moved to Silver Spring, Maryland, where they were soon joined by daughter, Carrie, age two, whom they adopted from Seoul, Korea.

The fall of 1969 was a difficult time: a young family, a new job, and long days that would end with Parker returning home, heading upstairs, and working "every spare minute I had, late into the night and through

Brent, Todd, and Carrie Palmer, 1973

the weekends, on that damned doctoral dissertation!" He finished the writing in late December 1969—an achievement he was able to celebrate a month later when he received a note from Robert Bellah that Parker still has in his files, saying, "You pulled the chestnuts out of the fire."

Once he finished the dissertation, Parker threw himself into the work of community organizing, which would occupy him for the next five years. He also had been invited by John Nason, then president of Carleton College, to join Carleton's Board of Trustees. The only trustee under the age of sixty, Parker was told by Nason that he had a future in higher education: "You're going to be a dean or a president." Professionally, Parker was on the fast track. In 1971, the dean at Georgetown University contacted him and offered him a position on the sociology faculty. Still finding deep reward in his community work, Parker negotiated a deal with Georgetown that allowed him to split his responsibilities between the college and the community with a focus on involving college students in his community work.

These were heady and generative times for Parker, times of intense action, yet he was starting to feel pangs of emptiness. As he remembers it, "At that point in my journey, I didn't have a conscious, reflective inner life. I didn't know much about the inner life traditions. I didn't know much about spirituality. What I had was a highly conceptualized religious belief system, which had been formed in me by some great thinkers. And I had some great exemplars of what it meant to live a life of faith. But there was nothing in my Methodist upbringing, and nothing in the theological traditions I had learned about at Carleton or Union, that was about inwardness as I now understand it."

Intrigued by this response, I followed up by asking Parker if he identified one moment or span of time that marked an awakening of his inner life. He described an encounter in a small bookstore in Dupont Circle.

> I used to haunt used bookstores even more than I do now. In the spring of 1970, I walked into one just off Dupont Circle in Washington, D.C., looking for Thomas Mann's *Magic Mountain*. The book wasn't there, but right where it should have been on the shelf was Thomas Merton's *Seven Storey Mountain*. I figured, "Close enough . . ." and bought Merton instead of Mann! I'm not sure I'd ever heard of Thomas Merton before. If you had said the word "monastery," I might have known something about it. But I had never been introduced to that spiritual stream that is inward and mystical and that flows through all the traditions.
>
> So I started reading this book and, like millions of people around the world, I was entranced. I couldn't put the book down. Today it's not a book that moves me deeply, but it was just the book I needed at that time. Then I started buying other Merton books, of which there are many. I think I own every book Merton ever wrote, and probably most books anybody ever wrote about him.
>
> Reading and meditating on Merton's work opened up the inner life in me. I started understanding what I now call "life on the Möbius strip," the way our inner and outer lives co-create reality. And I am glad I started to understand it because I needed it so badly! So much of me was in my head, so much of me was embattled with the world around me. I wanted to bring my heart fully into what I was doing, but that felt so dangerous. As I learned about the inner life, I realized that, yes, there are a lot of places in the world that aren't safe—but if you can find safety within yourself, you can be safe even in those places.
>
> Safety within yourself, I think, means clarity about your own mixed nature, your own complex blend of shadow and light. [It means] getting past the notion that your job is to save everybody else. It means seeing yourself clearly so you can see others clearly, not with a cynical eye, but with an eye that says, "Well, here's reality. Now, make some

good judgments about the possibilities that might emerge from that reality." So, the inner journey for me was about getting clear enough about myself that I could be clearer about the world. Then I could start to have what the woodcarver calls "live encounters."

The early 1970s proved to be a time of deep searching for Parker and his wife Sally. In a coauthored essay titled "The Paradoxes of Community" they describe the questions at the center of their deliberation:

> We had talked about community for years. How to create some "sense of community" where we lived? Whether to join an existing community—and which one? And what about the possibility of starting one with some of our friends? The longer we talked, the more barriers arose between us and any new way of life. Our family got larger, we all grew older, and as our needs increased our options narrowed. But the talk contained its own pressure, and by February of 1974 we knew it was time to put up or shut up. Our fantasies had become a source of frustration, not energy, and an honest look at ourselves revealed that we were beginning to protect life rather than live it.
>
> The need for community came from our feelings of isolation and fragmentation both at work and at home. Sally's concerns revolved around the difficulties of raising three children in suburban seclusion, and of forming purposeful relations with other adults amidst the logistical chaos of a family of five. Parker's needs came from the lack of community in academic life. . . . Together we felt a need for community to simplify and integrate the disparate pieces of our lives.[14]

I palpably feel the tension of Parker and Sally's quandary. As an academic with three children, a pretty home in the suburbs, and a lonely life in academia, I know from whence Parker and Sally speak. But what they did takes my breath way: they acted on their dreams with courage and daring. After visiting a number of intentional communities, they decided to move to Pendle Hill, a Quaker living-learning community near Philadelphia founded in 1930.

In the fall of 1974, Parker took a year's leave from his position at Georgetown University, and the Palmers enrolled as students in this communally organized adult study center, where they shared a daily life of worship, study, physical work, common meals, and recreation with about seventy people. In the spring of 1975, Parker resigned his position at Georgetown and became dean of studies at Pendle Hill, where Sally would soon become a crafts teacher and the Palmer family would spend the next decade.[15]

Parker and Sally Palmer in Finland, 1978

The Emerging Vocation

The Pendle Hill years were formative, and included a descent into a debilitating clinical depression and an ascent into vocational clarity. Sitting on his porch in Madison almost thirty years later, Parker described his eleven years at Pendle Hill: "When I decided to leave Georgetown to go to Pendle Hill, to become dean there and stay as long as I could, I was being moved by what I would now call 'imperatives of the heart and soul.' I wanted to be in a place where those imperatives could be honored, where there were other people who understood what heart and soul were all about. I knew of no university where I could find that understanding. But at Pendle Hill I had found many people who knew what I was talking about a lot better than I did."

As Parker embraced the rhythm, discipline, and practices of Quakerism, the ideas at the center of his future work began to emerge, influenced in part by his newfound friendship with Henri Nouwen, a Catholic priest and spiritual writer then teaching at Yale Divinity School. Nouwen, whom Parker calls "a spiritual virtuoso," had written eloquently about Merton, education, community, and other topics dear to Parker's heart. For more than a decade, Parker says, "Henri and I collaborated as colleagues in teaching and writing, and he quietly served as my mentor in the things I cared about."

Parker continued his study of Merton, adopted the Quaker practice of "meeting for worship" rooted in communal silence, taught classes of adult seekers in "a school [Pendle Hill] without grades or diplomas, where meaning was the only thing that counted," and began to devote large swaths of time to writing. His engagement with Quakerism and its way of thinking about "life together" became the basis for his thinking about transforming education. "Quakerism and Pendle Hill gave me a different angle, a different experience and a different language to think about the teaching and learning process."

In reflecting back on how Pendle Hill changed him, Parker says, "I'm eternally grateful to Pendle Hill because it gave me space and time to absorb some Quaker sensibilities into my own life. I had the rare experience of taking an inner journey in community by beginning each day with forty minutes of communal silence, a whole new thing for me. And in that silence, I discovered, I was compelled to come to terms with myself, with other people, with my work and with the world in a whole new way."

Pendle Hill Campus, 2003

In 1974, his first year at Pendle Hill, the thirty-five-year old Parker noticed a little plaque with an inscription from Martin Buber outside the meeting room: "All real living is meeting." This phrase became a touchstone for Parker, stirring him during his first year as dean of studies at Pendle Hill to write "Meeting for Learning," in which he asks, "How do we meet each other in a way that allows each one of us to meet ourselves?" He describes this oft-reproduced and anthologized essay as one of his favorite pieces:

> A meeting for learning is, in the first place, a genuine encounter between persons, a "meeting" in the literal sense. In conventional classrooms the focus is on the isolated self. The teacher addresses the individual student, treating him or her as a receptacle to be filled with knowledge. But in a meeting for learning the individual is always in relationship, and knowledge emerges in dialogue. It is not only what the student hears but what the student says back that counts. Here, learning happens *between* persons and not simply *within* the learner.[16]

In many ways, this essay contains the emergent threads of Parker's later works: the importance of an integral life, the centrality of community, pedagogies of transformation, and education for nonviolent change. In our effort to honor Parker the man, Parker the teacher, Parker the writer, and Parker the social activist, we authors in this volume have picked up on these themes.

The Touchstone: Inwardness

The touchstone idea of Parker's work, the linchpin of his worldview, is that all human activity emerges from our inwardness. For those of us who grew up with a secular, technocratic orientation to human development, Parker's belief in the utter sanctity and importance of the human soul is a radical premise.

Parker believes that our outward work in the world is a projection of our inner condition. How we relate to the work we do, and how we relate to others through our work, hinges on how well we know and understand ourselves. While Parker focuses on teachers and students in *The Courage to Teach,* his central tenet—"good teaching cannot be reduced to technique; good teaching comes from the identity and integrity of the teacher"[17]—can be applied to any of the roles we occupy in the world. Our way in the world depends on a still, small presence inside us that Parker views as the soul.

*Parker visiting Thomas Merton's hermitage
at the Abbey of Gethsemani in Kentucky, 2003*

This "inner teacher," as Quakers call it, speaks the truth about how we are with other people, about how we are with our work, and about how we are with ourselves: it yearns for congruence between our inner lives and outer actions. When we break faith or live in defiance of this inner voice, we live what Parker calls a divided life. The price for living a divided life is high. We feel fraudulent and uneasy, and our spirit sinks under the burden of duplicity. Our encounters with others lack genuine authenticity, which undermines our ability to form life-giving connections.

Wholeness is the opposite of the divided or wounded life. By "wholeness" Parker does not mean perfection, but a genuine embracing of our weaknesses as well as our strengths, our shadows as well as our light. He asks, "Once I understand the dividedness that marks my life, do I continue to live with this fragmentation or do I work to bring my inner and outer worlds into congruence?"

When he asks this question I have seen him calmly rise from his chair, stand to his full height of six-foot-three, look toward us and—moving his hands together and apart—offer an image of how our lives are wrested, tugged, and yanked. "We live in a gap, a tragic gap, between the way things are and the way they might be. There is no easy solution. There never has been and never will be. But we must learn to stand in this gap, faithfully holding the tension and negotiating between what *is* and what is *possible*."

Building on what he learned during his tenure at Pendle Hill, Parker began to think about what it would take to export Quaker principles and practices for "life together" into other arenas of the world. As he says in *A Hidden Wholeness*:

> We know how to create spaces that invite the *intellect* to show up, an-alyzing reality, parsing logic, and arguing its case. . . . We know how to create spaces that invite the *emotions* into play, reacting to injury, ex-pressing anger, and celebrating joy. . . . We know how to create spaces that invite the *will* to emerge, consolidating energy and effort on behalf of a common task. . . . We certainly know how to create spaces that in-vite the *ego* to put in an appearance, polishing its image, protecting its turf, and demanding its rights. . . . But we know very little about creat-ing spaces that invite the *soul* to make itself known [and do its work in our midst]. . . .[18]

In 1985, after eleven years at Pendle Hill, Parker and Sally accepted an invitation from the St. Benedict Center in Madison, Wisconsin, to help create an adult living-learning community modeled after Pendle Hill. After three years of intense work establishing the center, and Parker's second bout with clinical depression, the Palmers' personal lives hit a low. In 1988, after some years of struggle, Parker and Sally separated and, three years later, were divorced. Parker took an apartment in Madison and, with the help of a grant from the Lilly Endowment—whose vice president, Robert W. Lynn, had been a key mentor and friend to Parker for more than a decade—began working as an independent writer and "traveling teacher," giving speeches and workshops at campuses across the country.

Since 1983 and the publication of his book *To Know as We Are Known: A Spirituality of Education* (reissued in 1993 as *To Know as We Are Known: Education as a Spiritual Journey*), Parker had received a growing number of speaking invitations from college presidents, faculty, campus ministers, and foundation officers. They found his message honest and hopeful because he offered both a diagnosis and a prescription.

First, he pointed to the depletion and loneliness that many in higher edu-cation experience, calling it "the pain of disconnection." Mustering the cogent and meticulously constructed conceptual framework of a well-trained scholar, Parker drew upon the language of epistemology to diagnose the malady afflicting so many campuses as an obsession with objectified ways of knowing that are devoid of heart and self. He argued that this obsession creates a "one-eyed" life in which we see merely the measurable and predictable at the cost of blinding the "eye of the heart," which can see the "power of love" and the potential of community.[19]

Parker's remedy was to put forward a vision of education that honors the role of community in learning and a way of knowing that values "intuitions, our beliefs, our actions, our relationships and our bodies themselves." He advocated forms of relational knowing in which truth is discovered in co-creative relationships between students and teachers and their subjects.

Parker's message was radical, but he began to build a following. In 1987, Parker's career took a major turn when Sister Joel Read, president of Alverno College in Milwaukee and a board member of the American

Parker at age thirty-nine in the Minnesota woods

Association of Higher Education (AAHE), suggested that Parker be invited as a plenary speaker at the organization's national conference to be held in Chicago.

The speech he gave so riveted the audience of one thousand college administrators that Russell Edgerton, the president of AAHE, wrote a special article in *Change* magazine titled "Filling the Void," which attempted to explain the mystical and galvanizing aura that swept through Parker's audience that day: "You had to be there. . . . Palmer started. Soon the audience was very still. When he finished, a thousand people spontaneously rose from their seats to give him a prolonged ovation. He's on to something that people have felt but have not been able to articulate. He's giving voice to a broad-based concern on the part of a lot of people. . . . For a precious moment, Palmer filled the void. He took us along the exhilarating path of deep thought and more. He found the words to articulate how we felt."[20]

The speech, "Community, Conflict and Ways of Knowing,"[21] became the largest selling and most popular tape in the history of the organization. And the published version, which appeared in *Change* magazine, won a 1988 national Educational Press Association Distinguished Achievement Award.

Parker himself experienced the speech in a way quite different from the audience. At the time he gave it, he was in the midst of his second bout with depression. Here is what he says about that moment as he looks back on it sixteen years later:

> As I stood up in front of those thousand people, I was feeling very low and very empty. I wasn't nervous, but I certainly wasn't on fire! I remember feeling that I had nothing left to lose. I will never really understand what happened that day. But perhaps I was so empty, maybe so devoid of ego, that something much larger came through. So I gave the talk, and when I finished and said thank you, there was a very long moment of silence when I wondered, "What's happening?" And then, a thousand people stood and started applauding, and they went on and on and on.
>
> It was a huge turning point in my work in higher education. My phone started ringing off the hook, and I hear about that speech to this day. People say, "You know, I play that tape a couple times a year, as I'm driving to work. It led me to read all your books." Or, "I heard you in 1987, and I still remember that talk. Will you come to our campus and speak?" Had it not been for that moment, I don't think my work would ever have gotten on the radar screen of higher education to the extent that it did. And that led to an open invitation from *Change* magazine to

write for them, whenever I wanted, about any subject that was on my mind. So I did a series of five articles for them over the next seven years.

Parker was indeed on higher education's "radar screen." In 1990, he was featured in a *New York Times* piece titled "A Critic of Academia Wins Applause on Campus," and in a *Chronicle of Higher Education* piece titled "'Traveling Teacher' Inspires Professors with Talk of Truth, Love."[22] And during the same year, Parker published his fourth book, *The Active Life: A Spirituality of Work, Creativity and Caring*.

But the most important development for Parker was in his personal life: in 1992 he married Sharon Craven. Sharon has been his partner in work as well as life, serving as the first-line editor of everything he has written since they were married and as a close collaborator in the soon-to-be-born Courage to Teach program.

Putting Wheels on Ideas

The turn toward the Courage to Teach program came in 1991 after a series of conversations between Parker and Rob Lehman, the newly appointed president of the Fetzer Institute, a philanthropic foundation in Kalamazoo, Michigan. For a decade, the work of the Fetzer Institute had been focused on mind-body-spirit initiatives in medicine and science. When Lehman became president, he began to engage Fetzer staff and selected thinkers in conversations about how to expand the reach of Fetzer's mission into other professional arenas.

In November 1991, Lehman invited Parker to the Institute to explore the intersection between his work and Fetzer's emerging interests. Parker suggested that Fetzer's concern for the inner lives of doctors and patients be expanded to include the inner lives of teachers and learners in higher education, and Lehman proposed that the focus be on the world of public education. Despite Parker's initial reservations about working with K–12 teachers, a group about whom he knew little, Lehman convinced him to sketch out the design and rationale for a program for public school teachers that would advance Fetzer's new agenda.

Drawing on ideas and principles embedded in many of his prior works, Parker began by writing a memo to Rob Lehman, subsequently published as a Fetzer occasional paper, called *Reflections on a Program for "The Formation of Teachers"*:

> First, it is consistent with Fetzer's larger goal in education: to develop capacities in students and teachers that will help them live healthy lives. This includes the capacity for wonder, for reverence, for life-giving at-

titudes toward themselves and other people. Second, the emphasis on the formation of teachers is consistent with my own deepest conviction about the nature of good teaching: good teaching cannot be reduced to technique. Good teaching comes from the identity and integrity of the teacher. Third, this is the kind of support teachers yearn for. . . . [A] program that focuses on the state of the teacher's soul will be received with real gratitude.[23]

This remarkable memo then asks a question that anticipates what would increasingly become Parker's primary work from 1992 until the present. He asks, *"How can we move from this conviction about the soul-sources of good teaching into a program for the formation of teachers?"* Parker's answer prefigured many of the critical ideas that emerged in his most influential and widely read book, *The Courage to Teach: Exploring the Inner Landscape of a Teacher's Life* (1997).

In the memo, Parker begins with a careful diagnosis of the inward factors that diminish a teacher's personal wholeness as well as his or her capacity to teach well. He focuses on the role that fear plays in education and examines three sources of that fear.

The first source is our preoccupation with objectivist ways of knowing. By this, Parker means our "commitment to the notion that we cannot know *anything* truly and well unless we know it from such a distance that the 'object' of knowledge remains uncontaminated by our own subjectivity (whether that 'object' be a piece of literature, nature, history or human nature)." This cold, controlling, arm's-length way of knowing disconnects us from the world so that our knowledge cannot serve as a source of community and transformation.

The second source of fear comes from within our students. Our educational system has long used the fear of failure as an "incentive" to learn, neglecting two critical facts: that children come into this world as natural learners, needing no incentive beyond the joy of learning itself, and that fear in fact shuts down a child's capacity to learn. Parker argues that the silence and sullenness students sometime exhibit in class is not a sign of apathy or stupidity but a natural withdrawal from a situation that triggers their fears. He advocates a program of inner work for teachers that will increase their capacity to create fear-free settings where real learning can go on.

Then, with daring candor, Parker names a third source of fear, a fear that most of us who teach have felt: the fear of being judged by our students or, as Parker puts it, "our fear of the judgment of the young." Stagnation, cynicism, depletion, and, ultimately, burnout are the only possible outcomes when teachers internalize the daily experience of standing before "a sea of faces younger than one's own, faces that too often seem bored, sullen, even hostile"—especially when we elders fail to decode what is really going on behind those masks.

In the memo, Parker emphasized that his agenda was to encourage discussion about inner life issues that often get ignored but that are essential to strengthening teaching and learning. Then he offered a detailed vision of what a "teacher formation" program might look like.

After receiving the memo, Lehman asked Parker to lead a pilot retreat for public school teachers in January of 1994. Parker agreed, and 350 brochures were mailed to schools in Southwest Michigan. Eighty applications were received, and twenty-two teachers were selected to participate. The retreat was a rousing, poignant, and profound success. As John Doble, the external evaluator of the pilot retreat, reported, teachers called it a "life-altering experience" and "unlike anything they had ever attended." In his report to the Fetzer board, Doble wrote that teachers revealed a strong desire to "continue the process. Without this, they worried that the spiritual renewal of the retreat would be eroded by the outside forces and stresses of daily life. As one teacher said, 'You have awakened something in us. Now you have to take care of us.'"[24]

Enthusiastically supported by Fetzer, Parker's work with K–12 teachers began to grow at a rapid rate. The teachers from the January 1994 retreat signed on for a series of seven more retreats over the next two years. Dur-

Parker teaching on Bainbridge Island, Washington, 2004

ing this period, working closely with David Sluyter and Mickey Olivanti from the Fetzer staff, Parker decided to organize the retreats around the inner-life metaphors that can be drawn from the four seasons:[25]

- *Fall: The Seed of True Self.* This retreat focused on establishing an atmosphere of trust and openness that enabled each person to uncover and touch something of his or her true self. It was a time of self-encounter, self-revelation, and self-acceptance.

- *Winter: Dwelling in Darkness.* This retreat focused on the darkness and spiritual death that teachers often encounter in their work, created by such things as cynical colleagues and stagnant institutions, as well as by the deadly shadows we all carry within.

- *Spring: Embracing the Paradoxes.* This retreat focused on the fact that, despite winter's death and darkness, new life and vitality are always waiting to emerge. Here teachers had a chance to perceive "the hidden wholeness" by understanding how apparent opposites can complement each other, especially those that have special relevance to teaching (for example, subjective and objective knowledge, personal and professional commitments, cognitive and affective concerns).

- *Summer: Abundance and Harvest.* This retreat focused on living into the abundance of questions, ideas, and aspirations that the retreats had generated. Teachers were asked to look back on the past school year, to look ahead to the next, and to reflect on what they were learning about who they are, who they are becoming, and who they are meant to serve.

By the fall of 1996, new Courage to Teach retreat programs with newly trained facilitators were operating at four sites around the country: Coastal South Carolina; Seattle, Washington; Southwest Michigan; and Baltimore, Maryland. At each site, twenty to twenty-five teachers gathered in quarterly retreats of three days each over a two-year period. By 1997, the Fetzer Institute had agreed to fund the national Center for Teacher Formation to train facilitators to lead Courage to Teach retreats across the country, inviting Rick and Marcy Jackson to become the Center's codirectors. At the time of this writing, in 2004, approximately five thousand people have experienced versions of the retreat series programs in the United States.[26]

I entered Parker J. Palmer's world in earnest in 1998. After ten years as a public school teacher and high school administrator, I was in the final year of my Ph.D. program at Stanford University when I was hired by the Fetzer Institute to conduct an outside evaluation of the retreat program.

I began the interviews knowing very little about the retreats. In fact, I was a bit skeptical after reading the descriptions of the program; it felt elusive and soft. Yet after my first round of interviews with participants I was transfixed. The following is a representative sampling of the responses I received as I interviewed teachers and educational leaders.

One veteran educator told me, "It is a life-changing and altering program. It offers an opportunity to step out of your life to sit down beside the road and to be contemplative. It gives you time to consider how to *be* in this world and how to *be* with your students. It offers an opportunity to kindle and rekindle the sense of mystery and wonder about life and the precious lives of students."

Another comment came in the form of an impassioned plea to find ways to replicate the formation retreats for others. A veteran high school teacher said, "The CTT model is an incredible gift to public education because it gives us a way to replenish the sources of energy and wisdom inside us that can so easily be depleted by the relentless demands of students, parents, and school systems. It allows us to give back to ourselves so we can keep giving to the children. It encourages us to bring honesty and integrity to our work that is a very powerful model for the students."

The feedback Parker has received over the past decade of Courage to Teach retreats is extraordinarily gratifying to him because he finds himself so deeply moved by the role—and the plight—of public school educators. As he has often said,

> I think of public school teachers as being among our culture heroes. They're being asked to solve every problem that no one else in this society knows how to solve—and then being beaten up on a daily basis for their alleged inability to do so. The best of them are working under enormously adverse circumstances, with scant resources, and with hardly any public understanding of what it means to be a teacher or what problems teachers have to deal with. And yet so many of them are doing it with great passion, with great heart, with great commitment. I think my own inner movement towards this program was one of deep compassion for these folks who are doing such critical work in our society with so little outer or inner support.

As the Courage to Teach program has spread throughout the country and around the world, what has become clear is that the program is meeting a deep, abiding hunger in teachers. As a school administrator reported in an evaluation of the program, "What tired and burned out, good teachers need most is to 'rest' or to retreat. The CTT program offers seasoned teachers a chance to recall what brought them into the profession in the first place. To get in touch with one's inner teacher is invigorating and sustaining. This type of professional development is far more effective at improving the physical, spiritual, and emotional health of a teacher than traditional one-shot inservices. When teachers are living more fully, the students win because their teachers are more 'present' in the classroom."[27]

Not only does the program appear to "salvage a teacher's passion" for his or her work, as one administrator described, but it seems to catalyze individuals to work with more courage and commitment to issues that matter to them. As one twenty-year veteran told me, "I am no longer afraid, or less afraid, to become involved in conflictual situations with teachers, parents, students, administrators, or any combination thereof. I have learned ways to go into difficult meetings in a centered frame of mind, remembering that we all have the same goal: to feel successful and to help young people succeed. I am more fully aware that I will never be able to fulfill all of the requirements of the job—the best I can do is put people first."[28]

In his original memo to Rob Lehman, Parker argued that inner work was the missing link in our ongoing efforts to achieve genuine educational reform. "I strongly urge that the primary emphasis of the Fetzer program be on the internal factors that obscure or distort our identity. My rationale is simple: many, many programs are trying to effect educational reform from the outside in, but the greatest immediate power we have is to work for reform from the inside out. Ultimately, human wholeness does not come from changes in our institutions (as much as we need to work for such change); it comes from the reformation of our hearts."[29] For Parker, the success of the Courage to Teach program offers persuasive evidence that his core beliefs can be enacted in every professional arena.

By the mid-1990s, people in other professions—including law, medicine, higher education, philanthropy, and voluntary associations—had begun to participate in formation retreats, and the Center for Teacher Formation has expanded its role to accommodate this broader need. In the late 1990s, the Fetzer Institute funded the Center for Formation in the Community Colleges. And in 2000, the Accreditation Council for Graduate Medical Education (ACGME), the organization that certifies all 8,000 medical residency programs in the United States, created the "Parker J. Palmer 'Courage to Teach' Award" for program directors who demonstrate a commitment to physician education, serve as successful mentors, and are effective and innovative program designers.[30] Announcing the award, David C. Leach, M.D. and ACGME executive director, explained that the "ACGME recognizes that program directors face many challenges in administering a residency program. Those finding innovative ways to teach residents and to provide quality health care in this harsh environment should be celebrated."[31]

Tracking the genesis and growth of formal programs associated with Parker is one way to "chart" his influence. But most people encounter him through his books and public lectures rather than through formal retreats and workshops. While working on this book, I heard many stories from teachers and physicians who—upon reading *To Know as We Are Known* (1983), *The Courage to Teach* (1997), or *Let Your Life Speak* (2000), or hearing Parker speak—returned to their classrooms or clinics emboldened to let their identity shine through more clearly in their work and forge more meaningful connections with students or patients or colleagues.

By way of example, here is a reflection by Rob Kunzman—a wonderful teacher and former colleague of mine—on the encouragement Parker's words gave him:

> I teach several courses in which we grapple with controversial, uncomfortable—even painful subjects: equity, diversity, moral and political disagreement. I have always struggled with how to push students in their thinking and growth about these issues without creating a hostile atmosphere in which they feel threatened and judged. One semester I was challenged by a colleague whose teaching style was starkly confrontational—"you need to shake these students up, get in their faces. They're never going to recognize their ignorance unless you take them out of their comfort zones."
>
> My colleague's words struck at the heart of my uncertainty about the tension between emotional safety and growth. Some of my students, I knew, *did* want more room to challenge the status quo and even their peers; many others were already clearly at the edge of their psychic reserves. I myself felt deeply resistant to the prospect of a [free-for-all], but I wondered how much of that reflected my own fears of classroom confrontation and uncontrolled emotion.
>
> I first encountered Parker Palmer ten years ago through *To Know as We Are Known: Education as a Spiritual Journey.* Here was a perspective that resonated with my own sense of teaching as a deeply spiritual calling and endeavor. And it was to Parker's words that I returned during this time of pedagogical—and, in many ways, personal—crisis. He wrote, "A learning space needs to be hospitable not to make learning painless but to make the painful things possible, things without which no learning can occur—things like exposing ignorance, testing tentative hypotheses, challenging false or partial information, and mutual criticism of thought. Each of these is essential to obedience to truth. But none of them can happen in an atmosphere where people feel threatened and judged."

Parker with Marcy Jackson, Rick Jackson, and Sam Intrator, 2003

To make the painful things possible—here was the connection between growth and safety I had struggled to articulate to my teaching
self. A hospitable classroom was not an adequate end goal, but was a
vital ingredient in helping my students and me take chances, expose
ignorance, and grow beyond our necessarily limited perspectives. My
responsibility as a teacher was to provide this space where we could
pursue hard truths.

As Rob expresses with poignancy, teachers, physicians, clergy, politicians, and others who work at the intersection of personal and public life
find deep kinship and inspiration in Parker's writing. Yet from his earliest
days of building airplane models as a teenager in Wilmette to his days of
taking "sociology" to Silver Spring as a community organizer, Parker has
longed to put "wheels on ideas." As he told me with considerable passion,
having good ideas is only half the equation, the other half is bringing those
ideas to life.

What matters is not just the words that I speak or write, but how those
words relate to my own life. And, as I've often said, this isn't about
perfection. It's about acknowledging points at which my words represent something I'm not able to live and trying to be honest about my
weaknesses as well as my strengths. And "putting wheels on ideas" is

also about organizing energies and gathering resources that translate good ideas into projects and programs that other people benefit from. That's why the Courage to Teach program and the whole formation movement has been so important to me.

True Self Unleashed

One of Parker's favorite teaching stories is Rosa Parks' decision to resist the institutional racism that had ruled her life by refusing to yield her seat on the bus to a white man.[32] Parker has called attention to this kind of moment, when individuals who suffer from an intolerable situation have to choose between allowing their truth to be silenced or living with their identity and integrity intact.

In describing this moment, Parker quotes Rosa Parks explaining how she was tired of being complicit in her own diminishment: "People always say that I didn't give up my seat because I was tired, but that isn't true. I was not tired physically nor more tired than I was at the end of a usual working day. I was not old, although some people have an image of me as being old then. I was forty-two. No, the only tired I was, was tired of giving in."[33]

To Parker, Rosa Parks made a courageous choice for integrity when she decided she could no longer live a divided life. She acted in defiance of institutional structures that eroded her true self. Parker's understanding of how movements begin and gather momentum hinges on individuals who choose to live integral lives in which their actions in the world are congruent with their deepest values and beliefs. Movements begin when individuals make an inward decision to live "divided no more," and they start to gain power when those individuals discover one another and come together in what Parker calls "communities of congruence."[34]

The clearest and most poignant evocation of Parker's belief of what it means to unleash the true self on behalf of a movement is his response to Marge Piercy's poem "The low road" in *Teaching with Fire: Poetry That Sustains the Courage to Teach,* a book inspired by the Courage to Teach program:[35]

> I spent most of the 1960s in Berkeley, watching history-in-the-making, working on a Ph.D. and preparing to be a professor. But I found the social movements of that era so morally compelling that, having finished my degree, I moved to Washington, D.C., and spent the next five years as a community organizer working for racial justice.
>
> I never doubted the rightness of that work. But I grieved the loss of my vocation as a teacher, until I began to understand that organizing is

Parker with his granddaughter Heather Palmer, 2003

---

simply teaching in another form: the classroom is the community, the subject is real life, and the students are all who are willing to be engaged—and some who get engaged willy nilly!

I love "The low road" because it is a movement poem. It moves me through the gamut of feelings that come with passion for a good cause, not least the reform of public education. The first stanza is full of pain and fear. The second explodes into anger and the desire for revenge. The third brings things back down to human scale, and the saving grace of humor appears. And the fourth stanza gives me words to live by. Each day I ask myself:

- Do I still care enough to act, even when they say "No"?

- When I say "we," who do I mean?

- How can I reach out to someone else today—maybe even "the enemy"—so each day I can mean one more?

THE LOW ROAD

What can they do
to you? Whatever they want.
They can set you up, they can
bust you, they can break
your fingers, they can
burn your brain with electricity,
blur you with drugs till you
can't walk, can't remember, they can
take your child, wall up
your lover. They can do anything
you can't stop them
from doing. How can you stop
them? Alone, you can fight,
you can refuse, you can
take what revenge you can
but they roll over you.

But two people fighting
back to back can cut through
a mob, a snake-dancing file
can break a cordon, an army
can meet an army.

Two people can keep each other
sane, can give support, conviction,
love, massage, hope, sex.
Three people are a delegation,
a committee, a wedge. With four
you can play bridge and start
an organization. With six
you can rent a whole house,
eat pie for dinner with no
seconds, and hold a fund raising party.
A dozen make a demonstration.
A hundred fill a hall.
A thousand have solidarity and your own newsletter;
ten thousand, power and your own paper;
a hundred thousand, your own media;
ten million, your own country.

It goes on one at a time,
it starts when you care
to act, it starts when you do
it again after they said no,
it starts when you say *We*
and know who you mean, and each
day you mean one more.

—Marge Piercy[36]

At the heart of Parker's life and work rests a belief that the way to "right action" begins with an inner journey. He acknowledges that, at first, the turn inward may feel selfish or narcissistic. But if we go to the depths of the soul, he suggests, we will return to the world ready to offer life-giving leadership. If we do not take this inward journey, we are more likely to live divided lives in which our values and beliefs are at odds with our actions in the world— and our dissonance renders us incomplete and ultimately ineffective.

In his writing and speaking, Parker has been particularly transparent about his own journey toward living "divided no more." In *The Courage to Teach,* he describes how he views his own life's calling in regard to social movements. "I am a teacher at heart, and I am not naturally drawn to the rough-and-tumble of social change. I would sooner teach than spend my energies helping a movement along and taking the hits that come with it. Yet if I care about teaching, I must care not only for my students and my subject but also for the conditions, inner and outer, that bear on the work teachers do."[37]

Parker has always had a complex relationship with "outer conditions" or, said differently, with institutional contexts and circumstances. His path has been marked by conscious withdrawal from what we would call formal institutions. From leaving Union Theological Seminary to his difficult journey through the doctoral program at Berkeley to his realization that community organizing was not a match for his gifts to laying down his professorship at Georgetown to departing Pendle Hill and becoming a traveling teacher, Parker has always veered away from institutions.

But in spite of his vocational decisions to step back from institutional structures, he recognizes that institutions are the force field in which most people move: "I have to care about the institutional contexts in which people live and work, because that's where much of the work of the world gets done—and that's where the human heart either gets welcomed or thwarted or broken."

The Legacy of Life Lived True

An encounter with Parker, in person or in print, provokes us to confront ourselves in ways that range from profoundly uncomfortable to refreshingly stimulating. Perhaps that is why the reach of his work is so stunning. From the half-million books his publishers have sold to the tens of thousands of people who have heard him speak to the untold number of professionals who have encountered his work on syllabi or in reading groups, the impact of his vocation has been far-flung and powerful.

By way of a small example, during the span of time when I was working on this introduction, I attended an international conference of scholars in Hong Kong. The assembly included researchers and educators from every continent. At the opening meeting, the chairperson stood, held up a copy of *The Courage to Teach,* and said, "I read this book in one sitting. It said so many things that I have long felt inside but did not have the words to say. Reading it helped me envision my hopes and dreams for our conference. I hope we can join together as a community of scholars that puts into the center of our gathering ideas worth pursuing."

Though Parker has never sought the mantle of leadership, I believe that he is not only a leader, but potentially the most influential writer, thinker, and teacher in a movement devoted to reclaiming the sacred in the work of the professions. All across the world, teachers, physicians, lawyers, and others are locked in a contest with forces that seek to automate, measure, script, and narrow our humanity. Against these forces that would diminish creativity and deplete the heart, a resistance movement has emerged with Parker in its vanguard. He writes and speaks and teaches in ways that help us to know ourselves better, to work with and learn from each other, and to come together in common cause.

The organization of the essays in this book corresponds to what I see as the three key themes coursing through Parker's life and work. The first section, "This Live Encounter," features essays that focus on the quest for true self and explores the nature and contours of the inner life. The second section, "Moving the Heart to the Center," includes essays that offer visions and designs for creating communities of learning in which we can explore the inner landscapes of our lives. The essays in the third section, "True Self Unleashed," describe the social and institutional transformations possible when individuals decide to live and lead from a place of identity, integrity, and wholeness.

When I asked Parker what sentence he felt most effectively characterized his hopes for his work, he didn't hesitate. He said it was the mantra or litany for the work of the Center for Teacher Formation and the Cour-

Parker and Sharon Palmer on vacation on the Olympic Peninsula, 2004

age to Teach retreats: "We become teachers for reasons of the heart. But often, as time goes by, we lose heart. How can we take heart, alone and together, so we can give heart—which is what good teachers do."

And that is what Parker Palmer has done and continues to do.

NOTES

1. See the full bibliography of Parker's works at the back of this book.

2. "Leadership Project Award." *Change Magazine,* Jan.–Feb. 1998, p. 14.

3. Many of the quotes by Parker Palmer in this introduction are taken from this interview, conducted January 8–12, 2003.

4. *The Way of Chuang Tzu* (T. Merton, trans./ed.). New York: New Directions, 1965.

5. Wall, J. "Action and Insight: An Interview with Parker Palmer." *The Christian Century,* March 1995, *112*(10), 327.

6. Glasser, C., in conversation with the author, August 18, 2004.

7. Glasser (2004).

8. Glasser (2004).

9. Parker Palmer, interview by Mark Nepo, Generosity of Spirit Project, Fetzer Institute, April 18, 2003.

10. Palmer, P. J. *Let Your Life Speak: Listening for the Voice of Vocation.* San Francisco, Jossey-Bass, 2000, pp. 19–20.

11. Jacobson, E., Palmer, P. J., and others. *The Church, the University, and Urban Society: Implications for the University.* New York: Dept. of Higher Education, National Council of Churches, 1971.

12. Underwood, K. (ed.). *The Church, the University, and Social Policy.* Middletown, Conn.: Wesleyan University Press, 1969, p. 27.

13. Underwood (1971), p. 27.

14. Palmer, P. J. *The Promise of Paradox: A Celebration of Contradictions in the Christian Life.* Notre Dame, Ind.: Ave Maria Press, 1980, p. 59.

15. Palmer, P. J. *To Know as We Are Known: A Spirituality of Education.* San Francisco: Harper SanFrancisco, 1983, p. 1.

16. Palmer, P. J. "Meeting for Learning: Education in a Quaker Context." Philadelphia: Friends Council on Education, p. 1.

17. Palmer, P. *The Courage to Teach: Exploring the Inner Landscape of a Teacher's Life.* San Francisco: Jossey-Bass, 1997, p. 10.

18. Palmer, P. J. *A Hidden Wholeness: The Journey Toward an Undivided Life.* San Francisco: Jossey-Bass, 2004, p. 56.

19. The various short quotes in this paragraph are from Chapter One of Palmer, P. J. *To Know as We Are Known: A Spirituality of Education.* San Francisco: Harper SanFrancisco, 1983.

20. Edgerton, R. "Filling the Void." *Change,* 1987, *19,* 19.

21. Palmer, P. "Community, Conflict and Ways of Knowing: Ways to Deepen our Educational Agenda." *Change,* 1987, *19,* 20–26.

22. Wycliff, D. "A Critic of Academia Wins Applause on Campus." *New York Times,* Sept. 12, 1990, B8; and Heller, S. "'Traveling Teacher' Inspires Professors with Talk of Truth, Love." *Chronicle of Higher Education,* Feb. 28, 1990, *36*(24), A3.

23. Palmer, P. J. *Reflections on a Program for "The Formation of Teachers."* Kalamazoo, Mich.: Fetzer Institute, 1992. Available on the Center for Teacher Formation Website http://www.teacherformation.org/html/rr/index.cfm.

24. Scribner, M. "Our Common History: The Evolution of the Fetzer Institute 1990–1997" (internal report). Kalamazoo, Mich.: Fetzer Institute, April 24, 1992.

25. The rough sketch of this structure is supplied from a March 23, 1994, memo from Palmer and Dave Sluyter to Rob Lehman. The memo is titled "Teacher Formation Program: Notes Toward a Design."

26. Jackson, Marcy, codirector of the Center for Teacher Formation, Bainbridge Island, Washington. E-mail received November 3, 2004.

27. Intrator, S. M., and Scribner, M. (1998). *An Evaluation of the Courage to Teach Program*. Kalamazoo, Mich.: Fetzer Institute, 1998, p. 24.

28. Intrator and Scribner (1998), p. 28.

29. Parker, P. J. *Reflections on a Program for "The Formation of Teachers."* Kalamazoo, Mich.: Fetzer Institute, 1992.

30. See Paul Batalden and David Leach's essay in this volume and see the Accreditation Council for Graduate Medical Education Website for more information about the award: http://www.acgme.org/About/sitemap.asp.

31. See the ACGME Website: http://www.acgme.org/palmerAward/nomForm.asp accessed 10/25/04.

32. For a fuller treatment of the Rosa Parks example see chapter seven in Palmer, *The Courage to Teach* (1997), pp. 163–183.

33. As quoted in Palmer, *The Courage to Teach* (1997), p. 169.

34. For a fuller treatment of what Parker calls the "movement model of social change" see chapter seven in *The Courage to Teach* (1997), pp. 163–183.

35. Intrator, S., and Scribner, M. *Teaching with Fire: Poetry That Sustains the Courage to Teach*. San Francisco: Jossey-Bass, 2003, p. 190.

36. Piercy, M. "The low road." In Intrator and Scribner (2003), p. 191.

37. Palmer, *The Courage to Teach* (1998), p. 182.

LIVING THE QUESTIONS

For Parker J. Palmer,
teacher, writer, activist, friend.
With love and gratitude for a
lifetime of service to the inner life.

"*. . . have patience with everything unresolved in your
heart and try to love* the questions themselves *as if
they were locked rooms or books written in a very
foreign language. Don't search for the answers, which
could not be given to you now, because you would not
be able to live them. And the point is, to live everything.* Live *the questions now. Perhaps then, someday
far in the future, you will gradually, without even
noticing it, live your way into the answer.*"

—Rainer Maria Rilke, *Letters to a Young Poet*
(Translated by Stephen Mitchell)

"This Live Encounter"

THESE ESSAYS DESCRIBE the journey inward. The methods of the journey vary: some of the essayists venture forth in solitude and silence, others engage with meditative texts and excursions into settings that invite contemplation, and others find communities that engage them in conversations that matter.

Ultimately, a turn to a poem that Parker considers sacred, "The Woodcarver" by Chuang Tzu, gives a phrase that evokes the focus of these essays. There is much to be extracted from this poem, but the essence is that the Prince of Lu commissions a woodcarver to make him a bell stand. Khing, a master wood carver, creates a work that astounds all who view it. In awe of his craftsmanship, the prince asks the woodcarver, "What is your secret?" The woodcarver answers, "I am only a workman: I have no secret," but then paradoxically he describes an intricate process that concludes with this stanza:

> What happened?
> My own collected thought
> Encountered the hidden potential in the wood;
> From this live encounter came the work
> Which you ascribe to the spirits.[1]

Parker's work has been a quest to map that moment of the "live encounter." He refers to versions of this moment of grace in many ways; it is an occasion of "deep gladness," "hidden wholeness," "divided no more," "authentic vocation," and more. In *The Active Life*, Parker holds that the bell stand came to be not merely because of the woodcarver's technical precision but because he understood that right action and good work must begin with knowing and caring for ourselves: "He did not prepare for his work by conducting scientific study of the external properties of trees, though his years of woodcarving clearly had given him knowledge of wood. He prepared by going into himself, by penetrating the illusions that had him in their grip . . . in order to touch his own truth."[2]

One particular form of live encounter that holds great meaning for Parker and for the essays is the live encounter that comes from doing work in the world that matches your greatest beliefs. Parker is fond of quoting Frederick Buechner's generous and humane image of vocation as "the place where your deep gladness and the world's deep hunger meet."[3] For Parker, the notion of "deep gladness" is the complex sense of well-being and completeness that comes when we devote ourselves to something that flows from our identity and emerges from our integrity.

How do we get to this grail of deep gladness? Parker's answer is that it begins when we commit to embarking on a journey inward. He calls this the "individual quest for integrity." It is a voyage we must take if we believe, as he does, that "First, we all have an inner teacher whose guidance is more reliable than anything we can get from a doctrine, ideology, collective belief system, institution or leader. Second, we all need other people to invite, amplify, and help us discern the inner voice . . . because the journey toward inner truth is too taxing to be made solo."[4]

Although there are times we must persist through work that feels like drudgery, or hold jobs that pay money rather than evoke meaning in us, the journey to seek a vocation is a worthy search. As Parker reminds us, "If a work does not gladden me . . . I need to consider laying it down. When I devote myself to something that does not flow from my identity, that is not integral to my nature, I am most likely deepening the world's hunger rather than helping to alleviate it."[5]

The second chapter of essays in Part One is titled "Be Not Afraid." These essays honor and explore a great truth about the search for true self or right vocation: even if we find it, the bloodless logic of our institutional contexts can render us fearful, lonely, and adrift. Schools, universities, hospitals, and other institutions are riddled with fear in ways that shut down our capacity at work to stay connected, creative, and engaged. When we are scared to reach out to others we are diminished. Parker calls fear "a cultural trait work in every area of our common life.[6] We practice a politics of fear in which candidates are elected by playing on voters' anxieties about race and class. We do business in an economy of fear where 'getting and spending' are driven by consumer worries about keeping up with the neighbors. We subscribe to religions of fear that exploit our dread of death and damnation . . . fear is the air we breathe."[7] The essays in "Be Not Afraid" describe individuals who face their fear and step toward the shadows in an effort to enrich their work and lives. As Parker says, "be not afraid" does not mean we should not have fears—for that is an impossible dream. Instead, these essays suggest that we can be afraid without needing to *be* our fears.

NOTES

1. *The Way of Chuang Tzu* (T. Merton, trans./ed.). New York: New Directions, 1965, pp. 110–111.

2. Palmer, P. J. *The Active Life*. San Francisco: Jossey-Bass, 1990, p. 71.

3. Quoted in Niedner, F. "Home Court Disadvantage." *Christian Century*, Jan. 17, 2001.

4. Palmer, P. J. *Hidden Wholeness: The Journey Toward an Undivided Life*. San Francisco: Jossey-Bass, 2004, pp. 25–26.

5. See Jacobson, E., and Palmer, P. J., *The Church, the University, and Urban Society: Implications for the University*. New York: Department of Higher Education, National Council of Churches, 1971.

6. Palmer, P. J. *The Courage to Teach: Exploring the Inner Landscape of a Teacher's Life*. San Francisco: Jossey-Bass, 1998, p. 39.

7. Palmer, P. J. *The Promise of Paradox: A Celebration of Contradictions in the Christian Life*. Notre Dame, Ind.: Ave Maria Press, p. 59.

Chapter One

NOW I BECOME MYSELF

BEFORE YOU TELL YOUR LIFE what you intend to do with it, listen for what it intends to do with you. Before you tell your life what truths and values you have decided to live up to, let your life tell you what truths you embody, what values you represent.

—Parker J. Palmer

———o———

REFLECTIONS

Chip Wood

principal of Sheffield Elementary School and
cofounder of Northeast Foundation for Children.

To acquire a mentor at a point in your life when you are mentoring others is a rare and unexpected gift, to which many others in this book will attest. Having had the privilege of joining Parker in many retreat circles over the past five years helped open my heart to the deep questions and truths of what it means to be a mentor and to carry the light of mentorship while retaining one's hidden wholeness. I learned this from Parker by watching, listening carefully, reflecting, sensing all the time his holding us all in the tension of his own human frailty and wisdom, an open paradox, flawed and graceful, witty and shy—but certain of his calling, therefore available to all who felt called by him. I think this is how it is for his readership as well. I know I was called in a similar way years ago by *To Know as We Are Known*.

I suspect those who read this book are called to circles too. As a classroom teacher, my students and I sat in morning meeting circles. As a principal, I sit in study group circles, meetings with my staff, and parent seminars. In teacher workshops and professional retreats, we sit in circles that hold us and embolden us to go out into the world and broaden our circles.

Parker's *The Courage to Teach* continues to create ripples and circles throughout the world of education. I am proud to be a "contributing editor" to the rippling effect of Parker's voice in the world. Our classrooms, schools, and all of education need us now more than ever.

NOTIONS
OF PRESENCE

Chip Wood

*With Parker's permission, I am using four of his poems to
serve as illuminations alongside some of my thoughts
about children, teachers, and families after thirty-five
years in the field of elementary education.*

THIS WEEKEND, A MOMENT IN TIME. I attend my grandson's fifth birthday
party and cook for a baby shower for my daughter, who is expecting a
girl in a couple of months. Our high school girl's softball team has just
won the state Division II championship, a huge accomplishment for our
small, struggling school district. Impromptu, the fire trucks and police
cruisers and a cavalcade of fans escorted them down Main Street this afternoon. The sixth graders graduate this Monday from the elementary
school where I am the principal, and Tuesday is the last day of school.

Personal news hints at a professional life, where, like any of ours, meaning is woven out of the fabric of the everyday. Our daily circles expand
into broader conversations, webs of contacts, with people we come to
know and appreciate after months or perhaps years of interactions; where
the word *struggling* becomes shorthand for a lifetime of shared struggle
for social justice.

In the weave of this book, I know there is a shared fierceness for extraordinarily deep caring for others, especially children and others in need.
I know that those who read and have written here are a part of a tapestry that stretches back into shared histories of action and where, even
today, even now, loose threads are being lifted into place to produce important changes for the next generation.

A personal presence, like the one we honor in the pages of this book,
can sometimes have the effect of drawing us together around certain ideas,
issues, and threads. This has been one of the gifts of Parker Palmer for so
many of us. His presence has helped us reflect and share our own.

First Notion

What I would see
Mid all the stress and tension of these days
What I would see beyond my pain and, seeing, praise
Is how life works its way upon
Our thick, opaque obduracy
Presses down and pulls us out
To tissue-thin transparency:
Yes, praise.
I would not choose to stretch this way.
Unwillingly I find myself drawn membrane-thin
So others can see through and in.
I would prefer to hold my dark
To guard my secrets safe behind
A studied public face—
But stretched reveal a larger life
Admit a light beyond my own
And letting through these stronger, brighter rays
I praise.

—Parker J. Palmer

In the twilight of my career in education, I have stepped back into the daily devotion and difficulty of being a public school principal. Here I feel newly present to the paradoxical possibilities inherent in attempting to live less divided and to admitting a light beyond my own. Be open for what you wish.

For the twenty years prior to returning to this one public school, I worked with hundreds of public school teachers and administrators as an outside "school reform consultant." The ideas and strategies I helped develop and share with these schools were well planned, research-based, and field-tested. These approaches were successful in my own classrooms and those of my codevelopers. They helped in schools where I served as principal. They improved teachers' practices and enabled academic and social growth for students. Yet bringing these approaches to other people's schools produced mixed results. Innovation requires a certain shared passion and commitment in addition to good ideas. Outside expertise can appear opaque and obdurate in schools struggling against overwhelming poverty and the attending social issues, or in schools agonizing over state and federal mandates without a shared vision or stable leadership.

The people I worked with during the 1980s and 1990s were trying to figure out how to deal with institutional and cultural change at multiple levels, amidst aging and mostly monocultural teaching staffs, increasingly diverse and divergent family populations, and shifting educational demands. The schools that were most able to embrace and make positive use of new methodologies were those where leadership, staff, parents, and the broader school district were able to build an increased level of trust based on clear communication and shared expectations. In these schools, people tried to be the change they wished to see (to paraphrase Gandhi). New strategies sometimes helped establish an initial focus point for their work, but lasting changes occurred when strategies became the tools for rebuilding basic democratic structures for the institution.

Now it's my turn to try, at the same school, every day.

After the buses depart, I go to my office. The deep complexity of human interaction is reduced to piles of papers, schedules, requests, purchase orders, accident reports, proposals, and test results. I print and post the "Adult Community Guidelines" we have developed as a staff to help us with our work together this year. One of them is "Support others and feel safe asking for support." I think of how a paraprofessional I barely know helped me today when I stepped in to take over a classroom. I think of the empathy I felt so directly when I made a math mistake in front of the class and she deftly supported me and the student who corrected my mistake. Such a small and humbling moment of trust; a pebble casting a circle. I must remember to thank her when she comes in the next day.

We have only one hour a month, by past practice, to meet together as a staff, and by contract only the professionals are paid to attend. Paraprofessionals are paid hourly. A few stay voluntarily for that once a month meeting.

We are using this precious time strictly for reflection and communication. We meet in small, heterogeneous, or sometimes grade-level groups. At the beginning of the year, I introduced the idea of adult community guidelines, which we brainstormed together and refined in our leadership team at a later meeting. Soon thereafter I used a particular "council" strategy for the first half hour of one of our staff meetings, to give each person a chance to speak and be listened to about a schoolwide issue of interest (in this case, "My opinion about the student-of-the-month is . . ."). Each person had up to two minutes to talk.

At the end of each of these circles, there was time for comments and connections (as opposed to a lengthy discussion) among the eight or so people in each circle. ("When you mentioned how you felt like you were just stretching to include every student, I knew what you meant." "I connected with you, Marcia, when you talked about how the criteria for awards seemed really arbitrary." "I was surprised, Ed. I never knew you felt that way.") I set the rule to refrain from discussion in order to strengthen our ability to listen to each other more fully and to help us make better use of our limited time. "Council is an exercise that builds the muscle for dialogue," I mentioned, quoting author Rachael Kessler, from whom I learned this reflective practice. We begin to "lean into inquiry," as a mentor of mine, Rick Jackson, would say. At the end of our meeting, after fifteen minutes of sharing leadership team news, we go outside together for a spirited fifteen minutes of "four square" on the playground. The scaffolding for new structures begins to go up.

Second Notion

THE WINTER WOODS

The winter woods beside a solemn
River are twice seen—
Once as they pierce the brittle air
Once as they dance in grace beneath the stream.

In air these trees stand rough and raw
Branch angular in stark design
In water shimmer constantly,
Disconnect as in a dream
Shadowy but more alive
Than what stands stiff and cold before our eyes.

Our eyes at peace are solemn streams
And twice the world itself is seen
Once as it is outside our heads
Hard frozen now and winter-dead
Once as it undulates and shines
Beneath the silent waters of our minds.

When rivers churn or cloud with ice
The world is not seen twice
Yet still is there beneath
The blinded surface of the stream
Livelier and lovelier than we can comprehend
And waiting, always waiting, to be seen.

—Parker J. Palmer

As teachers, we know that what most distinguishes our work is being as present as possible to the hidden wholeness in our students, through moments of listening, recognition, and connection. What makes such presence possible is some momentary awareness of our own hidden wholeness. It is what attunes us.

Today, in our classrooms and schools the surface of the stream is a glaring and bitter winter ice jam, churning and grinding with misspoken political promises and impossible political expectations placed on teachers and children that keep us from all that lies beneath for ourselves and our students.

External expectations keep us blinded to the deep duality of daily experience that continuously offers us—adults and children—something extraordinary: the opportunity to use the structures of schooling provided to us in our democracy to teach and share with each succeeding generation the tools that mark a civilization's greatness. These tools—of reading, writing, scientific inquiry, artistic expression—live in school environments (where they are not constantly meddled with from the outside) in a purity of light, experimentation, and reflection that later produce "works of art" worthy of that status.

These tools, their workers, and their products are what will be noted in future centuries, not the weights and measures of each generation's educational marketplace. Over thirty-five years and a span of four decades of watching and helping children grow up in America, I have been struck by how much time so many of us have spent fending off the chess players who use our children—the flowering of our civilization—as pawns for their political gain. Each decade, regardless of political persuasion, interference in children's education, more than any other single factor, has impeded joy and justice for our grandchildren, and out to seven generations.

Third Notion

THE VIEW FROM FINDHORN

Six a.m.
an open field
in Scotland
and I, mid-field,
immersed in earth
saw suddenly a
different space.

The sky half-lit
but with
that dawning clarity
which neither night
nor noon
achieve,
for dark we need
to see the light
and light
if we would read
the dark:
to see both shores
we must be in
mid-stream.

Behind me in
that lucid air
the sun,
before me now
the moon:
both full-round
both standing low
both far and somehow   .
near
on the horizon.

And sudden
in the half-dark dawn
it was as if
a line were drawn:
one end anchored in
the moon
the other tied down to
the sun
while earth
with me atop it
rode steady
in between.

And with that line of sight
established

with this swift perspective
gained
I was able to see how
the earth and sun and moon
revolve,
to see that my place
my earth-share
is not (as it seems)
everywhere
but one place only
in the boundless air.

Yet having seen my place
in things,
knowing now just where
I stand,
I saw other places, too
down the earth's
fell land.
In the west I saw my home
halfway round
the globe
and saw that this same
setting moon
was rising there in
darkness made
as this one earth stood
in the shade
of this same
rising
sun.

For this one earth on which
we stand
receives the light and
blocks it, too
and sun that burns so
white at noon
reflects a dark light
off the moon
and just between the

moon and sun
(exactly where we stand)
comes this mid-field moment
dawn
where light and dark
are seen as
one.
                            —Parker J. Palmer

We all need these locations in our lives. As a teacher and educator, I am deeply aware and disturbed by how few children can find themselves, find their souls in the midst of their increasingly busy and frantic lives.

Children today do not know they were made for solitude; they think they were made for cybertude. The sounds and sights of Game Boys, Walkman, the Internet, cell phones, and television fill almost all available time slots and channels for learning about oneself these days. Everything visible is someone else's model of who you should become. For some children it is nearly impossible to look inside at all. Many have neither been taught nor given the time and space that might open them to their own souls.

Take, for instance, the pernicious practice of a "moment of silence" ritualized in some of our nation's schools, usually right after the pledge of allegiance to the flag. This moment of silence is just that—ten seconds on average, by my count—not just making a mockery of the idea of prayer, meditation, or musing but actually deconstructing children's ability to value or engage in such practice.

Where today can children be safely alone with the natural world, or even just with their own uninterrupted thoughts? Where are their Findhorns? One summer, a decade ago in Minnesota, I walked a group of preteens, of many cultures, inner-city and suburban kids, out from their cabins into an open field to see the stars. Lying on their backs, watching meteors race earthward, seeing the magnitude of the night sky, many for the first time in such a "mid-field" setting—they were afraid. Turning off their flashlights was an accomplishment; staying in the field for more than a few minutes, a challenge.

Over the years, I have helped schools install some formal "quiet time" in their schedule midday, or a brief "reflection time" at the end of the school day. Increasingly people tell me there is no time for such frills—fifteen or twenty minutes—where children can do as they will in the classroom, silently. Given time to read, draw, write, sleep, or daydream, children can find pathways to peace. Such a frill.

Childhood depression is dramatically on the rise as a warning sign that there is neither enough individual space nor meaningful connection in the lives of the young. Instead of creating such real spaces for children, we are providing them psychopharmacological solutions! One can only imagine the consequences of these spaces becoming fully extinct in the experiences of the young.

Most adults are too busy to hold an open space of reverie for children. To create such a space, adults must be willing to be present. Not just attending, but present. Not multitasking, cell-phone witnessing, but present. To preserve childhood, adults must be able to remember and understand their own need for interior space for silence and solitude. Only then will they grasp at a somatic level how such a space is increasingly endangered for children.

Thomas Merton wrote, "In silence we face and admit the gap between the depths of our being, which we constantly ignore, and the surface, which is untrue to our own reality. We recognize the need to be at home with ourselves in order that we may go out to meet others, not just with a mask of affability, but with real commitment and authentic love."[1]

Children easily recognize and respond to this need, but without the opportunity for solitude this awareness will wither and die. Solitude, by filling the reservoirs of patience, self-control, and understanding, strengthens all relationships and nurtures families, schools, and communities. Each child needs at least one adult who can show them how times of solitude and silence help each of us convey a presence that can kindle kindness and loving persistence in the world.

Fourth Notion

GRAND CANYON

They say the layered earth rose up
Ancient rock leviathan
Trailing ages in its wake
Lifting earthmass toward the sun
And coursing water cut the rock away
To leave these many-storied walls
Exposé of ages gone
Around this breathless emptiness
More wondrous far than earth had ever known

My life has risen layered too
Each day each year in turn has left

Its fossil life and sediments
Evidence of lived and unlived hours
The tedium the anguish yes the joy
That some heart-deep vitality
Keeps pressing upward toward the day I die.

And Spirit cuts like water through it all
Carving out this emptiness
So inner eye can see
The soaring height of canyon walls within
Walls whose very color, texture, form
Redeem in beauty all my life has been
The darkness and the light, the false, the true
While deep below the living waters run
Cutting deeper through my parts
To resurrect my grave-bound heart

Making, always making, all things new.

—Parker J. Palmer

A DUSTING IN DEEP PLACES
—for Parker J. Palmer

Flying the weak winter skies of late November,
I notice the thin, white lines down in the valleys,
deep in the crevices, lining the river beds and rivulets
where it has snowed into the barren, brown hills.

Only from mid-air are these markings visible,
tracing the landscape like a lover's finger
running along the lifeline of the beloved's palm.

What I think I see hints at what lays hidden,
that which you have taught us to attend to
in the silent and patient places.

I look again.
This time I see the dusting itself
making everything else so evident from so far away.

I look again.
Down in the hillsides themselves,
I imagine the young hunters following their fathers

and grandfathers, following the fresh print of deer on opening day, skipping school.

I keep staring out the window as the plane descends, dissolving metaphor into gritty runway snow.

—Chip Wood

NOTE

1. Merton, T. *Creative Silence in Love and Living*. Orlando, Fla.: Harcourt Brace, 1979, p. 41.

REFLECTIONS

○

Marianne Novak Houston
retired middle-school teacher and
leader in the Courage to Teach program

In the fall of 1993, I was engaged in reshaping the "gifted and talented program" at a large middle school. It was not an easy task. I was moving the district from a program that tested and judged children, choosing only a small number to be included in special activities designed for them, to a program that offered various enrichment opportunities to all children. It was a busy and challenging time, for change is always hard; parents and children were questioning, and even some staff seemed less than supportive. I was aware of the toll it was taking in my life. Then a wonderful thing happened: I responded to an invitation to experience a retreat, the very first Courage to Teach retreat, facilitated by Parker Palmer.

The weekend retreat brought together twenty-two teachers from a variety of schools and backgrounds; it was the seed that grew into the Courage to Teach (CTT) program. This was a truly reflective time with colleagues, away from the daily grind of the classroom, with time for silence and meaningful dialogue, and the presence of a quiet, inspiring, yet entertaining leader who valued each of us so much.

As we sat together and addressed questions that we never do in our teacher lounges, I realized the sheer goodness that resides in the typical educator's heart! Equally important was coming to know myself better and remembering who I am, what gifts I bring to my personal and professional life, and returning to some practices I had earlier used to center myself and work more peacefully.

I subsequently worked with Parker and other wonderful colleagues in developing the CTT Program, which has strengthened education in so many places and is now at work in other professional communities. Currently I facilitate retreats for educators on all levels, as well as for philanthropists, health care workers, and folks at work in their faith communities. My work of teaching/learning is not done, and indeed it may never be done. That suits me well!

LEARNING BY HEART

An Ode to My Vocation as a Teacher

Marianne Novak Houston

AS A SMALL CHILD, I caught the familiar feeling by the tail. My mother, Valerie Natalie Rys—eyes closed, and a smile teasing 'round the fresh, still-warm strawberry—would declare, "Ah, this is living!" I would recognize *her* feeling and dance with delight inside my own skin. My mother knew that she was born to savor the goodness of creation and that small pleasures were not small. Her knowledge radically imprinted my own life view, and in my own small world I felt kinship with her when the water held me wholly suspended in the public swimming pool. And again, when the apple tree branch supported my small behind as I sat among its blossoms in spring and its fruit in fall. It was *living!*

Nowadays, at an age far beyond my mother's in strawberry time, and after almost seven decades of my daily love affair with the real, I might describe the experience, "the feeling," as my *overflowing joy and sense of mystery, a treasured inner laughter* that bubbles up from time to time. It's there at the seasons' changing, on the first day of each returning winter, spring, summer, or autumn. It's there when I fold myself into the lake's fresh water, or when I savor a loved poem. It's also there in that sense of *wholeness* I experience in my current teaching work. Here educators, we students of life, search in solitary and community settings for meaning and wholeness. In that space and work, a familiar feeling of fullness frequently overtakes me—a deep, rolling sense of joy and assurance that, as Julian of Norwich recommends, "All will be well, all things will be well." *It is a holy blending of emotion and knowledge, holding my senses and my intellect, my heart and my soul, captive.* This work of teaching, it occurs to me, is my warm strawberry, rich, juicy, rewarding. Having my joy and my gifts meet the needs of a world hungry for learning is delicious, and it's a goodly part, from my present vantage point, of what makes my life worth the living.

The feeling of which I speak is larger by far than a fleeting, vague sense of happiness. It is an unspoken, subjective sense that teaching is, at least in part, what I was born to, and a contentment with that truth: it is healthy and fine to own it.

In sophisticated, more "academic" circles, one finds at times a reticence toward simple, subjective admissions; one absorbs an ambience of "objectivism" where it is not safe or suave to own the simple joys of one's own life. Childlike enthusiasm for what feeds one's soul is sometimes seen as childish and unintellectual. The not-so-hidden message of academe is that the *intellectual* ought to be divorced from the *emotional, heart-centered realities*. In such circumstances, one feels unsafe in *emoting* as one *ponders*. In my small hometown in Illinois, I think we'd have realized the inauthentic in this approach and would have said summarily, if irreverently, "Hogwash! If we can't invite the whole of ourselves—minds, hearts, and spirits—into our relationships and our work, what are we going to do with those elements that are 'left over'?" In truth, we prairie folk find ourselves to be in good company here: the renowned neuroscientist Antonio Damasio takes up the issue of the indissoluble relationship of mind and body in his two latest books, *The Feeling of What Happens* and *Looking for Spinoza*; in a body-and-mind-pleasing statement he writes: "No body, never mind." So, I teach because it *feels* good and right and *is* intellectually pleasing, for me.

For forty-five years, I have walked down the path called Teacher. How did I come to choose this path or profession? . . . or perhaps better, how did the profession choose me? What roles did my mind and heart have in the decision? Was this a wise thing to do with my "one wild and precious life"?

As I explore these questions, my life stories, my memories, crowd in on me, for my stories invariably illuminate the link between me and my life, my spirit and my work, my soul and my role.

Searching my memories, I am drawn back to my second grade autumn at St. Mary's School. Early in the school year, Sister Charlotte Ann said quietly to me, "Marianne, you can read, and these children can't. I want you to come out here each day with them and teach them to read." She had arranged eight tiny chairs along the hallway wall and led out eight little boys and me. Foreshadowing a lifelong habit of treading where angels fear to, I eagerly accepted the challenge. Thus began my teaching career, albeit shakily, for these little boys were not always the serious students one would have hoped. We played as much as we read, and often I had to chase them down the hall (when we weren't hanging out the hallway window seeing who could spit into the exact center of the large rock on the ground below!). But we also read daily, and repetitious reading together inevitably brought some change and growth. The learning for me was simple: Teaching Is Fun. (This, in fact, is how a second grader would define that "ecstatic feeling" we're pursuing in this essay.)

The teaching bug had bit, or at least it was sniffing 'round the edges of my life. My ninth summer was full of long and hot, sweet and sweat-filled days. My friend Johnny Burke and I would spend hours scouring on hands and knees the newly delivered pebbles spread over Wallace School's play-ground. These rocks somehow filled me with deep pleasure, and my pock-ets with weighty treasures, and tied me to the earth in some radical fashion. I imagined their forming and their journeys; I shared with Johnny what I knew of volcanoes and magma and gravel pits. We oohed and aahed and traded stones back and forth. This became another experience of teaching and learning in relationship with another, so profound that sixty years later, reflecting on it, I can still feel the pebbles cutting into my knees and the pleasure I experienced in the shared experience! (Now I wonder in retro-spect whether my considerable rock collection belonged to me, or I to it—just as I came to question in later years whether the "subject" I taught belonged to me or I to it.)

My tenth summer found our family the envy of our neighborhood friends. Our dog Sandy and our cat Mimi had each produced lovely litters—eight puppies, six kittens!—in opposite corners of our Illinois basement. The kids were ecstatic, our parents resigned. I watched Mimi and Sandy teaching their young important lessons, relating to them contentedly and in patient and generous ways, and I do not discount these hours of observation as I pon-der my personal preparation as teacher. Here were the beleaguered mother-teachers giving full time and attention to their young, and we captivated children observed the process with the generous full attention of the best stu-dents in our classrooms. Remembering the mothers' patience, and the hours we spent observing, teaches me again how significant a role time plays, in happiness as well as learning.

I was thus, so to speak, an early convert to the profession. No small influ-ence on me, from a formal perspective, were the teachers who patiently held and taught the talkative, active little girl I was. They were profound and strong models for me. Eventually I elected to join them in their work, and so after high school I entered the congregation of teaching sisters called Sisters of Loretto. They are a community of remarkable women whom I respect and love deeply and with whom I maintain close contact. Though I left vowed membership in 1966, after thirteen years I remain imprinted with the cha-risma of this extraordinary American order of sisters.

When I began my formal teaching career in 1958, fifty-two eighth graders graced (may I say *overflowed*) my small classroom at St. Pius V School in downtown St. Louis. I was also codirector of the almost-one-hundred-voice children's choir. These "upper el" boys and girls, who struggled valiantly with Church Latin and the neumes and punctums of ancient Gregorian chant, were my new treasures, my new playground rocks, my new pets. We bravely plowed through polyphonic music too—mostly very old and in mys-terious languages—and the beautiful music that came forth was a result of highly collaborative effort. Deeply connected by the music, we sang our way through the year, seeming to breathe together in a way that allowed us all to grow. This was destined to draw me again to the radical connection of my own heart with good and beautiful subjects—this time music, and children—and seal my fate as teacher. These children instructed me daily in the wisdom that I was not alone: that *all that is* is connected at some deep and inexplicable level; each sings its own melody into the harmony of the whole. I know this now in a way that the busyness of that time did not allow, but the familiar, deep pleasure was there, as was a grasp of the sacredness of our common work. Despite the challenges, the confusion, the frustration, the actual pain of my first years of teaching, I experienced a delight that has remained. The companionship with students and colleagues on the journey of, in Viktor Frankl's words, our "search for meaning" was bracing and enlivening. "Teaching is a profound experience," I might have said, "where my inner life and my outer life can be mutually fed."

Perhaps this is to say that one of the gifts of the teacher's life is that it allows me to access the "hidden wholeness" of which Thomas Merton speaks. To push the truth further is to realize that *part* is only a human way of speaking: there is only the whole. Divisions, parts, are in some way illusions; *undividedness* is the natural way of existing in the world, for me and for my students and for everyone. The discovery and rediscovery of this truth sweetens the living. It ties my *being* to my *doing*. Merton's hidden wholeness is reality, and the only real, authentic life is the undivided one.

I feel moved to say here, in the interests of truth, that though many more of my teacher days have been filled with love and light than have been dark, it is also true that the weeds of cynicism and despair have at times claimed their space alongside the flowers of optimism and hope. Although not always easily, particularly in the face of the tough realities of today's classrooms, the virtues of faith and hope have taken root, and they have been shored up by those tough allies, courage and perseverance. As is true with most teachers, the awe present in my teaching moments does not always feel like delight or joy, in the sense of fun. Sometimes it is pure wonder, or a raw satisfaction, or the presence of some nameless, inexplicable acceptance, or a dogged internal "Carry on!" command that fills me up. But there are those wonderful times when a silent song sings its way into my head, and the lyrics go something like "Ain't it grand! Sometimes the magic works!" . . . with honest admission that sometimes it doesn't.

There has been a slow but persistent growth in my awareness regarding this teaching vocation, helped along always by my students, and by studying the writings of numerous poets, philosophers, and storytellers, and also by increasing reflection on my experiences. I lived the life of the teacher meeting daily and yearly challenges, and as the years passed I found myself asking questions around my future work. I began by looking back: Where have I been on my life's journey? Which roads have I chosen, which left unexplored? What has brought me joy? Teaching and learning were always at the heart of it. I began also to consider the present, as well as my future work. Did my current teaching work fit my present state? Where was the road now leading my graying head and increasingly creaky joints? Slowly the next steps in my journey have become clear, and I have embraced the next iteration of my teaching life: facilitating teaching/learning circles of educators and others, in programs called the Courage to Teach and the Courage to Lead, where both personal and professional renewal is addressed.

You may judge it a bit of madness, this choice to continue teaching in another mode, given the current view of the teaching life. I have in fact more than once asked myself: Why continue my work in a profession that has come to be demeaned and unappreciated by so many? How is it that I sit now, in many circles of educators, when I could be warming my favorite chair with a good book in hand, or swimming the blue waters of Maho Bay? Why has formal retirement eluded me and meant instead the forging of this new "classroom"?

Maybe my mother-in-law, Louvenia Houston, had part of the truth, in her laughingly repeated "That Marianne, she just can't sit still!" But there is more. I have become my work; my work has become me. Not to teach would leave me hungry and thirsty; it is nourishment for the continuing journey. Engaging educators in a communitarian search for meaning is prime teaching. It's terrific soul food—or, if you like, warm and sweet strawberries—and I am a gourmand. *I relish it.*

There were other added ruminations that led me into this adventurous form of teaching. They focused on some pesky stumbling blocks against which I have faltered in recent years. First, the responsibilities placed on teachers today, particularly prekindergarten through senior high school, are enormous, and the need for perspective and renewal is great. It is as if our culture speaks to educators thus: "Here are our children. They are in great confusion and pain. We are puzzled as parents how to help them at home. Our churches seem powerless to lead them effectively. The social service and other government agencies are much less than helpful and in fact frequently exacerbate the problems. You. You take them. You fix them." But that's not all; the directives continue: "Do this work with decreased funds, larger classes, and less support. Make them well, please. Make them learn. And if you don't . . ."

Another series of considerations loomed larger for me as time passed. During my later years in the classroom, I began to notice the diminished trust and esteem with which the educator is held, both from without the profession and within (teachers frequently internalize the message: if only the schools—read "teachers"—would get their act together, all would be well!). I puzzled over the approach taken in well-meaning staff development programs. Why did most of them assume that teachers were beginning at the starting blocks? Why did most seem to carry the message that we were the *tabula rasa,* the empty slate, on which well-meaning "presenters" could and needed to write their new directives, so that our classrooms would be successful in the images of the current expert standing before us? Why were large groups of experienced teachers so often brought together and talked *at,* the presenters too rarely asking questions of us or attempting to use the wisdom and expertise present in their audience? Why were business leaders assumed to have all the answers for schools and teachers, in a field quite alien to their own? Why was there decreasing joy among teachers as well as students? Why was a sense of helplessness developing, the sense of "What can we do?" Where was the joy that had once accompanied our work in our classrooms?

Another important consideration was the current focus on standardized tests, high-stakes tests (standards and evaluation have always been important in education, and they remain so, but the focus has shifted, and your favorite educator can explain to you how), fact factories masquerading as schools, the concept that schools are businesses that ought to operate on the same model as our disease-ridden corporations, the recent suggestion by an emissary of our federal Department of Education that creative teaching approaches should be discouraged ("We know what works," she stated, in an unbelievable view that all children learn in the same way!) . . . all of this leaves little time for contemplation of what it is we are really about here as educators and effectively robs teachers and children of the joy inherent in authentic education.

Lastly is the current understanding in some quarters of what it means to teach, that is, something akin to the work of a technician ("open the head, pour in some facts, check the resulting product, and move the receptacle along to the next station"). This seems more closely allied to mechanics and engineering than to the holistic, organic process that education is at its authentic best. In fact, I believe that many noneducators, who currently have enormous power over the profession and practice of education, see it as an engineering feat not unlike what we are doing to our foods. In exchange for plastic perfection and a longer shelf life bioengineering often leaves us with produce drained of the juiciness, sweetness, and goodness. This view of education ignores the key principles of learning: it robs us of the all-important reality of relationship as the basis for all learning, and it puts statistics above students. We are in danger of producing a product that is less than wonderfully and happily human!

My teacher heart aches over these and other considerations. So I convene today these quiet learning circles into which I invite educators from all walks to enter into dialogue with their own teacher hearts. We explore together the mystery of our life on earth, the inner life of *being* as well as the professional, outer life of *doing*. We learn, at the very least, to confront our fears and sometimes even learn to accept them as friends that serve us along the way, and to experience the wonder of recognizing in our own fears those of others as well. Claiming time and space to pursue our own truth, we learn over time to create space for our students and our colleagues to do the same. We grow through solitary and communal work into our original selves and into the richer selves we are becoming; we find courage, light, and strength to live in an undivided manner, where what we do in our life and work is aligned with the values, virtues, and principles we hold dear.

"I don't need to be anything else . . . I don't need to be fixed. The basic work is remembering who I am," one teacher stated simply. "The more I return to my own truth the more courageous and honest I become in my classroom, in my school . . . and in my whole life," said another. The challenge, another opined, is the will to hold relentlessly to the truth, "to hold ferociously to what it is *to educate*."

As I consider the importance of this kind of being together, I am returned to a classroom of some years ago. Sixth graders were pursuing a study of C. S. Lewis's book *The Lion, the Witch, and the Wardrobe*. We considered a quote from the book: " 'But Professor, if something is real it's here all the time,' said Peter. 'Is it?' asked the professor." What did they think of this exchange? For an hour they mulled over its meaning, argued its truth, ranged into an amazing consideration of the good, the true, and the beautiful, of love and hatred, of life and death, of God and of evil, in genuine and unself-conscious dialogue. As he left the room later, Cory looked me in the eye: "Mrs. H., what *was* that we were doing?" he inquired. "I think you'd say we were philosophizing, Cory." "Oh. We should do more of that," he counseled solemnly, and promptly disappeared into the teeming hallway. Following him, Heather looked at me through her thick and filthy glasses and said, "Gee, Mrs. H., we got to say what we thought!" I confess that my heart not only broke open from the familiar full feeling—we had lived some moments of truth together—but it also just plain broke when I realized how few opportunities school affords students to actually reflect and speak from the heart.

I have come to realize that if we are to respond to our students' need to speak from the heart, to allow them space and time to pursue their own search for meaning, we teachers must have such time and space ourselves. It is just plain tasty—in strawberry language—this sitting together in our circular classroom, gaining strength from each other's courage and honesty, and learning to speak our truth. The questions that are posed by the conditions of our everyday life as educators are examined; others too float to the surface, and they are not ignored. One such question, posed decisively by a teacher, gave us food for much thought: "In so many workshops and conferences and conventions they effectively tell us we don't know, but if we don't know, what is this wisdom that keeps bubbling up here?" Her words rippled through the community, and a certain light filled the room. The remainder of our time together was spent in silent as well as vocal contemplation of these words and what they might mean, and the consequences of living into our teaching lives more fully.

The fundamental questions we are wont to confront in our circles are immensely rewarding, renewing, and regenerative—not to mention mind-satisfyingly interesting. Addressing questions full of meaning, in a context of deep and trustworthy community, tastes warm and sweet; it becomes a way of life, bringing growth and healthy change in its wake. "As I change, the world around me changes," said Gandhi; indeed, the circle experience transfers into a healthier and highly educational ambience in our schools and our classrooms.

In a fifth retreat, Marie, a thirty-year veteran of the classroom, wryly reminded us: "Questions explored in our community here aren't ordinarily dealt with in our faculty meetings or staff lunchrooms, friends, but they're so much more important." In another retreat specifically designed for administrators, a young principal confided: "It's really liberating to ponder together some of these fundamental questions, and doing it with my staff has made our school healthier and more truly productive for our children." A school district business manager—a very private person—offered this: "Just when you think you have penetrated your deepest layers, new ones come to the surface, and so I see the value of our coming together repeatedly." Cory and Heather would say: "We should do more of this!"

Thus for me the teaching life continues, and it's profound *fun*—almost as much fun as spitting from an upper window into the center of the rock below, or finding the perfect rock in the pebble-strewn playground. It is true that in my lengthening life nowhere has Merton's hidden wholeness been more present and tangible than in my role as teacher. Teacher, conceived of as teacher *and* learner, sharer *and* gleaner of wisdom, one who leads out the wisdom of another while allowing the other to lead out what lies buried deep within oneself—the role is both amazingly simple and amazingly complex. I have no doubt that its joys and challenges will keep me teaching/learning into my seventh decade and beyond.

"What do you want to do when you grow up?" I remember this question repeated so many times in my childhood. I did not know the answer then; it is not a question for the very young, I have learned. I don't recall ever pondering, planning, or charting my response to it, but I find myself living happily, daily, my answer to it. Through my teaching life, I am spared a lifelong hunger for fulfillment. My work is more than dry labor; it is virtue spiced by passion, it is a tantalizing main course set before me daily. It guarantees that I do not go hungry. It ensures that I do not live my life, in Mary Oliver's words, "simply having visited this world."

I am content that the teaching life found me so many years ago, for its gifts and its challenges bring the sweetness and saltiness that make for a delicious life. Teaching: a well-seasoned, balanced, nourishing meal. Ah, this is living!

REFLECTIONS

○

Henry Emmons, M.D.
psychiatrist and founder of
the Inner Life of Healers program

I first encountered Parker Palmer when I read *Let Your Life Speak*, which touched me deeply. It was written with such wisdom, openness, and acceptance. Reading it was like sitting down with a close friend—a really *articulate* friend. He had faced his life, accepted it, and allowed himself to be transformed by it. He gently offered that same possibility to me.

It was refreshing to encounter an author who was so endearingly human. My internal "truth meter" shot way up as I read Parker's words. Later, when I heard him speak, I had the same experience—only more strongly. I felt enlivened as I listened, and I knew it was still possible to work with the soul. Here was someone who was doing it!

I attribute much of what is best in my present work directly to Parker. This is true whether I am working with patients or teaching, writing, coaching executives, or leading a retreat. He offered me the initial spark of recognition: "Oh, *that's* the inner life!" He provided the means for doing it: "*This* is how you can work with the soul." He has also, blessedly, helped to sustain it: "Here is how one might feed and care for one's *own* soul while doing this work." One of those ways is through friendship, and I count Parker as a dear friend.

It is a tribute to Parker that I have learned more about deep healing from him and his work than from twenty years of psychiatric training and practice. Not only have I learned about healing, I have *experienced* it. My hope is to honor Parker by spreading this work to others as he has so graciously done for me.

INSIGHTS ON THE
INNER LIFE OF HEALERS

Henry Emmons, M.D.

AT THE BEGINNING OF A RECENT RETREAT for health professionals, we invited everyone to say why they had come. One of the physicians, a family doctor named Richard, said:

> It doesn't seem right that someone who is only forty-six years old thinks constantly about retiring. I thought I came into medicine for the right reasons. At first, I loved my practice. But the longer I do it, the harder it seems to get. The joy has gone out of medicine for me, and I don't know how long I can keep doing this. I came this weekend to try to answer this question: Should I get out now and do something else, or can I find a way to stay in medicine and make it good again? I think about this all the time, and I don't know what to do. I hoped that if I got away and had some time, I might be able to come up with an answer. I just know that I can't keep going on like this.

Richard is a devoted and caring physician in the prime of his life. But his work has long ago ceased to nourish or sustain him. He isn't so much burned out as he is parched. Whatever well he has drawn from has long since dried up. Richard's struggle reminds me of a cartoon by Gary Larson, creator of the Far Side series. As I recall, the image is of a few cattle grazing disinterestedly in a field. But one of them has stood up on his hind legs, and with an expression of surprised indignation says, "Hey, wait a minute! This is grass! We've been eating grass!"

Likewise, there are more and more physicians, nurses, therapists, and other health professionals who are standing up and saying:

> "Hey, wait a minute! This isn't what I wanted!"

> "I spend all my time doing paperwork."

> "I don't get time to know my patients anymore."

> "The money isn't compensation enough for all that this takes out of me."

> "I feel drained by my patients."

"I have nothing left to give to my family."

"I want to get out."

Malnourished at the Banquet of Life

One of the really striking observations from my work with health professionals is just how strong their sense of calling is. The need for meaning and the desire to be of service are woven into their beings as surely as is their DNA. Oh, to be sure, there are those who entered health care primarily out of an intellectual interest, or as an acceptable way to make money, or because of family expectations. But if you have seen the heart of a healer, you know how strong the pull is to somehow take all of one's individual gifts and attributes and make of oneself an instrument of service in a world of suffering. How troubling, then, to go through all the years of training and preparation, get established in a career, and then find out that this isn't so.

The irony is that, as physicians, we have a front-row seat to some of the greatest of life's dramas, yet somehow the joy and meaning of it elude us. It is as if we accepted an invitation to a rich banquet only to realize much later that we've been eating grass! This sense of dryness has become epidemic in medicine and presents a considerable risk to the field. Far too many physicians are dealing with the same struggles as Richard is, and they are contemplating an early retirement. We risk losing many skilled and compassionate healers at the height of their powers because the life has gone out of their work. Even if they continue to practice, doctors who are no longer engaged and enlivened by their work are less effective with their patients.

How could this have happened? Why have so many who felt such a strong sense of calling been nearly driven from their work? What can be done to replenish the deep internal reservoir that physicians need to sustain a lifetime of service?

Being Lost

Even at its best, medicine is a demanding profession. Physicians are under enormous stress today; this is increasingly recognized by hospital and clinic administrators, medical societies, and educational institutions. Recent surveys of physicians have found that an increasing number of them are unhappy and have become dissatisfied with their career. A 2002 California Medical Association survey found that a startling 51 percent of physicians plan to leave medicine within the next three years. A recent

Mayo clinic study found that 30 to 60 percent of practicing physicians experience burnout, as defined by emotional exhaustion, depersonalization, a sense of low personal accomplishment, and decreased effectiveness at work. Other surveys find that a large percentage of physicians would not choose to become a physician again, and an even higher percentage would *not* recommend the profession to their children. There are also studies suggesting that, despite fewer health risk factors, physicians have a higher rate of mortality than other professionals and are at greater risk for depression and anxiety, especially in their training years. What has gone wrong with the noble profession of medicine?

The usual explanations point to something external to ourselves. Indeed, there are many forces impinging on medicine today. Here is just a sampling of what you might overhear in a discussion among frustrated physicians:

- Health care has been taken over by big business. It's all about the bottom line. It has become high-tech and low-touch. Insurance payment favors technology and procedures over the amount and quality of time spent with patients.

- Regulations have taken precedence over caring. Physicians have lost control over decision making, and we have to fight for the care that we feel our patients need.

- Most of the increased dollars in health care go to higher administrative costs, drugs, and technology. Clinicians' salaries are stagnant or decreasing.

- We no longer have a long-term relationship with our patients. They change health plans every year or two and now relate to a "health care system" rather than to their own doctor, someone with a face and a name.

- We are bone weary from the twelve-hour days and the nights and weekends on call. A typical physician in a clinic may see twenty-five to thirty patients in a day, make hospital rounds, and respond to dozens of phone calls from patients and other doctors. All of this leaves many of us depleted and exhausted. As physicians, we see how our families often suffer because of so little time with us, and even when we are around there may not be much energy or attention left for the family.

- The stress of having people's lives in our hands becomes a heavy burden. At the same time, the public's intolerance of errors and their readiness to sue places so much pressure on physicians that it seems at times unbearable.

Medical societies are actively engaged in trying to address these issues. But how do individuals on the front lines of health care respond to all of this? There are those who direct their energy toward changing the system, becoming politically savvy or trying to retake control of the finances of health care. Others conclude that they simply need to withdraw, care less, or get out of the system entirely. More physicians are changing to holistic or alternative practices, in part because traditional healing practices still honor the need for time spent with patients to create the spaciousness needed for healing. Many just complain, or suffer in silence. The problems seem so vast that most simply don't know what to do.

A Heart Dis-ease

It is often said that there is a health care crisis in the United States. Typically, this refers to health care financing and delivery systems, which, unless they are addressed, could lead to an implosion of the health care system in this country within a few years. I think it is a legitimate concern. But I believe there is another kind of crisis from the perspective of the health care professionals, a crisis of the heart. There is not enough joy and love and kindness to sustain the hearts of those who serve. We know what happens when there is a blockage of the flow of nutrients to the heart; it closes down, and it causes pain. The public is mostly unaware of this, but many, many well-meaning and skilled caregivers are living and working today in pain of one kind or another.

In my view, a truly healthy response to all of this involves far more than working to improve the system. We can use this crisis as a call to look within. We need to become resilient again. We must rediscover what gives us joy and meaning, and hope that some of it is in the arena of work. We need to create the time and skills for reflection. We must learn to listen deeply and authentically, where we hear more with the heart than with the mind. We need to develop our innate capacity for compassion, to be an openhearted presence for someone in his or her suffering. The minds and the hands of today's health professionals are indeed finely trained. But when it comes to the heart, our development has been greatly wanting. We have been on our own in this realm and have not had the time, the inclination, or the ability to do much about it. These are not problems of the sort that can be solved by external means. This is an inside-out job.

A great need in the health care system is to attend to the inner life of those who would be healers. We have invested too much and the stakes are too high for us to lose a generation of talented and committed health professionals. In this human endeavor, we cannot rely on technology alone. We need our healers to be more and more human, to become more and more themselves.

Physician, Heal Thyself

It may just be in my nature to ask questions of this sort, or perhaps I lack the stress tolerance of many of my colleagues. Whatever it was, I didn't make it to midcareer before hitting the proverbial wall. During my medical training, I chose to become a psychiatrist, in part out of inspiration from the writings of Viktor Frankl, Carl Jung, and others who spoke about issues of soul and healing. I liked the idea of becoming a "doctor of the soul." But it didn't take long for me to realize that the apple of modern psychiatry had fallen pretty far from the tree of depth and meaning.

My first job was in a Minnesota HMO—a very good one actually, but a place where gains in efficiency often came at the expense of time and relationships with patients. My therapist colleagues called it "fast food psychiatry." Relatively few psychiatrists were responsible for a huge number of patients, so we were expected to quickly evaluate and prescribe medicines. Time for really listening and having an authentic relationship with our patients was mostly left to other non-M.D. therapists, if it was addressed at all. After a few years of this, I left and moved into a more community-based practice. Gradually, I realized that what I wanted no longer existed, or at least it was not common or easily found. Things had changed for most psychiatrists everywhere, not just in the HMOs. The field of psychiatry, once so filled with soul, had arguably become one of the driest branches of medicine. That was not what I would have chosen, but it was the role to which I felt consigned. As I listened to physicians from other fields, it became clear to me that this was not unique to psychiatry. I was beginning to realize that medicine had lost its way. The industrial model had taken hold of medicine and was not about to let go.

Just ten years into my career, I knew I had to make a change, quickly and significantly. I was fortunate to receive a sabbatical grant, a unique opportunity for physicians to step out of hectic clinical practice and learn something new. Importantly, this sabbatical program was intended as a time to slow down and reflect, so that the second half of one's career could be done differently, more sustainably. We physicians tend to be a driven bunch, and we have been for most of our lives. During the seven to ten years of medical training, we scarcely had time to eat, sleep, or maintain our significant relationships. In the four years of college before that, most of us were intense, focused overachievers. Anything less and we stood little chance to get into medical school. Of course, the seeds of overachievement were generally sown long before that. Most of us have *always* been hard working, compliant, nose-to-the-grindstone types. It is very often part of the physician personality. Slowing down and reflecting are foreign concepts to most of us. Yet they may be exactly what we need.

I used my year to study natural and alternative medicine in psychiatry and applications of mindfulness meditation to clinical practice. I also worked to develop programs of renewal for health care professionals. It was clear that I was not alone in struggling to maintain a sense of commitment and love for my work. Indeed, there were scores of physicians and others who were wondering how they could reclaim a sense of calling or an attitude of sacredness toward the healing arts. One of the most difficult aspects of being a physician today is the sense of isolation, carrying the weight of such difficult decisions and occasional mistakes, with precious few opportunities to talk about it. What a gift it could be, I thought, to be able to step back and examine, *with others,* the really important questions related to being a modern-day healer.

The Inner Life of Healers

As I studied and worked with these themes, I encountered Parker and his work. I listened to him speak one day about the Courage to Teach program and what it was doing for teachers, who have so much in common with health professionals. I heard Parker use a particular term in describing this work. He said that what they were really about was working with "the inner life of teachers." It really struck a chord in me, and I immediately applied it to the world I knew best, that of health care. It was like the moment when the woodcarver found just the right tree and saw within it the already completed bell stand. Out of this encounter, a program was born. The Inner Life of Healers was developed with the Center for Spirituality and Healing at the University of Minnesota, and since 2001 we have been reaching out to health professionals who feel there is merit in exploring questions of value and meaning in a community of like-minded professionals.

Each year since then, we have offered a retreat program based partly on the Courage to Teach model, modified for health professionals. We offer introductory programs of one day or one weekend, and also a cohort program of five weekends. In that model, the same group of fifteen to twenty people gather once a season for a year, and again for a final weekend six months later. In just three years, we have encountered hundreds of health professionals who are trying to better align their work in the external world with the designs of their innermost selves. We use meditation and guided imagery, poetry and art, journaling and self-reflection, small and large group discussion, solitude and community. People have opportunities to tell their stories, and also to listen and be touched by others. They are given the invitation to participate in a clearness committee, a Quaker process of quiet discernment, either as a focus person or a participant. Even those who have spent their lives listening are moved by the depth of the experience.

Why do they come? Sometimes it is with a deep question. Often it is to have a chance to slow down, to seek quiet and solitude, to have time for thinking or discernment. Occasionally it is because they recognize signs of depletion and are looking for ways to renew themselves. Others want to explore how to integrate the spiritual part of themselves into their work. A large number are looking for an experience of community. Some seek mentoring for their inner journey. Many express a desire to become more grounded or balanced, to feel more peaceful and less stressed.

Whatever their reasons for coming, participants usually encounter more than they expected or even realized was possible. I think this is because, with few exceptions, they come with such an openness and desire to grow, speak from the heart, and be authentic with one another. Although it cannot be scientifically measured, one knows when there is love in the room. I have experienced that in abundance while doing this work.

Deeply Listening

One of the great gifts of the Inner Life of Healers program, as with the Courage to Teach, is that we don't have to do this inner work alone. There is a lovely Buddhist term, *kalyanamitra,* which refers to "good friends," or soul friends, who journey together and aid one another along their spiritual path. It seems to me that this is what the cohort can become. If it is to happen, though, a great sense of "spaciousness" and safety with one another is required. To help create this, we spend a good deal of our early time together on the practice of "deep listening." Nearly everyone in our groups finds this to be a revelation. Many thought of themselves already as being good listeners but discover how often their listening is only partial. We are trained to ask certain questions and always be thinking of potential problems and solutions. We may be putting a lot of energy into focusing on the person in front of us, but this is hardly the same thing as true listening.

Participants find it delightful, and surprisingly hard, to *really* listen to someone, without distraction, without thinking about the next question or what they will say when it is their turn. They notice how much of the time, while listening, they are evaluating or judging what the other person is saying. In deep listening, they are asked to simply receive what the other is saying—fully attentive, accepting and open, hearing it not just with the ears or the mind but with the whole of one's being. Once they truly experience this, they realize what a rare and precious thing it is to be heard in this way. To share something personal—a surprise, a celebration, or a wound—with a group that is listening in this way can be quite profound!

At one of our retreats, a nurse with twenty-five years of experience shared with the group a story that she remembered only when we invited the group to reflect on their own experiences with deep listening. She began with a phrase to describe how she usually is at work: "I'm such a fixer." She went on to relate one of her earliest experiences as a nurse. She was working on an inpatient unit and was in the room of an older woman who was clearly dying, but no one wanted to acknowledge or talk about it. As the young nurse went about her business, the head nurse walked into the room and the patient said aloud, "I'm dying."

The charge nurse responded with a simple question. "Are you scared?"

As she continued to tell the story, the participant's voice began to crack with emotion that filled the room. "That was such an amazing moment for me. *I* was scared. I wanted to say, 'Oh no, you're not dying. You're going to be OK.' But the question made it all right, and the woman opened up and talked about her fear. I'll never forget what an impact that made on me. That taught me so much about listening."

The Healing Power of Presence

Making the shift from fixing or doing to simply being present with another is a real challenge, especially for physicians. After participating in a clearness committee, where two hours are spent listening and asking questions of the focus person, the doctors in the group often comment on how hard it is for them not to offer advice. They are so used to telling others what their problems are and how to fix them that, in one doctor's words, they "nearly have to be restrained" to keep from doing it. But having the opportunity to be a nonjudging presence for another, and experiencing firsthand how powerful it is, gives some the freedom to try it out in their work.

When a group comes back to meet after a three-month period of time, we usually ask them to relate some stories about what has changed, or what they have noticed since the previous gathering. Susan told a story that nicely illustrates what is possible when we trust that we offer healing because of *who we are* as much as what we do.

Susan is a family physician. Like every other primary care doctor working on the front lines, she has known the pressure of seeing twenty-five, thirty, or more patients per day, each seemingly more complex than the last. It became so untenable for her that she eventually opted out of the system and opened her own clinic offering holistic assessment and consultation. She felt sure that what she might sacrifice in income she would gain back in satisfaction. Early on in this endeavor, she encountered an elderly woman with a long list of chronic medical problems, and an even longer list of medications. She probably had ten or more medical problems she wanted to discuss. Yet most physicians have only fifteen to twenty minutes to sort this out, if they aren't running behind. This poor woman had reached the limit of what modern medicine could offer her, and still she was suffering greatly.

But Susan had made a conscious choice to work differently, being more attentive to her own needs and the needs of her patients. She scheduled an entire hour for this initial assessment and then went over the hour so that this woman could finish telling her story. Since they didn't have time to get to any solutions, they planned to meet again the following week. When the woman came in, she told Susan how much she had improved.

"But I haven't even given you any remedies yet," Susan said.

"Oh, I went home and told my husband that the good doctor had really *listened* to me, and I felt so much better afterward."

Most physicians wish they had more time and could really listen and try to address their patients more comprehensively. They try to give their patients the time they need, which is why they get so far behind. Often it is the best, most caring, and most competent physicians who attract the most patients with the most complicated problems. They want to serve their patients better, but they can only do so much when they feel the crush of too many patients, paperwork, phone calls, and the like.

Dealing with the Inner Winter

I am not suggesting that we strive for deep listening with every patient we encounter. Sometimes it isn't necessary. But if we want to be healers, it is an essential skill. One of its real beauties is that it is not something we do just for the sake of our patients. We also do it for ourselves. The real miracle is that it is healing for all of us. Physicians too are very much in need of healing.

Joseph is an outstanding physician. He is smart, caring, and careful, and he is sure to keep his skills refined by reading and attending conferences. Most would agree that he is a cut above the average physician in most every way. But now, in the middle of his career, he has run into a wall dreaded by every doctor. He is being sued for malpractice.

Joseph has been advised by his attorneys not to discuss the details of what happened. He can only say that a patient died and the family has blamed him even though he is sure that he did nothing wrong. In some ways, it makes no difference whether an actual mistake was made or not. The very allegation of a mistake, coupled with the seriousness of a life-and-death situation, cuts to the core of the physician's identity. It questions integrity, eats away at confidence, and erodes any joy that the physician still finds in the practice of medicine. The words used in a malpractice claim—*negligent, incompetent, blatant disregard*—are enough to bother anyone. They can destroy some physicians.

Of course, there are legitimate malpractice claims. But to be sued, rightly or wrongly, is a dreaded thing for a physician. I think we all know there are many lawsuits against physicians that are without merit or are outright frivolous. The public at large has no idea what an emotional trauma it is to be sued, or what a drain it can be to live with the constant awareness that, if we err, or if something goes badly wrong, we will be sued. The sad thing is that we carry this burden largely in isolation. It is hardly ever talked about. If there is any aspect of medical life that is shrouded in shadow, it is the area of medical mistakes and malpractice. We are human, and we know that we are not perfect. Yet we feel that we have to be.

Joseph cannot talk about the details of what went wrong. But at the retreat he could discuss what was going on inside him. He spoke of how the family's suit left him feeling hurt and betrayed. He was angry at the sense of injustice, when he had done no wrong. He was filled with fear, insecurity, and uncertainty. He grieved at the toll this was taking on him and his family. He was filled with shame, justified or not. He wondered if he would ever recover and be able to enjoy the practice of medicine again. His eyes filled with tears as he shared with us the burning sense of loneliness and isolation that he felt. Everyone in the room was riveted, for we knew whereof he spoke. We felt powerless to change much of what he described, but there was something we could do (and had already done). He was no longer alone in this.

Joseph's problems did not go away after talking about this. But neither did they feel so heavy, so dark. We *need* to tell our stories without fear of judgment, without having to hide our imperfections or insecurities. We need to bring our inner lives out of shadow, into the light of personal reflection, compassion, and community. We do need to live divided no more, in health care as much as in any human endeavor.

The Rebirth of Joy

Richard, the family physician described at the beginning of this essay who was unsure he could go on, came to me at the end of his first retreat. He apologized that he had not participated more verbally during the weekend. He assured me that he was deeply engaged in the process of the weekend and was grateful for it. "I'm not sure what happened, but somewhere in the middle of the retreat I realized that I really do love my work. I don't yet know how, but somehow I will find a way to be able to keep doing this for a long time. I got what I came here for. Thank you."

A Life Lived in Service

Every health professional at every stage of his or her career has an inner life worthy of attention. The soul is longing to be heard, but it speaks softly and is drowned out by the din and fray of our typical lives. Giving participants an opportunity to slow down means they can listen and learn from their inner teacher. Though this is a solitary journey in some ways, when it is done in groups where people feel safe enough to speak from the heart this work takes on added power. We experience our inner selves more deeply and enhance our capacity for community.

Whatever the circumstances in which we find ourselves, it is possible to take heart, reclaim our own wholeness, and renew our passion for healing. The effectiveness of the health care system depends ultimately on the quality of the human encounter when caregiver meets patient. The quality of that encounter depends on the state of the healer's heart at least as much as the healer's mind or hands. To paraphrase Parker, "We *heal* out of who we *are.*"

We need to rediscover and nourish what is most life-giving for each of us. Then, when we stand up in the midst of our career, we can say, with a look of deep contentment, "A life lived in *service*—who would not want that?"

REFLECTIONS

○
———

David J. Maitland
chaplain and professor of religion
emeritus at Carleton College

Perhaps the best way to introduce my connection to Parker is through his own words. On Sunday, October 26, 2003, in Northfield, Minnesota, Parker gave this eulogy for my wife, Betsy Maitland:

> The first Maitland I met was David. That was in 1957, when I arrived at Carleton College as an eighteen-year-old freshman, not long after David had taken his post as Carleton's new chaplain. From the moment I met him, David began giving me gifts of mind and heart and spirit. I am grateful for all of them, and some of them changed my life. But David never gave me a better gift than the chance to meet and know Betsy Maitland.
>
> Early in the first semester, I was invited, along with a few other first-year students, to have coffee and dessert with David and Betsy. I have a vivid memory of walking into the Maitlands' home and meeting this woman—this beautiful, vital, gracious, compassionate, and deeply intelligent woman.

Our relationship has persisted for a half-century as a personal and intellectual connection. When Parker was interviewed by the *Capital Times* of Madison, Wisconsin, in 1995, he responded to a question about the religious overtones in his work by saying that when he was in college, "I was influenced there by a chaplain who took the intellectual life very seriously. . . . He did not see himself at odds with it. He was interested in how religion could be critical of intellectual life while being part of it." As a teacher, friend, and chaplain, I am grateful that our lives have remained intertwined.

LATE OPENINGS?

David J. Maitland

RETIREMENT IS RARELY as uncomplicated as many anticipate. Although many conscientious retirees are satisfied with the benefits of improved diet and exercise, others begin to realize their need for something more. Rather than just enjoying their retirement as a long-deserved vacation, retirees often find themselves facing questions about meaning and identity. They ask themselves, How shall I present myself when no longer employed? They ask (along with Peggy Lee), "Is that all there is?" Still others begin to suspect that life after work might be more rewarding than they were led to believe possible. Some even seek challenges not imaginable earlier.

I've been struck by the media's growing interest in the changing lives of retirees. The reporting tends to confirm Ken Dychtwald's prediction in his book, *The Age Wave: How the Most Important Trend of Our Time Can Change Your Future,* that baby boomers would eventually, as they have in all prior life stages, transform the attitudes and practices of life's later years. As the boomers age, they have begun to try on various notions of aging, often challenging and expanding our notions of retirement. As they have every step of the way, the media continue to track the journey of this influential generation. Here are three such stories that recently caught my attention in the media.

The first appeared just last month as the lead piece in the *AARP Bulletin* of December 2002. The headline almost says it all: "Retirees Rocking Old Roles." The opening sentences of the study by Walt Duke and Trish Nicholson begin to flesh out their findings: "Across the nation millions of older active Americans are retiring old notions of what it means to be retired. . . . America's New Retirees [are] a growing army . . . who are using their late years to revitalize their lives. They are reinventing retirement. . . ."

These are important observations about radical initiatives coming from many like myself who are living longer than anticipated. For example, two women in their eighties are publishing for the first time an engaging novel, *Stones for Ibarra,* and a collection of poetry, *Ants on a Melon.* The latter's reflections on a husband's suicide decades earlier were striking. Such unprecedented longevity is not without complications (will earlier financial plans prove adequate? Will good health persist?), but the positive fact is that the desire to reinvent oneself is now socially recognized (and, I suspect, tenacious).

A much more specific phenomenon was discussed in our local paper.[1] Again, for our present purposes the headline may say enough: "The Emotional Impact of Regret Can Last a Lifetime." Most people regret some things done and some things not done. Regret has long been covered in ecclesia by reference to sins of commission and omission; this front-page piece suggests that by advanced age some people come to urgently feel the need to be at least somewhat freed from the debilitating effects of regrets long concealed, and often even denied. What such people discover is that they need a way to think of themselves beyond regret, which has often been central to their earlier self-understanding and self-presentation.

Although it will not assist all who need help, I find this prayer by the Rev. Reuel Howe, the late dean of Union Theological Seminary in Richmond, Virginia, to be potentially transforming: "Thank God, there's more to me than that!" These words regularly remind me of how easy it is to think of oneself in too limited a way and to allow others to diminish us. There is much more than regret to all our lives. As we mature, some of us are able to gradually bring such neglected "characters" onto the stage while retiring regret to the wings. Regret will probably never simply disappear but, as with other things gaining a more central role, regret can often be assigned an ever lesser part.

Finally, by way of reminding ourselves of the new tack being taken by the media, I call attention to a major segment of CBS's "Sixty Minutes." In the course of this long segment, which included interviews with academicians, extensive footage was given to men and women in their eighties and nineties who were finding ways out of the boredom of retirement and the self-destructiveness that often accompanies it. Central to the program were interviews with a Fred Hartman, who, through court struggles around charges of age discrimination, hires for his Needham, Massachusetts, operation only retirees who bring qualities comparatively rare in the larger workforce.[2]

The point of this brief review of media events is not to try to vindicate or confirm any of the presentations. Rather, I call attention to them at the outset because they suggest that promising things may be taking place among some older people. The stories are not the sort of copy that would have gained feature status a decade ago. Some changes seem to be afoot, and for reasons to which we'll now turn they echo my effort to expose and engage some potential late maturations, which have largely been neglected and even denied.

○

Such belated struggles for self-discovery, which are some people's alternative to boredom in retirement, remind me of Michelangelo's incomplete male figures, referred to variously as slaves or prisoners, at the Galleria dell'Academica in Florence. Whatever may have been his intention with these works—and art historians are not of one mind on this matter—the prisoners (which is how I think of them) illustrate brilliantly the thesis I advance in this essay.

For me, the larger-than-life marble figures are a metaphor for the incompleteness of our lives. Given the potential we all have at birth, it is inevitable—considering the limits of time and place—that much of what I think of as the *imago dei* will remain "buried in marble." Wherever and whenever one is born affects what one might be or do with one's life. Societies encourage the development of only parts of the vast human potential. Our marketing culture encourages only those skills that the system can most profitably employ. Such selective emphases are, for most people's working lives, apparently an unavoidable concomitant of life in society.

Because age lacks utility for marketing or consumption, we are not allowed to grow old. Inevitably we all do age, but, since it lacks societal endorsement, we are required to pretend that nothing changes with time. We do not age, we are not allowed to age, until we are finally, almost suddenly, and irredeemably old—and then we are shunted to the side.

Ignoring the tutelage latent in the passage of time, we are taught at least two pathetic lessons: to deny and to pretend. How deeply we may be trapped in such social "marble" depends, in part, on one's ability to embody these maturationally dysfunctional skills. Whatever maturations may be latent in life's later years are concealed, or at least they are radically minimalized, by most people until something like retirement or debilitating illness makes the fiction untenable. Fortunately, the skill to pretend doesn't always last a lifetime.

Though it is not my primary focus here, it is useful to recognize that there is also important potential instruction in illness and physical diminishment. They may remind us of vulnerabilities that, in extreme instances, can help turn a life around. The passage of time, which is my central concern, is ever universal, gentler, and more gradual than these radical assaults. One simply sees things differently than one did earlier.

Should the sixty-year-old, for example, be as uncritical a sports fan as she or he was at sixteen? Is that really possible? Ultimately, the passage of time opens some eyes: nothing continues to appear as it once did. Yet, in our ageist-tutored society, we must conceal and deny such changes.

Let me make clear my suspicion about the importance of the passage of time. Time is the "sculptor" who, in principle, might liberate everybody from the societal marble by which our potential growth is confined. That such liberation will not be experienced by all who grow old should not blind us to the latent tutelage potentially available to all. We know the ineradicable willfulness that leads some people to decline instruction capable of making a world of difference in their lives. Not everybody is at all times equally instructable. There are probably a variety of opportune seasons for different people. Who knows what it will take for a racist, a terrorist, a sexist, or whatever ideologue to move beyond his or her supposed absolute certainties? Tragically, most are immobilized.

For the majority, there is some hope. As one of Michelangelo's sculptures suggests, those who have experienced the passage of time the longest are most freed from the stone. Of the four figures, it is the oldest-looking who has emerged the furthest. This is not to claim—or even hint—that the aged are most in touch with their inner life and most available to others. Ideally, that's how it should be; but unfortunately not all are able to live into the gifts of time.

There is no single maturational curriculum for all people at all times. But since men and women born into a particular society at a specific time have been somewhat similarly shaped and misshaped, there may occasionally be some commonly held yearnings. This is how I would characterize the movement among retirees that underlies the media stories with which we began. Ever-extended lives coupled with the unchanged stimuli offered to seniors in this society are bound to leave some people dissatisfied. They are the sort (thank God) who begin to wonder about more rewarding ways to live out their later years within their changing reality. Most obviously, some of the diversions one may have enjoyed, such as physically active games, become simply too taxing. Though, quite understandably, it is deeply resented at the time, the onset of physical limitations may be an illuminating moment in the life of a person for whom competitive sports have been central. That such enlightenment is no assured thing is evident from the self-destructiveness of some former athletes. The transition from, say, tennis to chess, bridge, or adult education courses will not appeal to everybody who has had to abandon some long-satisfying activity. The person who does learn to let go will, in all likelihood, not do it quickly. Just last night, an acquaintance and once great athlete who has suffered systemic arthritis for a decade or more hastened to assure me that, come spring, he was going to be playing golf again.

Given the history of their self-presentation, which usually somewhat resembles self-understanding, many people go to great lengths to assure others that nothing has changed. In this society, whatever hidden wholeness may be seeking acknowledgment in us has to make its way through much denial of this sort. At best a person struggling with such issues, learning to let go of aspects of the past, may have to learn to say, "I am not what I was. What I may become is only beginning to take shape." Hardly an easy utterance in a society that prizes self-confidence and the absence of uncertainty.

———— o ————

The reality I wish to expose and indict is society's failure to offer stimuli appropriate to increasingly extended lives. The old diversions often simply fail to cut it. By this I refer not only to the absence of new avenues of pursuit but, more important, the failure to encourage initiatives that may be off the chart of our competitive, consumer-oriented society. Television is too addictive and deadening a drug to recommend in unlimited quantity. We must learn to honor activities that positively require the expenditure of that commodity in greatest availability among older people: time. No new equipment is required for the challenging work of reflection, writing, exchanging personal histories, for instance. (That there needn't be equipment to purchase may be the first hurdle for many to clear in their new life.) Learning to listen and talk revealingly with peers whose experiences are similar but not identical to one's own may be most important and difficult for people who know only how to give orders or take them. Both types will not find an easy adjustment to having time to think, talk, and listen!

The title of J. H. Oldham's *Real Life Is Meeting*, written before the middle of the twentieth century, says it all for me. So also does Martin Buber's classic of the same era, *I and Thou*. There isn't time to elaborate extensively why such books speak directly to what some retirees need to hear, but a sketch of their central theses may allow some people to break out of societal confinement. For example, Oldham insists that much of what we might call "life"—giving and taking orders in the interest of getting things done, which is often vitally necessary—is markedly less "real" than engaging lives with one another. What he believes matters most, and what takes us to ever deeper levels of one's God-givenness, is meeting. Unlike giving and taking orders, this is a two-sided process involving ever more accurate self-presentation and an endlessly improved ability to listen to the other. These humanizing capacities to gladly give and receive are developed in one's later years only to the extent that one brings authentic experiences of friendship to the task. Lacking such experiences, the prospects are dim.

What this means, and especially why it is so rare and important, is suggested by Buber's title, *I and Thou*. Apart from those who pathologically isolate themselves, everyone has daily dealings with others. But most of them are not between "I" and "Thou." Not only are most of our dealings with persons-as-objects (that is, men and women whom we think of as "its") but, when we're so oriented, we fail to bring ourselves into the engagement. The work, which enlarges and deepens one's self-awareness in the process, is to begin to see the diverse others out there less as objects than as beings in many ways quite like ourselves.

In a way, it's so simple: learn to appreciate the obvious! This is challenging and time-consuming because it requires turning inside out one's inherited understanding of what it means to be in the world. Societally tutored, there is no precious hidden wholeness in the other or even in ourselves. Only in aging may some people begin to assess the adequacy of such instruction. As one ages, though not necessarily as a consequence of that alone, some people find themselves capable of movement from conceal-and-deceive to reveal-and-celebrate. This is to move from tragic ignorance of the ambiguities of one's inner life to self-acquaintance. It may be only the latter, in which one begins to recognize at least one's internal contradictions—to say nothing of the sheer evil lurking in every heart—that will enable one to begin to see the other as thou. To see that whatever the race, gender, age, sexual orientation, he or she is, like myself, a flawed person with vast maturational potential. Given our numerous prejudices, of which ageism is foremost in my mind at the moment, this will be no snap growth. Indeed! As older people, we may have to first look more empathically at ourselves to recognize our vulnerable-but-promising humanity before seeing it in others.

More than once, I've advanced the socially deviant thesis that there inheres in the passage of time the possibility of illumination; or, if that's too strong, over time some people find themselves able to see things somewhat differently. Still, in our marketing society such modified sight is thought to be limited to the need for new ads each year because our sight is saturated and dulled from last year's appeals.

Through their actual experience over the decades, some people may begin to recognize how much more was involved in most situations than what they saw earlier. In aging, some people begin to realize that earlier, simple understandings must give way to appreciation for complexities previously obscured. Partly as the result of slightly deeper self-perception, eyes may open a little more to the inadequacy of earlier societal and personal simplemindedness.

Both individually and societally, we seem to be taken with simpleminded concepts and beliefs. As policy statements regularly remind me, even our governmental administrations are prone to simplifications of good and evil;

and regrettably, the majority of citizens prefer not to think beyond the identification of the bad guys. Naïvely assuming our contrasting virtue, we seem not to consider self-criticism a high priority.

Much of this may be due to America's youthfulness compared with most other societies. It is compounded by our adolescent refusal to grow up. That we've managed to acquire great wealth and amass unsurpassed power makes us as dangerous to the world as the reckless neighborhood teen with a driver's license or a .22 caliber rifle.

○

At least one more clarification is crucial to my argument. For some people, such as those featured in the media stories cited at the outset, the passage of time enables them to see how their shaping by society has also included some misshaping. After regular doses of this inadequate instruction (as with media emphasis on macho men and sexually alluring women), some people begin to acknowledge the cost to themselves and others of their efforts, successful or not, to embody recommended gender characteristics. They begin to wonder about the adequacy of the tutelage received. This can be a critical moment in the recognition of the something more within. It is in or from such moments that Reuel Howe's words may come vividly to mind: "Thank God, there's more to me than [just] that." As long as societal tutelage controls one's outlook, however, such fleeting glimpses of alternative self-understandings will not be acknowledged, and possibly not even recognized.

To become capable of encouraging some feature of the potential maturations in late life, one must first become something of a social critic. For example, attitudes and behaviors from which one seemed to benefit earlier may come to look as much like losses as gains, or worse. Those things once above criticism may begin to appear in all their ambiguity (or evil) later. This is what used to be referred to as the "wisdom" of aging, which is still recognized and honored in the greater part of the world. That such understanding is not fostered among us—indeed, thinking for oneself, deviating from the narrow platform of what's recommended and required, is disparaged—is at the heart of my critique. There have been few, if any, societies in which it was or is more difficult than in ours to keep one's head raised as one grows old. These conditions virtually prohibit pursuit of any hidden wholeness, which has been Parker's painful and precious discovery. That there might be such latency is aggressively and consistently denied. All that's encouraged in the aging is to be able to insist that nothing has changed, that is, to persuasively deny the passage of time. What a retirement send-off!

○

I may have discovered in medieval Christendom the source of our society's troubling relationship with ageism. Ageism is the contemporary expression of what was then recognized as the deadly sin of sloth. But sloth did not originally mean bone laziness nor lack of energy. Perhaps the best understanding for our late-twentieth-century minds of the deadly sin of sloth is the word *estrangement*. Through ageism, we denigrate those who are growing older because of their seeming inability to contribute to society. Yet our feelings of aversion go much deeper. Ageism is deadly because it expresses dissatisfaction with the way things are; time passes whether we like it or not. We age. Contemporaries in bondage to *acedia* (that is, those who abhor how God has fashioned the world) are endlessly seeking a way out. They are inconsolably unhappy with the unchangeable conditions for life. Sometimes their aversion takes the mystical exit sought by Marlowe's *Doktor Faustus*. Gifted in all academic disciplines, Faustus came to view all such achievements as "paltry." Nothing was of any value. He found no pleasure in life as it was available to him. His question, on which the balance of Marlowe's story hinges, is this, "Shall I have the spirits resolve me of all ambiguity?" That is quintessential sloth.

In medieval terms, such a person refuses to be what he or she really is. In contemporary terms, it is to abhor life's later years, to refuse the tutelage inherent in aging. Theologically, this is to reject the terms on which life is given in the creation; it is to abhor the Creator. People who are so bereft are left with the limited identity that society provides. Is it any surprise that, as time passes they sense society's rewards to be like quicksilver? They must hate the inevitability of aging.

A positive way to avoid such despairing self-hatred is to begin by paying attention to those assumptions which one unthinkingly imbibed as a child and eagerly embraced to enter adulthood. However, the ancient Delphic exhortation "Know thyself" may prove much more difficult than its brevity leads one to expect. Especially at the time one is (reluctantly) becoming aware of how restrictive the once-motivating societal lures to success have become, to recognize this may be deeply threatening. The understandings that looked so liberating from a distance may be terrifying close up. It becomes increasingly clear that the identity society rewards—of continuing to be an eager producer/consumer—has lost some of its appeal. At the same time, one cannot imagine anything more adequate: "For many, work is the most important form of production, and the cessation of work leads to a forfeiture of identity, of self-respect and of the respect of others."[3] Such moments as this give birth either to denial and a desperate effort to turn back the clock or to despair and a variety of self-destructive options.

Unfortunately, we do not often recognize or honor the learning that may occur as one ages. It is not primarily about developing retirement skills and interests, though they may prove useful. Nor is it about creating service opportunities wherein the healthy may provide for those less so, though such opportunities may also be good. The elusive new learning is much more radical and liberating than that; it is about recognizing how society taught us to value only selected parts of our God-givenness. Once this societal selectivity has been exposed, we begin to have access to our limitless resources. Reconnected to the *imago dei*—that indestructible key to our ultimate self-understanding—all men and women are free to get on with whatever they recognize as their distinctive agenda for the later years. They know what interests gives them pleasure, and they are moved to serve those more needful than themselves.

There are limitations, of course, though these are less dispiriting because people so connected to the depths of their being have taken back control of their lives. They do not need to wait for society to play tunes to which they're able to dance. They are their own musicians, and they know the sounds they like!

NOTES

1. *Minneapolis Star Tribune,* Jan. 5, 2003.

2. "Sixty Minutes," CBS, Jan. 12, 2003.

3. Simmons, H. C. "Ministry with Older Adults: Neither Known Nor Esteemed." *PACE,* Oct. 1989, p. 15.

REFLECTIONS

○

Mary Rose O'Reilley
professor of English
at the University of St. Thomas

I didn't understand my vocation as a teacher very well, nor its connection to my Quaker beliefs, when I first encountered Parker Palmer's works. His book *To Know as We Are Known* flared over my world like skywriting. I couldn't grasp it on my first reading. It was too abstract for me. Poets, like dogs, live with their noses to the ground, in a very concrete universe. Yet I came to realize that it was my business to try to make practical applications—as good a definition as any of *right livelihood*. Soon I came upon those famous words of his comparing the classroom to Quaker worship: "We prepare for meeting for learning by trying to become vulnerable to both hurt and healing in others and in ourselves. . . . Whatever the subject of study in the classroom, the shadow subject is ourselves, our limits, our potentials. As long as that remains in the shadows, it will block both individual and group from full illumination. But if both hurt and self-doubt can be brought into the light . . . then learning will flower."[1]

I read that passage over and over. Then I began to understand.

WHAT SOUND
DOES THE SOUL MAKE?

Mary Rose O'Reilley

THIRTY WHITE-TAILED DEER

This is the way
the beloved will stand:
a brown deer at dusk
on scrims of tamarack.

This is the way
your deep desire appears:
a brown deer on brown hills.
A country
where nothing moves
and you, dissolving in silence,
see nothing.

Then a flick of silk
in the woods
becomes presence,
eyes lock:
a landscape
where everything moves

has always
been moving.

PEOPLE WHO STUDY DREAMS tell us we should imagine that each character in a dream represents an aspect of the self. When I teach poetry, I often tell my students, "Think of a poem as a dream you had, and try to 'interpret' it from that psychic place."

"It's a dream the *poet* had," they often respond, bright students that they are. "How can we enter into the poet's mind?"

I am one who holds the tender hypothesis that we are connected to each other, members of one body. I think that, to go in another scriptural direction, "there are a variety of gifts, but the same spirit." In this economy, the poet dreams the dreams of the species—visions, nightmares, filaments of breath merely, sometimes surreal photographs of what the world half-knows. This is our job, and somebody has to do it. At least we get to sleep a lot. Awakened, over and over, by our souls. . . .

THE NOISE OF THE SOUL

I wake to her clip on the shingles:
small running claws of the soul.
She wanted me up an hour ago.
She is tired of waiting,
revealing her face to the mist;
souls get sick
and cry like Siamese cats;
bored, knock over furniture,
jump around on the beds.
They don't like to be left alone,
working long division
and practicing scales.
They start to run their invisible nails
over the blackboard,
get you to notice them,
get you to feed them,
get you to play catch.

This poem does not seem entirely successful to me, because the metaphor shifts so abruptly. First the soul is outside, running around like a squirrel. Then it is a petlike presence in the house; finally it misbehaves, like a child with tedious schoolwork. But the dreamer's job is different from the critic's; however clumsy the poem, it records what we know: the soul is demanding, unpredictable, and playful. I am making a mental list, as I write this, of all the things I learned from Parker Palmer, foremost among them, *pay attention to your soul*. It runs like a squirrel; it morphs into a cat or a bored child. Different souls make different noises at different times.

When Sam Intrator asked me to write an essay for this volume in honor of Parker Palmer, he called me at a time when I was spending a year in poet-mind. Those of you who vacation there will understand that it is impossible to travel back from poet-mind into the analytical space of the essayist. Sitting there at my rented e-mail connection, an hour's drive from my cabin in the Oregon woods, I nearly wept with frustration because I wanted so badly to contribute. "Never mind," said Sam generously, "just send some poems." I'm glad he let me do that, because Parker Palmer is such a foundational presence in my life; to tell the truth, he *saved* my life. Without my soul, I would be the hungry ghost of Buddhist mythology, though perhaps a more docile employee. As I look over these poems, as Sam has now asked me to do, trying to articulate the common threads that unite them to each other, and their spirit to Parker's, and all of us in a web of connection, I realize: he saved my life, and I bet I'm not the only one. What sound does a soul make when it is being throttled? Thanks to Parker, we do not know.

I started with an epigraph about contemplation, "Thirty White-Tailed Deer." Called to a vocation of inwardness, can one survive in the academy? When I was a young teacher, the answer was unequivocally no. Perhaps it is still no, if one's idea of contemplation involves quietism and withdrawal from the fray. Parker's special gift to me, I think, was his insight that contemplation and action are playfully united. Given his emphasis on the active life, it's paradoxical that Parker taught us so much about contemplation. But for him, there is no separation, no poisonous duality. We wait and hope for the advent of *presence,* the energy Sufis call "the beloved"; but the beloved is already with us. Space that has seemed empty has always been teeming with life. Palmer writes, "Contemplation happens any time that we catch the magician deceiving us and we get a glimpse of the truth behind the trick."[2] Later in the same work, he says, "Whenever we act in a way that brings us closer to reality, that action is contemplative."[3] Or active.

When I wrote these poems, I was living pretty much alone in the woods, visited every day by animals who seemed to regard me, behind my huge windows, as a kind of TV for animals. Deer, in particular, tolerate our kind and let us into their consciousness. We are privileged to overhear the prayers of animals:

THE DEER'S PRAYER

Sometimes I'm bigger
than my body;
I cannot help it.

Dawn stirs me this way
scent of fir tree and moss,
rivulets under the hoof.

Released from fear,
sometimes I slide into grace.
Having run far and fast

to preserve my hide,
I lie and let it all leave me,
the facts I tried to protect.

I feel the earth turn
like a faun in the belly
and lose the knack of telling

what I inhabit
from what inhabits me.

Deer—indeed, all animals—are images for me of Parker's "active-contemplative" life, the great surrender. I teach in, among other places, an environmental studies program, and I volunteer at a veterinary clinic devoted to wildlife rehabilitation. This latter job involves nursing animals who have encountered the rifles and automobiles and leg traps of humankind. Animals live with a wholeness that eludes us; in the Oregon woods, I kept trying to warn them away from me, away from the contamination humans spread. When, in my solitude, I began to imagine—or hallucinate—that I could understand the language of the visiting animals, I knew it was time for me to get back to the "real" world. ("You missed your chance!" a friend scolded.)

Out of the woods, I spent a day in Portland's Chinese Garden. One section of it replicates the serene architecture of a sage's home. Knowing of his love for Chuang Tzu, I offer this poem to Parker with a special smile.

CHINESE GARDEN

Crows fly over the scholar's garden.
He wants them to be ravens,
longs to see the thick beak and intelligent eye,
a bird poised for conversation
who will admire with him
an old calligraphy in its frame of space.

The scholar sips tea, tries his teeth on a nut shell.
He once knew a raven who spoke Mandarin passably well,
who tried to teach him the words of a far, dark people
across the sea.
That raven would sit every day over the moongate,
contrasting the scholar's measured wisdom
with some frantic, ardent,
evolving theology.

Just as the old man began to feel
the strenuous energy of conversion
coursing along the meridians
even down to the blue veins
under the nail,

the raven rustled and flew
as though he had gotten a letter.

Now the scholar sits on his silk pillow,
no hope to recover tranquility
due his years, his honors,
watching the sky.

I smile because I know that Parker Palmer will never be "retired." He taught us to listen to the scurry of our souls, to record and remember its nudges, as I know he has been storing up his own. No silk pillow for him, no crows; he will always be watching the sky.

Living in the woods, next to the richness of a tidal estuary, tempted to leave academic life for good, I dreamt a final dream. It's for you.

CALL IT A MATCH

From the hermit crab I could learn to own nothing.
Deer pick their way without mortgages up the slope,
Stellar's Jay cranks out his expectation of bread.

What am I trading for salary?
Christmas of all the world's dumpsters
sifts into the Goodwill store.
I think of my father, that natty man,
laid out in a paper dress. . . .

There is green light in the bone bleached by my door,
what body the bone belonged to I cannot tell,
what fears drove it, what grief,
how it flared out in its manner of loving,
what species of young it dropped in the wet grass.

Call it love anyway, call it a match:
green bone to spruce, feather: ephemeral leaf.

NOTES

1. Palmer P. J. "Meeting for Learning: Education in a Quaker Context." *Pendle Hill Bulletin,* May 1976, pp. 1–7.

2. Palmer, P. J. *The Active Life.* San Francisco: Jossey-Bass, 1990, p. 17.

3. Palmer (1990), pp. 17–18.

Chapter Two

BE NOT AFRAID

FEAR IS FUNDAMENTAL to the human condition and to academic culture. We will always have our fears—but we need not be our fears.

I am fearful. I have fear. But I don't need to be here in my fear. I don't have to speak to you from my fear. I can choose a different place in me, a place of fellow feeling, of feeling traveling, of journeying together in some mystery that I know we share. I can "be not afraid" even while I have fear.

—Parker J. Palmer

---○---

REFLECTIONS

○

Dawna Markova
author and cofounder of Smart Wired

Some people meet at intersections, some at thresholds, some at corners. I met Parker Palmer at a turning point, the turning point in a Möbius strip. We were brought together by a friend. She had told me he was a Quaker. The closest spiritual practice I identified with was Buddhism, but only because I had to believe in reincarnation, having experienced so many incarnations in this one life already: teacher, psychotherapist, consultant, author, poet, patient, healer, warrior, perpetual student. I told him I was a soul-in-wonder. He told me he was an educator-at-large. I knew then we were kin.

We meet in many places—Herman Miller, the Fetzer Institute, his living room—each time becomes a turning point in my life. Each time, Parker brings only his open mind and simple heart. Each time, I come dragging the long, flat strip I have been using to divide the world in two. Each time he stretches it out, shakes it clean and shows me both sides with a gentle smile. Then, like a cosmic magician, he offers a beautiful question that causes me to gasp. Hocus pocus! The ends of the strip twist, and Parker seals them together with tenderness and mercy. Each time, the world is made whole once again.

○

THINKING
OURSELVES HOME
The Cultivation of Wisdom

Dawna Markova

I write to fuse inside with out,
to salve wounds and broken dreams.
I write to understand the many things
no one has told me,
to stroke my moments clean,
to squeeze them into tiny mirrored fragments
shining with mindlight.
I write to turn my blood to ink,
to fertilizer, to sap.
I write so that my eyes can feel,
so that my heart can lick,
so that my soul can crawl from its hiding place
and gaze upon a mystery
which can be neither solved nor explained.
I write
to breathe my spirit live.

I AM TOLD THERE IS A BUDDHIST saying that the wisdom of a teacher can be best judged by the actions and motivations of his or her students. To honor what I have learned from Parker Palmer about the integration of inner and outer realities, I cannot just write about the role of contemplation in an active life. I cannot write this from an abstract place. I cannot fake it.

I start in solitude. I start in silence. I start from the truth of where I am now to engage in a live encounter with myself. I start thinking myself home.

I am doing more and it is meaning less.
I feel helpless against my own chaos.
My voice is for others. My listening is for others.
Am I making all this noise so I don't have to hear something deeper?
I am longing to belong to *both* the world and myself.
How do I find my way home when I am lost?

What is my poverty now, what is my real wealth?
How do I create meaning from the events that happen to me?
How do I create coherence in a chaotic life?

I imagine Parker's immaculate hands holding a strip of plain white paper. He calls it a "Quaker PowerPoint" and uses it to describe the relationship between our inner and outer lives. He holds it on edge to illustrate how we create walls to separate reflection and action. In a voice that reminds me of melted milk chocolate, he explains that we often feel forced to choose between the two. He joins the ends of the strip into a circle, showing how we alternate between them, paying attention externally until action becomes frenzy and then forces us to jump the wall to the inner world, trying to escape. Perhaps we take a vacation, or get sick, or self-medicate through drinking and eating.

The outcome of living such a divided life is being separated from one's self, alienated from the common ground where we all stand, the sense of connection that is referred to as the "hidden wholeness." It is the most painful way a human can live.

There is so much in the outer life to distract us from our true nature, isolate us in numbness and guilt, capture us in bonds of fear. Life calls asking for coherence, for meaning, for all the disparate notes to become a chord, a harmony, a mutual understanding. To respond to this, we need reflection, not escape, so that we can listen to the music of our lives amidst the noise, the cacophony, and the chaos. The inner world is a resonating chamber for our deepest longing, our search for wholeness.

I imagine Parker's long fingers holding the strip, giving it a single twist, taping the ends, and then tracing a line on the surface without lifting the pen. His soft voice says, "Although there is an outer and an inner surface, what seemed radically opposite can now be recognized as revealing a common space." The question he asks is, "How can one inform the other?" He calls this possibility the integrated life.

As Parker demonstrated, the Möbius strip is a map, an icon, a symbol of the way we can think ourselves home and cultivate our own wisdom. Each time we come to a turning point, an intersection between *either* and *or,* we have the opportunity to stop running and shift our attention, notice our breath, widen the space between impulse and response. Each turning point— whether it is caused by an unpredictable disturbance such as September 11, or cancer, or divorce, or burnout, or simply a hollow feeling of meaninglessness—brings us to this choice point where we can catastrophize, blame, worry, or open our minds and ask what is actually happening. As the swirl begins to settle, what emerges are questions, questions that come closer and closer to what is at the core of who we really are. The right question can carry us from the isolation of the wild to the companionship of our own hearth.

I was born shortly after Pearl Harbor was attacked. I grew up between the stunning parentheses of two predominant images: the mushroom-shaped cloud over Hiroshima and humankind's first view of the glowing green earth as a whole, photographed from space.

For decades of my life, I pursued answers. I masterfully hunted them down and hung them on the walls of my mind, where I could go and comfort myself with the belief that I *did* indeed know something. I had graduate degrees; there was no way I could be lost or stuck. I could answer questions. I could teach the answers to others who would pay me and love me for all those trophies I had collected: Mastery. Security. Identity. Control. I knew who I was, where I was, where I was going, and what I would do next.

Little did I know that I was stranded with those answers on the edge of an eroding cliff. Cancer crept into my life and dug away at the very ground I was standing on. It has returned several times in the past thirty years, bringing me to my knees again and again. Each time, I try to run from it, and then fight against it. Each time, I have less energy for the flight, the freeze, the fight, the opposition to what seems to be trying to take my life away. Inevitably, the fear gallops faster than I can think, and I have to accept that I cannot control it. I cannot control the cancer, nor the doctors who are as powerless as I am, nor the people who pity me and try to fix me by implying that somehow the illness is due to a mistake I made along the way.

Each time cancer comes calling, I am brought to the very edge of what it means to be a human being: I am vulnerable. I am fragile. There are things I cannot change no matter how many answers I have, no matter how many degrees or how much money. I used to believe this meant I was defeated. Either I control the situation or it controls me. Either I get rid of the cancer or the cancer gets rid of me.

Several years ago, while I was on such a knife edge, Parker listened to me complain about this intersection for thirty minutes. I kept waiting for him to intervene, to give me an answer, a direction. Instead, fully present, he just "listened me into speech" until there were no more words. We sat together in the silence for many lush moments before he said, "Dawna, it seems to me that your life is asking you, 'How can I live divided no more?'" My breath dropped deep in my belly. Parker didn't know, couldn't know, that my red and white blood cells were out of communication with each other, that I had spent my whole life divided between one side and another. The question he offered to me couldn't be answered. Instead, it became a bridge, a lifeline, a companion across any abyss that rose before me.

What brings us to wisdom is using our consciousness to reflect on our thinking. It doesn't just happen to us as we grow older. We can choose to "quest" ourselves forward. We can search for the larger questions that lead us beyond *either* and *or*. These evocative questions challenge how we think, how we diminish ourselves and fragment the world. They can cleave open the habits of mind that enslave us.

In my professional life, methodologies and processes have come and gone. Everything works and nothing works for very long. What has provided sustenance for me is the search for questions that cause us to live true to our purpose. I thought I was helping children at risk discover how they learn. I thought I was helping people who have been abused and challenged by disease and disruption liberate themselves from the limitations of their previous history. I thought I was helping organizations discover how to recognize and mobilize their intellectual capital. I thought I was doing research and teaching processes to expand the capacities we need to think really well together, to think through our right brains, our left brains, our hearts, minds, and bodies.

I have been doing all that, but underneath I realize that I was learning to offer to others the simple and profound gift Parker shared with me: I was learning to listen them into speech, learning to help them turn inward in reflection in order to recognize and follow the questions that live at the center of their lives.

But turning inward to confront these questions-that-have-no-answers isn't easy. At least not for me. The word *cleave,* to cut apart, also means its opposite, to cling to. As I struggle to let go of all my certainties, there is a harsh wind that blows through the place they occupied. I feel like a kite in that wind.

> There is nothing inside. Only emptiness.
> Emptiness spreads like a stain.
> I can't feel myself.
> My energy is spent on others, passes through me, out from me, leaving a
> hole.
> A gaping black hole in the middle of me.
>
> Calling, yearning, pulling, hungry, reminding me of what is seeping from me. Meaning.
> I feel mind-blind, heart-blind. I cannot see what
> matters.

I can only see what is the matter . . . with the world, with me,
with my work.
I can only see problems that call to be fixed, to be measured,
to be solved.
I cannot see a solution to this. I am stuck with my nose pressed
into a corner between *either* and *or*: Either I serve the world
or I serve myself. Either I give myself away or I withdraw from
the world. Either I abandon my own needs or I abandon
theirs.
How can I engage in action that is informed by reflection so it
doesn't become frenzy? How can I reflect in such a way that,
rather than escaping from the world, I serve the world in a way
that is authentic to me?

All of my wisest teachers have brought me beautiful open questions. The
first, my grandmother, used the same tool as Parker did, the Möbius strip,
to teach me how to relate to those questions that cannot be answered
quickly and simply. All I have to do is close my eyes and think about her
hands, her hands dusted white from the Sabbath bread she's been knead-
ing. "Grandma, Daddy says even though you can't read, you're very wise.
How do you get wise?"

She sits down at the kitchen table covered with a shiny red oilcloth and
folds one-half sheet of newspaper into a long strip. She makes a single
twist in it, and sticks the two ends together with a dab of bread dough.
Grandma calls it a Wisdom Trail.

She traces her bony finger around the outside of the loop, stopping at
the twisted place. "Wisdom grows inside of your heart drop by drop until
it becomes an ocean," she says.

"There's an ocean in my heart?" I ask. (With Grandma, you're allowed
to ask really dumb questions. She doesn't mind.)

"Yes, *ketzaleh*. An ocean, with a very peaceful island right in the middle.
All the things that have ever happened to you drop into that ocean. And
anything you really love and have memorized gets planted on the island."

Looking in her eyes, I could see it all and more. She takes my hand in
hers and leads my chubby finger around the outside edge of the newspaper loop, until it comes to that turning place.

"But how do you get into that wisdom ocean, Grandma? And what are
you supposed to do when you're there?"

A vein sticks out right above her temple. I watch it quiver, the blood
pulsing through as if it is a river of love. She looks down at the loop, then
slides her finger through the twist to the inside. Her words come slowly

as she explains, "You have to think in a different way. When you're about to swim in the ocean of wisdom, things get wobbly at first. Your thinking is like waves, and it splashes all over the place."

"So what are you supposed to hold onto?"

"That's just it, my darling. As you cross over into the ocean of your mind, you stop holding on. You let yourself sink down, down beneath the waves, way down."

I hang suspended in the pause between her words. Now her finger moves gently around the inside edge of the loop and her words are tender and hushed.

"There, close to the bottom, the water gets still. You just float around on the currents, even if the waves of thinking are splashing and crashing above you."

"But Grandma, when I do that, when I look out the window and just float around in my mind, my teacher says I'm not paying attention."

She hesitates for a long time before she speaks, but her finger keeps moving slowly around the inner edge of that strip of newspaper. Finally she says, "Maybe your teacher hasn't practiced swimming in her own wisdom yet, or maybe she forgets how. A lot of grown-ups do. Maybe they're afraid they'll drown in all the feelings they drop down there."

Her finger stops moving. "You can't drown in here, though. You just have to let your mind go as wide as a wing and you'll float. You may hear songs or see swimmy pictures or get ideas. Maybe you'll come back with an answer to a question you've been wondering about or a bigger way of understanding. Maybe you'll just feel easy with your question."

"And that's how you got wise, Grandma?"

"That's right, darling." She stops speaking and her finger dances through that turning point inside, then across it, and outside. I don't need to ask any more questions. In some way that words can't say, I understand. My grandmother knew, as Parker teaches, that we need to enter the cave of wonder to mine our wisdom.

An open question is a choice point, the twist in the Möbius strip. To achieve mastery, we are taught to answer questions that are asked. This leads us to the outside of the strip. But an open question cannot be answered. An open question takes us to the mystery of our inner world, where patterns and meaning unfold like petals. An open question leads us to what Einstein referred to as a "holy curiosity": a curiosity that is nourishment itself without the pressure of having to constantly fulfill our appetite for explanations and solutions. If we allow ourselves to slide wide and wonder with such a question, if we drop the stories we tell ourselves about who we are and are not, what we can and cannot do, what others want and don't want us to be, we can carry our harshest pain in curious hands to what is most true and genuine within us.

> I feel a swirling black hole in my solar plexus, turning clockwise.
> I can't catch up. There's too much to do. There is a hole at the center of everything, a black hole, sucking everything into it, sucking me into it. There is a whole at the center of everything. I can only find it by going through the hole, like Alice. Clockwise. Be clock wise.
> The minutes I'm being paid for are like dry sand through my fingers. I can't have them back. No matter how much I am paid, those moments are gone. I can't borrow more, or steal more, or buy more.
> Am I feeling sorry for myself? Self pity? "Poor me" instead of what I'd give to anyone else . . . compassion? Poor me, poverty of me. What is my poverty now? What is my real wealth?

Our culture trains us to think of the human state of mind called wonder as a disorder needing medication. This concerns me a great deal. More and more children in American schools and adults in the workplace are being medicated for this state of mind. This upsets me. It should upset all of us. What will the world be like without wonder? What will we be like as a nation when so many of us have been medicated out of curiosity?

Even as I write this, I am getting nervous. Every time I begin to speak about this on the radio or to a large audience, people get angry, explaining to me that wonder is not the way we are supposed to pay attention. They go on to explain that to succeed in this society a person has to be able to think at hyperspeed, to multitask, to concentrate on whatever is put in front of her nose, without her mind wavering for hours on end, even if what she is concentrating on is meaningless to her. They tell me they don't want their children to suffer the way they did in school. They tell me I have to be realistic, sensible, and come down to earth. They tell me this is the Information Age, after all.

I don't want to leave my son a legacy called the Information Age. I'd rather leave a legacy called the Age of Wisdom. Wisdom has always been birthed in wonder.

Each of us was born with the capacity to give our attention in many ways to both the internal and external world. Dee Hock, the author of *Birth of the Chaordic Age* and founder of Visa International, describes how thought changes as it is metabolized, if you will, by attention. Imagine a pyramid. At the base is data. As you move upward, data is processed into information, which is digested into knowledge. Distilling knowledge leads us to understanding, which is ultimately transformed into wisdom.

When I heard Dee talk about this, I thought of seeing a pointillist painting for the first time on a high school trip. I stood up very close to a canvas by Georges Seurat, fascinated with each tiny dot and its unique color. Then ever so slowly, I stepped back and the dots began to drift and float in space, then cohere until they were shapes, then forms blending together into a scene of people gathered on the shore of an island. Next, in some mysterious way, I entered into the painting to join those people on that Sunday afternoon. I knew exactly what the breeze felt like on my cheek. I could feel the peace of having nowhere to go.

Data and dots become information, then knowledge, understanding, and, if we step back far enough, wisdom. Dee says that many indigenous cultures of the world spend as much time in stepping back to cultivate wisdom as they do in processing data. In current Western cultures, we are so flooded with data that we spend most of our time processing it into information and go no further. Parker puts it this way: "The problem is that we begin to know so much that we lose sight of what is important and what isn't. . . . Part of the current turning to the inner life is a search for a set of principles or lenses through which to look at things. It's a way of discerning what counts and what doesn't."

Is it just the flood of data that keeps us from crossing over into wide and watery ways of attention, or is there more to it? I'm thinking of a man I worked with recently. Let's say his name was John. He was the COO of a major company. He called a meeting of senior leaders from around the world to "creatively explore our core purpose and strategy." He hired me to facilitate the discussion so he could participate fully.

For the hour the CEO was in the room, John was totally attentive. Within minutes of his leaving, however, John inserted a black plastic button into his ear that was connected to his cell phone and went into the hall. In the next three hours, he was in and out of the room eight times. Finally, earpiece still dangling, he returned.

We were at the point of our process where people had just spent an hour making a major decision about strategic direction. He sat on the couch with the rest of us, but as we moved to the next item on the agenda, he pushed the mute button on his phone. Apparently he was in two meetings simultaneously. As we began to move on in the discussion, John pushed the button again, and said, "Oh, by the way, you all didn't need to decide about strategic direction. I did that several months ago. Why don't you just go on to something else?" Then he pushed the little button and began to speak to the invisible people in the other meeting.

I won't tell you all of the effects of John's partial attention on the rest of us, or how that wasted hour cost his company at least $11,000, given our collective salaries and travel expenses. I will leave the gnashing of teeth, the rolling of eyes, the deflation of energy in the room to your fertile imagination. Months later, compassion blossomed in my mind. John is obviously capable of speaking and listening simultaneously. That kind of fragmented, continuous partial attention may be effective for reacting quickly at hyperspeed. It is not, however, the kind of attention one needs to create something new in the world or to think strategically at hyperdepth.

I watched a fourteen-year-old boy in Philadelphia play an electronic handheld game that required the same kind of reactive thinking John was doing. His mother proudly told me that her son could process data much faster than either she or her husband, and that a study she had read said this was true for most children his age. As I looked up this same study days later, I found that it also said that teachers reported these same children had much more difficulty understanding Shakespeare than those in years past. There's nothing wrong with being able to react to stimuli at hyperspeed. But must it be at the cost of hyperdepth?

When I was in graduate school studying clinical psychology, I was taught to recognize and categorize cognitive pathologies. One of them was called "hypervigilance." It was often found in the oldest children of abusive households. They seemed incapable of imagining; they had little or no capacity to think symbolically, in images or stories. They rarely had dreams. They didn't enjoy dancing or listening to music for its own sake. They lived on the surface of their lives, reacting in a jerky and frenzied way to everything around them instead of proacting from the inside out and creating what they wanted. Hypervigilance was thought to be a way their minds could be on continuous alert in order to defend against possible abuse. The suggested treatment, once physical safety was ensured, was to help these children learn to relax, and then regenerate their imagination and depth through art or music therapy along with slow, meandering walks in nature.

Forty years later, everything is like a sock turned outside in. Hypervigilence is considered normal, the sane way to be and do. Wonder and reflection are seen as pathology. Does living at hyperspeed really help us defend ourselves against the abuses around us? Is this truly the only way we can pay attention? Is attention a cost we pay? For what? How about holding or capturing someone's attention?

What if we considered attention to be something we could choose (or not) to give to others and to ourselves?

We give little of the kind of attention needed for pondering, discussing, wondering, contemplating, musing, reflecting. This is what makes it possible to notice patterns, stories, relationships, and interactions. This is the mode of attention Dee says can help us move from machine-crafting objects to what he calls "mindcrafting" wisdom. "In an open field, we open up too; ideas and feelings arise within us; our knowledge comes out of hiding."[1]

We can let our thoughts live us or grab hold of the kite string and allow our minds to open. We can choose to let the kite string out and wonder, *What's really important about this to me?* We can think a thought all the way through, think wide enough to understand the whole of something, think deep enough for chaos to cohere into patterns of meaning.

> Questions, beautiful questions I can't answer.
>
> Dangerous questions that will take me to places I haven't explored.
>
> Questions: wrap loosely around me, not like tentacles that clutch at me and demand answers, but wrap around me as if you are tender lover's arms. Caress me open so I can release this safe and known trapeze I've been swinging from.
>
> I need these spaces to ask myself dangerous and beautiful questions.
>
> Am I making choices that are life-diminishing, or life-enhancing?
>
> What's unfinished for me to give, for me to experience, for me to learn?
>
> How, in all the frenzy of a chaotic life, do I create the conditions so that the pain in me and the love in me can find each other?

This wide and wondering way of thinking is how we cultivate wisdom. It is not a disorder. It is not a deficit. It is not a waste of our time. It is one of our birthrights, one of our natural freedoms. It is how we can come to our senses and realize that life is its own meaning. It is the way we can think ourselves home.

This home is the place where our autobiographies write themselves. It is where the bits and pieces of our experience are tumbled in the kaleidoscope of our values, until they form patterns of meaning. It is where suffering can be transformed into the hard, free joy of jazz, dance, poetry, story. It is where souls reach for each other in an arch of mutual understanding. It is the rest in the place where wholeness is born.

But we cannot stay in any home without it becoming a prison. When I was studying the martial art of Aikido, the most frustrating experience was learning how to stay centered while moving. I practiced coming into the present moment, softening my eyes, shifting attention to my belly, widening my periphery, balancing between the forces of gravity and levity. Just as I would reach that delicate state, the teacher would whirl behind me and tap on my head. Immediately, my center of attention would rise upward, and when he pressed my shoulder, I'd topple over. Finally, in frustration, I asked him how I could stay centered. He paused a moment and then replied in a very gentle voice, "Centering is like coming home, yes? If you try to stay there, it becomes a tomb." He paused long enough for me to absorb his words. After I nodded, he continued, "The art of centering is to recognize when you have lost it and then know how to bring yourself back to center again."

Where I travel these days is less important than how far I am from home, how long I've been away, and how difficult it will be to get back. The Möbius strip provides a map of the journey. It can help us find our way to reflect on our active lives in a different and dignified way.

Thinking our way home is like a symphony. The first note is born in silence. It is called the key note, because it is home for the rest of the piece. Every other note is a journeying away as well as a longing to return to that first note. That home generates the meaning of the symphony, as it proceeds from the relationship of its many notes to that key note.

> I hang in silence. What if this were home? This warm and silent place. Inhale, space, exhale, space. My breath takes on the shape of the Möbius strip. I imagine sitting at the turning point, the encounters of the outer world on one side, the encounters of the inner world on the other, the questions lapping against the edges of my mind.
> I rest, realizing how much I need these moments, these in-betweens to digest and metabolize what has happened to me, what I have lived and what meaning it has for me. I need to notice how many moments have sifted through my fingers and wonder how many will be left to me.
>
> I let the questions wash softly against my chest, over my ears and eyes. I let it all be, listening, feeling my breath let go of what I no longer need, feeling the space between breaths, resting in the place where the music is born.

I float in the spaces between my questions. I know I'll never receive answers to all my beautiful questions. I do trust that I need to ask them again and again to find my way on this journey. I do trust that if I stop and listen for the inner wisdom that is evoked in response to these questions, I'll discover "a thousand ways to kneel and kiss the earth."

May we be drawn forward by profound and beautiful questions. May each of us discover the turning point at which the limitations of our previous history become the liberation of our collective future.

NOTE

1. Palmer, P. J. *To Know as We Are Known: A Spirituality of Education.* San Francisco: Harper San Francisco, 1983, p. 70.

REFLECTIONS

○
_____

Mark Nepo
poet and program officer
for the Fetzer Institute

Parker Palmer is that rarity among humans: authentic and sincere in a deep and lasting way that enables his mind to speak through his heart. He is more consistently who he is than anyone I know. This deep sense of being opens a space in which others can touch what matters, if they choose to.

Our friendship has been a fire by which we've told many stories and explored many questions. In truth, the conversation Parker and I have been entering for years has centered on understanding life as a transformative question we awaken into together. Through love and suffering, we all seem to be challenged, time and again, to understand and embody the changing tool we are: honed and eroded pieces of spirit working in the world.

I am deeply honored to pay tribute to Parker's spirit and life work by being part of this effort to extend this conversation. For my part, I hope to share the story of my own transformation over the years: as a poet, as a teacher, as a cancer survivor, as a spirit awakened to the world.

My aim is to speak about some of the deeper things I have learned and am still learning, including awakening to the paradox and true gifts of suffering, seeing obstacles as teachers, having the life of poetry and the poetry of life continue to blur, understanding creativity as an expressive form of healing, leaving the want-to-be-great for the great-chance-to-be, understanding how giving attention is more essential than getting attention, and awakening to the acceptance of our limitations and how we need each other to be complete and useful.

———— o ————

BECAUSE OF
MY NOT KNOWING

Mark Nepo

Because of my not knowing,
angels close their wings
and whisper in meadows
that call me into the open.

There Are Teachers Everywhere

I have learned, again and again, that it is the mystery of all I don't know
that leads me; that because of my not knowing, the world and all its teachers say, *now we will sing!* And I have learned that this is perennial. For
long before we were born, Hindu sages voiced the word *Upaguru,* which
means the teacher that is next to you at any moment.

And in my not knowing, it becomes clear that, from the rotting tree
felled by lightning to the water re-smoothing after the whale dives down,
everything is of equal sanctity and grace. From the darkness we can't see
through to the hidden tenderness of a grandfather afraid to speak, everything and everyone is a teacher. Each flower, each bird, each suffering
great and small, each eroded stone and crack in that stone, each question
rising from each crack—every aspect of life holds some insight that can
help us live. We can learn and deepen from anything anywhere.

Yet one of the paradoxes of being human is that no one can see or comprehend all of it. Thus, each of us must discover the teachers that speak to
us, the ones we can hear. This seems to be our job as initiates of being:
to pursue our curiosity and passion and suffering in an effort to uncover
our teachers. Just as different insects are drawn to certain flowers, though
pollen is everywhere, different souls are drawn to certain aspects of the living Universe, though God is in everything.

While the geography of stars pulsing in the night may help you discover
the peace waiting in your soul, digging in the earth may help your sister
know where she belongs; and yet, listening to elders speak of their life as
they near death unlocks for me the things I need to learn. Each is equally

a teacher, one no truer than the other. It's as if everything is holy so that we, in our limitations, will find it wherever we stop, fall, stumble, or give up. As if everything has to carry what is holy because each of us has only one set of ears and one set of feet to stumble on our way.

The moments that hold mystery, whether dressed in pain or wonder, wait for us to discover them, as if a message was carved in stone for you before you were born, and a storm has washed it ashore just in time, and you need all the help you can get to decipher its meaning. And we will be found by our teachers repeatedly—be they the moon, the thief, or the tiger—until we can uncover their meaning.

The moments that open our lives become powerful stories in our own personal mythology, the retelling of which renews our vitality. For me, such moments include God speaking of solitude through the waves of the sea, Grandma staring into eternity at ninety-four when she thought no one was looking, and waking after surgery to the miracle of freshly squeezed juice.

So, who and what have been your teachers? What stories carry the teachings? And what inner history do they form? How do you know that place inside that doesn't change? Who can you share this with? If no one, find someone. It's one of the few things that matter.

And where is your next teacher? In the loss about to happen that you won't be able to make sense of? Or in the stone in your shoe next month that has the imprint of a bird's wing?

It is all very humbling. For plan as we will, study as we may, search as we can, it is all a guess; a wild attempt to land ourselves in the open or in the dark until our teachers appear.

The Nature of the Dance

It seems that each person is born with an unencumbered spot, free of expectation and regret, free of ambition and embarrassment, free of fear and worry; an umbilical spot of grace where we were each first touched by God. It is this spot of grace that issues peace. Psychologists call this spot the Psyche, theologians call it the Soul, Jung calls it the Seat of the Unconscious, Hindu masters call it Atman, Buddhists call it Dharma, Rilke calls it Inwardness, Sufis call it Qalb, and Jesus calls it the Center of our Love.

To know this spot of inwardness is to know who we are, not by surface markers of identity, not by where we work or what we wear or how we like to be addressed, but by feeling our place in relation to the Infinite and by inhabiting it. This is a hard, lifelong task, for the nature of becoming is a constant filming over of where we begin, while the nature of being is a constant erosion of what is not essential. We each live in the midst of this ongoing tension, growing tarnished or covered over, only to be worn back to that incorruptible spot of grace at our core.

When the film is worn through, we have moments of enlightenment, of wholeness, of Satori, as the Zen sages term it, moments of clear living when inner meets outer, moments of full integrity of being, moments of complete oneness. And whether the film is a veil of culture, of memory, of mental or religious training, of trauma, of nationalism or sophistication, the removal of that film and the restoration of that timeless spot of grace is the goal of all therapy and education. Regardless of subject matter, this is the only thing worth teaching: how to uncover that original center and how to live there once it is restored.

How we move—from being covered over to worn open, from noise to silence, from confusion to clarity, from numbness to wakefulness—this is the dance of spirit and how it expresses us. Whether it appears as a cry of pain or a song of joy, this unseeable and repeatable cycle is the life-blood of our health. As blood must circulate through the body for the body to be vital, as water must pass through the gills for the fish to stay alive, the dance of spirit in all its forms must move through us if we are to know and feel our place in the mysterious scheme of things. In this way, the act of being who we are is at the heart of staying well.

So, let's talk about the nature of the dance. To begin with, why is being who we are essential to staying well? Because we must meet the outer world with our inner world, or existence will crush us. It is a spiritual law, as real as gravity. If we don't assume our space as living beings, the rest of life will fill us in the way water fills a hole.

Then, how do we assume our presence and inhabit our living space? How do we practice being here in a way that won't let the forces of the world collapse us? It seems that this requires another, more personal form of meeting in which our inner life helps to define our outer life; where who we are shapes what we do, where our being shapes our connections.

This personal alignment of inner with outer is a refreshing point of health we call integrity, and the condition of our integrity often determines our strength and resilience in meeting the outer world with our inner world. In a deep way, this is the purpose of integrity: to balance the outer forces of existence with the inner forces of spirit.

One of the most useful definitions of integrity comes from Rabbi Jonathan Omer-Man: "Integrity is the ability to listen to a place inside oneself that doesn't change, even though the life that carries it may change."[1]

Still, what do we mean by a place inside that doesn't change? For we are not defining integrity as a license to stubbornly adhere to our own point of view. Rather, we are offering a sense that goes deeper than what we've been taught or even what we've experienced. This deeper place inside that doesn't change serves as a threshold to an Original Presence we all share. It is an inlet to Wholeness and all that is larger than us. Given the chance, that place inside will speak to each of us. In essence, the soul's calling is to keep listening to that Original Presence inside that doesn't change, and to live accordingly.

Of course, being human, things get in the way. We often get in our own way, repeatedly. In truth, we all struggle with these recurring life positions:

> To journey without being changed is to be a nomad.
>
> To change without journeying is to be a chameleon.
>
> To journey and be transformed by the journey is to
> be a pilgrim.

It would be easy to see the first two positions as bad, or at least counter-productive. But all three are unavoidable. We cycle through them as part of the human process, as part of our unending path to and from integrity—both in our personal landscape and in finding our balanced place in the universe. It is our continual efforts to live from the pilgrim position that keep us growing into what is real.

In truth, listening deeply and inwardly allows us to keep meeting the outer world with our inner being, and this mysteriously keeps us and the world vital. Often, the nature of the dance cycles us from being self-centered to being other-centered to being balanced as an integral part in an integrated whole. And when blessed to experience those balanced, integrated moments, it becomes clear that everything is relational. Everything inside us and between us is circulatory—an ongoing exchange of what matters.

My own transformation as a poet speaks to this. As a young man, I started with the ambition to be a great artist. The everlasting poem was the goal. But when I had cancer, my writing became a rope of self-expression by which I climbed into tomorrow.

And so, greatness became irrelevant. Waking was a triumph. Now, my ambition, if you can still call it that, is the great chance to be. All my imaginings of great art have given way to a different experience of expression, one that goes beyond the writing of poems or the creating of art. I now see that expression—with ourselves, each other, and God—is a constant way of tuning our instrument of being, of staying faithful to that place inside that doesn't change. But expression is more than just the mouthing of words. It is the exchange of what matters between living things.

It leaves us with a simple and timeless question: Who will live your life? This is what the great choice comes down to: the great conflict between firsthand experience and tradition, between spontaneity and decorum, between compassion and obligation. Other life forms have no part in this. It is strictly a human affair. The sapling does not look to its elders for approval. It just grows toward the light. The bee feels its hunger and finds its honey and does not embark out of any sense of duty.

When I speak of these things, distrustful minds, against all intention of getting involved, blurt out, "But we have to live in the real world!"

And so it begins, continues, ensues. Their eyes grow gravely tense. Who will live your life? The answer is obvious. Yet the difficulty is not in knowing the course, but in accepting the many ways we give our life away, accepting the many ways we abdicate the one outright gift we have.

Too often, to live in the real world seems to require giving up all aspects of dream in the service of a survival that always looms as pragmatic. In truth, it is the opposite. Living in the world in a real way requires the evolution of an interior life, and much of our health depends on how we, at our porous best, negotiate the infiltration of the outer and the release of the inner.

Things No One Asks About

In our time on earth, we are given two continual chances to refind that incorruptible spot of grace deep within our being: we can shed what covers us over, or we can be broken open to what matters. Often, both happen at once and repeatedly. And this is the point of engaging our experience: to gain enough from what we feel to survive the pain in feeling it, to live through the thresholds that paradox offers, to live through the pain of breaking to the other side, into the rearrangement of nothing less than our very lives. We do not have to seek this sort of experience. We cannot avoid it. We have only to find the courage to feel the days keenly.

My breaking has, indeed, led me into an expanding love of being that is clearly God. I have been broken by disease and know fully that there are moments endured from which our lives will never be the same: severe, sweet moments beyond which everything is changed. No one asks for these moments. They simply happen, the way a merciless wind cracks a tree we never imagined would crack.

In truth, this experience has unraveled the way I see the world. It has scoured my lens of perception, landing me in a deeper sense of living. Though my story is framed around a particular crisis, cancer, I believe that crisis of the deepest kind somehow raises a common instinct to survive, and with that, a common set of tools—such as risk, trust, compassion, and surrender—becomes available to all. It is a constant challenge to find the current of life and to trust it, to behold the depth of what is, until a relaxation of intent and anxiety allows us to find the spaces in our individuality that we then know as spirit. Only through the passageways of spirit can we be lifted when we are heavy and rinsed of the exaggerations of our fear.

Still, it is next to impossible to do this alone. We need the loving truth of others to be well. Inevitably, when one is *thrust* into life, into crisis, into transformation—without notice or instruction—some come with us and are forever changed while others watch as we are forced out to sea. It is the power of love that enables those who come along. And in truth, a language of experience is unearthed that cannot be translated to those who stay behind.

It is the story of love, of how we hold each other up and listen, that enables a more substantial sort of living that holds nothing back or in. From here, we stumble into a more real sense of living that looks for the place where all boundaries disappear.

As a cancer survivor, I have been called heroic for merely surviving. It's like championing an eagle for flying to its nest. And I have been condemned as selfish for following the call of truth, which is like blaming a turtle for finding the deep. And I have escaped death more than once, but not the dying.

I have been worn slowly by experience and torn apart instantly by crisis and revelation. And all I can say is, Life is Food: to love is to chew; to forgive, to swallow. I cough up these bits: that the heart, like a wing, is of no use tucked, and distrust in the world, like an eye swollen shut, stops the work of love. Like a worried glassblower trying to refigure his clear and shattered heart, I have cut myself on all that I was, surprised that wisdom hides in the brilliant edges.

And as I look back, I confess that I have held the dying, have felt their life surge one last time like a surf, have held those not even a day old, have seen their eyes flicker out of focus at the coolness of this thing called air, and I have been the dying, held until I came back.

I have been crushed to center and left for invisible, and played like a sweet thing with broken strings, and in the hush after truth is shared, in the wake of all explanation and excuse, in the aftermath of illusions snapped like sticks, nothing matters now but the instant where all I am mounts like a wave for you. The instant my hand parts the air between us.

I tell you I have come so close to death that I forgot my name, and now all names seem useless. So nothing matters but emptying until the softness we call spirit bubbles through the tongue and words fail in utter adoration. Nothing now but this need to be . . . naked in the midst of what we feel.

Unraveling the Self

You see, in needing to survive, I've been forced to pare my life down to what is essential, and in doing that, I've been transformed, and along the way, my sense of writing and living has been transformed as well.

As it is, a funny thing happened on the way to being a poet. At first, I was excited to bear witness to the mysteries of life. But, feeling chronically insecure, I kept returning to an unspoken need to be recognized for my efforts, and out of this, I grew an ambition to be great, the way a camel grows a hump. All of this twisted my journey to one of getting attention instead of giving attention, to seeking recognition instead of recognizing the life around me. I wanted to be verified for every poem I wrote, when the vitalities of life only reveal themselves to those who verify what is living. In my neediest moments, I wanted to be great instead of being true.

But all of this changed with my experience with cancer. Here, I was desperate to stay alive, and so forgot about poems and manuscripts and publishers and overstatement. Now, I simply climbed that rope of expression, hand by hand, feeling by feeling, day by day, climbing my way into tomorrow. Now, my poetry became utter nonfiction. Here, the need to stay alive returned me to an expressive journey that drinks only of the Source.

And so, I learned rawly and through struggle that the center we all share is the same. And whether we find our way there by going out of ourselves completely or by going into ourselves completely, either way, we must find that vibrant center of truth that waits beneath all names.

In this, we are left with an ongoing cycle in both writing and in life, a cycle between self and other, through which we arrive, again and again, at mystery and meaning. Not by chance, though often surprising, the giving over of ourselves to the expressive journey yields the next phase of our inner curriculum. For each life is a language no one knows. With every heartbreak, discovery, and unexpected moment of joy, with every lift of music that touches us where we didn't think we could be touched, with every cut and confusion, another letter in our alphabet is decoded. Take a step, learn a word. Feel a feeling, decode a sign. Accept a truth, translate a piece of the mystery written in your heart.

So often, before living what is next, it seems as if there is some answer I need to arrive at. But daring to enter, I have been humbled to discover, again and again, that the act of living unravels both the answer and the question. When we watch, we remain riddles to be solved. When we enter, we become songs to be sung.

My experience as a poet and a cancer survivor has forced me to enlarge the notion of autobiography, beyond any narrative of events, to encompass an ongoing dialogue with the Oversoul from which we keep learning what our particular expression of spirit is to be in this life.

You see, when starting out, I wanted so badly to become a poet that I held it in view like some hill I needed to climb to see from. But getting to the top, something was missing, and so I had to climb the next hill. Finally, I realized I didn't need to climb to become a poet, I *was* a poet.

The same thing happened with love. I wanted so badly to become a lover, but climbing through relationships like hills, I realized again that I was a lover all along.

Then, I wanted to become wise, but after much travel and study, it was during my bedridden days with cancer that I realized I was already wise. I just didn't know the language of my wisdom.

Now I understand that all these incarnations come alive in us when we dare to live the days before us, when we dare to listen to the wind singing in our veins. We carry the love and wisdom like seeds, and the days sprout us. And it's the sprouting that's the poetry.

Yet there is another lesson that is more recent. It comes from a conversation I had with a very wise woman who was a mentor to me. She was the Jungian analyst Helen Luke. I knew Helen during the last two years of her life, and during what turned out to be our last conversation she said to me, "Yours is to live it, not to reveal it." This troubled me, for I have spent my life becoming a writer, thinking that my job has been just that: to reveal what is essential and hidden.

In the time since Helen died, I've come to understand her last instruction as an invitation to shed any grand purpose, no matter how devoted we may be to what we are doing. She wasn't telling me to stop writing, but to stop striving to be important. She was inviting me to stop recording the poetry of life and to enter the poetry of life.

This lesson applies to us all. If we devote ourselves to the life at hand, the rest will follow. For life, it seems, reveals itself through those willing to live. Anything else, no matter how beautiful, is just advertising.

This took me many years to learn and accept. Having begun innocently enough, there arose separations, and now I know that health resides in restoring direct experience. Thus, having struggled to do what has never been done, I discovered that living is the original art.

NOTE

1. Rabbi Omer-Man, spoken at a Common Boundary conference in Washington, D.C., 1999.

REFLECTIONS

○

Thomas F. Beech
president and CEO of the Fetzer Institute

Parker Palmer and I enrolled at Carleton College in the freshman class in 1957. We shared our college years and also attended Union Theological Seminary together. The friendship that began then has deepened over more than forty years, nurtured by shared experiences, shared values, wonderful opportunities to learn together, wacky and irreverent but always respectful humor, and abiding love.

In recent years, we've been drawn together in the Courage to Teach Program, and through Parker's role as a senior advisor to the Fetzer Institute.

I've had the opportunity to observe and learn from this master teacher through his stories, presentations, workshops, and consultations . . . and our friendship. In all of these roles, Parker gives himself unselfishly and unpretentiously, and the lives he touches (including mine) are richer for his gift of himself. In a real sense, this essay on learning is inspired by how much I've learned from him.

He describes himself as a teacher, and this is a valid description. His power as a teacher comes at the core because he is a learner: curious, always looking for new insights, and seeking new ways of knowing. He pays attention to his surroundings, to the context in which he lives, and he is attentive to the people in his life.

He also does not place himself at the center of his own life. His life is centered in his faith, his family, and his friends. His humor is genuine and refreshing because it is delightfully self-effacing. He is able to write and speak so clearly and beautifully about the power of the soul because of his own soulfulness. He is authentic in what he says about inner work because he does this work himself.

To be with Parker is to be in a learning environment, one that is open, inviting, and filled with light, hope, gentleness, and humor. It's this way because of who he is.

THE COURAGE
TO LEARN

Thomas F. Beech

OURS IS A SOCIETY filled with noise, overflowing with information and data. We extol the virtues of decisiveness, strategic thinking, and timely solutions. We celebrate but at the same time fear change. This worldview conditions our personal and vocational lives, driving us to focus primarily on the short run; to see the world as either-or; to abandon self-reflection and self-awareness in favor of self-protection; and to settle for quick fixes and sound bites rather than thoughtful, in-depth consideration that respects the complexity of our lives. The only way I have found to deal with this onslaught is to approach my own life as a learner, spiritually and intellectually.

I'm not able to do this as consistently as I'd like. All too often, I leap over obvious and useful learning opportunities in order to crash-land into a hasty decision. But when I can open myself to learning, I'm more able to respect the complexity, diversity, and uncertainty of life and appreciate the risks, the opportunities for experimentation, and the humor inherent in most situations.

Being a learner opens the possibility for relationships that are characterized by love and forgiveness. Being a learner opens the potential for me to know myself and therefore give myself in these relationships, more deeply and honestly.

Like most people, I learn in a variety of ways, but fundamental to all of them is the learning that comes from listening.

When I can't—or don't—listen, I shut out external voices and shut down internally as well. If I listen deeply enough, however, I hear not only new ideas and valuable information but also hopes and dreams, joys and sorrows. I hear what is not said as well as what is spoken. I hear people the way they want to be heard, the way they hear themselves. I hear *them*. This kind of listening involves more than my ears. It engages my eyes, my body language, and most of all my heart. Rarely, if ever, does it involve my vocal chords.

When someone really listens to me, I feel affirmed, and if I really listen in return, I reciprocate this affirmation.

The learning that comes from this kind of listening can be transformative. I gain a glimpse of what is truly meaningful, truly valuable for the person I'm listening to, and of course I become more aware of who I really am as well. This kind of listening is imbedded in all of the ways in which I learn.

Learning by Absent-Mindedness

One of my childhood memories is of a family gathering at our cottage in northern Wisconsin. I was about six years old, and the menu included hot dogs. I was there with my family and friends, talking, listening, daydreaming, looking out at the lake with a hot dog in one hand and in the other a small frog I had caught at the water's edge a few minutes earlier. I was lost in my own little world, thinking my own special thoughts, when out of nowhere my mother shrieked, "Tommy!" Shocked back into the present, I noticed that I was about to take a big bite of the frog instead of the hot dog. I dropped the frog, watched it hop away to live another day, and smiled sheepishly in response to the kindly laughter, pats on the head, and the shaking of many adult heads in acknowledgment to everyone that this wasn't the first time—nor would it be the last—that I'd exhibited this kind of behavior. The adults were prophetic.

Looking back on the occasion, I realize that this is one way I have always learned. I learn by absentmindedness in those times when my subconscious mind is focused on something that diverts my inward attention away from where I actually am, who I'm with, and what I'm doing.

In my experience, what is commonly referred to as absentmindedness is, in reality, awareness of a deeper "presentmindedness." I like to think of it as losing track of myself, getting my conscious self out of the way. It is this being present that makes music such a powerful force in my life. My absentmindedness is the gateway to melodies that seem to spring from nowhere inside me. Sometimes they stay with me long enough for me to write them down. At other times, they are gentle guests in my consciousness just for a moment or two. Being absentminded is one way I become aware of God's grace, the power of Spirit in my life. There's a kind of whimsy, an element of surprise in this absentmindedness. Some folks may look upon absentmindedness as being irresponsible or unreliable, rude, or perhaps even goofy. I think this attitude gives a bad rap to something wonderful.

Learning by Trial and Error

A second way that I learn, a close cousin of absentmindedness, is by trial and error.

Lewis Thomas, in his book *The Medusa and the Snail,* has some wonderful thoughts about the role of trial and error in our lives:

> We learn, as we say, by "trial and error." Why do we say that? Why not "trial and rightness" or "trial and triumph"? The old phrase puts it that way because that is, in real life, the way it is done. . . .
>
> We are at our human finest, dancing with our minds, when there are more choices than two. Sometimes there are ten, even twenty ways to go, all but one bound to be wrong, and the richness of selection in such situations can lift us onto totally new ground. This process is called exploration and is based on human fallibility. If we had only a single center in our brains, capable of responding only when a correct decision was to be made, instead of the jumble of different, credulous, easily conned clusters of neurons that provide for being flung off into blind alleys, up trees, down dead ends, out into blue sky, along wrong turnings, around bends, we could only stay the way we are today, stuck fast.[1]

Like the people Thomas refers to in this passage, I bear the marks of trial and error as a learning mode—nicks and bruises to my skin and ego. But I've learned something very important in the process: trying to be right all the time is not only impossible, it's suffocating! The hidden treasure in mistakes is the capacity to try something totally new, to embrace the unexpected.

It's taken me most of my life to unlearn the message that I have to be right all the time. I am only now beginning to discover that letting go of this expectation allows me to let loose of expecting it of others as well. The more I can accept myself, just as I am, the more I can accept others. If judgment is replaced by acceptance, a breath of fresh air opens up the possibility that, together, we will do our best, hoping for excellence but not demanding perfection. In so doing, I open myself to the wonder and possibility of learning something.

Accepting others and being open to learning is exceedingly important in my chosen vocation, the field of philanthropy. In this field, as well as in other helping professions, our mission is to make life better, to have a positive impact on the people whose lives we touch.

Certainly, there's nothing wrong with this. But in my experience, whenever this mission is confounded by an *overpowering* need to fix things, to be appreciated and to be right, I'm in trouble. This signals for me the early symptoms of one of philanthropy's most serious diseases: *chronic sincerity.*

My own experience of chronic sincerity occurs when I become over-whelmed with the seriousness, the weight, the importance of my work. More to the point, I become convinced that I alone carry the responsibil-ity to make all things right. I confuse the legitimate importance of the work I'm involved in with my own need for self-importance and perfec-tion. When I'm in this mode, service turns into suffocation.

A remedy that helps me break free of chronic sincerity is to remember the story someone once told me about why it took an entire Boy Scout troop to help an elderly woman across the street: she didn't want to go.

Learning by Example

A third way I learn is by example—not my own, thankfully. Throughout my life, some people—often without their knowing—have been inspira-tional examples for me. On occasion, others have served as a warning. To-gether they have helped me become more aware of the light and shadow in my own being.

The warnings come from people I encounter who feel they have a spe-cial corner on truth, and who are compelled to convert anyone within ear-shot to their way of thinking. Others who set off a warning signal within me are those who feel they've been dealt an unjust hand and can't let go of the events or people whom they think have harmed them or treated them unfairly.

I confess that being around both these kinds of people tests my earlier pronouncements about acceptance and being nonjudgmental. Truth be told, these encounters make me uncomfortable because they remind me of my own capacity to be arrogant and play the role of victim.

It's easier and more fun to talk about the people who have been an inspi-ration to me. I'll cite just two of them here. My Mom, Alice Lyon Beech, was a gifted artist with a wonderful sense of humor. She possessed a special way of looking at people, places, and occasions: the presence of light in the forest near our cottage in Wisconsin, the expression in someone's eyes, the tender-ness and texture of relationships. Her drawings and paintings were filled with her unusual and abiding awareness of natural and human beauty.

She sensed that music would be important to me, and though I hated choir practice and piano lessons as a kid she helped me discover a love of music that is one of the great gifts of my life.

She taught me by her own example that the root of a true sense of hu-mor is the ability to laugh at oneself. She radiated silliness and sophisti-cation at the same time. She also taught me that there's a close connection between my sense of humor and my sense of values. Losing touch with the former puts the latter at risk. Laughing at myself helps me not take myself too seriously, and it frees up the people whose lives I encounter to do the same.

Another inspiring example for me is James P. Shannon. Jim asked me to join him as assistant director of the Minneapolis Foundation when he was appointed its executive director in 1974. He became the most important person in my vocational life as well as a dear friend. While he was a bishop in the Catholic Church, Jim was on the receiving end of what can only be described as systematic and personal cruelty at the hands of people he trusted within the Catholic hierarchy. Yet he did not break his trust with them. He didn't respond in kind. He consistently and repeatedly forgave and prayed for his attackers and tormentors.

From Jim, I learned that trust, acceptance, and forgiveness are the bedrock of all relationships. These are not commodities that we can share or withhold at will. Jim taught me that the source of trust in my own life is not my strength or generosity of spirit. Whatever trustworthiness I may exhibit, as well as my capacity for trusting others, comes from God's grace, God's gift of love. So, paradoxically, although trust may be something I think I must earn, it is never something that I deserve or possess.

When we were together at the Minneapolis Foundation, and many times after that, I observed him interacting with others and marveled at the strength of his gentleness. He drew out the best from his coworkers and friends, partly because of his kindness, caring, and transparent goodness, and partly because, though he always was present, he made room for others to grow.

Jim was highly educated and profoundly wise, and he had a precise command of language. Yet he did not use these gifts to impress or impose his ideas on others. He participated with them in an exploration of alternatives, blending humility, humor, honesty, and hospitality so that he brought, to borrow one of his phrases, "more light than heat" to any situation.

Learning Through Relationships

I know that I learn from reflection and from solitude, but this aloneness must be balanced by interaction and relationship with others. Left to my own devices, I'll lapse into my default setting, which is governed by fear. Fear is the most powerful enemy of learning. As I anticipate dealing on my own with the small and large challenges that make up ordinary life, I invent the worst-case scenario, primarily out of fear: fear of failure, fear of not being accepted, fear of anger and criticism, fear of rejection, fear of abandonment. This fear shuts me down; it causes me to retreat into my shell and crowds out learning.

True learning, deep learning, is not only an act of intellect or will. It's an act of courage. It involves risk. The courage that "encourages" true learning comes from the experience of being supported in relationship with another person, or in being part of a community. The risk of error; failure; looking foolish, misguided, or mistaken is counterbalanced by the certain knowledge that I am loved, accepted, and valued—no matter what. This love, acceptance, and valuing was the basis of the relationships with my mom and with Jim Shannon, and still grounds my friendship with Parker.

Even before becoming a formal member of the Fetzer Institute community, I attended conferences at the institute's conference center, Seasons. The meetings at this remarkable place, called "a Center for Renewal," are guided by the values and beliefs that are also central to the institute:

- Every person is grounded with an inner source of truth, which is the root from which our capacity for loving and forgiving grows.

- Our inner life of mind and spirit is interrelated with our outer life of action and service.

- Just as we hold ourselves and others accountable for words and deeds, so also do we hold ourselves and others in our hearts. This is the basis for trust and freedom.

- The more we refrain from quick judgment and avoid the temptation to solve problems for one another, the more likely we are to learn with and from one another.

- Authenticity and integrity are based on respect for diversity.

The group settings and individual relationships in which these values and beliefs flourish melt away my fear and invite learning. What's actually at risk in these relationships are things I *can* bear: the risk of criticism, of having others disagree with me and challenge my ideas, the risk of struggling through uncertainty and pain. My self-hood, identity, and integrity are not at risk because I know that I am loved. This is what enables intellectual, emotional, and spiritual growth—true learning—to occur.

It is when I discover, or more accurately remember, this that I find the courage to learn.

NOTE

1. Lewis, T. *The Medusa and the Snail.* New York: Viking Press, 1979, pp. 38–39.

REFLECTIONS

○
———

Jane Tompkins
professor of English and Education
at the University of Illinois at Chicago

When I read *To Know as We Are Known* for the first time, I couldn't believe it. I wrote the author a fan letter, full of joy and adulation. Here was a kindred spirit, a person who thought and felt about education the same way I did. It seemed a miracle. Shortly thereafter, I met Parker at a conference. We had lunch. I heard his amazing deep voice, heard him laugh, and was delighted by his wry humor. I was a goner.

Since then, Parker has mentored me, encouraged me when I was down, and continued to inspire in me the love that is inspired by a truly great teacher—by which I mean someone who tells the truth about things. When students hear the truth at long last, they are so grateful that they give their hearts to the teacher.

LEARNING FROM
THE WORKPLACE

*Professional Life as an
Opportunity for Personal Growth*

Jane Tompkins

TWO YEARS AGO, I made up a new job for myself in the university where I was teaching (I'd been a professor all my life). The job was to create lounge and café spaces for the commuter students, who had no place to sit down before and after class. A year later, I was asked to take over classroom renovation. The experience of doing something completely new made me able to see myself in the workplace as I'd never been able to when I was a classroom teacher. This essay, which is based on observations I made about myself in the course of doing my work, deals with the topic of personal growth in the context of professional life. It is a revised form of a talk delivered in April 2003 as the DeGraaf lecture, to the students and faculty of Hope College in Holland, Michigan.

Moving from teaching into a kind of entrepreneurial activity within the university last year, and this year into administration, has made me realize how much I still have to learn about how to function in the workplace—even though I've been working on myself pretty directly for about fifteen years and have been holding down a real job for about thirty-six years.

This realization has not been a bad thing. The only thing worse than discovering, at age sixty-three, that you're still in kindergarten as far as knowing how to behave at work is concerned, would be realizing that you'd already learned pretty much everything you needed to know. Most of us long to be the person in the know, the authority, the one whom people turn to, and it does feel good when, now and then, we find ourselves in that position. But it's not good for us spiritually. Spiritually, we grow when we *don't know*; at least that's what I've found.

Looking back, I realize that my professional life has contained countless situations that gave me an opportunity to learn and grow, though I might not have been aware of them at the time. Among those I am aware of, there are some in which circumstances clearly did cause some internal change and development, and others—you might call them the cold case files of a career—where I never did figure out what went wrong or how I could have done better. One situation from the recent past produced a lesson for me that has become the focus of my efforts to act responsibly and in an enlightened way on the job.

My boss asked me to set up a system for planning classroom renovation and overhauling classroom maintenance, working with people who didn't like each other and who felt, in varying degrees, devalued by the university. I quickly saw that since I had no expertise in the issues we were dealing with, the only thing to do was to get the people who did have such expertise to bring their knowledge to the table. Something told me that to make this happen I had to focus on the people themselves; on how they were feeling; on their need for respect, for airtime; on their need to be listened to and have their concerns taken seriously. This meant that no matter how I might have felt about the issues, or about the people themselves, I had to set my own feelings aside, listen, and be responsive, respectful, and concerned. I had to forget about the plan we were to come up with and think only about the people who were in the room with me.

Somehow or other, I managed to do this; the information flowed. The plan wrote itself, or rather, one of the other people wrote the plan; all I did was revise it. This was how I discovered the principle that has occupied my thoughts so much recently: namely, the relationship is more important than the task. It means putting the welfare of the people you're working with ahead of your desire to get the job done. It means remembering that the human beings in the room with you are vulnerable, essentially pure and good, infinitely worthy of respect, *and,* at some level, the solution to your problems. The principle is easy to assent to, perhaps, but extremely difficult to put into effect. At least I find it so.

Over and over again this year, I have violated it: snapping at an assistant for not doing a job immediately, speaking harshly to a designer whose taste differs from mine. A particularly bad instance occurred one day when I was picking out carpet for my new office. Because my job was largely concerned with interior design, I felt I would be judged by how well I'd done with my own space, and since the carpet was the only new thing I could afford to buy it had to be right.

I'd brought to the carpet store a sample of the color I wanted, and when the salesman, a kind, good-natured older man who wanted to be helpful, twice picked out colors that didn't match, I insulted him, saying something like "That's not your strong suit," and went to find another person to help me. This was a perfect example of what I'd supposedly been learning to avoid. Getting the carpet color right was my task, and in my impatient desire to do it I ran over a human being.

Why is putting the relationship ahead of the task so hard to do?

One reason is our fixation on performance, on product, the result of our culture's obsessive goal orientation. When you're hell-bent on getting a job done, doing it right, and coming in on time, it's almost automatic to put the demand of the tasks first and human relations second. When we work this way, we work with blinders on, possessed by our own purposes, immersed in the details of our project, which blot out everything else. Our relationship to other people isn't even on the radar.

Of course, focused attention to a task in itself is not necessarily bad. In fact, it's essential to most demanding enterprises. The total absorption and laserlike concentration that one-pointed activity involves is profoundly satisfying, even thrilling. The trouble is that that kind of exclusive concentration can become the tool of unconscious psychological needs. The tunnel vision of all-absorbing work can feed the habit of wanting to see ourselves reflected grandly in our own achievements, of wanting to get an A on our test at any cost so that others may admire our worth. We have all been carefully taught this form of narcissism in the competitive environment of school, and even before that. It's been dinned into us from an early age, and our culture reinforces it at every turn.

To say that the relationship is more important than the task means violating this performance ethic, diverting attention from accomplishment (with ourselves in the starring role of the accomplisher) in order to pay attention to other people and other circumstances. This deflection of attention away from the task feels foolhardy, even dangerous, because it goes against the grain of our conditioning. If I forget about my job for a minute to pay attention to you, what will happen to me and my performance?

A second reason it's hard to pay attention to other people rather than to our own projects is that it means getting over any sense of superiority or entitlement we may be carrying around, setting aside our own purposes in favor of the needs of people whose intellects we might feel are less supple than our own, or whose values and behavior we do not particularly admire. Or they may be people we do admire but who *at that moment* are getting in our way. Giving up the conviction that we are right and must prevail if the work is to go forward is even harder than overcoming goal orientation; actually, it is another form of it.

But why, you ask, make such a fuss about behavior that is quite understandable, and even on balance defensible? Suppose the other people *are* getting in the way. Don't you have to stop them? Isn't it part of their job to know how to take the heat? What's the value of being nice if it means your work is going be bungled, or late, or otherwise screwed up? Are the only standards in play here the finer points of human interaction?

What about doing a good job and getting things right? If you put relationships ahead of the task, you're likely to end up with half-baked projects *and* a reputation for being a pushover, aren't you?

My answer to these objections is, we must still put relationship first, because doing so trumps the value of the task: people's feelings are more important than bringing a project in on time. Interestingly, the quality of the relationships involved affects the outcome of the task in subtle ways. Having said that, I'll add that it's also true that a promise to do something and do it well constitutes a relationship, a relationship to yourself and the person to whom you've made the promise. The concept of relationship includes these relationships as well. Integrity demands that you do your job to the best of your ability, while wisdom and compassion require that you find a way to do it without hurting another person's feelings. This means paying attention to how other people feel—which is easier said than done.

Talking about relationships rather than about product means shifting away from an instrumental view of the workplace, from work as a means to an end to work as an end in itself—relationship, creativity, celebration, service, spiritual practice—work as what we do with our lives every day. This concept of work would require assessment different from the one we normally use: the measure of productivity. The new way of measuring how well a job is being done would consider not only our output but our relationship to other people, and also our relationship to the task itself.

When, one year into a completely new kind of work, I accepted a whole new layer of responsibilities, my relation to the job became one of anxiety punctuated by terror. I was without a clue. I had a boss who flattered me, listened to me, and made me feel good but who was vague—almost unbelievably vague—about what it was, exactly, that I was supposed to do. When I asked him a question, his favorite reply was, "Let's just see how things unfold."

For those of you familiar with the Myers-Briggs Type Indicator (a Jungian-based personality test), this "let's see how things unfold" attitude is a sign of "perceiver" behavior. A strong perceiver in this typology is a person who doesn't need closure, doesn't like a fixed agenda, hates to hem himself in with detailed plans, but likes instead to wait and see what's around the next corner, go with the flow, let the universe take charge. The opposite of the perceiver is the "judger," who wants to have all the reservations made months in advance, nails things down ahead of time, doesn't like loose ends, always has a fallback position, gets to places early, knows what her bank balance is, and takes the car in to be fixed at the first sign of a suspicious noise.

Though I myself am a strong perceiver, the *laissez faire* behavior of my boss left me floundering. What was my job? My role? What exactly was I supposed to be doing? When was I supposed to have it done? With no articulated expectations to work with, I set unrealistic expectations for myself that I then proceeded not to meet, thus causing gut-wrenching guilt and a sense of failure. Add to this the fact that I was making a lot of money and had moved into a large corner office (for which I bought that new carpet in a time of budget crisis) and you get the picture.

The lessons came slowly. After three or four months of agonizing self-recrimination, I finally realized a simple truth: I do not function well in an unstructured situation. To feel secure, valued, and productive, I have to have my task spelled out for me so that by doing it I can know I am worthy of my hire. Without external benchmarks by which to measure my worth, I collapse psychologically, disappearing into a void of intangibility and amorphousness. (Ever the goal-oriented worker, I cannot exist on relationship alone.)

As a result of this experience, I began to see what it must have been like for some of the students in my experimental courses when I asked them to organize and conduct entire classes on their own. How terrified they must have been. When you're the one calling the shots, telling the people who report to you to do their own thing seems enlightened; you see yourself as the great emancipator. But freedom without signposts or boundaries can be frightening if you are the one expected to produce something, only . . . what? when? how?

I learned the horrors of being set afloat on an unknown sea with no particular destination and nothing to navigate by. But there was another side to the story. I also learned that I could navigate without a compass and find dry land on my own. I could figure out what to do, little by little, by doing first one thing and then another. Even doing something that turned out to be a mistake was better than floating in the void. You can usually correct a mistake, and then one thing leads to another and eventually you arrive somewhere. Having arrived, you get your bearings and set out again, correcting your course. In effect, being willing to act without knowledge—a relationship to the task that you might call faith—is more important than the task itself, because often the task is unclear and will emerge only *through* the relationship.

Around January, I experienced the deep sense of relief that comes when a task has finally assumed a definite outline: concrete steps have been taken, results have been produced, and they have been received and discussed by others. But the period of anxiety and not knowing was when the learning occurred. It was when my relation to the task was all-important, because at that time there *was* no task to speak of, only a desperate hope that the task would sooner or later materialize. My initial relation to the job, a relation of anxiety, called forth another, parallel relation, of faith and trust. I had to believe that somehow things would work out. There was simply nothing else to do.

During the period I am speaking of, I experienced a great deal of fatigue and feelings of ill health, some of which no doubt were occasioned by job stress but whose ultimate source remained a mystery. With the ill health came doubt about whether I should have accepted the new responsibilities in the first place. I thought my fatigue was a sign that I'd made the wrong choice.

Doubt—as I should have remembered—is just one of the five hindrances that in Buddhism are said to prevent mindfulness. (The others are agitation and restlessness, sloth and torpor, aversion, and grasping and clinging.) Doubt, the fifth hindrance, was just one of the regular lions in the path; nothing to get worked up about. I had been through the mill of doubt before. But when it arose this time in the context of my job, I failed to recognize it, so I lived with the doubt day by day, twisting in the wind.

The doubt called forth a deeper level of trust than the anxiety had. When you don't know what you're doing *or* whether you should be doing it at all, it forces you to a keener sense of your own limitations. You have to begin trusting in forces larger than you are, relying on the wisdom inherent in the energies of a moment, surrendering to the shape of a situation. It is this last lesson, the lesson of surrender, that involves taking things lightly and not trying so hard; this is the most difficult. For those of us whose identity is all bound up with the notion that to work hard and stay in control is to be a good person, allowing the universe to take its own course threatens us at the core.

Gimpel the Fool

These days, when I think of the maxim that the relationship is more important than the task, I think of the lines that the rabbi speaks in Singer's short story "Gimpel the Fool."[1] The story is tough, as many of Singer's stories are. The life it depicts, in the miserable little Eastern European settlement of Frampol, is nasty, brutish, and short, the people generally selfish, underhanded, and base. They have learned that the boy Gimpel has a believing nature and is easily taken advantage of. They play mean tricks on him, ridicule and humiliate him, exploit his innocence in every conceivable way; they even bully him into marrying a woman who, unbeknownst to Gimpel, is pregnant with another man's child.

Only when Gimpel goes to the rabbi to seek advice are we offered another perspective. The rabbi says, "It is written, better to be a fool all your days than for one hour to be evil. You are not a fool. They are the fools. For he who causes his neighbor to feel shame loses Paradise himself." We are glad to hear these words, though they are not very comforting. The way Singer sets it up, either you're a fool like Gimpel, suffering the contempt of your fellow men, or you're one of his tormentors. There's no comfortable place in between.

As Gimpel's wife dies, she confesses that none of their six children was fathered by him. Finally, in retaliation for the deceptions that have been visited on him all his life, Gimpel is tempted by the devil to deceive his fellow townsfolk. He is a baker; he will urinate into the dough and sell the bread to the villagers. But his wife appears to him in a dream, her face black, saying: "You fool! Because I was false, is everything false too? I never deceived anyone but myself. I'm paying for it all, Gimpel. They spare you nothing here." On hearing this, Gimpel divides his money among his children, kisses them goodbye, and leaves. He becomes a wanderer in the world, spinning stories, and he looks forward to death, for "whatever may be there, it will be real, without complication, without ridicule, without deception."

Whatever the story in its totality may mean, I like it because it presents life in two dimensions: the day-to-day world, where people take advantage of each other or are taken advantage of, trying to get ahead by small contrivances; and the eternal world, where all that matters are the truths of the spirit. I like it because little by little, in my own work, I'm coming to see that the fool's way is best—the way of trusting and believing. Late in the story, the rabbi says to Gimpel, "Belief in itself is beneficial. It is written that a good man lives by faith." I've come to believe that it's better to relate to your work from faith and trust and to act than it is to operate from your competence and expertise.

Though we may work for them long and hard, competence and expertise are relatively easy to come by, given the right conditions. But faith and trust are another story. Mostly, we're robbed of them at a young age and spend our lives trying to avoid being taken advantage of again by learning to act cannily in our own interests. The story of Gimpel shows what a mistake that is.

Don't let your work be only about succeeding on the job. Let your work, in addition to teaching you competence and expertise, teach you something about your own nature. Let it be an education of the heart and of the spirit. Everywhere around you are opportunities to learn at this level; recognizing them is the trick. The trick is to look not at the content of the task at hand but at your relationship to it. If you can learn to switch your attention from the job to your own reactions to the job, you can learn a great deal.

Before I end, there's one more observation I'd like to make. By recommending that you pay attention to your own growth and development, whatever form this may take, I don't mean to be suggesting it's actually a way to achieve worldly success by another route. I am not saying or implying that cultivating inner qualities will give you an insight into yourself and others that makes you skillful at interpersonal relations and thus leads to your advancement. Whereas it's possible, in the course of attending to your emotional and spiritual growth, to become a high achiever by standard measures, it does not necessarily follow. Flannery O'Connor said somewhere, "You shall know the truth, and the truth shall make you odd." Self-knowledge and integrity carry with them no particular guarantees. The reward for this kind of work lies not in external achievement but in the quality and depth of your experience. Since this is where happiness lies, it's a good deal.

NOTE

1. The quotations from "Gimpel the Fool" are from Singer, I. B. *Gimpel the Fool and Other Stories* (S. Bellow, trans.). New York: Farrar, Straus & Giroux, 1957.

REFLECTIONS

○

Margaret J. Wheatley
president of the Berkana Institute

I have to admit, one thing that consistently intrigues me about Parker is his name. Just the subtle shift from *r* to *l*. I've often wondered how Korean and Japanese colleagues handle it. Years ago, I had an MBA student who named his child after Parker. But to this day, I can't remember if his son's name is Parker, or Palmer.

I first met Parker through his book *The Active Life*. I used it in the ethics class I was teaching at Brigham Young University. Then, miraculously, Parker appeared on BYU's campus for a weeklong exploration of spirituality and education. I still treasure my notes from those sparkling days.

During that week, Parker came to my home for dinner, to meet those of us who had just founded the Berkana Institute. Parker gave us trenchant advice about Berkana that helped us over many years. That very week, I had received the first two copies of *Leadership and the New Science*. I had no idea how the book would change my life, but I had the good sense to give one of the two copies to Parker.

In later years, we would sometimes be together speaking, which was always a joy. But as I look back on all that transpired in the brief visit in June 1992—the formation of Berkana, the exploration of spirituality and teaching, the beginning of my own journey—I can still hear the rustling wings of the many angels who were present that week.

THE TRUE PROFESSIONAL

Margaret J. Wheatley

I LOVE EVERYTHING PARKER HAS WRITTEN, and I eagerly refer people to his many books.

But I was first stirred and taught by *The Active Life*. For four years, I used it in the ethics class I was teaching to master's-level students who would become city managers, business leaders, entrepreneurs, and consultants. I never grew tired of the book, and I always discovered something new each semester.

When I was asked to contribute to this volume, I didn't want to write anything that would focus on me. It seemed too small and limiting. I only wanted to illuminate the wisdom and voice of Parker. I also could not begin to express what I have learned from Parker in prose form. The depth, complexity, and grace of his being is what has blessed us these many years, and poetry is the only medium I know that might begin to mirror these qualities.

What I've written is termed "a found poem." Every phrase and word is Parker's, all of them residing in *The Active Life*. But of course, I chose the phrases and words to work with, and therefore these choices reveal me. In this poem, I play with concepts and language that illuminated for me the landscape of being a true professional. They have remained fundamental to who I am, and I willingly give Parker all praise for shining this light onto the path.

As I worked with Parker's words, it was astonishing how much new meaning popped out of familiar phrases. I thought I knew this territory, yet there it was, bright with ideas and sensibilities I had not yet seen, glowing with new clarity.

This found poem has only deepened my gratefulness for the many gifts of Parker.

A "FOUND POEM" TAKEN FROM
PARKER'S WORDS IN *THE ACTIVE LIFE*
Recomposed with love and gratitude by Meg Wheatley

"The true professional is a person whose action points beyond
his or herself to that underlying reality,
that hidden wholeness, on which we all can rely."

Illusion

Too much of our action is really reaction. Such doing does not flow from
free and independent hearts
but depends on external provocation.

Such doing does not flow
it depends on external provocation.

It does not come from our sense of
who we are and what we want to do, but from
our anxious reading of how others define us

   our anxious reading of how others define us
   our anxious reading of how others define us

and of what the world demands.

        When we react in this way we do not act humanly.

The true professional is one
who does not obscure grace
with illusions of technical prowess,
the true professional is one
who strips away all illusions to reveal

a reliable truth
a reliable truth in which
the human heart can rest.

Can rest.

Unveil the illusions
   unveil the illusions that
      masquerade
the illusions that masquerade
as reality and reveal
 the reality
 behind the masks.

   Catch the magician
deceiving us
   get a glimpse
     a glimpse of the
   truth behind the trick.

   A glimpse.

Contemplation happens anytime we get a glimpse of the truth.

Action

Action, like a sacrament,
is the visible form of an invisible spirit
an outward manifestation of
an inward power.

> An expressive act is not to achieve a goal outside myself
> but to express a conviction
> a leading, a truth that is within me.

An expressive act is one taken
because if I did not
if I did not
if I did not take it
I would be denying
my own insight, gift, nature.

Action, like a sacrament, is the visible form of an invisible spirit
an outward manifestation of
an inward power. But as we act,
we not only express what is in us
and help give shape to the world.

We also receive what is outside us
and we reshape
   our inner selves.

When we act, the world acts back.

The world acts back
and we and the world,
we and the world are

co-created.

> Right action is a process of birthing that cannot be forced

but only followed.

Surrender

When God's love for the world pierces our armor of fear
it is an awesome experience of calling and accountability.
When God's love pierces our armor of fear
it is awesome
it is awesome to be pierced by God

to be called to accountability
to be called by God's love
for the world.

The true professional is one
who does not obscure grace
with illusions of technical prowess,
the true professional is one
who strips away all illusions to reveal

a reliable truth in which
the human heart can rest.

Reveal a reliable truth.

Let our human hearts rest.

Moving the Heart to the Center

WHEN WE ARE DISCONNECTED from ourselves or from others, we feel vulnerable, fearful, and wounded. This ubiquitous sense of disconnection plaguing our culture disrupts what Parker calls our "web of being." The antidote to the disconnected life can be found in engaging each other and belonging to communities devoted to honoring genuine interaction with each other. For Parker, "Community is the outward and visible sign of inward and invisible grace, the flowing of personal identity and integrity into the world of relationships."[1]

The essays in this section focus on two aspects of community important in Parker's work. The first set of essays, "Learning in Community," explore what it means to know, teach, and learn within communities pursuing knowledge and understanding. These essays explore what it means to gather together to learn and to contest ideas with energy and rigor. The authors describe efforts to propel a search for truth and meaning in schools, in the public space, and in the workplace.

The essays affirm Parker's vision of a learning community in which the "hard" virtues of cognition coexist with the "soft" virtues of community: "Without the soft virtues of community, the hard virtues of cognitive teaching and learning will be absent as well. Our ability to confront each other critically and honestly over alleged facts, imputed meanings or personal biases and prejudices—*that* is the ability impaired by the absence of community."[2] Learning in community is open, public, and energized by candor.

The second set of essays, "Opening Space for the Inner Life," explore the role community can play in supporting the inner journey. In *Let Your Life Speak,* Parker describes an evolving relationship with the aphorism that began in his early thirties:

> I ran across the old Quaker saying, "Let your life speak." I found those words encouraging, and I thought I understood what they meant: "let the highest truths and virtues guide you. Live up to those demanding standards in every thing you do." Because I had heroes at the time who seemed to be doing exactly that, this exhortation had incarnate meaning—it meant living a life of Martin Luther King Jr. or Rosa Parks or Mahatma Gandhi or Dorothy Day, a life of high purpose.
>
> So I lined up the loftiest ideals I could find and set out to achieve them. The results were rarely admirable, often laughable, and sometimes grotesque. But always they were unreal, a distortion of my true self. . . . Today, some thirty years later, "let your life speak" means something else to me, a meaning faithful both to the ambiguity of those words and to the complexity of my own experience: "Before you tell your life what you intend to do with it, listen to what it intends to do with you. Before you tell your life what truths and values you have decided to live up to, let your life tell you what truths you embody, what values you represent."[3]

How can we discover and lead a life congruent with the truths and values that we embody? One answer is to set forth on a spiritual journey of solitude and silence. It is often suggested that the spiritual path requires solitude over interaction, solo journeys rather than communal engagement, quietude more than animation. These images, as Parker points out, devalue the energies of the active life and discount the indispensability of others in the work of living and discerning an integral life. The journey for Parker hinges on community that allows an individual to experience "being alone together."

When we are alone, we can listen deeply to our life and we have much to learn from within; but as Parker warns us, "It is easy to get lost in the labyrinth of the inner life. We have much to learn from others." We must never lose sight of our connections to each other. Yet the tension between community and solitude is a true paradox for Parker: "Solitude does not necessarily mean living apart from others; rather it means never living apart from one's self. It is not about the absence of other people—it is about being fully present to ourselves, whether or not we are with others. Community does not necessarily mean living face-to-face with others; rather, it means never losing the awareness that we are connected to each other."[4] The authors in Part Two appreciate this tension and explore what it means to open up a space hospitable for the soul. In *The Hidden Wholeness*, Parker challenges us to think about what it would take to create spaces that invite the "soul to make itself known." He writes

> We know how to create spaces that invite the intellect to show up, analyzing reality, parsing logic, and arguing its case. . . . We know how to create spaces that invite the emotions into play, reacting to injury, expressing and celebrating joy. We know how to create spaces that invite the will to emerge, consolidating energy and efforts on behalf of a shared goal. We certainly know how to create spaces that invite the ego to make an appearance, polishing its image, protecting its turn and demanding its rights. But we know very little about creating spaces that invite the soul to make itself known. Aside from the natural world, such spaces are hard to find—and we seem to place little value on preserving the soul spaces in nature.[5]

NOTES

1. Palmer, P. J. *The Courage to Teach*. San Francisco: Jossey-Bass, 1998, p. 90.

2. Palmer, P. J. "Community, Conflict, and Ways of Knowing." *Change*, Sept.–Oct. 1987, p. 25.

3. Palmer, P. J. *Let Your Life Speak: Listening for the Voice of Vocation*. San Francisco: Jossey-Bass, 2000, pp. 2–3.

4. Palmer, P. J. *A Hidden Wholeness: The Journey Toward an Undivided Life*. San Francisco: Jossey-Bass, 2004, p. 55.

5. Palmer (2004), p. 56.

Chapter Three

LEARNING
IN COMMUNITY

THE GREAT GIFT WE RECEIVE on the inner journey is the certain knowledge that ours is not the only act in town. Not only are there other acts in town, but some of them from time to time are even better than ours! On this inner journey we learn that we do not have to carry the whole load, that we can be empowered by sharing the load with others, and that sometimes we are even free to lay our part of the load down. On the inner journey we learn that co-creation leaves us free to do only what we are called and able to do, and to trust the rest to other hands. With that learning, we become leaders who cast less shadow and more light.

—Parker J. Palmer

REFLECTIONS

○

Jean Feraca
distinguished senior broadcaster, Wisconsin Public Radio

The first time I met Parker, I knew right away this was a man I wanted to talk to forever. Over the course of the thirteen years of *Conversations with Jean Feraca,* my public radio talk show, Parker returned again and again to explore universal themes based on bedrock spiritual principles that inspired deep, resonant conversation.

Radio broadcasters live in dread of "dead air." But Parker once insisted that we start a program about the benefits of silence with one full minute of dead air. That was a very long minute, as I watched the second hand stagger around the clock.

People who center themselves in silence know how to talk. Their words have clarity and weight; they surface like found objects from a deep well. Parker means what he says, and because he is so attuned to silence, he knows how to listen. He attends; he leans into what is being said; he lives through the questions.

Parker once described my program as "Jean Feraca's Flying Circus" because of my intuitive leaps and nonlinear interview style. But it is really Parker who creates the feeling of being under a big top, a space where you feel safe enough to be real and talk about things that matter. Conversations that take place in such a context can be powerful; they can bring forth new ideas, and fresh insights—and even change lives.

It was during one of my conversations with Parker that I had an epiphany. The program was called "Karasses and Granfaloons," and we were talking about invisible communities. Suddenly, it came to me. What we were doing was in itself a form of invisible community. Where else but on the radio do we keep the company of strangers? That was the beginning of what I began to call Earth Radio, a project that Parker endorsed and supported from its very conception, and that has led me to this very threshold: the launch of a program never before attempted, global call-in radio, *Here on Earth.*

CROSSING
THE GREAT DIVIDES
The Power of Radio to Connect
People Across Boundaries

Jean Feraca

I HAVE A DREAM.

Imagine a radio program with a mission to search out and chronicle the evidence of our interconnectedness, transpersonal, transpolitical, and transnational. A program that would profess what we do not yet possess: a global brain, a new genesis, the earth as one interwoven through technology. Earth radio. The voice of an emerging planetary society. A program that respects our differences while it pulses clear and steady evidence of our common humanity, that what we hold in common is greater than what divides us.

Imagine a consortium of world citizens in search of new forms of freedom, carrying on a global conversation and practicing the rituals of community on the radio. Imagine a living classroom of the air operating through synergy and dialogue, practicing global thinking as a commonplace of everyday reality. Where the highest common denominator is assumed along with the deepest respect for human capacity. On such a program we might meet and interact with Nobel laureates, MacArthur geniuses, practical visionaries and spiritual masters, world-class artists, writers, poets, inventors, social architects, healers, and heads of state. People with the big picture. But a guest might just as likely be the lady down the street who gets angry about the toxic waste dump in her neighborhood, gathers together a group of neighbors, and starts a revolution in her kitchen.

People using their native ingenuity and resourcefulness to think through problems collectively and set new directions. People inspired and enabled through Web-enhanced radio to continue online the conversations that begin on the air, to seek each other out, link up, form groups, networks, and allegiances. Words open the mind; they tenderize the heart; they lead to deeds.

Adapted from the keynote address by Jean Feraca delivered at the radio conference "A Transnational Forum," University of Wisconsin, July 28, 2003.

Imagine a program where, instead of the conspicuous poverty of the world, we might discover its hidden riches. Where instead of judging the standard of living in places like Oaxaca, Mexico, on the basis of per capita income we might instead come to understand what it is about a way of life that inspired its people to defend their *zocolo,* the ancient town square, and drive out the threat of McDonald's by passing out free tamales. We might learn how family structures and the rituals of community allow people to survive in places like Afghanistan in the absence of civil society. Or what it is about the human spirit that prompted the people of Sarajevo to stage a beauty pageant in the middle of a war.

Imagine a program that might displace Americans from their notion that their lives are more valuable than those of non-Americans, their way of life more precious and salutary, their institutions and form of democracy sacrosanct and exclusive. A program that might dissuade us from our overreliance on military solutions. A program that would open our ears and our minds, extend our reach and our embrace, increase the circle of the human family, and be sweet medicine for what ails us. A program with heart that might replace our fear of the other with fascination for the other, and rekindle our sense of adventure and delight in the world.

Imagine a program that in linking the courage of Shazia Mirza, the Muslim woman stand-up comic, with Philippe Petit, the Frenchman who walked a tightrope between the twin towers of the World Trade Center, with the chutzpah of a Sarah Chayes, a former NPR correspondent turned humanitarian who regularly stands up to her local warlord in Kandahar, we might discern the dim outlines of what might be called the Poem of the World.

Now imagine such a program originating right here in Madison, Wisconsin. *Here on Earth.*

"Truth," Parker Palmer tells us, "is an eternal conversation about things that matter conducted with passion and discipline." Why not have that conversation on the radio? An impossible dream? Perhaps. But now, thanks to British radio historian Chris Priestman, we have a name for it. It is called the Dream of Radio's Great Global Conversation.

How did this dream come to root itself in me? Radio itself put it there. In the thirteen years in which I hosted *Conversations with Jean Feraca,* a wildly eclectic weekday news, lifestyle, arts, and cultural affairs call-in program that was broadcast throughout the upper Midwest every weekday morning from 9:00 to 11:00 on the Ideas Network of Wisconsin Public Radio, radio has been my teacher. Hosting *Conversations with Jean Feraca* was the equivalent of an ongoing liberal arts education, and it was a privilege to interact on a daily basis with guests as thoughtful as Parker

Palmer. But what I learned from interacting with callers, men and women from all over the Midwest, was maybe even more important. And what I came to believe in, ultimately, and to trust implicitly, was the collective genius of ordinary people.

I was raised Roman Catholic in the pre-Vatican Church of the fifties when the Mass was said in Latin and all eyes were trained on the altar. You never had to hug your neighbor or hold hands in those days. You were never expected to so much as glance at your neighbor. That was discouraged, in fact. All you had to do was talk to God, and most of that was strictly private. People went to church to talk to God, not to one another.

It was easy enough to love God. After all, God was lovable. But thy neighbor? Thy neighbor was the guy you could never get along with. The Irish kids who egged your brother. The Greeks who moved in next door and spoiled all your fun. The Yankee Doodles your father hated who were so mean they would begrudge a day laborer a glass of water. In my visions of heaven, there were angels and saints. Mother Cabrini and Father Damien. Maybe even a leper or two. But there were no neighbors. I had to wait to be on the radio to meet my neighbors.

I hear voices. One of these voices is gruff and craggy, tobacco-laden and coated with whiskey. It wears a fedora and it calls me "Jeannie" just as my father did. It belongs to Vito the Bartender, who enters the conversation whenever things get a little too abstract and academic. That's when Vito uses his favorite word, "Mendacity." I imagine how he shakes his shaggy head and I can hear him muttering, "Mendacity, Jeannie. Mendacity."

Another voice belongs to a Vietnamese factory inspector in Racine, Wisconsin, who improved her English by listening to my program on headphones while she was at work. Thanh once sent me a dozen tea roses during a pledge drive and then called in the following Monday to ask, "You get the roses I send you?"

Another caller, suspicious of my Republican roots, once called me a poor little rich girl. And then there was my nemesis, the son of a Pennsylvania labor organizer, a disappointed Marxist who used to call in from Middleton, Wisconsin. Mike could always be counted on to correct me whenever I got a little too sentimental about America, and whenever he failed to call I discovered I had internalized his voice.

Now the love of our neighbor, according to the French philosopher Simone Weil, simply means being able to say to him, "What are you going through?" but to say it in such a way that it feels real, that the person is made to feel that he really exists, not as a specimen but as a person exactly like you, who might just happen to be marked by a special stamp of affliction. The other/my brother. Only she who is capable of attention can do this. The soul empties itself of its own contents in order to receive into itself the truth of the other. I learned to do this on the radio. I listen. I pay attention. I have learned to gauge the conversation from the blind side, the way a tailor works the cloth.

We are all blind on the radio. That's the beauty of it. In the absence of vision, we are free from those fatal assessments that we all make continually, discounting and rejecting one another in a flash strictly on the basis of looks. All we have on the radio by which to judge one another is the voice. And the voice carries the essence. It goes directly to the heart, as poets will tell you. It bypasses the censors.

"If you find your life tangled up with somebody else's life for no very logical reason," says Bokonon, the mythical founder of a new religion in Kurt Vonnegut's novel *Cat's Cradle*, "that person may be a member of your karass." A karass, he tells us, "is a group of people who don't know each other, who have never met, who don't even know they are on the same team, but who somehow manage to do God's will without ever intending it."[1] That is exactly the way I experience my radio talk show, as a karass. There are truck drivers in it, farmers, cheese makers, criminals, nuns, clergymen, lawyers, doctors, transsexuals, teachers, housewives, physicists, molecular biologists, at least one bloodhound that I know about, and God only knows who else.

Like a town meeting, a call-in talk show is one of the truest contemporary forms of democracy. Properly conducted, it cuts across class, race, gender, age, and nation. It doesn't give a hoot whether you managed to get your eyebrows on straight, or whether your tie matches your sport coat. In my radio karass, a program broadcast out of a studio in Madison, Wisconsin, might end up in France, or Kazakhstan, or Istanbul, without anyone ever directing it. Words travel. Sound has no respect for boundaries, not even the boundary between the living and the dead. Vito the blind bartender keeps coming in loud and clear, even though he's now been dead eight years.

I never set out to become a talk show host. I have no formal training as a journalist. I am a poet schooled in literature and the liberal arts. When I arrived at Wisconsin Public Radio twenty years ago to take on the job of humanities coordinator, I felt displaced. I was an elitist from the East who found herself in a Midwestern culture of enforced egalitarianism. As such, I had no real sense of community. It was radio that brought me out of my tribe.

Left to my own devices, I would never have learned to look for wisdom in the ghettos of our inner cities, where solutions to many of our social problems can be found rising from people oppressed by poverty, living in some of our most dangerous neighborhoods. I would never have dreamed that anything as rough and vulgar as a call-in talk show would become for me a form of meditation, a collective daily spiritual practice. Without it, I would have been deprived of the aristocratic company of Luther the Jet, King of the Hoboes; of the friendship of a Haitian voodoo priestess; of the wisdom of Ye Fu Twan, the erudite Chinese geographer; and Jim K., the ex-con whose ideas about prison reform were formed firsthand behind bars. I would never have made friends with my garbage man, or discovered a closet mystic in the Iron County mailman scribbling frantic notes on his dashboard while he listens to my program. I would have overlooked altogether the intelligence of farmers. And I surely would have shunned all association with known misogynists, Marxists, and members of the Aryan nation.

> You shall listen to all sides
> And filter them yourself.

A listener once sent me that quote from Walt Whitman [*Leaves of Grass*] with a note attached that said, "This is what you do." I keep the company of strangers.

Miracles can happen when you keep the company of strangers. Let me tell you about two miracles that happened on the radio.

"State-of-the-art medical clinic built on the banks of the Amazon as a result of an interview conducted on Wisconsin Public Radio." That was the message I read off a strip of Associated Press wire copy that chanced across my desk. I blinked. I read it again. My God, I thought to myself, that's my interview. That's my story.

The real story, of course, was the doctor herself. Linnea Smith went to Peru on an ecotourism vacation in 1990 and was so moved by what she found among the river people living there that she made a dramatic decision. She abandoned a thriving medical practice as a general internist in Sauk City, Wisconsin, and moved to the Amazon rainforest, where she began delivering babies, snakebite serum, penicillin, and birth control free of charge to the Yagua Indians, operating out of a one-room dispensary with a thatched roof, no electricity, and nothing but a rickety cot for an examining table. An architect from Duluth, Minnesota, happened to hear Linnea tell her story on my program. He got hold of his friend, a retired surgeon and fellow Rotarian, and the two of them set out for Peru to check this lady out. When they came home they rounded up their buddies, raised $130,000 from three groups of Rotarians, and dispatched forty of their own charter members, men, women, and children, from Duluth to Iquitos. From there they hauled their lumber and gear upriver, slogged through primordial mud, Amazonian rain and heat, and hammered the damn thing together, solar panels and all, in the space of three weeks right in the middle of somebody's buffalo pasture. Yanamono Clinic is now in its twelfth year of operation, having saved the lives of countless river people who regularly make the trek on foot and by dugout, sometimes carrying each other in hammocks to visit La Doctora.

Another radio miracle: In January of 1991, a friend of mine named Willow Harth saw a headline in the newspaper declaring an end to the Cold War. President Bush senior was calling on Americans to come to the aid of the Russian people, who were facing hunger that winter, queuing up in long bread lines that too often ended in empty shelves. For my friend, this was a moment of epiphany. She conceived the idea of ending the Cold War with hot soup—a grassroots initiative that became known as the Russian Winter Campaign: Hands Across the Heartland. It brought together a coalition of politicians, military personnel, Physicians for Social Responsibility, Nurses for Social Justice, United Methodist Churches, a group of conservative businessmen, even a volunteer truck driver.

What gave this idea wheels was a single hour on the radio in which Willow—who became known in Washington's military circles as "that dingbat from Wisconsin"—was given the golden opportunity to present her plan live on the radio to the man who was then serving as head of the Armed Services Committee, the late Les Aspin, our Democratic representative in Congress. He joined us on the air by telephone from his office in Washington. In the presence of thousands of Wisconsin Public Radio listeners, Les Aspin pledged to make the Russian Winter Campaign a reality. And on the wings of that promise, Wisconsin sent five hundred tons of food and twenty-eight of its citizens to Moscow in a C-5 Galaxy, the Pentagon's largest military transport plane, designed to carry Humvees, not hot soup. The Russian Winter Campaign helped some hungry Muscovites make it through a lean time, but what pleases Willow most about her mission is the fact that it shifted the mind-set of hundreds of Americans from a Cold War mentality to thinking about the Russians as our neighbors and friends rather than as our enemies.

Such stories give us clear examples of the power of radio to cross great divides and connect people across boundaries.

A few years ago, I was one of a number of journalists invited by the International Studies Institute of the University of Wisconsin to participate in a symposium called From Shanghai to Sheboygan. Its purpose was to delve into the ways in which news from abroad is covered in the American media. The consensus our panel reached was that international news in this country is almost invariably news of breakdown: genocide, ethnic cleansing, civil wars, political corruption, plagues, earthquakes, and other natural disasters. What is more, this news is usually filtered through the lens of an American journalist with an American perspective, and a centrist worldview. To give you a recent example of what I'm talking about, an issue of the Sunday *New York Times* magazine, published just after President Bush returned from his trip to Africa, showed no less than forty-two images of starving African men, women, and children on its cover. Looking at them, it occurred to me that I have been seeing those images all of my life, and I ask myself, *What else do people do in Africa besides starve to death? Does anybody know?*

Oh, yes, I forget. They hack each other up with machetes, they chop off each other's hands and limbs, they die of AIDS and rape little girls in the mistaken notion that intercourse with virgins will save them, and they are subject to corrupt and cruel regimes ruled by vicious ugly despots. But they do have nice giraffes.

Was anybody else besides me surprised to discover in the buildup to the latest war in Iraq that Baghdad actually has a symphony orchestra? What a discordant image to set beside rubble and disease, the specter of chemical and biological warfare, and house-to-house combat.

The point I am making here is that whether intentional or not, this reporting serves to reinforce our already deeply entrenched American attitudes of moral superiority and cultural imperative. What could we possibly learn that we don't already know from boatloads of drowning Haitians and truckloads of Mexicans and shipwrecked Chinese who regularly spend their fortunes and their lives to reach our shores? Why go anywhere else when everybody is literally dying to come here? Why learn anybody else's language, read anybody else's literature, see anybody else's movies? With hip hop in Holland, country music in Russia, rockabilly in Italy, McDonald's in Russia, and blue jeans in Milan, we're already everywhere.

The danger inherent in such complacency, arrogance, and indifference was made all too clear the morning of the great awakening, September 11, 2001. Unfortunately, instead of opening a window on our ignorance, what it did was shut it. Under the shadow of Code Red, Code Orange, and Code Yellow, we now live in a climate of fear, distrust, and mutual suspicion, encouraged to go about our daily affairs in the constant expectation of another terrorist attack, another catastrophe. We are encouraged by our government to spy on one another and to turn each other in. We who lived through the Cold War and the demise of the Soviet threat are now being systematically deprived of our own freedoms by our own government, which has suspended the writ of habeas corpus, silenced dissent, and is rapidly turning our media into tools of propaganda.

Last weekend I met an eighty-nine-year-old man, a renowned psychiatrist, Dr. Joel Elkes, who lost his family and all the people in his hometown of Kovno in the Lithuanian holocaust during World War II. He spoke to a group of us in July 2003, at the Fetzer Institute in Kalamazoo, Michigan, about the industrialization of fear: "Emotions represent huge reservoirs of human energy, which can be harnessed for good or ill. The dominant emotion of our age is fear. The industries driven by fear are formidable, and have become so much a habit of thought that only massive denial allows us to pursue the routines of daily living."

Daily, in our newspapers, on our radios, and on our televisions, we get story after story of who we are at our worst: from images of mutilated corpses thrown at the U.S. embassy in Liberia to the casual story of a woman who bludgeons her husband to death with the spike of her heel, to the children who go to the prom one night and go to kill their classmates at point-blank range in a shootout the next morning.

"The plethora of violence seen in the media," says Joel Elkes, "and the bias toward reporting it, has created an addiction of the general public toward this kind of coverage. Market force and advertising operate in its favor. . . . Against these huge negative emotions, one can only respond in kind."

"Positive emotions must be experienced and harnessed on the same pervasive scale, not as an afterthought on the last page or a feel-good toss-off at the end of a program. This cannot happen by exhortation or propaganda, but must grow out of the deep soil of daily personal experience." The darkness is only getting darker, he warns us. "We must learn how to garden in the middle of the night. We must assume that . . . in this divided, crazed world there is a hidden wholeness."

The threat of disaster is a powerful catalyst. I want to light a candle in the midst of this darkness. Like Linnea Smith in her tiny medical clinic on the edge of the vast illimitable darkness of the Amazonian rainforest. Like my friend who took to heart her president's exhortation and found a way against all odds to help the Russians through a perilous chapter in their history. Joel Elkes is calling for a good news channel. He believes there are countless undocumented and unreported stories all over the world, not just of practical visionaries like Sarah Chayes working to rebuild Afghanistan and save the honor of her country, and Earl Shorris, founder of the Bard College Clemente Course in the Humanities on Manhattan's lower east side, lifting poor people out of poverty (a project that has now been replicated all over the world), but of ordinary people doing extraordinary things, evoking the collective genius of ordinary people.

Such stories are not rare; they are commonplaces of everyday reality. What is rare is that they come to light at all, because, sadly enough, somebody once decided that when we are at our best we are not newsworthy.

I'd like to do my little part to change that. I'd like to help erode our xenophobia and replace the fear of the other with fascination. I'd like to introduce young Israelis, for example, to Palestinians who don't throw rocks, and Palestinians to Arik Asherman, the founder of Rabbis for Human Rights.

The argument that nobody would listen to such a program has already been empirically tested in my radio laboratory experiment, where we chronicled a steady stream of stories that enlivened listeners and inspired hope for the future, faith in people, and positive action. People love that kind of programming. They support it, they demand it, they will rearrange their schedules to accommodate it, and they will tell you from time to time that it saved their lives. Words have the power to heal and give life as well as to kill. In public broadcasting, we are still free from the coercion and corrupting influence of commercial interests and the tyranny of the bottom line. We know from our research that public radio audiences are intellectually curious, high-minded, and socially conscious. Why not raise the bar, then, instead of lowering it? Why not enrich content rather than dumb it down? What better way to serve such an audience than to deliver the news of who we are at our best rather than our worst as human beings, our yet-to-be realized potential as a species, and how much we have in common? One world, one race, one people. *Here on Earth*.

NOTE

1. Vonnegut, K. *Cat's Cradle*. New York: Harcourt Brace (orig. Holt, 1963), p. 2.

REFLECTIONS

○

Bardwell Smith

professor of religion and Asian studies
and dean, Carleton College

I met Parker Palmer early in the fall of 1960, when he was a senior majoring in philosophy and sociology and I was a freshman faculty member at Carleton College. Immediately I was impressed by this person and wondered, *If all Carleton students are of this caliber, I'm in trouble.* Fortunately, not all students were as impressive.

Early on, we became friends, beyond the categories of student and faculty, and though not articulating it then I suspect we each saw ourselves as resistant to the normal categorizations of which these were obvious examples. I have always found Parker to be stunningly honest and open-minded. His self-deprecating humor is but one delicious ingredient of this honesty. His impact on me derives from the fact that he has been, quite unknowingly to him, a kind of litmus test for me of what being human can mean. As is always true in such cases, his instance reveals the beauty of knowing that we are all imperfect, that we are at best learners. After all, at our best we are all "works of art in progress."

INTEGRATING
LIFE AND THOUGHT
As Teacher, Student, Colleague, Friend

Bardwell Smith

TO BE HUMAN is to experience the absence of integration. We yearn for wholeness but live and breed fragmentation. Yearning for wholeness, ironically, becomes the problem. In Buddhist terms, it is the pitfall of striving to be Buddha. In social terms, it is longing to be admired above others. In each case, it is the yearning, the striving, the longing that trips one up. Desiring wholeness becomes a diversion, a hankering after substitutes—kudos, riches, or power.

The antidote comes in part through living (albeit uncomfortably) with ambiguity, incompletion, uncertainty. In Reinhold Niebuhr's words, "Man's problem is not that he is finite, but that he has difficulty living with his finitude." Judging by the nature of modern society and its cultural values, it's almost as if Niebuhr never existed. Rare are today's social critics who take seriously society's self-delusions and pretensions without resorting to cynicism. Parker Palmer, in his life and work, examines the paradox of how our questing can both trip us up and also spring us loose—one type seeking confirmation from others, the other refusing to settle for external approval. A classic instance of this double-bind may be glimpsed in Parker's satori-like realization of why he wanted to be Swarthmore's president. Put simply, it was to see his accomplishments chronicled in the *New York Times*! How often we have been refreshed and chastened by how his delicious humor punctures his own—and our—proclivity to posture and to buttress our intellectual, religious, and political attachments.

Coming to terms with my own journey, I have become increasingly attentive to the interdependence of existence, the necessity of learning to unlearn, the importance of recognizing the subjectivity and learning capacity of students, and the necessity and the art of learning together.

The Interdependence of All Existence, in Life and Thought

Centuries ago, Mahayana Buddhists talked eloquently about the fact that there are no self-originating forms of existence, and that all forms of life exist in infinite patterns of interdependence. In the Buddhist sense, there is nothing but interdependence. Quite literally, independence from this network of connections does not exist. We can feel independent and we can strive to be independent, but the consequence of doing so socially, politically, and environmentally is hazardous. In today's body politic we are graphically aware that tremors in one part of our obviously connected, yet often disconnected, world have profound repercussions.

As a young Marine serving in China in 1945–46, I had my first taste of being connected to the lives of a people about whom I had previously been ignorant. "Poverty" had been an abstraction until I saw how real it was to their society and to the few Chinese I came to know well. The contrast of my affluent upbringing in suburban Chicago with this kind of suffering was striking. The reality of that became central to my expanding world. I had begun to discern the depths of my ignorance, only later realizing how much this experience was a prerequisite to genuine learning.

Subsequently, I discovered a parallel to this on a more sophisticated level through Rachel Carson's insight that the damage societies do to the environment arises from a failure to appreciate the limits of our comprehensibility. In *The Edge of the Sea,* Carson recounts her experience of nature's *otherness* as she walks by the water's edge at night with her flashlight and spots a small ghost crab. In a singularly specific experience, she grasps the limits of her own understanding of that world. In Vera Norwood's words, "The night, the individual crab, the alien seascape all conspire to deny her a comfortable sense of identification with the world she sees."[1] This sense of nature's otherness deepened her respect for its intrinsic worth, separated totally from whatever utilitarian value it may have for humans.

Hers was an axial shift of thinking about human perspectives on the natural world. The tragedy lies not simply from an insensitive ethical stance but from a distorted epistemology.[2] It was Carson's genius to turn conventional ideas into themselves. Her lack of epistemological arrogance is the prerequisite to genuine learning of any kind.

The Paradoxical Art of Learning How to Unlearn

My awareness of paradox has been fed over the decades by Buddhist and Taoist traditions in which paradox is a way of life aspired to, as well as a mode of thinking. As one conjures the tension between so-called opposites, the more interconnected one's life experiences become. Within these differentiated experiences, one stumbles upon evidence of "hidden wholeness." This occurs as one encounters the limits of one's understanding and the irony of one's self-deception.

Celebrated examples are found in the riddles of Lao Tsu: "To die but not to perish is to be eternally present"; "Difficult and easy complement each other"; and "Work is done, then forgotten. Therefore it lasts forever."[3] Paradoxical expressions are puzzling because we tend to categorize in oppositional terms what we fail to see as part of a larger whole: "life" and "death," "good" and "evil." If we think in linear fashion, we regard these supposed opposites as being at contradictory ends of a one-dimensional spectrum. In actuality, they call each other into being.

An unexpected experience of inclusiveness occurred to me when Katagiri Roshi, the late Zen master in Minneapolis, made the following statement after one of his meditation sessions at Carleton: "It is more often true to say that thought comes from life than to say that life comes from thought." This simple distinction was intended not to disparage thinking but to emphasize that life's impact on thought enhances our ability to think in a more holistic and lucid fashion. When the two are working harmoniously, there is no need to elevate one above the other. When they are out of sync, each is impoverished. In academic circles, this point of view is sometimes held with suspicion; thought is supposed to reign supreme. One way to see their interface without being regarded as anti-intellectual is to let paradox have its play. Thought enriched by life is what Pascal means when he says that "the heart has reasons of which the mind knows not." This is vintage paradox.

Among the many reflections of the literary critic Austin Warren that altered my way of thinking is his telling observation that "everything outer must become inner . . . only everything is enough." When I first read this thirty years ago, it accelerated my journey from a primary preoccupation with the outer world of society to a quest for some sort of balance between what we call outer and what we gradually discover as the inner dimensions of that outer. Unless involvement in the world is balanced by inner wrestling of the spirit, suffocation is the result.

I thought I understood this when, in the 1950s, I read Nicholas Berdyaev's *Solitude and Society*,[4] only to discover, when I reread it later, that the interplay between these two is subtler and more dynamic. Solitude and society do not stand still; nor does the relationship between them, or the one within myself. The boundary between them is evasive and fluid. It is like the blend of sound and silence in a monastic setting. Or like the inner tug of war between self-concern and compassion.

I came to recognize that the known and the unknown are not contraries; the unknown lurks not beyond, not alongside, but actually within the known. It is the agnostic safeguard, the irritant within the known, that challenges us constantly to rethink what we think we know. Without the persistence of this quality, the known remains static, is taken for granted, becomes doctrinaire, and begs to be defended.

The Teacher as Learner; the Student as Subject

The saying goes that so-and-so is a born teacher. I don't subscribe to such a contention. It strikes me that the path to becoming a true teacher is marked by lots of bumps and turns (lest one forget those times when a discussion or a lecture truly bombed). No one ever fully arrives. Nor does one become an effective teacher without continuing to learn how to learn, or without practicing the difficult art of unlearning. When Shunryu Suzuki titled his well-known book *Zen Mind, Beginner's Mind,* he had no illusions about the ease of attaining a beginner's mind. In fact, he says, the "most difficult thing is to keep your beginner's mind."[5] It is to rediscover the capacity of thinking afresh instead of being shackled to old ideas or ways of thinking.

Learning and relearning how to learn is a demanding, never-ending task; it can also be the most rewarding of vocations. The learner/teacher sees his or her students not as receptacles but as fellow subjects engaged in a process of learning how to deal with the subject matter at hand. When asked about my criteria for straight A papers, I always answered that they were papers from which I learned and profited considerably—not so much by way of content as by their perspective and insight. The old adage about not teaching subject matter but teaching students is only a half-truth. What actually takes place is a triadic relationship among the subject matter, teachers who practice the art of learning, and students who in learning how to learn become able to be teachers of each other and of us.

When I was Carleton's dean of the college (1967–1972), a diverse but representative group of about twenty students met at our home every Sunday evening to discuss all kinds of issues. Among the topics of concern in 1969–70 was how students might be involved in evaluating faculty. One student argued for a course evaluation booklet. Having seen the abuses of this approach at Yale, I said, "John, you're certainly right in saying students should be involved in such a process, but let's discuss how this might occur." This led to several productive sessions and to many meetings of the faculty along divisional lines. The result a year later was approval of a means for student assessment of faculty to become part of a complex process of evaluation.

In this process, the dean sent a letter to students that asked them to provide a paragraph discussing their criteria for effective teaching. Students were then invited to assess a particular faculty member with their own criteria in mind. Reading these confidential letters year after year, one readily saw how thoughtful the students were and how adeptly they gauged the different styles of good teaching. In the mind of the perceptive student, there is no fixed standard of what constitutes good pedagogy. One indirect consequence of this system of shared evaluation is that there are seldom major differences between student and faculty judgment in the hiring process or in assessments for tenure.

Among the qualities that exemplify an effective learner/teacher is a kind of strength that gives birth to a willingness to reveal one's vulnerability. "Strength through weakness" gives license to see and acknowledge one's lack of mastery. Significant competence, yes; omniscience, hardly. One is liberated from the need to posture, and from what Parker labels as the "climate of fear" that constitutes much of academic life (indeed, professional life more generally). This climate of fear is what spoils a classroom's mood, undermines collegial relations, and engenders preoccupation with status in one's profession.

Many of my real-life models are teachers who run the risk of being seen as a learner principally, and only secondarily as a teacher. Austin Warren, whom I knew only through some of his graduate students in early American literature at Michigan, struck me as an emancipated risk taker (though there was no doubt about his competence). Some episodic remarks of his, in no particular order, typify his approach as a learner:

> "I want, in a sense, to teach something that I have not yet learned."
>
> "An author should take his art seriously, but not himself."
>
> "A writer has to be spiritually naked; that is why some people prefer to be scholars, to keep their clothes on."
>
> "Assume what interests you interests others—one of the most generous and spiritual of maxims."[6]

The art of imagining ignorance (one's own and that of others) is the quality not only of a gifted teacher. It is the wisdom of one who recognizes that genuine learning always begins afresh as one practices the difficult art of unlearning, which is the process of emptying. Far from being easy, it requires immense discipline. When practiced, learning becomes joyful, and fear of risk taking is dispelled. As one listens to others, learning is shared; all become engaged as subjects in the activity of teaching each other.

Collegiality, or the Art of Learning How to Learn Together

We are familiar with conditions and presuppositions that tend to hamper creative teaching and engaged learning. Various patterns of shaping academic life are useful, but many need questioning, such as how knowledge is characteristically packaged (courses, departments, disciplines, programs); the disjunctions between teaching and learning by age level; the very designation of *higher* education as though it is more important than what precedes it; the question of alternative incentive systems for faculty and students in schools and colleges; how teaching and research might complement each other more effectively; and the means by which faculty could benefit by sharing teaching experiences with each other.

About a dozen years ago, after more than a year of careful study, Carleton created a Learning and Teaching Center. The fact that we reversed the standard names for such a center was symbolic of what we sought to create. The primary intent was not to help faculty become better teachers (though that might happen as a by-product); the goal was to create a reciprocal process whereby faculty and students could learn from each other.

In one such instance at the center, a panel of four women students discussed with candor and perception a course given the previous term. The class, consisting of about twenty Carleton women and a few men, was an overseas seminar in Paris focusing on well-known European lesbian authors. The panel's focus was how the course had been perceived by the straight, bisexual, and lesbian women in the class and how members of the class interacted. The instructor encouraged the panelists and other students from the class who attended the meeting to discuss openly the problematic as well as the successful features of this experimental course. Her idea was to have a postmortem session that also included students and faculty not involved in the course. It was a remarkable gathering; words were not minced. It was clear that even though the educational process was far from easy or smooth, the overall experience was rare and demanding. The great majority of students listed this course among the best they had taken.

This was just the sort of interchange the center was intended to foster. Prior to the center's emergence, there were no regular means for discussing alternative ways of shaping the learning process. A faculty member might have had a private discussion with a close colleague about how things had or had not worked in a course, but to have such a discussion shared openly with interested others was a rarity. Run by faculty, not by administrators, the center has nothing to do with faculty evaluation. Word got around that such conversations were an important catalyst in facilitating faculty and student discussion about the learning process as experienced in particular courses. Many tales began to circulate about how the center contributed to a freer climate of exchange.

I have also found that a greater sense of collegiality with students and teachers has been a central factor in my becoming a better learner, therefore a better teacher. Of particular importance have been situations where I sought to modify my role by making it less directive, but not necessarily less active.

Some examples are prominent. First, on five occasions during the 1970s and 1980s I organized a pass-fail course on forms of Buddhist meditation. Twice the principal instructor was a Rinzai Zen priest-scholar; two other times the sessions were conducted by a Soto Zen roshi or Zen master; and the fifth time the leader was a former Thai monk in the tradition of Vipassana meditation. Each of these courses was open to about thirty students, who agreed to meditate as a group for ten weeks under the instructor's leadership for hour-long periods early in the morning, Monday through Friday. Regular attendance was expected, and absence was rare. Required readings relating to psychological, social, and cultural aspects of the meditative practice were discussed weekly in small groups. Consultations with the instructor were encouraged but not required.

Keeping a journal was the main academic part of the course. The journals were submitted at three-week intervals to make sure the work was being done and to encourage individuals in a practice that to most was not an easy experience. The general reaction at the end of the course was that this ten-week process of developing greater mindfulness helped them become more attentive to their own thoughts and feelings, with unexpected but welcomed consequences for their academic work and their personal relationships.

As in the case with studio art, applied music, and physical education, these educational goals and forms of learning are not identical with those that occur in the standard classroom. Yet it is often through art, music, theater, and athletics that we learn to see, think, and understand differently. More to the point, participants agreed that what took place cumulatively in these sessions was a valuable form of connecting their life with their academic work. In fact, many became more open to surprises—a quality that is fundamental to learning, as any scientist can attest.

In the second instance, over a period of thirty years of being involved in overseas programs in India, Sri Lanka, and especially Japan, both directing and teaching in academic programs, I have realized how field-study approaches to learning can be a profound way of integrating life and thought. My most satisfactory experience has been in the Associated Kyoto Program (AKP). This is a junior-year, ten-month program that Carleton and Amherst created in 1970 and that now includes fifteen institutional members, all of which teach four years of Japanese. Students live with homestay families throughout their year in Kyoto and take intensive Japanese language along with other courses on Japanese society and culture in En-

glish. Most students have completed two years of classroom Japanese before coming to Kyoto and are therefore able to make increasing use of their
language ability as the year unfolds.

Twice while teaching an AKP course on Japanese religions and culture,
I incorporated into the semester a two-week period during which the class,
ranging from thirty to forty in number, participated in a famous Buddhist
pilgrimage. This particular thousand-year-old pilgrimage, located on the
island of Shikoku, is approximately one thousand kilometers long; it normally takes two months to walk the entire length. By mid-October, when
students undertook this walking pilgrimage, they had already read a good
deal about Japanese religions and begun doing fieldwork in the Kyoto area.

The purpose of this pilgrimage was to give all of us, including faculty
and staff, a group-learning approach to studying interrelated aspects of
Buddhist myth, symbol, cosmology, ritual, sacred geography, art and architecture, sociology, and history. In such a setting, the integrative process
occurs daily. One experiences this learning both in a personal manner and
as a group with its varied interests. Over the two weeks, a sense of common purpose begins to develop. The tough walking—eight to ten hours a
day for fourteen days, with a heavy backpack, up and down mountains,
through river valleys and farm fields, and along paved roads—contributes
to a regimen that tests one's mettle.

To grasp the uniqueness of walking this pilgrimage, one needs to know
that virtually 99 percent of the many thousands of Japanese do not walk
it but instead go by temple or tourist bus, or in their own car. Dressed in
conventional pilgrim garb, these American students were treated with respect by Japanese pilgrims for having chosen to walk even a shortened,
two-week form of this longer journey. Local people would often give gifts
as a way of manifesting appreciation to the student pilgrim, or *henro,* for
helping to maintain this tradition. In exchange, the students gave one of
the pilgrim slips of paper (*ofuda*) with his or her name, age, and country
of origin written in Japanese phonetic syllabary (katakana) to the other
person. This custom, called *o-settai,* is an ancient and moving practice or
ritual that symbolizes a sense of reciprocity.

On returning to Kyoto, each participant wrote a twenty-page paper,
based on the journal kept over this two-week period. Having read seventy-
five of these papers, I found it clear that this experience was to students
and faculty and staff alike among the high points of their year in Japan. A
common thread from this experience was how the pilgrimage was a practice that honed and polished each person's ability to concentrate on what
he or she was doing and thinking. Each step along the way called for concentration; it became a contemplative exercise.

We had many discussions, but we refrained from imposing any normative framework. No one was told what he or she should get out of this tough, culturally significant journey. It was intended that they experience this rich texture for themselves. As Austin Warren observed, "The boundaries set to a course should be delicate and evasive." Learning from each other and through participating in an important cultural practice, students, faculty, and staff engaged in forms of learning that required unlearning preconceptions and becoming active in their own discoveries. Such a challenge calls forth the beginner's mind, that hidden potential for fresh discernment.

As a third example, creating a Japanese garden may also strike one as nonacademic, but for more than twenty-eight years it has not seemed so to me. Having promoted the creation of a Japanese garden at Carleton; seen that it was properly designed, created, and maintained; and frequently given talks at this garden, I came to recognize its impact on students, faculty, staff, and returning alumni, as well as the Northfield community. Because we resisted attributing to the garden any specific meaning or saying what it symbolized, those who came to enjoy the garden's quiet beauty discovered qualities within themselves that were stimulated by their own experience in relating to this space.

The whole point is the work itself. Even visually elegant symbols tend to impose a meaning on the garden. In the process, the viewer refrains from reflecting on what the garden means to him or her. Gardens that speak powerfully are those that invite one to look and listen, not to impart meaning but to animate inner reflection. Through this quality of invited contemplation, Eliot Deutsch writes, we as viewers are transformed.[7] We are taught nothing; we are called into being in ways we could not have anticipated. We end up being surprised, which is often the font of joy.

A garden thus experienced serves as gentle iconoclasm. It lessens one's thirst for beliefs on which to cling. Prominent among the properties of Japanese gardens is the suggestion of deeper levels of mystery. Explanation limits what one derives from cumulative experience. By imposing *meaning* on the garden, one detracts from its deeper significance, which cannot be put into words. It is to be rediscovered, again and again.

For these many reasons, the Carleton Japanese garden, created in 1976, was not named until it became clear how it was being received by those who visited it. Following a gestation period of fifteen years, its name, the Garden of Quiet Listening (Joryo-en), came naturally to mind. As one student put it: "The Japanese garden is a beautiful, secluded spot on campus—perfect for sitting and thinking and gradually slipping away from the hectic Carleton pace for a few minutes." In this indirect way, the garden has been a source of education in its most generic sense. It has helped lead people out of themselves to experience their own interconnection with the many worlds around them. It has had a *humanizing* influence. This is perhaps the most basic form in which learning occurs.

Epilogue

T. S. Eliot may be right in saying that we return to the place from which we started, as though for the first time. The practice of imagining ignorance, one's own and that of others, I now see clearly as central to the twin arts of learning and teaching.

The forms of collegiality I have valued were not limited to those I knew at Carleton; they included colleagues at other institutions with which Carleton has a close consortial relation. These associations have been vital to my own development as a person, teacher, colleague, and friend. They have helped me discover how life and thought interact in more ways than one can imagine.

In his deeply personal book *Let Your Life Speak,* Parker makes an observation that offers me a good place to end: "Embracing one's wholeness makes life more demanding—because once you do that, you must live your whole life."[8] This essay has never implied that embracing one's wholeness was easy, but it is in fact the real and continuing point of departure.

NOTES

1. Norwood, V. L. "The Nature of Knowing: Rachel Carson and the American Environment." *Signs: Journal of Women in Culture and Society,* 1987, *12*(4), 740–760; quote is on p. 751.

2. Norwood (1987).

3. Feng, G., and English, J. (trans.). *Lao Tsu: Tao Te Ching.* London: Wildwood House, 1973, numbers 33, 2, and 2 respectively.

4. Berdyaev, N. *Solitude and Society.* London: Geoffrey Bles, 1934.

5. Suzuki, S. *Zen Mind, Beginner's Mind.* London and Tokyo: John Weatherhill, 1970.

6. Warren, A. *A Recognition of Austin Warren.* Collected by T. Stoneburner and others, privately printed, ca. 1966.

7. Deutsch, E. "An Invitation to Contemplation: The Rock Garden of Ryoanji and the Concept of Yugen." In *Studies in Comparative Aesthetics.* Honolulu: University Press of Hawaii, 1975.

8. Palmer, P. J. *Let Your Life Speak: Listening for the Voice of Vocation.* San Francisco: Jossey-Bass, 2000.

REFLECTIONS

○

_____

Ian G. Barbour

professor emeritus of science, technology,
and society at Carleton College

From 1957 to 1961, Parker Palmer was an undergraduate at Carleton College in Minnesota, where I was teaching. I saw him occasionally on campus or in our home. It was only later in my life that I found in his writing and in his workshops a strong encouragement of my quest for intellectual and personal wholeness. Earlier I had earned a Ph.D. in physics, chaired the physics department in a liberal arts college, and done graduate work in theology and ethics. At Carleton, I was teaching in both the physics department and the philosophy department. Later I helped to found a new religion department. I was beginning to try to fit together these diverse aspects of my own life and to write about ways of relating science and religion.

In the 1970s, I was also exploring relationships between ethics and technology. In the late 1970s and 1980s, as I was belatedly rethinking my teaching methods and trying out some alternatives, I attended four workshops Parker led at Carleton and elsewhere. I was greatly impressed by his sensitivity to the role of emotion as well as reason in the lives of teachers and students. Above all, he presented—and represented—a vision of intellectual and spiritual integrity among persons in community that I have continued to seek in my own life.

WHOLENESS IN SCIENCE
AND PERSONAL LIFE

Ian G. Barbour

PARKER PALMER HAS REFERRED to me as one of his mentors during his college days because he felt I showed in practice that religious commitment is not incompatible with intellectual inquiry. But my debt to him in subsequent years, through his writing, speaking, and leadership, is far greater. He has helped me see the importance of the heart as well as the mind—intellect as well as emotion—in the experience of both students and teachers. He has presented vivid examples of exciting teaching and active learning. He has been an inspiration to those of us in higher education who seek to overcome the fragmentation of disciplines that is prevalent today.

Parker has written frequently about "a hidden wholeness" in the life of each person.[1] In accordance with this theme, I will start by recalling the quest for wholeness in my own life. He has also reflected on the wholeness of the world and has cited some examples from science.[2] So I will then in successive sections explore some indications of wholeness in three areas of science—physics, biology, and neuroscience—and describe some implications for education. These new views in science may seem to involve the mind more than the heart, but I hope that the opening section will place them in the context of my own life.

Wholeness in Personal Life

I was a physics major at Swarthmore College in the early 1940s. Influenced by my contact with Quakers, I registered as a conscientious objector in 1943 and spent three years divided between fighting forest fires in Oregon and working with mental patients in a North Carolina hospital. A happy event was the joy of meeting on the Duke campus an undergraduate named Deane Kern, whom I married soon after her graduation. After the war I went to the University of Chicago and was a teaching assistant under Enrico Fermi, who directed the first sustained atomic reaction. There I wrote a Ph.D. thesis on an experiment in high-energy physics. My first job was teaching physics at Kalamazoo College, and I was subsequently appointed chair of the department. Deane and I were active in an interdenominational Student Christian Center and had discussion groups in our home. We were also enriched by an adult meditation group that met every week to share readings and silence.

In 1953, I received a Ford Fellowship in a program designed to give faculty members a year of graduate study in a field other than that of their primary expertise. I took this opportunity to study theology and ethics at Yale Divinity School and was so fascinated by courses there that I asked for my leave to be extended to a second year. By then, I knew I wanted to complete a degree and spend at least part of my time learning and teaching in religious studies. Carleton College offered me a job teaching physics half-time and teaching religion half-time in the philosophy department (there was no religion department at the time). In 1960, Bardwell Smith joined the faculty, and we started a new religion department, which grew to five members in a few years, including specialists in Judaic, Roman Catholic, and Asian traditions.

With the demands of chairing the new department, I could no longer continue teaching and conducting research in physics. But I did occasionally teach philosophy of science and did some teaching and research on the relation of science and religion—aided by a sabbatical year at Harvard. What started as an attempt to find wholeness in the two halves of my own life became a wider intellectual inquiry in which I found that many other people were interested. My book *Issues in Science and Religion,* published in 1966, was widely used as a college text at a time when there were few systematic volumes relating the two fields. Subsequently, I explored questions of methodology in science and religion and the implications of evolution, genetics, neuroscience, and the artificial intelligence of computers for our understanding of human nature.

In the 1970s I initiated at Carleton a program on science, technology, and public policy, which drew students and faculty from a wide variety of disciplines. My own courses in this program examined ethical, environmental, and political issues related to such technologies as energy, agriculture, computers, and genetic engineering. Such interdisciplinary courses are a wonderful opportunity for learning from others because a variety of perspectives and areas of expertise can be illuminating. I was especially grateful for the seminars dealing with a particular process in which we really did learn from each other. Students would read each other's papers as well as reports of cooperative projects and would often refer to them later in their take-home final exams. For me, this was a valuable experience of Parker's dialogic pedagogy and participatory learning, contrasting with the more common view of education as the transfer of objective information from a teacher to passive students.[3]

Through the years, I have also come to a greater appreciation of Parker's interest in combining contemplation and action.[4] On several occasions, Deane and I have been at Iona Abbey off the coast of Scotland for memorable weeks of work, discussion, and worship. The Iona community has brought together the journey inward and the journey outward in response to social injustice and human suffering; it has also written some powerful contemporary hymns set to Celtic melodies. We have been grateful for retreats at Kirkridge in the mountains of Pennsylvania; the ARC community (Action, Reflection, Community) in Minnesota; and several stays at Pendle Hill, the Quaker center near Philadelphia where Parker was at one point dean.

In Northfield, we have found in the United Church of Christ (Congregational) a community of acceptance, commitment, and concern for social justice, centering in the person of Christ and the work of the Spirit but remaining open to differences in theological interpretation. The theme of sin and forgiveness has, of course, been central in the Christian tradition, but I have learned from Paul Tillich and others to appreciate some pairs of contrasting terms that go beyond sin and forgiveness, namely, alienation and reconciliation, bondage and liberation, and especially brokenness and wholeness. The invitation to the communion table given by our minister for many years, Gordon Forbes, describes what I take to be the heart of the Gospel:

> If you know the brokenness of life, its fractures within and its division without, then you have participated in the broken body of Christ, and you are invited to share in the breaking of bread.
>
> If you desire to know the love of God that overcomes indifference and despair, if you desire the reconciliation that overcomes estrangement and alienation, then you are invited to share the cup of the new covenant.

Wholeness in Physics

Parker urges us to find wholeness within and in our relation to other persons, but he also points to the wholeness of the world that science studies. In elaborating on this theme myself, I would note that the Newtonian view, which dominated science until the twentieth century, understood the world to be a collection of self-contained particles. But in quantum physics today, enduring particles have been replaced by shifting patterns of waves that combine at one point, dissolve again, and recombine elsewhere. A bound electron in an atom has to be considered as a state of *the whole atom* rather than as a separate entity. As more complex systems are built up, new properties appear that were not foreshadowed in the parts alone. New wholes have distinctive principles of organization as systems; they exhibit properties and activities not found in their components.

The Pauli Exclusion Principle states that in any atom no two orbital electrons can be in identical states (with the same quantum numbers specifying energy, angular momentum, and spin). To this remarkable and far-reaching principle can be attributed the periodic table and the chemical properties of the elements. This "exclusion" does not resemble any imaginable set of forces or fields. In quantum reasoning, any attempt to describe the behavior of the constituent electrons is simply abandoned; the properties of the atom as a whole are analyzed by new laws unrelated to those governing its separate parts, which have now lost their identity. An orbital electron is a state of the atomic system, not an identifiable entity.[5]

The energy levels of an array of atoms in the solid state (such as a transistor) are a property of the *whole system* rather than of its components. Again, some of the disorder-order transitions and the so-called cooperative phenomena have proven impossible to analyze through the behavior of the components—for example, the behavior of electrons in a superconductor. Such *system laws* are not derivable from the laws of the components; distinctive explanatory concepts characterize higher organizational levels. Interpenetrating fields and integrated totalities replace self-contained, externally related particles as fundamental images of nature. The being of any entity is constituted by its relationships and its participation in more inclusive patterns.

Recent experiments confirm a form of holism known as *nonlocality,* or *quantum entanglement.* Two particles originating in a single event show correlations (in spin, polarization, or other properties) when they reach detectors too distant from each other for a signal to travel between them at the velocity of light while the particles are in transit. Evidently the two particles (or wave packets) must be described by a single inclusive wave function even when they are many kilometers apart. But the experiments lend no support to claims of the possibility of mental telepathy. The nonlocal correlations are only evident statistically and retrospectively; they cannot be used to transmit information instantaneously.[6]

In the *act of measurement,* the multiple potentialities of a quantum state become one actuality. Physicists have been puzzled by the sharp discontinuity that occurs when the wave function (the "superposition of states" representing alternative outcomes) collapses to the one value that is observed. Along the route between the microsystem and the human observer, where does the initially indeterminate result get fixed? Some physicists hold that quantum results are fixed only when they enter somebody's *consciousness.* Others assert that this is an observer-created universe; the collapse of the wave function is the product of intersubjective agreement in which the key feature is not consciousness but human communication.[7] I would argue that it is not the human mind that affects observations, but the *process of interaction* between the detection apparatus and the micro-system. The experimental results might be automatically recorded on film, or on a computer printout, which no one looks at for a year. Holism is evident, not mentality.

The Tao of Physics, by the physicist Fritjof Capra, was the first of a series of books claiming that physics and Eastern mysticism make similar metaphysical claims about the *wholeness of reality.* Quantum physics points to the unity and interconnectedness of all events. In relativity, space and time form a unified whole, and matter-energy is identified with the curvature of space. Eastern thought also accepts the unity of all things and speaks of the experience of undifferentiated oneness encountered in the depth of meditation. There is one ultimate reality, referred to as Brahman in India and the Tao in China, with which the individual is merged. The new physics says that the observer and the observed are inseparable, much as the mystic tradition envisages the union of subject and object.[8]

I think Capra has overstressed the similarities and virtually ignored the differences between the two disciplines. For example, Asian traditions speak of undifferentiated unity. But the wholeness and unity that physics expresses is highly differentiated and structured, subject to strict constraints, symmetry principles, and conservation laws. Space, time, matter, and energy are all unified in relativity, but there are exact transformation rules between them. The mystic's structureless unity, in which all distinctions are obliterated, seems very different from the organized interaction and cooperative behavior of higher-level wholes. Capra says little about the difference in the goals of physics and of mysticism, or the distinctive functions of their respective languages. The goal of meditation is not primarily a new conceptual system, but transformation of personal existence, a new state of consciousness, an experience of enlightenment.

In *Wholeness and the Implicate Order,* physicist David Bohm is more cautious in delineating similarities between physics and Eastern mysticism. He proposes that mind and matter are two projections or expressions of a single deeper reality, an "implicate order." Bohm also finds in Eastern religions a recognition of the basic unity of all things; in meditation there is a direct experience of undivided wholeness. Fragmentation and egocentricity can be overcome in absorption of the self in the undifferentiated and timeless whole. Here is an ultimate monism and determinism, which contrasts with the greater pluralism of Western religions.[9]

In short, the holism of quantum physics is impressive, but any elaboration of a metaphysical system must draw on other sources as well. I believe that Western thought has given too much emphasis to the individual, while Eastern traditions have overemphasized wholeness at the expense of human freedom and individuality. Parker's understanding of the integrity of persons in community (individuality without individualism) seems to strike a better balance than has been present in the dominant traditions of either East or West. Perhaps a similar balance between parts and wholes is present in the quantum world.

Wholeness in Biology

Consider first the transition from inanimate to living systems. Most physical and chemical systems return to the most probable, disordered, equilibrium state if disturbed from it. But sometimes, if they are unstable and far from equilibrium, a *new level of collective order* appears and achieves a stable form. Ilya Prigogine won a Nobel Prize for his work on dynamic systems far from equilibrium. One of his examples is the sudden appearance of an ordered vortex in the disordered turbulence of a flowing river. Another is the appearance of a complex pattern of convection cells in the circulation of a fluid heated from below. In such cases a small fluctuation is amplified and leads to a new and more complex order that is resistant to further fluctuations and maintains itself with a throughput of energy from the environment.[10]

Prigogine has analyzed many inanimate *self-organizing systems* in which disorder at one level leads to order at a higher level, with new laws governing the behavior of structures showing new types of *complexity*. Randomness at one level leads to dynamic patterns at another level. In some cases, the new order can be predicted by considering the average or statistical behavior of the myriad components. But in other cases, Prigogine shows, there are many possible outcomes, and no unique prediction can be made. Multiple divergent solutions arise from these nonlinear instabilities. Formation of such self-organizing, self-perpetuating systems at the molecular level was perhaps the first step in the emergence of life. As in quantum theory, we must look at larger wholes and higher levels of organization, not just at the component parts.

Living organisms exhibit a *many-leveled hierarchy* of systems and subsystems. A level identifies a unit that is relatively integrated, stable, and self-regulating, even though it interacts with other units at the same level and at higher and lower levels. One such hierarchy of levels is identified structurally: quark, nucleus, atom, molecule, macromolecule, organelle, cell, organ, organism, and ecosystem. A more specialized information-processing hierarchy is that of molecule, synapse, neuron, neural network, brain, and body. Human beings also exhibit many-leveled hierarchies in all the social and cultural interactions studied by the social sciences and humanities. In each case, a discipline or field of inquiry focuses attention on a particular level and its relation to adjacent levels, and it tends to ignore more distant levels.

The presence of a hierarchy of levels has been important in *evolutionary history*.[11] Each level represents a relatively stable unit that preserves its own identity even as it interacts with other similar units. Modular construction facilitates assembly of various higher-level configurations without starting each time from the most elementary components. Past advances in complexity can be conserved and used in new ways.

Bottom-up causation occurs when many subsystems influence a system. *Top-down causation* is the influence of a system on many subsystems. Higher-level events impose boundary conditions on chemical and physical processes at lower levels without violating lower-level laws. The state of the upper-level system is specified without reference to lower-level variables.[12] Correlation of behaviors at one level does not require detailed knowledge of all its components. Network properties may be realized through a great variety of particular connections. The laws of chemistry limit the combinations of atoms that are found in DNA, but they do not determine them. The meaning of the message conveyed by DNA is not given by the laws of chemistry. Niles Eldredge and Stanley Salthe speak of an "upward influence" when many lower-level subsystems work together as necessary conditions of a larger whole, and a "downward influence" when many subsystems are constrained by the boundary conditions set by higher-level activities.[13]

Of all the sciences, *ecology* is the most holistic. Every creature is seen as part of the interdependent community of life (illustrating in nonhuman life Parker's theme of community as a form of wholeness). Ecologists have traced cycles of elements and compounds, food chains, and behavioral interactions linking diverse species. Ecological stability is not a static concept, but a dynamic balance of flows with feedbacks that compensate for certain changes. Diversity within and among species contributes to the stability and adaptability of ecosystems. Human actions can have unintended and indirect consequences distant in time and space. So ecologists urge humility and cooperation with nonhuman nature, rather than the goal of "conquest of nature." Since Rachel Carson's *Silent Spring* (1962), many writers have combined a scientific account of the interdependence of life with a sense of our spiritual unity with nature (reminiscent of the Romantic poets of the nineteenth century) that goes beyond the findings of science.

Wholeness in Neuroscience

Neuroscience is the scientific study of the physiology of the brain. Since the 1980s, educators have been impressed by research on *brain lateralization*. The behavior of patients who had brain lesions or who underwent surgery severing connections between brain hemispheres (to control severe epileptic seizures) suggested a specialization of functions. The left hemisphere evidently has a major role in serial processing and logical and temporal reasoning. The right hemisphere seems crucial in recognizing patterns (including faces) and visualizing images and spatial relationships—all of which are forms of *holistic understanding*. These studies led David Sousa and others to advocate educational strategies to ensure the use of both hemispheres, by including more visual activities along with verbal and mathematical skills in the classroom.[14]

More recent research suggests that information processing in the brain is more complex than theories of lateralization assumed. Stephen Kosslyn, Michael Gazzaniga, and others have shown that visual imagery, pattern recognition, and spatial reasoning involve several levels of interpretation drawing from *both hemispheres*.[15] John Bruer uses such findings to argue that educators should not claim support for their theories from neuroscience.[16] But Ron Brandt replies that there is much to be learned from neuroscience, so long as educators also draw from other sources, such as cognitive science, behavioral research, and experience in the classroom.[17]

A series of books by Renate and Geoffrey Caine advocate "brain-based learning." They accept Paul MacLean's depiction of the triune brain: a brain-stem system of physiological routines that goes back to the reptiles, an emotion-laden limbic system that we share with mammals, and the more recent cognitive systems of the neocortex. They cite evidence that under stress both animals and humans—including students in the classroom—revert to more primitive responses. They are impressed by the capacity of the human brain to perceive and generate meaningful patterns connecting parts and wholes. Such findings lead the Caines to criticize pedagogies requiring memorization of isolated facts and to explore ways of integrating content and context. They hold up examples of integrative and experiential learning through drama, stories, role playing, and group and individual projects that engage a student's interest. They suggest themes that cross the usual disciplinary lines. They defend whole-language learning of vocabulary and grammar together and propose socially interactive activities that encourage cooperation and mutual respect.[18]

Parker's conviction that teachers should pay attention to the whole student, including the emotions, receives considerable support from neuroscience. Antonio Damasio has studied the relationships between *emotion* and *cognition* in people who have undergone damage in the prefrontal cortex. He cites the classic case of Phineas Gage, who recovered from a severe brain injury and retained his intellectual abilities but underwent a personality change in which he was unable to make decisions or observe social conventions. One of Damasio's patients with a prefrontal brain tumor was totally detached emotionally. When he viewed films depicting violence, he could describe appropriate emotional reactions but said he could not feel them, and he was unable to make decisions in daily life. Damasio argues that the cortex and limbic system (especially the amygdala) work together in constructing emotions. He suggests that both Descartes and modern cognitive scientists have neglected the role of emotion in cognition. He describes the self as a many-leveled unity: "The truly embodied mind does not relinquish its most refined levels of operation, those constituting soul and spirit."[19]

Joseph LeDoux uses elevated blood pressure and heart rate as indicators of the emotion of fear in rats when they hear a sound to which they have previously been conditioned by association with an electric shock. He finds evidence of *direct* neural paths from the auditory system to the amygdala, which allow rapid response (which would have been valuable in evolutionary history). He also finds *indirect* paths to the amygdala by way of the cortex, which are slower but permit interpretation and discrimination among sounds. LeDoux distinguishes between emotions as neural responses and brain systems on the one hand and the subjective feelings associated with them on the other, which he says are inaccessible to scientific study.[20]

Leslie Brothers has shown that monkeys *respond emotionally* to the emotions expressed in the faces of other monkeys. Particular neurons in the brain of one monkey respond selectively to expressions of fear on a video of the face of another monkey in a neighboring room, and its body undergoes similar physiological changes.[21] This seems to be an early forerunner of *empathy*, the capacity to feel and respond to the emotions of another being. Human infants are attentive to adult faces because they are prewired by evolutionary history to respond to relevant facial signals, and in their moral development they can learn to care about their effects of their actions on others (including potential victims). Putting yourself in the place of another person has both cognitive and emotional dimensions. Daniel Schacter has shown that people have a better memory of events that had an emotional impact on them. Subjects shown slides or videos of a variety of situations can recall more accurately the details in images arousing emotional responses. For example, most citizens can remember when and where they first heard of a tragic event, such as the news of President Kennedy's death.[22]

A variety of approaches to human emotions have been pursued by psychologists. William James and his followers held that emotions are simply perceptions of *physiological processes* of which we are directly aware (pounding heart, faster breathing, tense facial muscles, and so on). The *behaviorists* ignored internal emotions and studied correlations between directly observable variables such as stimulus and response. *Evolutionary psychologists,* along with sociobiologists, portrayed the adaptive advantages various emotions might have offered for survival in earlier evolutionary history.[23] But a major group of psychologists has stressed the *cognitive aspects* of emotions. Whether an animal or a person flees in fear or fights back in anger may be partly an instinctive reaction, but it also reflects cognitive appraisal of the situation and unconscious judgment about its potential danger. Psychologists in this tradition talk about the beliefs, interpretations, expectations, and goals that contribute to emotional responses.[24]

A final group of authors emphasizes the role of culture in the *social construction* of human emotions. Emotions and their expression are shaped by cultural meanings learned in infancy and in later life. For instance, anger may reflect the belief that the other person is to blame for an offending action. Guilt is an acknowledgment that one has violated one's own norms, whereas shame is the feeling that one is not worthy in the eyes of others. Some studies suggest that when children learn words for emotions and culturally approved actions to express them, their emotional experience is itself affected. Whereas physiologically oriented authors have usually confined themselves to six basic emotions (anger, fear, happiness, sadness, disgust, and surprise), social constructionists also consider more complex emotions such as guilt, shame, embarrassment, and anxiety in the face of uncertainty.[25] They join the cognitivists in studying the close connections between beliefs and emotions, but they stress the social sources of those beliefs. Such studies do not contradict the findings of neuroscience but instead put them in a wider context.

Howard Gardner has argued that there are a variety of kinds of intelligence. In addition to logical, mathematical, spatial, kinesthetic, and musical abilities, he also includes self-knowledge (awareness of one's own feelings) and interpersonal skills (in nurturing relationships, resolving conflicts, and so forth).[26] Daniel Goleman's influential book *Emotional Intelligence* suggests that there is an identifiable group of emotional abilities that are relatively independent of IQ: the capacity to identify one's own emotions, manage them, recognize them in others, and use such abilities in constructive interaction with others. Goleman holds that because emotions are so important in understanding oneself and one's relation to other people, they should receive greater attention in education. He suggests that literature and drama offer valuable opportunities to talk about the feelings of the characters—and of the students. Helping students listen to each other, consider alternative responses, and think before they act can contribute to conflict resolution outside the classroom.[27]

What are the *religious implications* of neuroscience? Eugene d'Aquili and Andrew Newberg claim that particular areas of the brain are important in the religious experience of the timeless unity of all things—which is perhaps the ultimate holism. They did brain-imaging studies of Buddhist monks and Franciscan nuns while they were deep in meditation. The studies show increased activity in the frontal lobe, which is the seat of attention even in the absence of sensory input. By contrast, activity decreased both in the right parietal lobe (associated with causal and temporal ordering, as we have seen) and in the left (associated with integrative, holistic, and spatial relationships). Reduction in temporal ordering activity evidently accompanies loss of awareness of the passage of time that is reported by mystics in many cultures. Reduction in spatial ordering occurs in parallel with the sense of unity, loss of individual selfhood, and obliteration of all boundaries described by the mystics. Disciplined meditators report an experience of timelessness, oneness, serenity, and joy. They assert the ultimate goodness of reality and their loss of anxiety and fear.[28]

These findings might be interpreted as evidence that brain networks cause us to imagine the idea of God or a transcendent reality. Alternatively, one could say that the brain wiring developed in evolutionary history as our ancestors responded to a transcendent reality. Articulation of every claim about reality—whether of a table, an electron, another person's love, or the divine—requires neural activity in the brain. The reality of the referent of our symbols can never be determined by examining the brain. On the other hand, the claims of the mystic inevitably go beyond the experience itself and involve interpretations influenced by language and cultural assumptions and concepts. Moreover, myth and ritual have been as important as religious experience in religious history, and mysticism is not the only form of religious experience. The numinous experience of awe, holiness, and the otherness of the sacred has been as common as the sense of unity and identity with the sacred. Ethical dimensions of religion have also been important. Both Catholic saints and Buddhist bodhisattvas are judged as much by their lives of love and compassion as by the intensity of their experiences. I believe brain studies have only a limited value in understanding religion.

Finally, let me consider the philosophical and theological implication of neuroscience for a holistic understanding of human nature. A *dualistic* view of body and soul has been dominant in Christianity since the Middle Ages.

A sharp distinction of mind and matter has been prominent in philosophy since Descartes. Historians have shown that these dualisms came into Christian thought primarily from Greek thought, through the neo-Platonism of the church fathers in the Hellenistic world. By contrast, the Hebrew Scriptures (Old Testament) regard heart, mind, and soul as aspects of *a personal unity*, a unified activity of feeling, thinking, and willing. When belief in life after death emerged in the New Testament, it was held to occur through resurrection of the body, not the immortality of the soul. Lynn de Silva writes: "Biblical scholarship has established quite conclusively that there is no dichotomous concept of man in the Bible, such as found in Greek and Hindu thought. The biblical view of man is holistic, not dualistic."[29]

A dualistic view of human nature is also called into question by neuroscience. All of our capacities, including human love and spirituality, are dependent on the functioning of the brain. Chemical imbalances can alter our moods and our personalities. We are *psychosomatic embodied selves*. In reaction to dualisms of mind and matter, many scientists accept only the reality of matter, and they end with philosophical materialism. But if we reject reductionism, we can acknowledge a hierarchy of emergent levels, as indicated earlier. We can also insist, as the Bible does, that we are *social selves*, persons-in-community. We are formed and live our lives relationally—including our relation to God, in the biblical view. We are who we are as husbands and wives, parents and children, and members of a covenant community. It is consistent with Parker Palmer's holism to acknowledge that human life is rooted in and dependent on both brain and body, and at the same time to appreciate the importance of religious traditions and forms of religious experience that take us beyond the domain of science without contradicting the findings of science.

So I am grateful to Parker for holding up for us a vision of wholeness. Most important, of course, is his encouragement of the search for wholeness in our own lives as teachers, as students, and as people in a variety of vocations. For teachers, his writings and workshops have borne fruit in efforts to integrate diverse fields of knowledge so often pursued and taught in isolation. I have suggested that, within the sciences, the wholeness of knowledge is a reflection of the wholeness of the world that is evident even in particular sciences such as physics, biology, and neuroscience. For me, these themes come together when we express in practice as well as theory our conviction that a human being is not primarily a rational mind, or an eternal soul, or merely a biochemical mechanism, but rather an embodied self in a community of persons. With others we search for more inclusive sources of meaning. The quest for integrity in my own life has been expressed primarily in exploring ways of relating science and religion. Parker's sensitivity to diverse dimensions of human experience has been for me, as for so many others, an inspiration in an ongoing intellectual as well as personal pilgrimage.

NOTES

1. Palmer, P. J. *The Active Life*. San Francisco: Harper San Francisco, 1991, pp. 29–34.

2. Palmer, P. J. *The Courage to Teach: Exploring the Inner Landscape of a Teacher's Life*. San Francisco: Jossey-Bass, 1998, pp. 95–99.

3. Palmer (1998), pp. 24, 132.

4. Palmer (1991), p. 15.

5. Barbour, I. G. *Religion and Science: Historical and Contemporary Issues*. San Francisco: Harper San Francisco, 1977, pp. 173–175.

6. Barbour, I. G. *When Science Meets Religion*. San Francisco: Harper San Francisco, 2000, pp. 82–83.

7. Wigner, E. *Symmetries and Reflections*. Bloomington: Indiana University Press, 1967, p. 172; Wheeler, J. A. "The Universe as Home for Man." *American Scientist*, 1974, 62, 683–691.

8. Capra, F. *The Tao of Physics*. New York: Bantam Books, 1977.

9. Bohm, D. *Wholeness and the Implicate Order*. Boston: Routledge and Kegan Paul, 1980.

10. Prigogine, I., and Stengers, I. *Order out of Chaos*. New York: Bantam Books, 1984.

11. See Barbour (1977), pp. 230–233.

12. On top-down causation, see Peacocke, A. *Theology for a Scientific Age* (enlarged ed.). Minneapolis: Fortress Press, 1993, pp. 53–55.

13. Eldredge, N., and Salthe, S. "Hierarchy and Evolution." In R. Dawkins (ed.), *Oxford Surveys of Evolutionary Biology 1984*. Oxford, England: Oxford University Press, 1985.

14. Sousa, D. A. *How the Brain Learns: A Classroom Teacher's Guide*. Reston, Va.: National Association of Secondary School Principals, 1995; see also Jensen, E. *Teaching with the Brain in Mind*. Alexandria, Va.: Association for Supervision and Curriculum Development, 1998.

15. For example, Chabris, C. E., and Kosslyn, S. E. "How Do the Cerebral Hemispheres Contribute to Encoding Spatial Relations?" *Current Directions in Psychology*, 1998, 7, 8–14.

16. Bruer, J. "In Search of Brain-Based Education." *Phi Delta Kappan,* May 1999, *8*(9), 648–657.

17. Brandt, R. "Educators Need to Know About the Human Brain." *Phi Delta Kappan,* Nov. 1999, *81*(3), 235–238.

18. Caine, R. N., and Caine, G. *Making Connections: Teaching and the Human Brain.* Reading, Mass.: Addison Wesley, 1994; and also by the Caines, *The Brain, Education, and the Competitive Edge.* Lanham, Md.: Scarecrow Press, 2001.

19. Damasio, A. R. *Descartes' Error: Emotion, Reason, and the Human Brain.* New York: Putnam, 1994, p. 252.

20. LeDoux, J. E. *The Emotional Brain: The Mysterious Underpinnings of Emotional Life.* New York: Simon & Schuster, 1996.

21. Brothers, L. A. *Friday's Footprint: How Human Society Shapes the Mind.* New York: Oxford University Press, 1997.

22. Schacter, D. *The Search for Memory.* New York: Basic Books, 1996, esp. chapter seven.

23. Cornelius, R. *The Science of Emotion: Research and Tradition in the Psychology of Emotion.* Upper Saddle River, N.J.: Prentice Hall, 1996.

24. Lazarus, R. "Progress on a Cognitive-Motivational-Relational Theory of Emotion." *American Psychologist,* 1991, 46, 819–834.

25. Harre, R. (ed.). *The Social Construction of Emotions.* Oxford: Basil Blackwell, 1986.

26. Gardner, H. *Multiple Intelligences.* New York: Basic Books, 1993.

27. Goleman, D. *Emotional Intelligence: Why It Can Matter More Than IQ.* New York: Bantam Books, 1995.

28. D'Aquili, E. G., and Newberg, A. B. *The Mystical Mind: Probing the Biology of Religious Experience.* Minneapolis: Fortress Press, 1999.

29. De Silva, L. *The Problem of Self in Buddhism and Christianity.* London: Macmillan, 1979, p. 75; see also Brown, W. S., Murphy, N., and Malony, H. N. (eds.), *Whatever Happened to the Soul? Scientific and Theological Portraits of Human Nature.* Minneapolis: Fortress Press, 1998.

REFLECTIONS

———— o ————

Joel Elkes, M.D.
distinguished service professor emeritus
at the Johns Hopkins University

I met Parker at one of his workshops to which he had invited me. I do not recall the meditation, but I do distinctly recall the silence that followed, and throughout this silence the superb economy of his work. A word, a story, or joke. The timing was always perfect. *This man is an artist,* I thought. It was as if somehow he sensed our collective waves emanating from each of us, and in his responses he always managed to reach the center of our being.

I saw an image while I was with him: a total scintillating nexus of waveforms filling the room—a gently pulsating, shimmering, transparent organism. This alchemy resonates with the dance of molecules, which are my business.

I knew I had acquired a friend of the heart in that first session.

LIVING THE
NIGHT INTO DAY

A Response to Dark Times

Joel Elkes, M.D.

"AN AUTHENTIC MOVEMENT is not a play of power; it is teaching and learning writ large. Now the world becomes our classroom, and the potential to teach and to learn is found everywhere. We need only be in the world as our own true selves, with open heart and mind."

Thus ends Parker Palmer's classic *The Courage to Teach*.[1] For more than thirty years, Parker has labored, exploring the inner landscape of himself and those around him, inventing quietly as he went along. Having been in a group with him, one is moved again and again by how *little* he does. This stillness moves huge boulders. One feels privileged to witness the power of "formation." We are all in his classroom, and what he offers is profoundly relevant at this time, for his work speaks to identity, morale, and hope, the very sinews of human resilience. It is odd that so little attention has been paid by the authorities to this vital factor of human survival.

The published plan for Homeland Security is replete with detailed and expensive suggestions for safeguarding life and physical plant.[2] The measures suggested are mainly retrospective, rather than proactive; in addition, *conservation* and enhancement of human capital is relegated to a brief section on the treatment of victims. A recent article in *Scientific American* points to more proactive measures taken after September 11, 2001, but these measures, even in the medical field, do not take into thought the psychological effects and needs following 9/11.

Yet it is the strengthening of human *resilience* that survival is for, and about.

It is the purpose of this essay to point to the timeliness and import of groups and formation to our lives. The process holds profound lessons for an agenda for the future, and our ultimate homeland security.

The Industrialization of Fear

Emotions represent huge reservoirs of human energy, which can be harnessed for good or ill. The dominant emotion of our age is fear. The industries driven by fear are formidable and all-consuming. Fear has become so much a habit of thought that only massive denial allows us to pursue the routines of daily living. As for the most deeply sought aspirations of mankind: they are shelved, or denied, or postponed to a better "never, never" future.

These habits of thought have been with us for generations, and over time they have assumed a life of their own. They have left a huge, ominous physical residue, which remains—all honest efforts for their removal notwithstanding. Imagine the paranoid overdrive of governments that produced more than twenty thousand nuclear warheads, enough to incinerate life on the planet many times over; or the one million shells of nerve gas, stored quietly in Sochi, Russia, each of which, it is reported, can be accommodated in a small suitcase.[3] One could be conveniently stolen. If exploded, it can kill a hundred thousand people. The disposal of the total arsenal—given maximum means, and unlimited goodwill on both sides—would take six years.[4] In the interim, the likelihood of acquisition by terrorists remains high. So does their use.

Negative vis-à-vis Positive Emotions

Against these huge negative emotions, one can only respond in kind. Positive emotions must be experienced and harnessed on the same pervasive scale. This cannot happen by exhortation or propaganda, but must grow out of the deep soil of daily personal experience. It is submitted that the most solid defense against the hopelessness of terrorism are groups who know their own mind: groups composed of informed, aware, sturdy, and open individuals brought together in mutual work, affection, and love. Thus Parker's contribution may be very relevant to our times. *Formation* is a universal verb.

The Relevance of Formation to Our Present Crisis

Parker's idea of formation arose out of the needs of teachers who suffered burnout. It involves a process of self-discovery, and a sharing of common spiritual ground. It has deep roots in Parker's sense of his own identity and journey. In *The Courage to Teach* he alludes to the stages of the process. He determined at the outset that he himself would be the plumb line of it all—as each of us must be in our own lives. If that line was "true," and he had something worthwhile to share, the students would feel it. If it was "skewed," his teaching would feel it also.

This integrity was arrived at through prolonged and painful trial and error. Rejection at the beginning proved grist to his mill. He knew the paradox that was him, and little by little he accommodated to the paradox, rejecting the *either* and the *but*, accepting the *also* and the *and* into a complementarity of peaceful coexistence. He saw through the divisive trapping of words. He was taught to "think the world into pieces," and taught himself to think the world "together again."[5] He knew that he would have to take the partnership of good and bad into his heart, and he succeeded magnificently in his self-imposed task. Again, it is this simple quality of comprising the paradox that made him the leader he has become. We can all take heart from his example.

Living in the Twilight

We are living in the twilight of historic change; only full recognition of the paradoxical complexities of our times will give us the capacity to bend without being broken. We must assume that, obscure in this divided and crazed world, there is a hidden wholeness.

Community is a large word, compounded of manageable entities of neighborhoods and groups of all kinds within those neighborhoods. Supposing that in each neighborhood everywhere, groups were to form in relation to particular tasks and interests: schools, churches, hospitals, day care centers, and so on; and suppose that each group were to engage in a formationlike personal process related to their particular task.

The beginning would be slow, but as the process took hold cohesion and sharing could grow, and relationships among the members could deepen. Teachers could be leaders of each group, as could leaders of Boys and Girls Clubs of America, the Service Corps, the Peace Corps. What these groups would have in common would be a profound respect for the person, a spiritual core and a continuity between this core and the outer engagement. There would be a fostering of independence and of personal freedom and autonomy. Each group would be committed to the task, come what may. The task would be far from easy.

The groups would meet, and go on meeting, directing their attention to day-to-day practicalities—and, most important, to the inner problems (issues?) of participants. This threat of disaster could be a powerful catalyst. Honesty and openness in the face of diversity would slowly do their work. The groups could, over time, become a strong and reliable home for the person; they could constitute an island of integrity, if and when disaster strikes. Groups form a powerful defense; they are, to use an immunological metaphor, the lymph nodes of society.

Night Falls Fast

It takes only a few hours for a terrorist to totally transform the givens of a communal living. Fire, biological, chemical, or nuclear attack will rend the social fabric. Yet a group, once formed, is a resilient structure. It could grow the moral leadership and exemplify, for all to see, its viability. Practical work will tell: food distribution, courses in schools, work in hospitals, in small businesses, old people's homes and the local radio or TV stations. The tattered social fabric could be restored into some kind of functioning order. The idea of public service as an acceptable career would grow. Life would continue.

Living the Night into Day

This process would continue for some years, during which time many changes are sure to occur. Overarching all will be a growing appreciation of the value of the intangible, deeply personal elements of friendship, and a seeking out of these friendships in common acts of kindness and mutual service. The group's work will be seen as a powerful antidote to despair, arising out of violence and crime. Slowly a consensus of a determined "never again" will form and extend into actions making recurrence less likely. Very slowly, communities will move through the night toward a spiritual morning. I believe that sometime in the middle of that apocalyptic night the word *love* will regain its old, deep, and universal meaning. It will simply be an affirmation of all that has gone before. Love will be talked up, and talked about, having acquired obvious, new, fresh, urgent, and matter-of-fact practical meaning. As the new day breaks, its power and virtue will be apparent to all. Love and the spirit of forgiveness will infuse decisions in a new idiom. In this they will be supported by ordinary people, capable of extraordinary wisdom when needed.

Daybreak: Putting Love and Forgiveness to Work

These images flow out of one basic assumption, namely, the power of a small, well-informed, aware, and open group to assume control of the destiny of the community it serves. Thousands upon thousands of such groups could form in the country during the present emergency. Their presence and ongoing function would immeasurably strengthen morale and the ability to withstand the onslaught of any coming disaster.

NOTES

1. Palmer, P. J. *The Courage to Teach*. San Francisco: Jossey-Bass, 1998, p. 183.

2. *Homeland Security, 2002*. Washington, D.C.: Office of Homeland Security, July 2002, p. 12.

3. *Homeland Security, 2002*, p. 12.

4. Sen. Richard G. Lugar, in testimony before the Armed Services Committee, U.S. Senate, July 29, 2002.

5. Palmer (1998), p. 61.

REFLECTIONS

○
_____

W. Douglas Tanner Jr.
cofounder and president of the
Faith and Politics Institute

I came of age during the civil rights movement. My own soul was forged
in it. I later managed a friend's successful campaign for Congress, came
to work in his office, and in doing so experienced the challenges that
politics pose to personal wholeness. When the seeds of my present work
were germinating during a sabbatical season, I met Parker Palmer. My
life has been graced ever since by Parker's friendship and wisdom. His
teaching has profoundly informed and shaped our work at the Faith and
Politics Institute.

SOUL AND ROLE,
POLITICIANS AND POLITICS

W. Douglas Tanner Jr.

I WORK WITH MEMBERS of Congress, their staffs, and others closely connected to Capitol Hill through the Faith and Politics Institute, an organization I helped to found in 1991. We seek to help those with whom we work integrate "soul and role" in a setting rather unfriendly to such a notion. We organize and facilitate small weekly "reflection groups," occasional weekend retreats, periodic evening sessions with outside speakers, and pilgrimages to places where conscience, courage, and compassion have created new political possibilities. We return regularly to Alabama, where events of the civil rights movement in Birmingham, Montgomery, and Selma changed the nation—and, I believe, helped it take a critical step toward integrating soul and role. I share here three stories from my work with members of Congress. In interwoven but distinctive ways, they reflect Parker Palmer's teaching and spirit.

Congressman Glenn Poshard and Campaign Finance

I met Glenn Poshard in 1988, about a month after he was elected to the U.S. House of Representatives from his district in southern Illinois. Glenn had been a high school American history teacher and an Illinois state senator. We were seated at the same table at a dinner, and when Glenn learned I was a clergyman he shared some of his own religious identity. He came from a fundamentalist background, attended a Southern Baptist church, read a lot of Thomas Merton, and made regular retreats to Gethsemani, the Trappist monastery near Louisville where Merton lived and wrote. The combination struck me as unusual, and I took notice.

Several months later, Glenn called and asked if we could have dinner. We met at a small restaurant on Pennsylvania Avenue, and he opened a window onto his soul. He was feeling the typical freshman's loneliness, exacerbated by the fact that his wife, Jo, had remained behind in Illinois to teach school. He was also yearning for spiritual companionship. He had begun to feel the pull of political pressures more strongly than ever in the state senate, and he was troubled about where that might take him. He didn't have anyone in Washington with whom he felt free enough to air his anxiety and to sort things out. I told Glenn I would be glad to be present with him in such a way.

We got together a couple more times, just the two of us. Then I asked Glenn if he'd like me to seek out one or two other people who were both experienced in politics and consciously seeking their own spiritual growth; we could form a small group to meet regularly for mutual discernment and encouragement. When Glenn said yes, I recruited kindred spirits Anne Bartley and Joe Eldridge. Anne was an experienced political player whom I had come to know in a class on prayer at the Church of the Saviour's Servant Leadership School. Joe, whom I had known for more than a decade, was a fellow United Methodist minister and a longtime human rights activist.

The four of us began to meet from 7:30 to 9:00 on Wednesday mornings in Glenn's office in the Cannon Building. We would sit in silence for a few minutes, listen to a brief reading from Merton or another spiritual master, and sit in silence again until someone felt moved to speak. Then we would essentially follow wherever the spirit led us, speaking and listening from our depths, and usually managing to keep the conversation at a level that was quite personal. It was not a place for abstract questions on ethics and values in the political realm. It was, rather, a place for each of us to share things with which he or she was honestly wrestling. We didn't try to fix one another. Rather, we created a space within which each of us could learn to listen to the voice within, and count on others asking enough questions to ensure that we were hearing it clearly.

In October 1989, Glenn shared a deeply personal, spiritual, and ethical dilemma that gave rise to the real drama of our life together.

"I need you guys to help me with something," he said one Wednesday morning. "I'm supposed to be raising money for my reelection campaign, and I just don't want to do it. One of my colleagues has told me that my goal as a freshman should be to raise $1,000 a day. The DCCC [Democratic Congressional Campaign Committee] is telling us that we should have at least $100,000 in the bank by the end of the year to scare off an opponent. You know, the first time I did it like everybody said to. I raised $430,000 [at the time about an average figure for a Congressional race]—almost $250,000 of it from PACs. And I just hate the thought of doing it again.

"My district is almost 20 percent unemployed." (Shut-downs of southern Illinois coal mines had given Glenn's congressional district the highest unemployment of any rural district in the country.) "I can't ask my people for that kind of money. If I have to raise money, I'd much rather do it to buy jackets and shoes for school kids back home who need them, than to pay it to media consultants and TV stations. I can raise campaign money from the PACs, but I'm uncomfortable with that. I feel like I have to commit myself before I've had a chance to study their issues thoroughly, so I don't really know where I stand in my own heart and mind.

"I'd like to try to do it differently. I'd like to not take more than $50 from anyone and not buy any TV time, but instead debate my opponent in all twenty-two counties in my district, and rely on local weekly newspapers for coverage. And I don't want to just scare off an opponent; I think my people deserve a choice."

Anne, Joe, and I looked at each other in amazement, thinking this was Mr. Smith-come-to-Washington-and-going-back-to-Illinois-pretty-soon! Was he serious? We knew fundraising could be a pain, but what did he mean, he didn't want to scare off an opponent? Surely he didn't mean he wasn't going to take full advantage of his status as an incumbent.

Yet, as Glenn talked about campaigning on a minimal budget, his expression reflected a powerfully compelling charisma. By contrast, when he talked about having to go out and raise half a million dollars, he looked like a wet, worn-out dishrag.

By the end of the meeting, we weren't necessarily convinced that Glenn would win with such an unconventional approach. But we were clear, knowing Glenn and his spirit, that he should follow his energy on this. That energy was in doing it differently—radically differently—from conventional campaign wisdom. "This seems politically crazy to us," we told our freshman friend, "but we believe you need to do it, and we're with you."

Glenn won that campaign. In the campaigns that followed, Glenn modified his approach a bit, but not a whole lot. He took no PAC money and set his limit for individuals well below the figure federal election law allowed. He was reelected four times, was outspent by ratios as great as five to one, and each time increased his margin of victory.

In the congressional redistricting that followed the 1990 census, Illinois lost two seats. As usual, there was a measure of heavy-handed wheeling and dealing behind the scenes when the new district lines were being drawn. In this case, Glenn had been left with the short end of the stick. In addition, he was thrown into a primary battle with another incumbent Democrat with plenty of campaign money and—supposedly—a stronger base in the new district. Glenn was angry and resented the way he had been treated. He doubted he could win, but he was ready to run anyway on the energy of his anger.

Gradually making his way past his bitterness, Glenn threw himself into the race with his heart fixed on the ideals that had guided him into politics in the first place. Staying true to his conviction about campaign funding, he made up for his lack of a heavy mass media communications budget by a lot of hard work and old-fashioned organizing. He won 62 percent to 38 percent, surprising everyone in Washington who didn't know him well enough to appreciate how effectively he could connect with voters.

The week afterward, Glenn and I sat down in his office. We spent a couple of hours savoring the success of his faith in his convictions and in the electorate. I asked Glenn which factors he thought had been determinative.

"The issues," he stated with quiet confidence, "had to do with the broader state of the union in regard to representation and trust. . . . The campaign was one of integrity because we told the hard truth. People intuitively knew what it meant for the long haul. We in Congress generally don't trust people's judgments with the bigger picture. Instead, we wrap ourselves in security blankets. . . . If Congress is going to help save the country, it has to stop worrying about saving itself."

"Glenn, where did you find the clarity—and the courage—to begin to do it differently from most of your colleagues?" I asked.

"A lot of it came from the group," Glenn answered, referring to our regular Wednesday morning gathering. "The time with you guys has been critical. You were the ones with whom I felt enough trust to talk about the fundraising issue and to make that decision. I don't think I would have stayed with it without you. There were a lot of times I was tempted to change my mind. If there hadn't been someone to whom I held myself accountable on it, I probably would have.

"Everyone in this place encourages you to vote safely for political reasons. All the time I hear, 'Your first job is to get back here.' No one asks, 'Where is your gut? Where is your heart? Where is your soul?' But our group does.

"The group is the place that pulls me forward. I can go to my family for comfort, but not for that. You guys strengthen my capacity to listen to my inner voice. You give me the encouragement I need to follow through. No one else around here holds me accountable to the truths I know most deeply.

"One of those truths is that there's nothing creative about acting vindictively. In the final days of the redistricting process, when I learned about the map [of the newly drawn district], I felt so betrayed. My first reactions were anger and vindictiveness. Our group gave me a space and way of dealing with that until I had put it in perspective. When I finally decided to run, I saw it as a chance worth taking. By then, I wasn't doing it out of blind vengeance. I think I would have lost if that had been the case. If I had gone in angry, I wouldn't have been able to focus on the whole. All that involved some heavy soul-searching. When I made the decision, I had a profoundly positive spiritual experience of abandoning my own self to it. Ultimately, every time you have the courage to believe in that, you become a vessel for something greater, and you bring people along."

Parker couldn't have said it better himself.

Encountering the Civil Rights Movement in Alabama

Both Glenn Poshard and Parker Palmer revere Thomas Merton, the Trappist monk whose writings represented the essence of contemplative wisdom in twentieth-century America. In the spirit of Merton, Parker has defined contemplation as "anything that penetrates illusion and touches reality." My second story is of a profound penetration of illusion and touching of reality that occurs with some regularity on our pilgrimages to Alabama.

Two truly outstanding members of Congress co-chair the board of directors of the Faith and Politics Institute. One is John Lewis, a Democrat from Georgia. The other is Amo Houghton, a Republican from upstate New York.

John Lewis, as many readers will know, is an African American and a genuine hero of the civil rights movement. Under the tutelage of Rev. Jim Lawson, he became committed to nonviolence not only as a tactic for social change but also as a way of life. He led sit-ins to integrate public facilities in Nashville, Tennessee, and participated in the freedom rides that broke the color barrier aboard buses traveling through the South. He chaired the Student Nonviolent Coordinating Committee in the early 1960s, was beaten by mobs on numerous occasions, and went to jail perhaps even more times than he was beaten. On March 7, 1965, John led a peaceful march across the Edmund Pettus Bridge in Selma, Alabama, that was violently and viciously broken up by state troopers on horseback. More than any other event, that "bloody Sunday" and the subsequent march by Martin Luther King, Jr., John Lewis, and thousands of others from Selma to Montgomery led to enactment of the Voting Rights Act of 1965.

Following his retirement as CEO of Corning Glass, Amo Houghton had intended to move to Zimbabwe and assist in the administration of a mission school, but instead he was persuaded to run for an open seat in Congress. A devout Episcopal layman, he brought to Capitol Hill a gentle openness of spirit that made him exceptionally admired and appreciated on both sides of the aisle throughout his eighteen years in office.

In 1998, under the leadership of Congressmen Houghton and Lewis, the Faith and Politics Institute conducted its first congressional civil rights pilgrimage to historic sites of the civil rights movement in Alabama. With ten members of the U.S. House of Representatives and the chairs of both the Democratic and Republican National Committees, we flew into Birmingham and began the weekend at its Civil Rights Institute. John told his own stories as we walked through the institute's museum. We felt ourselves truly walking into the history and experience of "the movement."

The next day we went to Kelly Ingram Park, where Police Chief "Bull" Connor had turned fire hoses and dogs on peacefully demonstrating children. We sat in the sanctuary of the Sixteenth Street Baptist Church, where four teenage girls at Sunday School had been killed by a bomb.

Then we boarded a bus for Montgomery, watching en route videos from the documentary *Eyes on the Prize* with running commentary from John. In Montgomery, at the Dexter Avenue Baptist Church, we heard Deacon Nesbitt describe how he recruited Martin Luther King, Jr., to come as the pastor, and how Dr. King soon found himself leading the bus boycott. We walked silently up the hill, laid a wreath at the Civil Rights Memorial, and joined hands to sing "We Shall Overcome." Tears fell quietly down our cheeks and into the water that flows over the names of the movement's martyrs and the dates of their deaths engraved into the granite circle. We then went to visit former Gov. George Wallace in his home, in what turned out to be the last year of his life.

The next morning our pilgrimage took us to Selma. We again watched the documentary en route, and when we entered First Baptist Church we met individuals whose courage and clarity of spirit had amazed us in the historical footage of *Eyes on the Prize*. We worshiped at Brown's Chapel AME Church and joined the annual reenactment of the march across the Edmund Pettus Bridge. John eloquently described both the context and his personal experience in 1965, when he was beaten unconscious and hospitalized for three days.

On the bus ride back to the Birmingham airport, we all knew we would never again be who we had been when we first flew into that city. We had been touched by a sacred encounter with a profound time in our history that had shaped the soul of our nation. We had begun to receive a new vision for personal engagement in the political arena. People in the movement had exhibited spontaneous joy, freedom of spirit, and clarity of purpose in spite of the obvious dangers and the fear those dangers engendered. They were led by their faith to an expansive vision of political possibilities, many of which were realized. We were captivated by them. We had seen the power of the choice to live—in Parker's words describing Rosa Parks—"divided no more." We had also been struck by the relative shallowness of most of the political battles fought daily on Capitol Hill.

Two stories of individual responses are worth telling here. One occurred on that first pilgrimage, when Jim Nicholson, then chair of the Republican National Committee and later ambassador to the Vatican, stood up to speak in Selma's First Baptist Church. "I was a ranger fighting in Vietnam in 1965," Jim said, "and I missed this. I read a bit about it in *Stars and Stripes,* and by the time I got home, it was pretty much over. I know what it's like to find the courage to weigh into the fray. What has amazed me and what I want to learn more about is how to find the courage to do it nonviolently."

The second occurred two years later. Congressman Mike Forbes came on the institute's third pilgrimage as a Republican from Long Island. He was struggling intensely with how to cope with the major differences he had with his party's leadership in the House. Mike walked through the history and across the Pettus Bridge with John Lewis, Fred Shuttlesworth, Bettie Mae Fikes, Bob Zellner, and Bernard Lafayette, all of whom had put their lives on the line in the sixties. "If John Lewis can find the courage to do that," Mike concluded, "I can find the courage to be true to myself about my changing political convictions." A couple of weeks later, he switched parties. A nationally coordinated and funded campaign was waged against him in the next election, and Mike lost his seat in Congress. But he had listened clearly to his true self and been prepared to pay the political price. Mike had no regrets about the decision and returned on another pilgrimage the year after he was defeated.

Parker could hardly be surprised by either Jim's or Mike's response. Each engaged in profound contemplation; each penetrated illusion and touched reality.

The Promise of Paradox: Learning in South Africa

One of Parker's books is *The Promise of Paradox.* A chapter in another, *Let Your Life Speak,* is entitled "Leading from Within." My final story is of the wisdom so well contained in these writings.

In May 2003, the Faith and Politics Institute entered international waters for the first time when it coordinated a visit of fourteen members of the House of Representatives, their spouses, and selected additional guests to South Africa. The primary purpose of the trip was to learn from South Africa's experience in ending apartheid, resolving conflict, and promoting reconciliation between those who had been on opposite sides in a long, painful, and often bloody political struggle.

We traveled to Pretoria, Johannesburg, and Soweto, then to Cape Town, the township of Guguletu, and Robben Island. We met with religious leaders, government officials, members of Parliament, individuals deeply involved in efforts to combat HIV/AIDS, business and labor leaders, major figures in the process of negotiating the end of apartheid, and members and staff of the Truth and Reconciliation Commission, which sought to help heal the nation's heavy wounds.

We received unforgettable lessons in both the fundamental reality of paradox and the power of leadership that flows after deep soul-searching reveals transcendent truths. South Africa's painful experience is yielding profoundly hopeful political possibilities that merit close attention from the rest of the world, perhaps especially from the United States at this point in our history. The most promising dimensions of both the pain and the possibilities, I believe, are in keeping with Parker's teaching and the wisdom he draws from the Quaker tradition.

I recount here one instance of our encounter with those lessons.

At a dinner the evening we arrived in Cape Town, former South African President F. W. de Klerk and Tokyo Sexwale (a guerrilla warrior and political prisoner under apartheid, then the African National Congress premier of Guateng Province and now a leading international businessman), spoke to the delegation. De Klerk described the Afrikaner worldview that had prevailed until the late 1980s and how it began to change:

> We [Afrikaners] clung to the concept of being free as a nation with our own culture, with our own language, in our land . . . but we failed to bring justice. And we had to take a deep hard look at ourselves.
>
> What prompted the dramatic paradigm shift from apartheid to a new vision? It was the admission that you cannot build the interest of your core group on the basis of injustice to, in our case, a majority of the population. . . . It was not pragmatic reasons. It was a deep soul-searching process.
>
> Politics and faith should go hand in hand. But, at all times, we should be critical because, in faith and in religion, you can go the wrong way, and in politics you can become obsessed with the wrong ideas and the wrong principles. In the final analysis, what was the dominating philosophy which brought reconciliation to South Africa, which avoided a catastrophe, which gave us hope for the future, was the realization that you must go to basic principles. And the guiding basic principle which for me was the dominating philosophy to which I adhered, and against which I tested everything we tried to do, was that you cannot build the future on the basis of injustice to an important section of the

community. Therefore . . . those fundamental principles—justice, integrity, love, forgiveness—should be the guiding light if you talk about reconciliation, not the fine script of agreements. . . .[1]

Parker has written how Nelson Mandela used his twenty-eight years in prison to prepare inwardly for leadership instead of drowning in despair; "Under the most oppressive circumstances, people like Mandela . . . go all the way down, travel through their inner darkness—and emerge with the capacity to lead the rest of us toward community, toward 'our complex and inexplicable caring for each other.'"[2]

Sexwale spoke of the courage it took for Mandela to call his fellow prisoners from Robben Island—including Tokyo—and tell them it was time to negotiate. On video materials from the institute, Sexwale continued:

Leadership, I learned over a long period of time, in exile where I once served for several years, in the underground where we were operating in this country as fighters, . . . in prison where I was sentenced for treason and terrorism and conspiracy to overthrow [pointing to De Klerk] *his* government, to eighteen years and served fifteen on Robben Island . . . I learned—everywhere we were—leadership is about courage.

The courage of a leader is to dissent, not so much against your opponents, but amongst your friends. The essence of leadership is to debate, to test ideas amongst your supporters.

And I learned since then that one quality of leadership, and I will use Nelson Mandela as my standard, is the ability to use five words: A leader has got to be able to say *nevertheless*. A leader has got to use the lexicon of saying *however*. A leader must have the ability to say *but, notwithstanding,* or even use the phrase *having said that.* Those are the key words for me of leadership. And I have seen struggle, I have been in the most difficult circumstances, where body and soul of man are brought very close sometimes to death. It is these words that helped us survive.

That is the South Africa of Nelson Mandela, but also the South Africa of de Klerk . . . one was engaged in soul-searching, you heard him very well. The other, a prisoner somewhere, was also engaged in soul searching, and he called us and he said: "I think we must confront the problem. We cannot sit here in prison and rot and not confront our enemy and stop them in their tracks." It required courage to take the first step, the ability to say nevertheless, notwithstanding. . . .

The message of reconciliation coming from South Africa is that there is still faith in politics. . . . Government can and does work, provided that a critical element of courageous leadership remains.

How did this happen? I say, walk outside the cell of Nelson Mandela and listen to your own heartbeat. We say as you walk there, peace comes at a price, and the price of peace is compromise.

I have been around members of Congress for more than twenty years, and I can't remember when I have ever seen such an enthusiastic, spontaneous response from both Democrats and Republicans. Some threw their arms around each other's shoulders. One looked at another and said, "Nevertheless . . ." to which the other immediately responded, "However. . . ." One grinned, "But . . ." and the other beamed "Notwithstanding. . . ." Then both simultaneously declared, "Having said that. . . ."

They knew that their political battles, on numerous issues that are truly important to the American public, often rage on and on, with little substantive accomplishment. They hungered, I believe, to have what they knew deep down publicly validated, that progress toward the common good requires both courage and compromise. This is far from the highly charged, often acerbic, partisan posturing that has become the dominant note in Congressional politics.

To break this pattern requires finding the clarity and courage to live divided no more and the wisdom to recognize a particular paradox: successful compromise also requires clarity and courage.

Referring to Rosa Parks, Vaclav Havel, and Nelson Mandela as leaders who decided to live "divided no more," Parker writes: "They decide no longer to act on the outside in a way that contradicts some truth about themselves that they hold deeply on the inside." They are able to do this, he adds, because "they have come to understand that no punishment anyone might inflict on them could possibly be worse than the punishment they inflict on themselves by conspiring in their own diminishment."[3]

Parker concludes an essay on "Leading from Within" with these words:

> We do not have to lead from a place of fear, thereby engendering a world in which fear is multiplied. We have places of fear inside us, but we have other places as well—places with names like trust and hope and faith. We can choose to lead from one of *those* places, to stand on ground that is not riddled with the fault lines of fear, to move toward others from a place of promise instead of anxiety. As we stand in one of those places, fear may remain close at hand and our spirits may still tremble. But now we stand on ground that will support us, ground from which we can lead others toward a more trustworthy, more hopeful, more faithful way of being in the world.[4]

Nelson Mandela couldn't have said it better himself.

NOTES

1. The lines from President F. W. de Klerk and Tokyo Sexwale are taken from materials recorded by the Faith and Politics Institute.

2. Palmer, P. J. *Let Your Life Speak*. San Francisco: Jossey-Bass, 2000, pp. 81–82.

3. Palmer, P. J. *The Courage to Teach*. San Francisco: Jossey-Bass, 1998, p. 171.

4. Palmer (2000), p. 94.

Chapter Four

OPENING SPACE FOR THE INNER LIFE

WHAT SORT OF SPACE gives us the best chance to hear soul truth and follow it? A space defined by principles and practices that honor the soul's nature and needs. . . . What is that nature, and what are those needs? My answer draws from the only metaphor I know that reflects the soul's essence while honoring its mystery: the soul is like a wild animal.

Like a wild animal, the soul is tough, resilient, resourceful, savvy, and self-sufficient: it knows how to survive in hard places. . . . Yet despite its toughness the soul is also shy. Just like a wild animal it seeks safety in the dense underbrush, especially when other people are around. If we want to see a wild animal, we know the last thing we should do is go crashing through the woods, yelling for it to come out. But if we will walk quietly into the woods, sit patiently at the base of a tree, breathe with the earth, and fade into our surroundings, the wild creature we seek might put in an appearance. We may see it only briefly and only out of the corner of an eye—but the sight is a gift we will always treasure as an end in itself.

Unfortunately, *community* in our culture too often means a group of people who go crashing through the woods together, scaring the soul away. In spaces ranging from congregations to classrooms, we preach and teach, assert and

argue, claim and proclaim, admonish and advise, and generally behave in ways that drive everything original and wild
into hiding.

A circle of trust is a group of people who know how to
sit quietly "in the woods" with each other and wait for the
shy soul to show up. The relationships in such a group are
not pushy but patient; they are not confrontational but
compassionate; they are not filled with expectations and
demands but with abiding faith in the reality of the inner
teacher and in each person's capacity to learn from it.

—Parker J. Palmer

o

REFLECTIONS

○
_____

Shirley H. Showalter
president and professor
of English at Goshen College

I recall meeting Parker over styrofoam-cup coffee in the breakfast nook of a hotel in Valparaiso, Indiana. Both of us were attending a conference sponsored by the Lilly Fellows Program for Humanities and the Arts at Valparaiso University. He was a keynote speaker, and I was the senior fellow in that program for 1994–95, on leave from my position as professor of English at Goshen College.

At that time I had already read *To Know as We Are Known* and that book had begun to change both my pedagogy and my identity as a professor. For me, *AP* means After Parker, when I more fully claimed my vocation in the classroom and with my colleagues. I took more risks with students, revealing more of my own inner life. I began to expect the text to offer us a connection not only to meaning but to more meaningful lives. I challenged myself to grow, published more, and urged my students to go deeper.

Parker took me into his life with a graciousness that remains my model for mentoring. He understood the dark night of the soul I went through in my forties, and he has led me through two "clearness committee" meetings over the phone. He spoke at my inauguration and has made a deep impression on many others at Goshen College.

I love to hear Parker laugh. When he does, for a split second the universe opens up and swallows all kinds of dichotomies. He is always pointing us not to himself but to "the great thing," the subject. Behind everything he writes, I hear inaudible music. This essay is the vibration.

"HOW CAN I
KEEP FROM SINGING?"

Seeking the Wisdom of Sound

Shirley H. Showalter

For twenty-five centuries, Western knowledge has tried to look
upon the world. It has failed to understand that the world is not
for the beholding. It is for hearing. It is not legible, but audible.
—Jacques Attali, *Noise: The Political Economy of Music*[1]

WHENEVER I READ A Parker Palmer book or essay, a moment arrives when I close the book and sigh. I get a sudden, strong urge to choose Huck Finn's quintessentially American path: to quit institutions and "light out for the territories."[2] It's difficult to live Parker's creed of "divided no more" when you participate in institutions that, by their very nature and even at their best, seem to support the whole over the parts, the choir over individual voices. It is even harder to do so when you are the institution's president.

Parker loves to tell a story about the time when he was offered the presidency of a small educational institution. Like a good Quaker, he did not make the decision by himself. Nor did he cede the decision to others. Instead, he entered into a "clearness committee" meeting, "a process in which the group refrains from giving you advice but spends three hours asking you honest, open questions to help you discover your own inner truth."[3] When asked what he would like about being a president, Parker began a litany of the things he would not like. Repeatedly reminded that he was not answering the question, he found the courage to speak the truth: "I guess what I'd like most is getting my picture in the paper with the word *president* under it."[4] This admission caused silence to fall on the whole group while Parker inwardly groaned. Finally a "weighty friend" in the room asked another question: "Parker, could you think of an easier way to get your name in the paper?" Every time Palmer tells that story, he throws his head back and roars with laughter, and his audience laughs with him.

Though Parker managed to escape from running an organization, he certainly has not turned away from those who do. In fact, at first his writing originally focused on the very group he would have led, had he taken the presidency: "faculty at church-related colleges and seminaries, professors of religion, and people involved in religious education."[5] As one who took the "road not taken" by Parker (a presidency of a church-related college), I can contribute a view of education from that perspective. From my experiences, I have discovered that in the deepest places—the place where education meets wisdom—we must start and end with sound.

The hymn text of my title, written by Robert Lowry just before the beginning of the Civil War, in 1860, offers a compelling vision of what education could be, combined with a haunting melody that captures that yearning:

> My life flows on in endless song, above earth's lamentation.
> I catch the sweet, though far-off hymn that hails a new creation.
> Through all the tumult and the strife, I hear that music ringing.
> It finds an echo in my soul. How can I keep from singing?[6]

Within my own soul, music has become the best metaphor for knowing as we are known, or knowing by loving. Music is a metaphor we literally feel in our bodies. We need to create and re-create spaces that make music possible—sounds that enter the spirit and connect us with each other and with life everlasting. Our scholarship should reverberate with sound and also allow space for silence; our classrooms and residence halls and chapels should "make the air with music ring."[7]

Parker has pointed us to an "inner landscape." What if we began to think about our own lives, our work, and our campuses as potential "inner soundscapes"?[8] I believe we would find a new kind of spiritual energy and knowledge. Toward that end, I will explore some "sound" educational practices—sound scholarship, sound spaces, and sound leadership that encourages both. First, however, I will share the history and experiences that have deepened my convictions.

A Musical Autobiography and Ethnography

Because I was born into a Mennonite community, I entered the world attuned to music. My mother loved to play hymns on the piano. She has a clear soprano voice and encouraged me to learn alto so we could harmonize as we washed and dried the dishes. But it was in church that music really came alive, as worship and as communal communication. The men sat on one side of the shoebox-shaped church and the women on the other. The separation benefited young people as they tried to learn their "parts." When you hear only altos and sopranos, the basses and tenors do not seem as intimidating, and it is easier to pick out the notes that harmonize with your range. It was there in church that I sang "I Owe the Lord a Morning Song of Gratitude and Praise" nearly every beautiful spring Sunday morning. It was there, thirty years later, that I felt a direct, electric bodily message while singing "Come, Come Ye Saints" during the funeral of my father.[9] It was there, in the lives of some remarkable adult mentors, that I first learned what it was to shape one's life around the invisible presence sensed in the overtones of music.

If something is hidden yet real, how do we know it? How do we teach it? There are many ways, but I can think of no better one than music. As the philosopher and rabbi Abraham Joshua Heschel has said: "To sing means to sense and to affirm that the spirit is real and that its glory is present. In singing we perceive what is otherwise beyond perceiving."[10] An even more profound description comes from philosopher Simone Weil: "This tearing apart, over which supreme love places the bond of supreme union, echoes perpetually across the universe in the midst of the silence, like two notes, separate yet melting into one, like pure and heart-rending harmony. This is the Word of God. The whole creation is nothing but its vibration. When human music in its greatest purity pierces our soul, this is what we hear through it."[11] When I read these words, I understood why musicians are often mystics and why it takes a mystic to describe the powerful connection between music and spirit. Long before any physicist developed the idea of string theory, Weil described a poetic version of it.

Most of us lack the poetry of a Simone Weil or Abraham Heschel. But language is only one form of knowing. The Mennonite community that shaped me taught me much that does not transfer readily into written language. I experienced it in the body. An anonymous expression I heard recently illustrates the limitation of words for physical and spiritual experience: "Writing about music is like dancing about architecture." Language is only one form of knowing.

Music does not require language, and it can speak truth without words. When we make music together, we start the creation over again. What was torn can be mended, at least for the moment. No matter how small or large the group that sings, no matter how well or poorly gifted or trained, they can tune themselves to each other. They also know that music can be both intimate and powerful.

Whatever truth I have learned about loving, learning, and leading has been enhanced enormously by the experience of singing in many settings. Many others have also learned this way. In fact, if we go back far enough, we find music at the very center of the curriculum. In the earliest of Western educational curricula, the trivium and quadrivium, music was one of the four highest subjects in the catalogue of all the culture that was valued, along with geometry, mathematics, and astronomy.

We can recover this ancient wisdom without discarding all the new disciplines and approaches of the academy. The best way to bring music's wisdom to the curriculum is not to rely solely on the discipline of music itself. The best approach is to find new ways for all faculty and students to experience the pleasure of listening to their own and others' voices together. As Wordsworth said of Coleridge in his long biographical poem "The Prelude," "what we have loved others will love, and we will teach them how."[12] As a Quaker, Parker knows deeply what it means to honor the wisdom of silence; he taught us how to love what he has loved. We return the favor when we teach others what we have loved. As a Mennonite, I would like to offer a complementary kind of wisdom: that of the human voice singing its way to love and resonating with other hearts and voices as together they move beyond time.

Mennonites began a century before George Fox, the founder of the Quakers, was born. They were part of the "radical reformation" of the sixteenth century. The two groups are both united in viewing the gospel as a call to peace and against war. Mennonites, however, are less silent in worship than their Quaker brothers and sisters. They are noisier because they sing, as they always have done. Their early history is filled with suffering. The übertext of the faith, *The Martyr's Mirror,* records martyr stories of more than eight hundred early Anabaptists, as they were called then.[13] Many of these martyrs sang as they were being readied for the fire. The singing was so disconcerting to the magistrates and so seductive to new converts to the faith that eventually tongue screws were employed to silence the voices of those about to die. Contemporary Mennonite poets have gone back to this source often and have found ways to situate them in the present, as in Shari Miller Wagner's poem.

A CAPPELLA

As we gasp between lines
a chasm opens
from the older hymns.

I sense a darkness
like what I heard
at an Amish barn door,

the entrance to a church
or a cavern
where my ancestors

droned the poetry
that could not be uttered
in the village.

In sixteenth-century
dungeons
they sang these hymns

as a way to connect
flesh chained to walls
and rack. We hold

these broken ones
in our voices
like bread that could

bless us. Grandma Mishler,
whom we buried
the Easter when hyacinths

bloomed inside ice, leans
behind my left shoulder
and Shawn with the quick

laugh who died
giving birth
sits beside Grandfather

on the couch. They listen
with their eyes closed.
All of the old ones

are here in the dark
room of a house that
stood where corn grew

because God sent
the sun. We end with
"Praise God from Whom

All Blessings Flow"—
the version with echoing
alleluias and amens.

We don't need the book
and no one sets the pitch.
We've sung this one

at every marriage
and funeral. Even in-laws
with eyes on the last

five minutes of a game
join in from their corner.
From every direction

there are voices within
voices, husks beneath
husks. The dead sing

in a house so haunted
we breathe
the same breath.

    —Shari Miller Wagner[14]

The movement in this poem is from old to new, past to present, death to life, but the moment of insight comes when the person recognizes that these are not separate realities and that "there are voices within / voices" in the music. The sufferings of the ancestors, though hundreds of years old, are "sensed" in the darkness still present in the lugubrious music of the Amish. There is no thought of revenge for the suffering, only the desire to make it meaningful by keeping memory alive. The image of holding broken ones in our voices enlarges the human voice box and vocal chords to a spacious room that can hold others. The power of the others to "bless us" like bread is obviously sacramental; the sacrifice becomes the power to transform within the voice of another.

The family members, both dead and alive, are tied together with a sound-filled faith. The visual images are all subordinate to sound. The most interesting people are the in-laws, who may not only be from outside the family but outside the faith as well, who join in the singing even though their eyes are still on the last five minutes of "the game." They are the only ones who are looking; the rest are listening and singing. The "game" they are watching might be any visual distraction, perhaps even the metaphorical "game" wherein the material, visible world is all there is. The poet seems to celebrate simultaneously the deeper knowledge of sound contained in the biological family formed in faith, but she seems also to warn of the possibility of exclusion. If the in-laws cannot join in or do not want to join in, the music will lose its power to connect.

In "A Cappella," the visible world is a sign of the invisible, like the corn that grows because God sent the sun. The poem is metaphysical, and like the metaphysical poet John Donne, Wagner uses puns to help strengthen the overtone of the poem. The literal corn grows because God sent the sun. The metaphorical corn grows because God sent the Son. The darkness of the past and of the room is not overcome, but the sound makes the darkness bearable. Just as the darkness of the crucifixion was not overcome by the death of Jesus, his voice just before the end still has the power to push back the darkness.[15]

The poem ends with sound and the origin of sound and life: breath. The dead "sing" in a "haunted" house. It is "so haunted" that the dead are alive, and "we breathe / the same breath." This ending seems deliberately ambiguous. One could read it as a reverse form of necrophilia, or even cannibalization. The dead are so alive that they take over the bodies of the living.

I don't read the poem this way, though the possibility of this interpretation challenges the reader to face "the shadow" of community life. Other subcultures can relate to both the sunshine and the shadow, especially if suffering was part of their past. African American spirituals, Jewish laments, gospel, blues, and folk music of many cultures have their own versions of this kind of knowledge.

Part of the magic in music is that it synchronizes the participants into one whole. The field of neuroscience today is helping us understand why and how this happens. According to William Benzon, "for individuals sharing a common musical culture, there is a strong and systematic similarity between the tonal flow of music and its neurophysiological substrates that allows a tight coupling between the brains of those individuals. While participating in music those individuals constitute a community of sympathy."[16] Benzon goes so far as to say that such practice is essential: "When we deliberately coordinate our nervous systems with each other—this is when we become human."[17] He came to the conclusion that Descartes and others who begin with individuals and the rational mind as the basic building block of reality and philosophy were wrong. He did not begin his research with this thesis. Rather, he says, "it was forced on me as I thought about how people make music in groups. I do not believe that you can understand human community by starting with individuals and trying to derive interaction and community from rational self-interest."[18]

Benzon's conclusions seem nearly self-evident from where I stand. Taken as a whole, my experience in family, church, and school, including higher education, brought me into a "community of sympathy" long before I was ever conscious of it. The implications of this for what learning could be are staggering. If we can learn to "listen each other into speech,"[19] we could also listen each other into song, which would go beyond the individual voice and the rational self-interest flesh is heir to, and bring it into meaning that can only be grounded in groups. If we are to apply what music teaches us to the field of education in the twenty-first century, what new song can we hear? I propose that we strive to hear a new sound in our scholarship, our spaces, and in the leadership we desperately need in higher education.

Sound Scholarship

I had been my whole life a bell, and never knew it
until at that moment I was lifted and struck.
          —Annie Dillard, *Pilgrim at Tinker Creek*[20]

The university has placed research—quantified in the production of essays, papers, and books—at the pinnacle of scholarly inquiry. Ernest Boyer tried valiantly, and somewhat successfully, to stretch those categories by describing four kinds of scholarship.[21] Yet even these four types rely on use of publications for legitimacy. I believe we need to recognize another form of scholarship, the kind that, like music, seemingly disappears into the air when sound subsides but that lives on in the mind and heart of another person. I have named this practice "oral scholarship."[22]

Oral scholarship starts with hospitality in the classroom, the office, and one's own home. It includes living acquaintance with the subject and willingness to face doubts directly. It means giving away ideas instead of hoarding all of them for private research. It sets high standards for thinking—one's own and one's students'—and sustains us in our difficult times but does not allow us to give less than our best. It crosses boundaries between fields and exults in many. It encourages theological thinking in all disciplines. In the midst of conflict, it seeks peace. It may mean putting the community ahead of one's own career.

In the last hundred years, some of what might have become published work was instead shared with students, colleagues, and church members. There was often joy in this because whatever sacrifices resulted were shared sacrifices. What was gained—thoughtful talk, service projects, some books and articles, going abroad to study—was also shared. There was as well pain and loss.

One of my predecessors in the Goshen College presidency, J. Lawrence Burkholder, for instance, wrote a summa cum laude dissertation at Princeton but did not publish it until years later because of the discouragement of the established scholars in the field of Mennonite studies in the late 1950s and early 1960s, whose primary concern was a cohesive church. Today it would be a rare scholar who defers to the church in such a way (as it would be rare for the church to care so much about the content of a single dissertation).

The senior faculty of Goshen College, when I arrived in 1976, included not only Burkholder, who was president, but Carl Kreider, Mary Oyer, Mary Eleanor Bender, Frank Bishop, Atlee Beechy, and John Oyer. These are people whose names are and were known to almost every educated Mennonite. Among their students are scholars teaching at the best research universities in the world. I have heard these graduates testify that they searched the whole world over and never found character as deep as (nor minds more subtle and original than) those of the faculty who shaped their early adulthood at Goshen. By the standards of the academy then and now, we had greater talent here than a small institution "deserved." Such is still the case.

From the lips of oral scholars fall statements that go on reverberating in the minds of others. During the 1999–2000 academic year, I had the pleasure of connecting Katherine Lemons, a young Stanford undergraduate who transferred to Goshen College for that year, to one of the best oral scholars I know, a professor emerita of French, Mary Eleanor Bender. While in Goshen, Katherine spent many hours in Mary's living room talking about art in relation to ethics. She recalls one statement with pristine clarity: "Your statement, so honest and so effortless, that no one would have the heart to feed the hungry never having been witness to beauty for its own sake, stems from an instinct which is as rare as it is important and as clear as it is risky."[23] Katherine heard and felt something in Mary's presence for which she craves words:

> Words are the instruments of reason for me and for passion: they are the slippery grade that I scramble over as I make sense of myself and as I become my thoughts and become familiar with my thoughts, and it would be both a deep pleasure and a profound honor to have the opportunity to use these little parcels of attempts at meaning to articulate what happens when we talk together in your living room, the traffic outside punctuating in its ebbs and flows, synchronizing the continual fluctuation of the light from red to green to red to green, our words as they dance and dip, almost visible as they rise from our lips.[24]

When oral scholarship eventually is published, sound becomes visible. Lemons herself has begun to recognize the beauty, depth, and durability of the primary, oral language translated into visual reality. Several renowned scholars have dedicated books to Mary Eleanor Bender, who never wrote any herself. Nor did Socrates. Nor Jesus. Orality has a grand but rapidly fading tradition. It should not be lost, even as we recognize the need to preserve what can be captured in print.

Sound Spaces

The magic that happens in the best oral scholarship, which might be called the music of the intellectual life, happens most fully in certain kinds of spaces. One of these spaces is the classroom. When in 1993 my professor husband and I took a group of twenty-three students to Côte d'Ivoire, our group met in a small classroom with good acoustics. When Monsieur Yapo, an ethnomusicologist from the University of Abidjan, spoke to us, he asked us to sing. We sang in four-part harmony the hymn sometimes known as the "Mennonite national anthem" (the hymn referred to in the poem "A Cappella" as "Praise God from Whom All Blessings Flow,"—the version with "echoing / alleluias and amens"). We sang for M. Yapo. We sang from our hearts, and the music filled the room. M. Yapo closed his eyes and entered a rapturous state of intense listening. When he opened them, they were moist with tears and wide with delight. Then he began to instruct us. He picked up a bent branch from a tree, strung with a single bow. He said six words: "This is how the world began." He began to use both his mouth and his hands to set up vibrations and sound, and soon the room that still had our notes hanging in the air began to vibrate like a drum. We were all inside the drum, the cave of the earth, and we were feeling the energy of creation.

We might understand the needs of good "soundscapes" better if we paid attention to the field of acoustical engineering. One of the most exciting projects of my life began with a group of alumni and friends singing together in a conference center room in Colorado. Out of the intimacy that comes only when voice and spirit find the right partners in the right space came the spontaneous offer to help fund a much-needed and long-awaited music center at Goshen College. Exactly five years later, we dedicated the completed project, including a new concert hall, recital hall, rehearsal spaces, practice rooms, and community music school. When building a concert hall or a rehearsal hall, one designs space in such a way so as to create acoustical conditions that approach perfection. The acoustical engineer we chose was Richard Talaske, who not only produced quality sound spaces but also gave us an education in the science of sound in the process. Talaske describes ten acoustic characteristics that he aims to perfect, or eliminate, as he designs:

1. *Clarity,* the quality of sound that supports the comprehension of detail and the distinct separation of individual musical notes and articulations

2. *Loudness,* the overall quantity of sound, as heard by a listener

3. *Liveliness,* the sense of the persistence of sound as heard during ongoing speech or music

4. *Reverberance,* the perceived lingering of sound following the cessation of music

5. *Echoes,* distinct and audible repetition of sound (generally undesirable and detrimental to clarity)

6. *Dynamic range,* the ability to experience both pianissimo passages with clarity and fortissimo tutti passages without harshness

7. *Envelopment,* the sense of being surrounded by sound

8. *Spaciousness,* the perceived width of a sound source, such as an orchestra (it sounds larger than it actually is)

9. *Warmth,* the tonal quality resulting from an abundance of low-pitched (bass) sound within a room

10. *Silence,* the total absence of continuous or intermittent extraneous noise

Each of these characteristics applies not just to the literal performance of music but also to the "community of sympathy" that we try to create on a college campus. Talaske explains that qualities of sounds result by distinguishing between the source, the path, and the receiver. . . .: "The secret lies within the path throughout the room!"[25] Every room in which there are at least two learners present holds the potential for sound education, and the applications extend far beyond the literal. This is why another of the spaces in which sound education takes place is the home of a professor, such as what Katherine Lemons described in her letter to Mary Bender.

Probably the most influential sentence in all of Parker Palmer's work is one he penned in *To Know as We Are Known:* "to teach is to create a space in which obedience to the truth is practiced."[26]

The original metaphor of space came from the writings of the desert fathers, particularly Abba Felix. Parker uses the desert as the image of openness and the monk's cell as the image of boundedness, both of which are essential to a good learning space. The other essential ingredient is hospitality. To bring the ancient practices of religious men and women into the public space of a pluralistic culture was one of Parker's great contributions to epistemology and pedagogy in the twentieth century.

One way in which openness, boundaries, and hospitality are brought together in Parker's books and practices is through silence. Again, music offers us new ways of knowing this truth: "Silence is never more audible than when the last sound of music has died away."[27] In silence, students and teachers alike find their voices and create community. They honor the "great thing," the truth that is beyond any single person's comprehension and yet can be known through loving. This is where the wisdom of the Quakers and the wisdom of the Mennonites come together, for without silence there could be no music. It is one of the most profound of the ten acoustical characteristics. A room conducive to learning needs to be capable of silence. A college that never ceases to emit sound will not be able to take advantage of intentional silence, without which sound loses its meaning. Spaces that that are conducive to silence and that magnify the human voice are spaces that invite the presence of wisdom.

Sound Leadership

If we recover the oracular voice in education and build soundscapes (literal and figurative) on our campuses but do not change our leadership, we will leave the promise of a recovery of sound unfulfilled. Preaching about the need for sound scholarship and sound spaces without committing ourselves to sound leadership will make little difference in the end.

The best leaders I know in higher education are searching for new and better ways to serve their communities. Thinking of sound, silence, and all the acoustical elements might help direct our paths. I was called to be president while on sabbatical leave from my position as an English professor at Goshen College. The prospect of applying the many ideas I had about education to a much larger classroom thrilled me. But there was so much I did not know, given the fact that I had never held a senior administrative position before. Coming from my own campus, working among colleagues and mentors, would have some benefits, but it would also mean being willing to take responsibility for making difficult decisions that were sure to displease people I cared about. Even if they respected my leadership, they would never be my friends in the same way again. And yes, I was the first woman to hold the role. Sometimes thinking about the risks made me break out in cold sweat. I had an enormous amount to learn. When I told my colleagues at the Harvard Seminar for New Presidents in 1996 that I was moving from professor of English on sabbatical to the presidency, I could see the ill-concealed disbelief on their faces.[28]

The longer I stay in the job, the more I marvel at the trust that was placed in me then. I was protected to some degree by my ignorance. Until then, I had never met a challenge that hard work, a vivid imagination, and lots of help from good friends could not overcome. I was sure the community was calling me. I felt my inner teacher telling me to take the risk. "Go." "Let go." "Listen!" "Learn!" were the voices I heard. Automatically, I reached for music. When I was presented to the community as the president-elect in April 1996, I began by striking a tuning fork in the key of E and holding it against a guitar used as a resonator. Though no one could hear the striking of the fork against my hand, they could hear the note when it was amplified through the chamber of the guitar. I brought my fears into the space of the circular sanctuary and committed myself to give all I had, to be one note willing to sing if the community were willing to be the amplifier, not only for my voice but for all our voices.

Leadership is sound only when it moves beyond the ego. Yet leaders are notorious for large egos. Many of us, if pressed, would have to admit that we are happy to see our picture in the paper with *President* written underneath. That's why we need to sing. Singing will teach us that our voice is just one—and nothing without the voices of others. It teaches us that we can make mistakes and recover. It teaches us to match our voice with the ones around us. It teaches us the benefit of sitting next to a strong alto or tenor or bass if we want to learn our part. It takes us to a place we cannot find alone or by some other means. It also readies us for the moment when we need to sing out alone, and sing out strong. It teaches us that we get this strength not from our own effort but by trusting in the voice that made every living thing—the voice that spoke the world into existence and sustains it note by note, voice by voice:

> No storm can shake my inmost calm
> while to that Rock I'm clinging[29]

NOTES

1. Attali, J. *Noise: The Political Economy of Music.* Minneapolis: University of Minnesota Press, 1985, p. 3.

2. Twain, M. *The Adventures of Huckleberry Finn.* New York: Bedford Books, St. Martin's Press, 1995.

3. Palmer, P. J. *Let Your Life Speak.* San Francisco: Jossey-Bass, 2000, p. 45.

4. Palmer (2000), p. 46.

5. Palmer, P. J. *To Know as We Are Known.* San Francisco: Harper San Francisco, 1993, p. xi.

6. Lowry, R. "How Can I Keep from Singing?" In *Hymnal: A Worship Book.* Scottdale, Pa.: Mennonite Publishing House, 1992, p. 580. (Originally published 1860)

7. Clayton, W. "Come, Come Ye Saints." In *Hymnal* (1992), p. 425. (Originally published 1846)

8. Stephen Webb, associate professor of religion at Wabash College, first suggested the idea of "soundscape" in contrast to "landscape" in an essay, "The Size of a College and the Sound of a Voice," published electronically Dec. 13, 2002, in *LiberalArtsOnline*, 2(11). He wrote, "Colleges are, in a way, an architecture of sound, designed to promote verbal exchanges. Their soundscape is every bit as important as their landscape."

9. I have described this experience more fully in the essay "The Miracle of the Three Plowshares." In *Godward: Personal Stories of Grace.* Scottdale, Pa.: Herald Press, 1996, p. 15.

10. Quoted in *Prayers of Those Who Make Music* (David Philappart, comp.). Chicago: Liturgy Training, 1995, p. 17.

11. Weil, S. *Waiting for God.* New York: HarperCollins, 1951, pp. 123–124.

12. "William Wordsworth." In M. H. Abrams (ed.), *The Norton Anthology of English Literature* (6th ed.), vol. 2. New York: Norton, 1993, p. 286.

13. The term *Anabaptists* continues in present usage to describe distinctive theological emphases on peace, justice, community, service, and simplicity—quite similar to distinctive Quaker values—but perhaps more rooted in a strong Christological tradition. It also is used as an inclusive term for all groups who trace their roots to the radical reformation: Mennonites, Amish, Church of the Brethren, and Hutterites.

14. Wagner, S. "A Cappella." In *Evening Chore.* Telford, Pa.: Cascadia Publishing House, 2005.

15. In a performance of Bach's *St. John Passion* at Goshen College on April 4, 2003, the evangelist sang "it is fulfilled" as the story of the crucifixion was told in music. A member of Apollo's Fire, a Cleveland chamber orchestra that plays with baroque-era instruments, was so moved that she wept, even as she stroked the strings of the gamba. The audience wept with her.

16. Benzon, W. *Beethoven's Anvil: Music in Mind and Culture.* New York: Basic Books, 2001, p. 44.

17. William Benzon, lecture at Goshen College, Apr. 12, 2003.

18. E-mail from Benzon to author Showalter, Apr. 28, 2003.

19. Morton, N. *The Journey Is Home.* Boston: Beacon Press, 1985, pp. 55–59.

20. Dillard, A. *Pilgrim at Tinker Creek.* New York: HarperCollins, 1974, p. 34.

21. Boyer, B. *Scholarship Reconsidered: Priorities of the Professoriate.* Princeton, N.J.: Carnegie Foundation for the Advancement of Teaching, 1990, pp. 15–25.

22. Showalter, S. H. "Conclusion: The Life of the Mind as a Life of Service." In D. W. Zuercher (ed.), *Minding the Church*. Scottdale, Pa.: Herald Press, 2002, p. 259.

23. Letter from Katherine Lemons to Mary Eleanor Bender, Jan. 29, 2001, quoted by permission.

24. Lemons to Bender.

25. Richard Talaske, FASA, acoustics consultant, in "Understanding the Qualities of Concert Hall Acoustics," a pamphlet published by the Talaske Group, Inc., Consultants in Architectural Acoustics and Audio Systems Design, p. 2.

26. Palmer, P. J. *To Know as We Are Known*. San Francisco: Harper: San Francisco, 1993, p. 1.

27. Picard, M. *The World of Silence*. Chicago: Regnery, 1989, p. 27.

28. Showalter, S. H. "The Call." In Mary Swartley and Rhoda Keener (eds.), *She Hath Done a Good Thing*. Scottdale, Pa.: Herald Press, 1997, p. 170.

29. Lowry, R. "My Life Flows on." In *Hymnal: A Worship Book*. Scottdale, Pa.: Mennonite Publishing House, 1992, p. 580.

REFLECTIONS

○
───────

Marcy Jackson
codirector of the
Center for Teacher Formation

I first came to know Parker through participation in a weeklong retreat he led for Kellogg Fellows and their significant others. I was an "other" and probably approached the retreat from that perspective. But what I noticed right away was how Parker extended welcome and hospitality in such a way that there really were no others. We were simply a circle of equals, women and men seeking, questioning, and learning together in solitude and community. After relaxing into that space of hospitality and trust, I noticed something more. I felt as if I had come home—home to myself first of all, but also home to a way of working, being, and leading that was modeled with such integrity and compassion by Parker. I knew then that I wanted to embody this kind of leadership in my own work.

After the retreat I came to know Parker as a friend. The theme of friendship weaves through much of Parker's writing. He speaks of friendship and love as the basis for vocation, and how his best work has been done in the company of friends. As codirectors of the Center for Teacher Formation, Rick and I work with Parker to develop and lead formation programs, in education and within other serving professions. This essay celebrates the threads of vocation, integrity, trust, and love woven through our friendship and shared work.

Rick Jackson
codirector of the
Center for Teacher Formation

After seminary, my good fortune was to begin work at the University of Minnesota YMCA, where students and faculty met in community service and weekend retreats to reflect on the deeper lessons of social activism. I loved this combination of action and contemplation, especially with young adults whose questing and questioning attitudes were so courageous. Early in my U-Y years I "met" Parker Palmer through an essay titled "Campus Ministry: A Pastoral and Political Vocation." I was struggling to maintain the tension between two seemingly opposite roles—political activist and pastoral counselor—in the midst of a university culture that kept them apart. Parker's essay held the inner life of mind and spirit and outer life work and service in cocreative, paradoxical relationship. The vocation of campus minister, Parker suggested, was to profess wholeness, proclaiming and calling forth all dimensions of being human. The uniting of pastoral and political roles posed the image for my lifework.

THE THREADS
WE FOLLOW

Marcy Jackson and Rick Jackson

THE WAY IT IS

There is a thread you follow. It goes among
things that change. But it doesn't change.
People wonder about what things you are pursuing.
You have to explain about the thread.
But it is hard for others to see.
While you hold it you can't get lost.
Tragedies happen; people get hurt
or die; and you suffer and grow old.
Nothing you do can stop time's unfolding.
You don't ever let go of the thread.

—William Stafford[1]

BELOVED POET WILLIAM STAFFORD wrote this poem in August 1993, the month of his death at age seventy-nine. Here was a man at the end of his life still contemplating and trying to explain to himself—and others—the significance of the thread he followed and the vital necessity of holding on to it. The thread represents a "lifeline," a connection to one's deepest sense of self and truth. For him, this was simply how things work. There's no need to quarrel, or quibble about it; it's just "the way it is."

We too have seen this manifest in our own lives and work. Not that there's just one thread; there are *threads* we follow—sometimes consciously, many times unwittingly. Sometimes it seems the thread is following us rather than the other way around.

It may be easier to perceive the threads of our lives in retrospect—the perspective of age allowing us the long view and serving to highlight the contours and junctures of our life's journey—but our threads are at work in us and through us at every stage of our lives. There is a trajectory to our lives, if we take the time to pay attention to it. Paying attention can make all the difference in living a conscious, compassionate, and committed life—a life with meaning and purpose. This is not simply self-serving or just a nice idea. We desperately need people and leaders in our world who demonstrate greater consciousness, extend compassion even in the harshest situations, and have the capacity for sustained commitment when the going gets tough.

In our fragile and fractured world, it is all too easy to imagine that our lives are like the small silver balls in a pinball machine, initially sprung with promise but then at the mercy of all manner of obstacles and distractions, propelled by nothing more than dumb luck and random events. Our experience affirms that something much different is at play. We each have the opportunity and responsibility to participate in the unfolding of our life, and the sense we make of it. In an article on personal renewal, John Gardner affirms personal responsibility for finding meaning in this way:

> Meaning is not something you stumble across, like the answer to a riddle or the prize in a treasure hunt. Meaning is something you build into your life. You build it out of your own past, out of your affections and loyalties, out of the experience of humankind as it is passed on to you, out of your own talent and understanding, out of the things you believe in, out of the things and people you love, out of the values for which you are willing to sacrifice something. The ingredients are there. You are the only one who can put them together into that unique pattern that will be your life. Let it be a life that has dignity and meaning for you. If it does, then the particular balance of success or failure is of less account.[2]

Threads of Vocation

A common thread in our professional lives has been working with others who are sometimes on the margins, who are hurting in one or many aspects of their lives, who haven't had much encouragement or many opportunities to find their place in the world. In our early professional roles (for Rick, youth worker, YMCA program director, nonprofit executive; for Marcy, bereavement counselor, child and family therapist, tribal mental health counselor) we felt very connected to those with whom we were working, as we witnessed and cheered their steps toward healing, wholeness, independence, and accomplishment. For some, progress was hard won; for others simply staying alive was a victory to be celebrated. In doing this work, we often struggled to maintain our own bearings, stay hopeful, be of use.

As we embraced challenging and rewarding work, and as we experienced joys and tragedies particular to our own life journeys, we discovered the importance—and necessity—of finding ways to sustain ourselves, our passions and commitments. This too became a thread we followed! We sought opportunities for solitude and silence in order to listen within, to pay attention. We set aside time for regular connections with friends and colleagues to explore our questions, stories, and callings. We found ways to give voice to unlived parts of ourselves through journaling and creative expression, to let the used-up parts take a rest while discovering that we are more than what we do. None of this is particularly earth shattering, and yet it made all the difference in our ability to continue working in difficult situations, to keep doing work we cared deeply about.

Our early vocational threads and the recognition of what it takes to stay healthy, whole, and hopeful naturally led us to want to work with others committed to challenging but important work in the world. Since 1996, we have had the privilege of creating opportunities for personal and vocational renewal for some of our most self-sacrificing public servants: teachers. Under the guidance of Parker and using an approach to personal and professional renewal called "formation," the program Courage to Teach (CTT) was launched. As codirectors of the Center for Teacher Formation, charged with developing and expanding CTT programs, we serve a network of Courage to Teach facilitators who work with teachers and leaders in their own communities.

Courage to Teach

Living with greater consciousness, self-awareness, and integrity is a worthy goal for any human being. But for those who dedicate their lives in service to our children as teachers, principals, counselors, and early childhood educators, it is critical. These are the people who are influencing and shaping the hearts and minds of our future, the ones whom we expect will meet the learning needs of each and every child, to leave no child behind. Yet we have been leaving teachers behind at almost every turn, most importantly in terms of respect and understanding of what they do and the enormous role they play in our society.

When asked, many teachers say that all they have ever wanted to do is teach (one of their lifelong threads) and to make a contribution to the world, one student at a time. So the pain in the heart of a teacher who feels alienated from his or her work can be overwhelming. The deforming forces in public education are legion: underfunded schools and crowded classrooms, elected officials who have a political agenda to "fix schools" but who seldom talk to educators, family and community dysfunctions that should be addressed elsewhere but get played out in schools, and isolating working conditions in which adults rarely have time to speak with other adults.

Over the years, we've listened to the poignant and compelling words of many teachers and educational leaders as they've struggled to stay committed to their chosen vocation:

> Friends urge me to move to an "easier" school, but I want to find a way to cope with the stress and enable myself to continue reaching out to these kids. I know that there are people out there who can do this and thrive. I want to be one of them. (Middle school teacher, fifteen years' experience)

> Is not quality public education the foundation of true democracy? Are not children our future? Do we really value all children? If public education is going to be a true road to a meaningful life and healthy community membership, we must nurture educators so they do not despair beneath overwhelming demands, but maintain an inner gyroscope and persevere. We all need to be more attentive to the needs of the soul—our own and that of children. Without this deeper perspective, all the well-meaning reforms will wither along with the teaching staff. (Elementary school teacher, eighteen years' experience)

To address this critical time in public education—and the challenge of finding and keeping good teachers, principals, and superintendents—we need to provide sustained and meaningful support for educators so that they can continue to show up fully day after day to do the very hard work of teaching, leading, and investing in our children's future. Courage to Teach was designed for just this purpose.

Courage to Teach invites teachers and leaders to explore the inner landscape of their lives as educators by going back to the deep well of their calling. Each Courage group consists of twenty to thirty educators who gather for quarterly weekend retreats over a one- or two-year period.[3] In large-group and small-group conversation, and in times of solitude and reflection, participants explore aspects of their own wholeness and professional identity and integrity by reflecting on their personal and vocational journeys. Through introduction of poetry, teaching stories, evocative questions, and insights from various wisdom traditions, they begin to reclaim their passion for teaching and find greater balance in their lives. This approach to personal and professional development, which we call "formation," involves creation of a quiet, focused, and disciplined space—a circle of trust—in which the noise within us and around us can subside and we can begin to hear our own inner voice. Both a personal and a communal process, formation invites educators to reclaim their wholeness and clarity of vocational commitment, and it encourages connections between nurturing a teacher's spirit and revitalizing public education.

As with many things, talking "about" something is entirely different from the lived experience of it. But perhaps this description of an opening circle in a CTT retreat can offer a glimpse into the depth of speaking and listening that occurs—the kind of sharing that nearly all participants report to be utterly unique in their years of experience as educators.

Twenty-five teachers and administrators sit in a circle, giving their full attention as an elementary teacher speaks passionately, and poignantly, about her love for her students and her commitment to reach each and every one of them. She goes on to tearfully describe the personal toll this is taking on her own life: creeping guilt at not having enough time or emotional energy to give to her own family, bone-deep exhaustion, nonstop worrying about the safety of some of her students, the weariness of facing an always burgeoning mountain of papers and projects to grade, a sense of increasing isolation from friends and colleagues because there is simply no more to give. The listeners sit quietly, respectfully, as she finishes, each reflecting on their own version of her story.

The next teacher speaks of the debilitating effects on the morale of his colleagues as more and more pressure is being placed on him and his school to raise test scores at his school, or else! Teaching was once a labor of love, but it is now becoming an onerous task as the nearly singular focus on standardized testing dominates all communications among faculty and administrators. More silence.

The next person to speak, a newly appointed principal, describes her recent attempts to mediate an explosive situation involving a student, his parents, and a teacher. Amid helping the parties work through their threats and misunderstandings, she has become aware of the heavy burden of responsibility she carries. Yet in telling her story, she is also recognizing a growing confidence and inner sense of authority, grounded not in her role as a new principal but in her personal integrity. On it goes, each person relating stories and examples of how their complex journey as teachers and leaders has unfolded since the last time they were together, a few months ago.

Creating and holding a trustworthy space—in which honest and vulnerable sharing such as this can occur—looks deceptively simple but is actually complex and demanding. You'll notice in this brief description that no one rushed in to save, or fix, or "problem-solve." Instead, each person's sharing was simply heard and respected. The kinds of issues and dilemmas raised by these educators are not unusual or extraordinary to people working in schools these days. What is unusual is the opportunity to share their fears, burdens, and humble successes with trusted colleagues who take time to listen and receive them.

Threads of Integrity

The word *integrity* comes from the Latin adjective *integer,* meaning whole or complete. In the ancient world, the word *integrity* was used in the garment industry. A piece of fabric that was woven from one end to the other as a *whole piece* of cloth—a seamless garment—was said to have integrity. But when we apply this to a human life, "whole" or "complete" does not mean perfect or flawless. Implied in the word is the notion of integration, of the less developed or desirable parts of ourselves with the more vibrant or gifted parts. It is in the process of recognizing and attending to all the parts, and how they come together to serve the whole, that the true beauty of the overall fabric of our lives, and of a work, is created.

For teachers, the importance of integrity can't be overstated. Another word for integrity is "authentic." Students know right away when they are being led and listened to by an authentic human being. In the profession of teaching, the messenger and the message are both crucial components of the learning exchange. Educational researcher Sam Intrator describes teachers as "the pivot on which all else swings . . . the pivot on which everything turns in American education." He goes on to say: "Teachers are the ones who set the tone, they're the ones who decide what's taught, they're the ones who forge the relationship. . . . So as we think about what we need to do in terms of improving schools, to make those schools places that inspire kids to learn better and think more broadly, we need to focus on those adults who are the pivot—the teacher."[4]

> Students respect integrity and can sense hypocrisy. To be a valuable and effective teacher, one must know oneself. . . . Courage to Teach helped me gain and celebrate that knowledge. It is essential to be willing to share enough of yourself and to admit areas where there are challenges—to be able to teach from the heart. Students certainly respond and learn more from that safe space. (Elementary school teacher, nine years' experience)

> Courage to Teach is not a Band-Aid. It deals with the very core of the issue of education: the soul of the teacher that touches the soul of the student. Without caring for the heartwood of a tree, the branches will fall off, the bark will peel, and the roots will rot. Without caring for the soul, the teacher will become frustrated and ineffective, and the students will fail. (High school principal, twelve years' experience)

In establishing the Center for Teacher Formation, our instinct was to commit to stewarding a "chain of integrity"—from the process of preparing new CTT facilitators to maintaining the quality of Courage to Teach and the essence of the formation approach, to the way we organize to do business and participate in a growing movement. As the number of facilitators and programs has grown, and our work has become better known within education and increasingly in other serving professions, we are urged to "ramp things up" and "bring them to scale" (using the current vernacular for all-too-many school reform initiatives). This may be an understandable external response to success, but our efforts continue to be guided by the qualities and conditions that are foundational to the integrity of this work. Growth with integrity demands that each new part be in service of the whole.

The process of formation is hard to articulate—particularly in the world of education that so wants to box it in, create a rubric for it, and develop a curriculum around it. This lack of easy categorization leads people to compare it to what they already know. In some ways, it is easier to say what this *isn't* than what it *is*. There are many approaches that are "kindred" in some way, but in and of themselves they do not adequately or accurately define the formation approach. Here is a list describing some notions of formation work:

- *Not team building,* though with time and trust a strong sense of community naturally emerges in a Courage circle

- *Not therapy,* though this approach results in greater self-awareness and self-acceptance for participants, sometimes accompanied by a sense of deep inner "healing"

- *Not diversity work,* yet greater understanding of "otherness" in all its manifestations, and a deeper appreciation of the richness of differences, is a hallmark of most retreat groups

- *Not a vision quest,* though the journey of the inner life often leads to greater clarity of vision and purpose

- *Not a meditation practice,* though the practice of being together in silence fosters mindfulness and contemplation

- *Not a spiritual smorgasbord,* offering a chance to dabble in a range of spiritual/psychological practices; yet words of insight and inspiration from diverse wisdom and spiritual traditions enrich our communal dialogue on some of life's most challenging questions

- *Not creativity training,* though the creative spirit is released when individuals begin to claim their gifts and act on what brings them joy
- *Not leadership training per se,* yet by offering multiple invitations and experiences for people to "author" their own lives they begin to take greater responsibility and leadership in their lives and work
- *Neither* "sage on the stage" *nor* "guide on the side," but rather something altogether different: a kind of "being" and "leading" that emerges from the inside out

Much of the essence of formation work is embodied in the subtleness of facilitation that helps create a trustworthy space within which others may explore their own inner landscape. This understanding has led us to develop a thoughtful discernment process regarding selection of facilitators, and to pay careful attention to how we prepare and mentor formation facilitators. It is their integrity and capacity to create a safe and hospitable space that invites the process of transformation for others.

Teachers and leaders, CTT facilitators, educational researchers, and doctoral students are increasingly giving voice in word and print to CTT's importance and lasting impact on participants. Parker's inestimable written contributions, along with others, continue to enlarge the discourse within education and other professions about the importance of renewing vocational vitality and honoring the "person" in the profession.[5]

Threads of Trust

While leading our initial CTT retreats, we quickly learned that not only was it necessary to trust ourselves and each other; we also needed to deeply trust that the individuals with whom we were working had the capacity to slow down, quiet themselves, and listen within—to believe that the voice of truth within, the "inner teacher," will in fact show up if given the time and space to do so.

Facilitating and creating safe spaces that welcome the soul, and inviting people into tender and sometimes risky territory, is only possible if there is a foundation of trust. When you ask people to speak honestly; to be vulnerable; to look at fears and failures, hopes and dreams that are closely held but rarely see the light of day, it is trust that shows the way. A high school principal described the power of risking a conversation about fear and failure with peers and colleagues in a Courage retreat:

> A poem about fear led to an amazing conversation about the fears in our own lives. Very capable and accomplished professionals shared

openly and honestly. People with multiple graduate degrees and years of experience and awards in their professions shared their fear of being inadequate. Their fear of failure. Their fear of letting people down. Sharing that vulnerability, in a way I still don't completely understand, helped to strengthen all of us. But somehow knowing we were all indeed quite human and quite apprehensive about being able to meet the challenge of educational leadership actually made us bold to keep on trying. (High school principal, twenty-six years' experience)

People are often initially skeptical and fearful. They want to explore their lives and work in depth, yet they are reticent to do so with "strangers." (This is why the ground rule that no one can be *sent* to these retreats— they must choose it for themselves—is so important.) Additional guidelines, sometimes called "touchstones" or "boundary markers," begin to establish norms for how we will be working together. The most important one is the fundamental principle of "no fixing." Instead of problem solving, we practice listening with care and without judgment to ourselves and others in the circle. Rather than share our advice or good ideas, we ask honest, open questions to help each other discover our own inner truths. In practice, this is a much more daunting challenge than it may seem. Another essential boundary marker is that participation in every portion of a formation retreat is invited but not demanded. Parker frames it this way: "This is not share or die!" It's hard for people to believe that we trust them to know best what their own needs and limits are.

In a world where there are so many fearful and untrustworthy places, a space where trust can be restored, modeled, and experienced can be profoundly healing. Time and again it has been our experience in retreats that when people are trusted (by us initially, and by the group as time goes on) they begin the harder task of trusting themselves, which in turn leads to greater trust with their colleagues, students, and administrators. An assistant superintendent (and CTT alum) believes development of trust, individually and collectively, to be one of the most important outcomes of this work:

The teacher in the classroom and the principal at the head of the teachers are going to set the climate of building relationships. Trust between teacher and student and between teacher and principal has to be there in order to be successful. If you look at the schools that are really successful, it's not only about good strong instruction, it is about what happens to the people in that building. If you're not healthy inside yourself, if your staff is not healthy and your children don't believe that they are being loved and cared for as individual children, then you are not going to be able to achieve those goals of accountability no matter how you try to improve your instructional program. (Assistant superintendent, thirty years' experience)

A recent study of school reform calls trust the "connective tissue" that holds improving schools together. Documenting the critical role of "relational trust" in improving student achievement, the researchers contend that "the fulfillment of obligations entails not only 'doing the right thing,' but also doing it in a respectful way, and for what are perceived to be the right reasons."[6] The researchers found that when trust is high there is a more vibrant and healthy school climate, and the effectiveness of a school's central endeavor—teaching and learning—is greatly increased.

Numerous research studies have documented that Courage to Teach makes a lasting contribution toward good teaching and learning by helping teachers and educational leaders develop more trusting relationships. Teachers who once hunkered down in their classroom behind closed doors as a way to cope with the stresses and dysfunction in their school are more willing to assume a leadership role to create a healthier school climate. Most important, they are more fiercely determined to seek and support the innate gifts within each of their students. Through their own inner work, they have found renewal for themselves and compassion for their students and colleagues.

Threads of Love

The title of a hit song by Tina Turner asks an important question: "What's love got to do with it?" In the world of education, love has a whole lot to do with it—from the love of a certain subject or body of knowledge to the love of creating moments of discovery, learning, and engagement around that subject, to the love of individual students even when they sometimes act unlovably. Teachers use such words as "passionate," "wholehearted," and "being on fire" when they describe themselves teaching at their best. For many teachers and school leaders (we would argue, the best of them), the business of education is not just about the mind; it's a matter of heart.

We recently received a letter from a teacher who was in our first CTT group (1996–1998), who had been struggling with a decision whether to continue teaching in a diverse, urban school:

I remain convinced that love is the essential ingredient in all worthwhile endeavors and am so grateful it remains in the core of my teaching. I so often feel both humbled by the task and in awe of each young child—so many walk a path wrought with challenges too daunting, yet what else can they do?

Chip Wood, a nationally respected educational leader and writer, and also a CTT facilitator, has spent his life trying to improve education for *all* children. Looking back over four decades of work in public schools, and now returning to service as the principal of a poor, rural elementary school in western Massachusetts, he observes:

> I had spent years as an educational reformer creating structures to help build understanding in the multicultural community of our public schools, to help educators teach social skills together with academics . . . in Courage to Teach circles, it became clearer to me that without time for reflection in busy school settings there is less possibility for awareness of others, for empathy, love, forgiveness. And without such awareness there can never be peace.

Many educators come into Courage circles feeling as if their heart has been trampled, their love of teaching and desire to make a difference in a student's life betrayed by conditions and mandates that have turned life in school upside down. We have heard heartbreaking tales from teachers around the country that are essentially versions of the same story: the love that brought them into this profession is being wrung out of them by forces largely beyond their control and by people who pay little attention to their ideas or input about how things could be done differently. Over the years, we have seen an increasing level of despair and discouragement among educators coming into our groups. For us and for our facilitators around the country, this only reinforces our belief that creating circles of trust for teachers and school leaders is needed now more than ever.

Now a decade into our work with educators, we are hearing from people in other serving professions who are searching for ways to bring greater wholeness and vocational renewal to their organizations and professional communities. We remain committed to deepening our work in education, but we are also harvesting the lessons learned in creating and leading Courage to Teach as we respond to the growing interest in creating circles of trust within other professions.[7]

Weaving Threads

When we began working with Parker and Fetzer Institute staff (who generously sponsored and supported this work from the beginning), we were drawn by the promise of meaningful work that would contribute to the renewal of public school educators. We learned about the art and craft of formation through doing our own inner work and experiencing Parker's strong but gentle facilitation. Eventually, we set up four sites around the country to try out the Courage to Teach model that Parker piloted with Michigan teachers.

Parker gave each of us a tremendous gift by entrusting this emergent creation to our untested hands. Because of his confidence in us, we were able to rise to the opportunity presented to us. The "experiment" was successful; the efficacy and power of the formation process passed the test. We were awed and inspired by the transformation we witnessed in our first Courage to Teach groups. Each of us was experienced in other realms of professional and organizational development but had never encountered ways of working that fostered so much depth and richness, and that honored the soul and solitude of each person in the circle while surrounding us with a community of support and encouragement.

We have known Parker for more than twenty years, and we have worked closely with him during the past ten. Even though we have had the privilege of "putting wheels under his ideas," Parker has never imposed his own agenda on us. Instead, he has been steadfast in supporting our own clarity of selfhood and vocation. Over the years, we have grown a trusting and loving friendship, one that has led to much fruitful work. In partnership with Parker and Sharon Palmer, and numerous friends and colleagues around the country, we have served a common work that neither of us could have imagined on our own, let alone carried out. Together we have conspired in a range of cocreations, from retreats to book projects to forming organizational structures, all in support of the larger movement of countless good people who are dedicated to soulfully revitalizing their schools, communities, and professions.

In the beginning we didn't foresee, or imagine, the interweaving of threads, connections, trust—and love—that would develop over time. In retrospect, we now see how threads of love and friendship have been integral to the strength and vibrancy of the fabric of the work we have created together. In *The Prophet*, Kahlil Gibran writes that "work is love made visible."[8] So it has been for us.

NOTES

1. Stafford, W. "The Way It Is." From *The Way It Is: New and Selected Poems*. St. Paul: Graywolf Press, 1988.

2. Speech by John Gardner titled "Personal Renewal," delivered on November 10, 1990, to McKinsey & Company in Phoenix, Arizona.

3. Parker Palmer piloted the program with a group of Michigan teachers from 1994 to 1996. To build on the early foundations of this work, the Fetzer Institute established the Center for Teacher Formation in 1997 to develop, deepen, and expand Courage to Teach programs and formation work (for more information, go to www.teacherformation.org).

4. Interview with Sam Intrator, by the author, Nov. 2003.

5. See especially Parker Palmer's most recent book, *A Hidden Wholeness: The Journey Toward an Undivided Life.* San Francisco: Jossey-Bass, 2004.

6. Bryk, A. S., and Schneider, B. *From Trust in Schools: A Core Resource for Improvement.* New York: Russell Sage Foundation, 2002.

7. The Center for Teacher Formation prepares formation facilitators in education and other serving professions (including medicine and health care, law, philanthropy, nonprofits, and community leaders) through a program called Formation Facilitator Preparation: Creating Circles of Trust.

8. Gibran, K. *The Prophet.* New York: Knopf, 1923, p. 28.

REFLECTIONS

○
———————

Sally Z. Hare

Singleton Professor in Teacher Education
at Coastal Carolina University

A Kellogg fellowship in the early 1990s created the opportunity for
me to meet Parker Palmer. My mind goes back to the warm summer's
day in 1992 on Little St. Simon's Island, a small piece of heaven off
the coast of Georgia. Beginning my second year of the fellowship, I was
there to participate in a seminar on leadership and spirituality with
Parker and some other Kellogg fellows. I had no idea that this week
would change my life. Parker introduced me to the Quaker process of
the clearness committee, and I literally changed my path. I "undeaned"
from my position as dean of the Graduate School at Coastal Carolina
University, as I connected to the knowing that my birthright gifts were
incompatible with the hierarchy of higher education administrator.

A few years later, Parker invited me to join him and a few others in
implementing his vision for teacher formation. Now I have difficulty
telling where Parker stops and I start, as his teaching comes through
me and shapes my work in the world.

THE LEHRERGARTEN
A Vision for Teacher Education

Sally Z. Hare

I REMEMBER MY FIRST YEAR of teaching. I had wanted to teach for as long as I could remember. Playing school with the neighborhood children from the time I was five, I felt that I was born to teach. And yet, that first year in my own classroom, I felt overwhelmed and underprepared. The gap between what I had learned in my teacher education program and what I needed in the public school classroom (even one more than thirty years ago) was a huge chasm.

My undergraduate training taught me various teaching techniques and strategies as well as how to create lesson plans and bulletin boards, and even a bit of classroom management. I soaked up the philosophy and the theory, and I loved the curriculum and methods courses. However, I still felt so uncertain and vulnerable in the sea of seven- and eight-year-old nonreaders assigned to me, the new teacher, that I left at the end of my first year to return to graduate school. There I learned only more theories and techniques, which did little to assuage my sense of being inadequate and alone in the classroom. My experience still holds true today: most teacher education programs focus on techniques and strategy, educational philosophy and theory, skills and assessments, with little attention to the inner resources that teachers need to survive in the profession.

I am deeply troubled by the desperation I see among today's new teachers, not to mention the sheer discouragement and seeming loss of heart among the experienced teachers. The distressing statistics show a record number leaving in the first five years of their careers, and many veteran teachers taking early retirement. All across the country, we are facing a critical shortage of teachers.

Our linear model of teacher education is inadequate to meet the daily needs of and demands on today's teachers. We train teachers to work with a particular subject or grade level, with little attention to the cyclical nature of human growth or the interconnectedness of subjects. We isolate the teaching of reading from the teaching of writing, American history from world geography; and we isolate teachers, often in one room with one age group. Little attention if any is paid to current research on the brain and emotional intelligence, or to all we are learning about how humans learn, to the importance of the learner's feelings of belonging to the larger community, to the need for lifelong learning in a world in which adults may change careers several times.

For too long, teacher education has been only about bringing the outer world of skills and techniques, of facts and content, into the preservice teacher, the person being prepared to teach. Certainly, competent teachers need knowledge and skills, but the good teacher is so much more than external influences and learned techniques. Teaching must be grounded in the teacher's identity and integrity, as good teaching requires the strength and openness to be who we are, in the public space of the classroom, the school, the community.

I urge us to consider another way of thinking about how teachers are prepared for their important work, how they gain the inner resources to withstand the pressures of the job, and how they find the literal courage to teach. I want to reframe the role of teacher education as one of creating a space in which the preservice teacher can learn to bring her own inner knowledge and resources, as well as skills and facts and techniques, out into the work of teaching.

I call my vision for such a teacher education program the *lehrergarten* (from German, *Lehrer,* teacher, and *Garten,* garden), a garden in which we nurture the seeds of future teachers; the teacher educators who prepare these teachers of courage are *lehrergartners,* "teacher gardeners." I have intentionally turned for guidance to the German philosopher Friedrich Froebel, who created the kindergarten, and his wisdom about the parallels in the laws of nature and human development. "We grant space and time to young plants and animals," he wrote, "because we know that, in accordance with the laws that live in them, they will develop properly and grow well. . . ."[1]

The Principles of the Lehrergarten

The preservice teachers who walk into my classroom are still idealistic about making a difference in the lives of children and teens, in spite of the negative messages they have already received about teaching. They know about low salaries, public distrust, and parents in crisis. Many of my students come with their too-busy lives, as they juggle jobs, families, and coursework. Yet they come with a sense of optimism and resilience, an inner hunger to work in the field of education, to prepare young people for the unknown future.

The core purpose of the lehrergarten is to develop good teachers with a strong sense of identity and integrity, excellent teachers who can sustain their career in education. A good teacher education program must provide the theory and foundation of education, the methods and techniques, the knowledge and skills, but in addition to the *what,* the *how,* and the *why* it must also develop the *who* that teaches.

1. We teach who we are. Craft, skills, and techniques are important and necessary to our teaching, but who we are, our seed of true self, is more important to how we teach than any method or procedure.

2. Learning is a lifelong cyclical process, not a linear one. The pace of learning is organic, requiring not only enough time but also attention to the cycles of work and rest, experiences and reflection, just as nature attends to the cycles of light and dark, winter and summer.

3. Every person has access to an inner source of truth, a source of strength and guidance that is the place of truth within us where we know the difference between reality and illusion. A vital relationship exists between inner clarity and sustaining our work in the world.

4. Creation of a quiet, focused, and disciplined space is essential for teacher education students to hear their own inner voice. The practices of reflection and journaling, silence and solitude are important elements in creating that space.

5. There is an interdependent, reciprocal relationship between teaching and learning. We learn best when we are teaching. When we are open to learning, the roles of teacher and learner are dynamic, with the student often becoming the teacher.

6. Opportunities for embracing paradox, for seeing the world as both-and instead of either-or, abound in education. The teacher who can move with ease between the poles of seeming contradictions holds a key to sustainability in the profession.

7. The relationship between education and community is vital. Preservice teachers need the opportunity to experience this relationship, develop the skill of dancing along the continuum of the individual and the community, and stand with grace at the intersection of education and community. Learning is social; perceiving oneself as belonging to a learning community makes a difference for learners of all ages.

With these principles as the foundation, I use my knowing of nature's seasons and the seasons of human development to find the appropriate metaphors to frame the lehrergarten.

The First Season: The Seed of True Self

In a recent introductory course, I taught Jackie (who was absolutely certain she wanted to teach young children but had no experience at all), Linda (who had worked in a day care center and was the single mom of a four-year-old), and Jason (a retired military officer who wanted to teach as a second career). During a semester in which they spent time in various settings with children, they explored questions of identity and vocational fit. Jackie came back from her first practicum assignment touched by the affection of the young children and enthusiastic about her experience. Linda, on the other hand, was questioning whether she had "what it took" after she tutored some children in a group home. Although she had dreamed for years of teaching young children, she felt overwhelmed by the emotional neediness of these nine-year-olds as she tried to help them with reading skills. Jason's first try at instilling military discipline in a middle school math class where he was serving as a mentor left him wondering about his career choice as well. In the first stage or season of teacher development, students can run the gamut of emotions from passion to fear, from vocational certainty to evident doubt—sometimes in the same day—as they explore the seed of true self.

The lehrergarten provides the space to explore the fears and doubts as well as the passion and commitment on the developmental journey to remembering and discovering true self. The self is the seed of all growth, inward and outward, planted traditionally in education in the autumn of the year, the time when nature is planting her own seeds of regeneration. True self is also relational, and in reconnecting with the self the individual also touches others in the community.

Liz entered my education course as a shy and withdrawn young woman, one I later learned was a victim of sexual abuse. In the same class, Mark was an outgoing extrovert who kept us laughing but rarely allowed himself to feel. For each of them, as well as the others in that group, boundary markers were crucial to creating the kind of space that honors and invites the inner teacher. Perhaps the most important marker is one that creates such clear boundaries that no one feels invaded. The space must be hospitable, with the absolute ground rule of "no fixing" each other. This countercultural concept means that teachers and students are in the program together in ways other than the usual mode of giving advice, criticizing, and judging. The practice of deep listening and asking open, honest questions are other markers of such a space.

The inner self is shy but resilient. To have the best chance of accessing our inner truth, we need a safe space. How do we prepare teachers so that

they can create such a safe space for their students? We, the lehrergartners, first have to create a space in which it happens for our preservice
teachers. The space must be invitational, always inviting people into relationship with the self and others, but never creating a situation that is
"share or die" (that is, an individual always has the right not to speak or
to reframe a question). For example, I invited Liz and Mark and the other
students to share what gave them energy or made them feel most alive.
Rather than moving around the room in typical linear fashion, students
shared as they felt moved to do so. I remember a period of silence, after
several students had given their responses of "walking in the woods" and
"being with my boyfriend" and "listening to music," out of which Liz
said, "I can't remember the last time I felt really alive." The supportive silence that followed seemed to invite Liz into a place of safety, a place from
which she could continue to find her voice.

In the early stages of the teacher education program, the safe space is vital
as teacher educators encourage and support preservice teachers in "remembering" who they are and recognizing their birthright gifts. Education at its
best teaches us to recognize what we love, what makes us feel most alive; it
teaches us to know how to be and do what we love in the world. "Many of
us became teachers for reasons of the heart, animated by a passion for some
subject and for helping people learn," Parker Palmer writes in *The Courage
to Teach*.[2] An important part of the teacher education program is to help
students remember those reasons of the heart, and to illuminate that passion. Recalling stories from childhood, remembering teachers who touched
us and significant moments in learning, and inviting in the heart as well as
the mind are all part of this process.

Reflection, listening to one's own inner teacher, is also critical. Journaling and other self-exploring practices are important in creating an environment for reflective practice, as is silence—learning to still the external
noises, even to quiet the internal noise so that students can hear their own
inner wisdom. A class journal can be fun, one that moves around the
room, so that students can share their observations and reflections, anony-
mously or by signing them and claiming authorship. The last ten minutes
of class is a good time for students to write an "exit observation," creating a safe place to express something they might not say aloud. But these
processes only work if the pace is slow enough for the participants to take
the time to hear themselves and each other.

Poetry and insights from various wisdom traditions, as well as stories
from students' own experiences, may open the space. What's important is
not just what the author or poet has to say, but what each participant hears
from her own inner teacher in response to the text. For example, I have used

May Sarton's wonderful poem "Now I Become Myself"[3] with students as a way into identifying their own paths to becoming themselves. Preservice teachers are often still struggling with issues of identity, of self-esteem, of establishing their own voice. They particularly identify with Sarton's word picture of wearing "other people's faces." I have also used Palmer's *The Courage to Teach* and *Let Your Life Speak,* as well as Sam Intrator's *Stories of the Courage to Teach,*[4] to encourage students to see how their own "small stories" intersect with the writers' stories, to see others' perspectives, and to evoke their own memories and truths through the words of others.

Another important component of the lehrergarten is the opportunity for preservice teachers to discern their vocation as they move through the program. The first opportunity comes during this season, as students become more aware of their own identities and gifts and also grow in their knowledge of the demands and requirements of teaching.

Jennifer, who was in my classroom last year, volunteered for a clearness committee, a process based on Quaker tradition. Her question was, "How can I be open to my students and still maintain control of the classroom?" The clearness committee, composed of five of her peers, gave Jen the space to work through for herself what was required of her as a teacher. In the safety of clearness committees, preservice teachers experience the paradox of better access to self by being in community, through the nonjudgmental, honest questioning and deep listening of other students and teachers. Dialogue with mentors and other teachers also creates intentional occasions for students to explore the questions of vocation and calling. Of course, the possible discovery from this dialogue that one is not called to teach is as legitimate and acceptable as affirmation of the calling.

The Second Season: Dormancy and Darkness

In the next season of the teacher education program, as in nature, there must be time for dormancy and rest. After the initial excitement and activity of landing in one's preservice site, these teachers-to-be often experience a crisis of confidence, of vocational choice much deeper and darker than the initial doubts of the first stage. Now that students are facing the busyness of a teacher's life and running up against impediments of school culture, a period of darkness is not uncommon. The lehrergarten honors this darkness as a natural stage in the preservice teacher's development and promotes the opportunity for stillness and silence, so necessary to hear one's true self.

The lehrergarten provides a space in which faculty and students learn to still the outer and inner noise in the practice of listening to their inner selves. Teacher educators have to move slowly into this space of quiet and reflection with students, allowing their students time to live through the stages of fighting the silence and on into tolerating it, to finally valuing it and even demanding it. After an intense practicum or service learning experience, teacher educators might create the space for silence, for slowing down, for remembering. Time in silence may expand after student teachers spend time in the classroom—and then return to the campus, to the sacred ground of silence in community, for reflection, for listening to their own inner teacher.

Our culture tends to deny that darkness and shadow are an inevitable part of life, of growth. But nature in winter knows the importance of darkness so that seeds can germinate. Embracing the joys of winter, the nights for "hunkering down," the gifts of "snow days" and hot chocolate and candlelight helps teachers understand balance, a critical notion for a sustainable career. When Roland struggled with whether he was making any difference with the boys he was mentoring in a fifth grade practicum experience, a walk in winter observing nature enabled him to perceive that what may look dead is often only dormant. He decided he needed more time with the ten-year-olds, and that he needed to give himself time as well. He came to value his time in building relationships with the boys, taking precious minutes to read to them and play Monopoly, instead of always supervising homework or reviewing multiplication tables. He shared with us that this new sense of time well spent came from an insight about his own joy when he gave himself permission to hunker down on a winter night with a good book instead of feeling that he always had to study. Journaling about how to winter through is one way for new teachers to realize how much they already know, what inner resources they already own.

Through their understanding of darkness as a vital part of nature, preservice teachers come to value darkness as playing a significant role in rest and renewal. They will be better prepared for the darkness to be encountered in the years ahead, darkness created by resistant colleagues and institutions, hard-to-reach students and defensive parents, and the inner shadows that we all carry. They will learn the value of their own inner resources, for only in the classical winter of the inward journey does one learn to winter through, to find knowing in not-knowing, to claim the faith that comes only through doubt.

The Third Season: The Flowering of Paradox

The next season is a time of renewal, spring in the natural world, the flowering that follows the death and darkness of winter. Education students at this stage have had opportunities for mentoring and tutoring, experiences with children and teens in various settings, even as they are taking more classes in theory, method, and curriculum. They come into my classes, excited and passionate, with questions about gaps between what they are learning at the university and what they are seeing in the classrooms, about "best practice" and "real life."

Student teachers need to explore many paradoxes, but especially those that they meet in teaching: the personal/professional, teacher/learner, cognitive/affective, individual/community, subjective/objective, and abundance/scarcity. Our responsibility in teacher education is to help teachers develop the ability to embrace paradox, as well as to build a strong foundation in content, methods, and theory. For example, exploring Einstein's statement that "everything that counts can't be counted, and everything that can be counted doesn't count" can yield insight into educational measurement and assessment; it can enrich teachers-to-be in their understanding of the importance of finding how to show what is happening with their students, to be accountable and yet maintain their authority, literally being the author of what is going on in their classroom.

The dance with paradox begins early in the teacher education journey, as students develop an awareness of the seeming contradictions that pervade the profession. As students have experiences in the classroom and grow in their skills in the craft of teaching, teacher educators can create the space to allow them to move more deeply into the complex relationship with paradox. The paradox of "we teach who we are" paired with best practices (methods and techniques that research has shown to be most effective) offers fertile ground for preservice teachers to acknowledge both their own gifts and the available knowledge and research. Through poetry and stories, through mentoring and service learning experiences, students can grow in their ability to turn what often seem to be external pressure or commands for excellence, diversity, and standards into their own internal choices for those same goals.

Another paradox for both the faculty and the students to grapple with is readiness (the idea that learning particular skills takes place at certain critical times in development) alongside lifelong learning (the idea that human beings never stop learning). As we moved from the Dark Ages to the Age of Enlightenment through the Industrial Revolution and the Nuclear Age to the Age of Technology to the Age of Information, embracing this paradox has become even more vital. Technology and access to information have changed the lives of students much faster than we have changed the ways of education. Learning how to learn and having a love of learning are essential for thriving in our world, but too often students learn the opposite in schools feeling the pressure for high test scores and quick fixes.

In claiming the natural cycles of our lives through the seasonal metaphors, we can open ourselves to knowing that death and life, darkness and light, are not opposites but go hand-in-hand in the manner of paradox. "I wouldn't give a fig for the simplicity on this side of complexity," wrote Chief Justice Oliver Wendell Holmes, "but for the simplicity on the other side of complexity, I would give my life." Embracing paradox is the simplicity on the other side of complexity. Most of us will need the rest of our lives to grow into the place of living comfortably in paradox, but it is of great importance to at least begin this understanding in our education of teachers. Preservice teachers must move beyond the deforming tendency of our culture to see the world as warring opposites—and begin to grasp and trust the wholeness of life, seeing how seeming opposites can actually complement, complete, and even cocreate each other.

The Final Season: Embodiment and Abundance

In the final season of the teacher education program, student teachers are exulting in the light at the end of the tunnel—and facing the scary reality of finding a teaching position and being on their own. Turning once again to nature, our guide is the summer, a time of embodiment, of fullness of being. In the human world, embodiment, writes Parker, means understanding that none of the ideas we have explored in the previous seasons can merely be thought; all of them must be lived.

Leigh Ann shuffled into my office one day near the end of her internship. She was one of my best students, with so many gifts that pointed to the rightness of teaching as her vocational choice. Her eyes filled with tears as she described a devastating student teaching experience; "Now I feel I've wasted four years and my parents' money," she concluded. Kristi had the opposite experience, as she gained confidence in her skills under the wise mentorship of an excellent cooperating teacher. For each of them, the lehrergarten must constitute the space to look at how she now takes her inner work into the outer world.

I often use the words of the poet Rilke with my students at this point, inviting them to ". . . have patience with everything unresolved in your heart and try to love *the questions themselves* as if they were locked rooms or books written in a very foreign language. Don't search for the answers, which could not be given to you now, because you would not be able to live them. And the point is, to live everything. *Live* the questions now. Perhaps then, someday far in the future, you will gradually, without even noticing it, live your way into the answer."[5] Faculty in the lehrergarten can best develop reflective practitioners by inviting students to reflect on the questions they are holding and on how to live into those questions in their lives as well as their work.

We want to create the space in which it is safe for preservice teachers to explore not only who they are, but who they are becoming, as they move toward their life after their teacher education program. Mentoring relationships are an important part of the lehrergarten, as students literally discover themselves in the eyes and words of others. Opportunities for community engagement and service learning are other ways for teacher education students to strengthen their ability to live at the intersection of education and community, as well as to embody what they have been learning.

Nature in summer is filled with abundance. Again the seasonal metaphors offer rich opportunities for deepening inner resources as the teachers-to-be recognize the abundance around them and experience gratitude. The practice of gratitude is a key to renewal, and to inner strength. The end of the teacher education degree program is another opportunity to affirm the cycle of beginnings and endings, the time for gathering the harvest after the seasons of growth.

In her poem "The seven of pentacles," Marge Piercy tells us that "this is how we are going to live for a long time: not always; / for every gardener knows that after the digging, after / the planting, / after the long season of tending and growth, the harvest comes."[6] After the harvest, nature starts over. Lehrergartners must commit to continued support of their graduates, acknowledging that learning and teaching are lifelong processes that don't end with graduation or certification. Opportunities for renewal and connection should be offered for alumnae and for graduate education students at least annually, perhaps in the form of a weekend Courage to Teach retreat or a summer weeklong program. Book groups or quarterly seasonal retreats could also offer a way for graduates to come together more frequently for mutual support and growth.

Piercy also exhorts, in "The seven of pentacles," to "Live a life you can endure." To do this, she advises: "Live as if you liked yourself, and it may happen: /reach out; keep reaching out, keep bringing in." The lehrergarten gives new teachers an experience of reaching out and reaching in, a chance to strengthen their identity and integrity as well as their knowledge of content, skills, and methods. It gives them the best chance of living a life in the classroom they can endure.

Notes

1. Froebel, F. *The Education of Man* (J. Jarvis, trans.). New York: A. Lovell and Co., 1885, p. 8.

2. Palmer, P. J. *The Courage to Teach*. San Francisco: Jossey-Bass, 1998, p. 17.

3. Intrator, S., and Scribner, M. *Teaching with Fire: Poetry That Sustains the Courage to Teach*. San Francisco: Jossey-Bass, 2003, p. 79.

4. Palmer, P. J. *The Courage to Teach*. San Francisco: Jossey-Bass, 1998; Palmer, P. J. *Let Your Life Speak*. San Francisco: Jossey-Bass, 2000; Intrator, S. *Stories of the Courage to Teach*. San Francisco: Jossey-Bass, 2002.

5. Rilke, R. M. *Letters to a Young Poet*. New York: Random House, 1984, p. 34.

6. Intrator and Scribner (2003), p. 101.

REFLECTIONS

———○———

Paul Batalden, M.D.
Center for the Evaluative Clinical Sciences
at Dartmouth Medical School

I first met Parker Palmer about twenty-five years ago in his book *The Active Life*. I held an adult discussion group to study what he was trying to say. Soon after, he led a weekend retreat for adult educators. What he opened then for me was the authenticity of the teacher-person I was.

I work as a professor and teach about improving the quality, value, and safety of health care. My work involves inviting the whole person who is the health professional to show up, and to keep showing up, in relationships with patients and in the contexts of interaction between people (professionals and patients).

Parker has helped me make sense of what I do as a teacher and as a physician deeply committed to forming and developing health professionals at all stages of their lives. Parker and I have laughed together. We have struggled together as we searched for our truths. He has taught me to appreciate poetry and the artistry of careful words. He has helped me appreciate the value of stillness and silence in the midst of busyness and noise. I deeply respect him and value his friendship.

David C. Leach, M.D.
executive director of the Accreditation Council
for Graduate Medical Education

I first encountered Parker Palmer by watching a videotape of his speech to the Institute for Healthcare Improvement in 1998. Parker spoke of the undivided life, the heart of social change, and the desire of good people not to attack institutional life but to prevent those institutions from falling into their most degraded state. The message connected with my personal search for wholeness as well as my desire to see the goodness of medicine restored.

Subsequently, I played the video to my board of directors, who were equally moved. I then called Parker and said, "You don't know me, but your work is becoming important to the profession of medicine. I call to ask permission to steal your name and the title of one of your books, to establish the Parker J. Palmer Courage to Teach Award for outstanding program directors." Thus began a dialogue that has deeply enriched my life.

There are about one hundred thousand resident physicians in the United States who are in active formation as physicians. Parker's work informs our own and has the potential both to enhance physician formation and to improve patient care.

THE INNER AND OUTER LIFE
IN MEDICINE

*Honoring Values, Relationships, and
the Human Element in Physicians' Lives*

Paul Batalden, M.D. and David C. Leach, M.D.

MEDICINE IS A COOPERATIVE and integrative art; it cooperates with the body's natural tendency to heal and integrates cognitive knowledge, technical skill, and ethical values in the particular context of a patient. The real "productivity" of medicine (yield for effort, investment) must be measured in ways that honor this cooperative and integrative nature of the work. Yet in recent years medicine has been framed as a narrow, "objectlike," piece-work productive activity, complete with attendant metrics ("cases seen per unit of time," "relative value units," "panel size," amount of revenue generated).[1] The inherent nobility of medicine—individual physicians applying their intellect and will to help vulnerable fellow humans—as well as the capacity of the profession to attract outstanding health professionals to work effectively toward the aim of improving patient care have both been compromised by this limited view of productivity in medicine. Health professionals, who come to their vocation as committed healers, are forced to measure their services by these narrow definitions rather than by their ability to connect and heal. They are forced to lead divided lives. Something they know deeply to be true is being violated, and they do not know how to correct it.

The message of Parker Palmer's work speaks to this inner but unspoken knowing and offers "space" to discover a path forward, from the strength of our profession as physicians.

In medicine, the quality of the care delivered is to some extent dependent on the quality of the relationships supporting that care. Yet relationships between the physician and patient, between the physician and colleagues, and between medicine and society—all marks of professionalism—have been flawed, and both patients and doctors have suffered because of it.[2] Patients hunger for a meaningful conversation with their physician; physicians, attracted to the rigors of medicine by idealism, also hunger for conversation with both colleagues and patients.

In the absence of these conversations, doctors and patients alike have become cynical and suspicious. No one feels empowered to change this context of care or work, but thoughtful medical leaders find the ideas Parker Palmer has explored (the courage to teach; the skills of the head, the hands, and the heart; life on the Möbius strip; the power released by living divided no more) a welcome tonic.

The relationship between Parker's work and our own constitutes the theme of this essay. It cannot be explored as deeply as it should be; yet this modest beginning is in order. Parker may be retiring, but his inquiry, his ideas, and their effects are not.

Connecting with Parker Palmer

On his way home from a retreat with Parker, a distinguished senior surgeon said, "I probably have about five years of competence left. I would like to devote the rest of my life to this [invitation from Parker to integrate the learning of the head, the hand, and the heart]. It is important. Medicine understands the skills of the head and hands but needs to know much more about the skills of the heart. If you tell doctors they need to develop skills of the heart, they won't understand; we need a new language to communicate these ideas."

After fours years of college and four years of medical school, physicians are awarded an M.D. degree; yet they all acknowledge that they lack the practical experience needed to practice independently. Hence they enter postgraduate training programs of three to seven years' duration. This phase of medical education is known as residency, or graduate medical education. Physicians in residency programs are known as residents or house officers, reflecting an earlier era when physicians lived "in the house" to be available to patients at all times. There are seventy-eight hundred residency programs in the United States that together house about one hundred thousand residents. Each program is led by a program director. In recent years, the program director turnover rate has risen to 20–30 percent annually. As part of a larger effort to understand and reduce the turnover in program directors, the ACGME (Accreditation Council for Graduate Medical Education) turned to Parker Palmer's work in teacher formation and his books and ideas. In 2001, ACGME established the Parker J. Palmer Courage to Teach Award, given annually to ten outstanding program directors who demonstrate some of Parker's ideals.

The first year yielded ninety nominees for ten awards, the second two hundred for ten awards again. Residents and colleagues identified quiet, effective physician-teachers who demonstrated the courage and power of "living divided no more." Descriptions in the nominating materials included language about fidelity to values, consistent support of classic traditions in medicine and yet enthusiasm for innovation, outstanding mentoring relationships, a focus on things human in patients and doctors, gentle courage, and resilience.

The February 2002 award ceremony provoked reflection about the importance of Parker's work and how many parallels existed between the work of the program directors and the teacher formation movement started earlier by Parker. This led to a retreat for the award recipients, the leadership of ACGME, and the leadership of the American Board of Medical Specialties in May 2002 at the Fetzer Institute. The group, facilitated by Parker, explored a patient case associated with medical errors. We learned to use new language as he led us to ask new questions: "Who was the moral agent?" "Isn't this really a failure of the heart?" Every physician in the room knew we were reflecting on and speaking with truth.

We also explored how we could become a community. Through silent meditation, reflecting together on the truths in poems, a clearness committee, and small group reflections, we all experienced the beauty and power of honest, attentive conversation.

After the retreat, some of us struggled with how to share the experience with others. Everyone was deeply moved by the time spent together, but no one knew how to describe it. We knew using words such as "moral agent," "skills of the heart," "courage," and "living divided no more" without some preparatory work would cause many physicians to disengage and marginalize the importance of the language and the ideas. We wondered how this could be made attractive to the best physicians—particularly those who identify themselves as hard-core physician-scientists.

We drew on Parker's invitation to pay attention directly to the inner life and to the connection of that life (or our souls) to the life of our outer lives (our roles). Rather than subject such an important thing to new and unfamiliar language that would invite classifying the message with the vagaries of faddish trends, we sought to root it firmly in established traditions that would open receptivity among our colleagues. Aristotle came to our rescue. We found that his concept of the intellectual virtues—particularly his concept of *phronesis* and the importance of integrating episteme, techne, and phronesis—gave us a way to convey this important message.[3]

Aristotle and Phronesis

*Phronesis is knowing exactly which rule to break and exactly
how far to break it to accommodate the reality before you.*
—John Kostis, M.D.[4]

*To teach is to create space in which the obedience to truth is
practiced.* —Abba Felix, Desert Father[5]

The real value that physicians add to society is found in their capacity to make good clinical judgments. Knowledge and skill are prerequisite but not sufficient. The "right thing to do" usually does not derive from general principles but rather from the particular details of the case before you. The virtue of phronesis is usually translated as "practical wisdom," and sometimes as "prudence." Aristotle defined it as "a true and reasoned state of capacity to act with regard to things that are good or bad for men."[6] He distinguishes it from all other intellectual virtues and from related intellectual qualities. Practical wisdom includes excellent deliberation, and excellent deliberation is correct practical thinking, which can quickly reach the correct conclusion from the correct premises by means of the correct inference.

Appreciation of the particulars of a given case toward the end of distinguishing the highest good for a patient is at the heart of good medicine. To see the particulars and the highest good takes true prudence and involves all human faculties, not just the intellect. Gathering the particulars of a given case involves a special kind of relationship with patients, not just checklists of questions. "Skills of the heart" are needed for this practical wisdom.

Parker has suggested that teachers create "space," set boundaries within which exploration and learning can safely occur, and offer "hospitality" for the exploration of what is not yet clear, known, or discovered. Coincidentally, the word *doctor* comes from the root word meaning "teacher." Physicians too can create a safe space where the patient's vulnerability is explored. A frame of inquiry can help open the space. The space is kept open by the physician who is able to listen carefully and formulate causal hypotheses in temporal synchrony with what the patient reveals. The physician offers respect and hospitality for the pursuit of discovering and exploring the underlying problem the patient presents.

When it is framed as necessary to enhance one's capacity to make good clinical judgments, the message in Parker's work becomes immensely attractive to physicians and other health professionals. It speaks to the idealism that drew people into medicine, yet it focuses on the practical applications that are so much a part of the daily work of patient care.

The Stories of Medicine

The physician's goal in the clinical encounter remains the discovery of what is going on with this particular patient. Events of body, mind, family history, and environment are reconstructed as the physician constructs the case. Scientific knowledge is necessary, logic is essential, but they take their place in an activity that is narrative and interpretive. The clinician must grasp and make sense of events occurring over time even as he or she recognizes the inherent uncertainty of this quasi-causal, retrospective, but unavoidable strategy. Piecing together the evidence from the patient's symptoms and the physical signs to create a recognizable pattern or plot is imprecise and subject to all the failings of historical reconstruction, but it is the best—the logical, rational best—they can do. This is not science, and if it is an art, it is a very particular kind. Those who know Aristotle's distinction recognize it as phronesis.   —Kathryn Montgomery Hunter[7]

Doctors' lives are filled with stories. Kathryn Montgomery Hunter has written eloquently about these stories. She helps us understand how young doctors learn to elicit the patient's story—a story of meaning. It is in the patient's story that the doctor learns about the illness and its burden in the life of the patient. Then the doctor must create a "doctor story." A doctor's story is a story to attract resources and to take action. It is a story that must be faithful to the patient's story, a story that other doctors can learn from. It is retold as the doctor mobilizes resources for the patient; it must allow the right resources to connect with the patient's need. The doctor's story—along with the patient's story—helps doctors remember and learn. Stories develop the language of the head, the hands, and the heart and their integration for doctors. Reconnecting the doctor's story with the patient's story—closing the communication loop—is fundamental to good patient care. When the patient understands the connection between his or her story and what the doctor's story and attendant "sense making" is all about, patient satisfaction and patient-physician agreement about what must be done is possible.

Each story is a story of sense-making for the persons involved. Getting good at stories—their formulation, their telling, and their analysis—is at the heart of good doctoring. Teaching about this involves modeling the practice and respecting the learner, what Parker Palmer calls honoring the "small stories and the big stories," the first efforts and the polished ones, the little "cases" and the big "cases."

Experienced physicians have a repertoire of stories, the particular details of cases they have seen, that contribute to their tacit knowledge and inform the explicit and more external knowledge accepted as best practice that is based on science. Life on the Möbius strip, living divided no more, and using deeply held inner truths to inform external behavior have a parallel in the physician's professional life: using tacit experienced-based knowledge informed by the stories of medicine to complement the limited technical rationality and incomplete science of medicine to produce the best judgments of medicine. It is the difference between the science of pneumonia and what to do when "Mary Smith" gets pneumonia. Always compatible with science but going beyond it, the art of medicine derives its power from stories, tacit knowledge, and the particulars of a given case. Regarding medicine, the "courage to live divided no more" means restoring the balance between art and science. It means listening to the informed heart, as well as the informed head.

Life on the Möbius Strip

> *Rodin does not "think about" his work, but remains within it: within the attainable . . . it seems that the ultimate "intuitions and insights" will only approach one who lives in his work and remains there, and whoever considers them from afar gains no power over them.*   —Rainer Maria Rilke[8]

The poet Rainer Maria Rilke invites us to the same "living divided no more" that Parker Palmer and Rosa Parks invite. Recall that it was Parks who launched the American Civil Rights campaign in 1955 when she decided to sit in the front of the Montgomery, Alabama, bus because she was tired of living divided: one life on the outside (a compliant, "lesser" black person required to move to the back of the bus) and another life on the inside (someone of value and self-respect).

Physicians often have conversations about the science of disease biology. Sometimes they converse about the science of clinical practice. Occasionally they link these two fields of rational inquiry. Rarely do they have conversations integrating these dimensions of their outer social role with their inner personal journey of meaning. Provoking dialogue about the physicians' lives on the Möbius strip is essential to their ongoing authentic formation as health professionals. These are the conversations that inform the daily work of offering and improving patient care. It is "life within the work"—not from afar, as Rilke observed—that is at the heart of gaining intuition and insight about that work. When we are able to act on the poet's insight, we recognize the limits of "knowledge alone" or "technique" or "decision rules" for practicing and improving medicine. We realize the truth and benefit of accepting Aristotle's invitation to integrate episteme, techne, and phronesis and Parker's invitation to integrate the learning of the head, the hand, and the heart—living on the Möbius strip.

Physicians are challenged by the question, "What do you make?" They frequently begin by answering, "Healthy patients." When that answer is further explored, they realize that they themselves actually make information, services, procedures, and a safe environment for patients seeking to limit the burden of illness in their lives. This is not external, object-creation work. This is work that depends on the person who is the physician. It is that physician-person who connects to the other person with the need. These are not only mechanical, rational transactions. They are composites that arise from the inner person of the physician and the outer scientist who is also the physician. It is life on the Möbius strip.

We gladly join those who honor Parker Palmer by faithfully seeking the truth we believe he is seeking. Parker's concepts and inquiry add value to medicine; they do not compromise the science of the profession. Rather, they help bring practical wisdom and prudence to the table, inviting restoration of the profession's capacities and appreciation of the abundant energy available for the formation of physicians as professionals.

NOTES

1. Reinertsen, J. L. "Leading Clinical Quality Improvement: The Tyranny of Piecework—Political and Practical Milestones, Part 1." *Healthcare Forum Journal*, 1994, *37*(4), 18–21, 23–24.

2. Husser, W. C. "Medical Professionalism in the New Millennium: A Physician Charter." Journal of the American College of Surgeons, 2003, *196*(1), 115–118; Kuczewski, M. "Developing Competency in Professionalism: The Potential and the Pitfalls." *ACGME Bulletin*, Oct. 2001.

3. Flyvbjerg, B. *Making Social Science Matter*. Cambridge, England: Cambridge University Press, 2001.

4. John Kostis, M.D., personal communication with David C. Leach, M.D., January 2002.

5. Palmer, P. J. *To Know as We Are Known: A Spirituality of Education*. San Francisco: Harper San Francisco, 1983.

6. Ross, D., Ross, W. D., Ackrill, J. L., and Urmson, J. O. (trans.). *Aristotle: The Nicomachean Ethics* (Oxford World's Classics). New York: Oxford University Press, 1998.

7. Hunter, K. M. *Doctors' Stories: The Narrative Structure of Medical Knowledge*. Princeton, N.J.: Princeton University Press, 1991.

8. Comments in a letter dated June 28, 1907, in Rilke, R. M. *Letters on Cézanne*. New York: North Point Press, 2002.

REFLECTIONS

○

Douglas Orr
president of Warren Wilson College

Parker's first intersection with my life's journey began when he spoke at the Presidents' Institute of the 1993 Council of Independent Colleges and recipient of the CIC Outstanding Service Award. He was being recognized for his significant contributions to independent liberal arts colleges.

In the course of his address, Parker, in his vintage self-deprecating humor, recounted his earlier Outward Bound experience of being frozen in place as he was perched precariously on the side of a cliff during one of the program's challenging "rappelling" exercises—a metaphorical perch that college presidents know all too well. After interminable nervous frozen moments, Parker recalled being asked by staff members on the ground, "Is anything wrong?" and replying in a high, squeaky voice, "I don't want to talk about it." As a fellow Outward Bound graduate, and one who gained profound teaching and learning lessons through the experience, I was determined to get to know this kindred spirit.

In subsequent years, his writing, teaching, friendship, and gentle poetic spirit have repeatedly inspired my own life and work. My wife and I attended his spiritual retreat at the Fetzer Institute for college presidents and spouses (in which poetry served as our daily text). Parker gave our preeminent annual lecture, which calls on the speaker to share life's vocational journey (it became the second chapter of *Let Your Life Speak*), led a faculty retreat workshop, participated with his wife, Sharon, in our college's summer music workshops, and served as our 2001 commencement speaker. In the process, I've given away a library's worth of copies of *The Courage to Teach* to each new faculty member and copies of *Let Your Life Speak* as a gift to graduates. His insights and guidance are a living part of our campus community.

○

A JOURNEY
OF THE HEART
Seeking the Questions Worth Living

Douglas Orr

*We are crossing the water our whole life through, we are making
a passage that we hope is true, every heart is a vessel every
dream a light, shining through the darkness of the blackest night.*
—Bill Staines, singer-songwriter, "Crossing the Water"

It's never too late to be what you might have been.
—George Eliot

THE PLACE WHERE I LIVE and work is a small college nestled amid 1,135 acres of forest, farm, and river, enveloped by the highest peaks of the Blue Ridge Mountains and part of the Swannanoa Valley, a place the earlier Cherokee inhabitants named, meaning "land of beauty." There is an old Cherokee tale that whenever a member of the community was despondent and lost in the darkness of life's passages, the tribal elder would pose several profoundly symbolic questions: "When in your life did you stop singing?" "When in your life did you stop dancing?" "When in your life did you stop being enchanted by stories, particularly your own life story?" "When in your life did you start being uncomfortable with the sweet territory of silence?"

There is not a culture in the world that doesn't include singing, dancing, and storytelling, or that doesn't honor silence. Singing, dancing, storytelling, and silence are the four universal healings held in the crucible of the arts; they were significant to the Cherokee in the literal and metaphorical sense. They believed that whenever you've stopped singing or dancing, or being enchanted by stories, or you feel uncomfortable with the sweet territory of silence, you have begun to experience loss of soul and spirit.

As those of us in higher education try to be faithful to the sacred trust of teaching and mentoring young people during their formative college years, we search for the relevant questions to guide their journey, quite aside from the steady barrage of information and simplistic answers. In many ways, the ancient Cherokee elders were the spiritual antecedent to those of us who try to probe the deeper meaning and questions within a liberal arts education. Certainly, the gifted wisdom keepers of today (Parker J. Palmer is among the best to grace our lives) are all part of the same family tree of such teachers.

Meanwhile, there is an alarming trend throughout higher education toward "white-collar vocationalism," which forsakes education for training and simply shapes young people to be cogs in an economic engine. It indeed corrupts the true essence of *vocation,* which stems from the Latin word for voice, as in a life's calling, rather than a goal one pursues.[1]

Our colleges and universities need to raise the basic questions of calling and selfhood, and thereby allow students to find the pathway to a life full of meaning and service in a free society.

A few years ago, Parker served as commencement speaker at Warren Wilson College. Commencement addresses these days are all too often formulaic, with a kind of seven-step set of answers to life in the "real world." Throughout commencement week, students everywhere are quizzed on the usual what-next questions. Parker summed up the typical litany: "What do you plan to do this summer?" "What do you plan to do next fall?" "What do you plan to do the next decade—or two or three?" "Just what is your plan for the long and awkward passage between graduation and Social Security?" It is an annual interrogation repeated by parents, grandparents, faculty, and college presidents, usually followed by a recommended sage game plan.

Parker cut across the grain and suggested to the graduates that they politely decline the well-intended inquiries: "It is too important a question to dishonor with a definitive answer. Tell them that, instead of looking for answers, you are looking for questions—questions that are worth living, questions that you can wrap your life around. . . . Since ten or twenty years from now the questions you choose to live will have become the shape of your life."[2]

The graduation ceremony was the culmination of these seniors' unusual educational experience. Warren Wilson College has a unique niche in American higher education, with a liberal arts curriculum, a fifteen-hour-per-week work program for each student that helps operate the college, an off-campus service-learning experience of one hundred hours for every student, an international academic field course, and a campuswide commitment to environmental programming and stewardship. It is an ambitious, time-demanding, value-centered program that tends to draw students nationally and internationally who possess a passion for bettering the world. The program challenges students to find their individuality within a community context. It also can draw a romanticized view of a kind of utopian, holistic educational nirvana. The fact is, such a multifaceted program is characterized by its "messiness."

Parker indicates one of the shadows through our inner journey is a fear of the chaos of messiness, and yet the insights we gain from these experiences lead to creativity, innovation, challenge, change, and empowerment.[3] Indeed, some of the most significant breakthroughs in the creative endeavors of humankind have occurred through such a rich, chaotic stew of inventiveness.

This full college program also represents a very active life that students attending Warren Wilson lead, and the critical need to find balance between action and reflection. This in microcosm becomes a secret to living a life that is fully engaged and alive; it calls to mind the paradox of opposites, the profound truths of the need for community and the need for solitude.[4]

Perhaps never in human history has this been a more daunting challenge. Yet a liberal arts college—with the reflection time of classroom study, readings, and the creative writing of senior letters—can be a good laboratory for finding such an equilibrium. This is especially true when work and service elements are part of the mix, not to mention other activities of college life such as athletics, theater, music, and socialization.

The required senior letters usually reveal that students have blossomed under this challenging mix of programs. Perhaps they are better able to continue a life's journey that is bound to have its share of messiness and chaos, its twists and turns, but always with a full measure of passion. I make it a practice toward the end of commencement to read a cross section of students' immediate plans for after commencement. (Yes, our students do fill out such a survey at commencement rehearsal.) It invariably is a rich tapestry of journeys of the heart: Peace Corps, school teacher, ecologist, VISTA, artist, trail guide, small business entrepreneur, Head Start, Americorps, homeless shelter staff, park ranger, musician, organic farmer, Witness for Peace, "something amazing," and of course graduate school and summer travel to the four corners of the globe. Therefore, when Parker posed some "questions worth living" such as the birthright gifts of service to others, beauty in nature, authenticity of self and life's amazements, these new graduates were already on their way.

Another lost art, thanks to the preoccupation with educational training that undercuts reflective learning, is a loss of a sense of the moment. Crossing the waters and shoals of life is made up only of moments, something that older cultures may understand better than our own. Most of these graduating seniors seem to have learned that lesson well. Graduating senior Mia Cohen shared this poem in her senior speaker comments:

And when you ask me what I'm doing after graduation
And I reply "Ask me after graduation"
It is only because I want to breathe in the sweetness of springtime
I want to taste this ripening strawberry
I want to walk across Dogwood
Sing at midnight at River Bend
Dance under the full moon
Sit under the canopy of trees in my hammock.

I want to be here now with all of you
Our teachers, even bosses, mentors, friends
This community
My mom, brother, friends, your families, our community
All of us, here right now—weaving together a web of life
Breathing together words that aim toward wisdom
In this valley of Swannanoa in the Appalachian Mountains
At Warren Wilson College
Home in ourselves.

If you see me today and ask me what I'm doing after graduation
And I whisper, "I'm not telling"
It's only because I want to taste these precious moments
And savor today here with you.

Yet the growing cross-currents of society pull us elsewhere: on a fast track to stay ahead of the next guy, for instant gratification in an MTV generation, and early economic achievement or fame. Sandy Astin, of the UCLA School of Education, conducts an annual survey of freshmen college students to test incoming college students' interests and values. When initiated in the 1960s, the survey indicated that students' first priority for attending college was to find meaning and purpose in life. A lower priority was maximizing opportunity for economic well-being. By the 1980s, with the "me generation" students, these priorities reversed and have generally remained so to today. However, for Warren Wilson students, the "life purpose" objective has unrelentingly remained the top priority for the college experience.

Many educators find this prevalent student trend cause for concern, especially given the fact that we are in an age of mind-boggling change. Author and sustainable enterprise advocate Paul Hawken has called this the "Age of Discontinuity" and contends that it is just as significant as earlier eras, such as the Agricultural and Industrial Revolutions, and that the computer is revolutionizing our lives as did the printing press.[5]

The term *discontinuity* implies that the historic linear progression of things no longer applies, that we are now in an age in which the twin forces of technology and globalism can generate change at an exponential rate. One calculation hypothesizes that with the accelerated rate of computerized data generation, the amount of information available will double every seventy-five days by the year 2035! Whether precisely accurate or not, such a trend has profound implications for the way we learn, work, and travel through life's many pathways. Not only will job changes multiply but career changes are expected to occur several times over for each individual.

Consequently, the day of the teacher as the "sage on the stage" is ending, being replaced by the teacher as a facilitator, mentor, and learning companion. It calls for the classroom to be much more interactive in nature and for the professor to find the courage to reveal his or her own humanity, questioning and bringing together self, subject, and students into one tapestry. As Parker points out, we are born with this birthright of selfhood, yet it is often trained away or lost in our attempt to live up to others' expectations to be something we are not.[6]

Therefore, the ability to stay in touch with one's selfhood affects both a choice of vocation and the manner in which we practice a vocation such as teaching. In many ways, it calls for our academic institutions to reconnect within as a community of colleagues: overcoming the "privatization" of teaching behind closed doors and using faculty mentors, holding more honest and open discussion of teaching problems, arranging for "in-house teaching consultants," supporting the informal coffee gatherings, encouraging availability of teaching workshops, and drawing in colleagues from other campuses through professional associations.

Those of us in leadership positions—presidents, deans and department chairs, and school administrators—must encourage the conversation and be faithful to the tenets of good teaching: openly creating a hospitable space in which mutual support flourishes, setting a tone, revealing our shared passion in this noble profession, and showing the same sense of self that faculty are asked to bring to the classroom. Too often we are not mindful enough that faculty, like the students they teach, are conflicted in their life's vocational quest and need to be reconnected with the basic tenets of their calling. One faculty member told me that she shared excerpts from *The Courage to Teach* with her students and advisees, indicating that it reflected "where she was coming from and her aspirations." Faculty have discussed the book among themselves and acknowledged that the academic affairs component of the campus has by and large forfeited the transformative aspects of the learning experience to other parts of the campus.

I'm always exhilarated to witness teaching that emphasizes the "companioning" principle, whereby the teacher displays a shared passion and love for a subject as much as simply imparting technical information. Artists and musicians do this very well because their vocation tends to be a passionate avocation as well. One of my favorite examples is that of the late legendary Appalachian fiddler and close friend, Ralph Blizard, who for a dozen years taught fiddle classes in our college's summer music workshops, the Swannanoa Gathering. Ralph's vintage fiddling in the Tennessee long-bow style, complete with slide and blues bowing notes, brought him worldwide recognition, including a prestigious National Heritage Fellowship award from the National Endowment for the Arts. Students of all ages flocked to Ralph's classes, even though most will never be able to master the long-bow technique. Basically, they were entranced by his "theology of fiddle playing," which combined a passion for creativity, improvisation, experimentation, and space to try things and fail. To make creative mistakes. Ralph had an instinctive sense of "companioning" with his students and of giving them the courage to stretch and find their own individuality with the fiddle bow. We often say that "Ralph never played the same tune the same way once!" That is especially true of his signature fiddle tune, "Blizard Train," adapted from "Lost Train Blues," which in many ways is a metaphor for the long train journey of musicianship that was unique to his musical soul and identity. It seems to me there are lessons here for all of us as we coalesce our vocational and avocational callings.

At this hinge of history, our nation's colleges and schools have a particular responsibility to help students find their own voice as they journey through a fragmented society and are bombarded with outside expectations. Students generally come to college (or begin the first day of school at any level) with two fundamental apprehensions: (1) Can I make it academically? and (2) Will I be accepted? Each August we welcome a new set of first-year students, accompanied by families who are as anxious about letting go as their sons or daughters are about new beginnings. They assemble in the college chapel for the usual welcome, introductions, and orientation remarks. To break the tension a bit, I call on my wife, Darcy, and a couple of musical colleagues to (informally and unaccompanied) sing a song titled "Come from the Heart":

> When I was a young man my mama told me
> A lesson she'd learned it was a long time ago
> If you want someone that you can hold onto
> You're going to have to learn to let go.
> You've got to sing, like you don't need the money

Love, like you'll never get hurt
Dance, like nobody's watching
It's got to come from the heart if you want it to work.[7]

The response always includes a collective sigh of relief. I suppose they are thinking, *If they're nuts enough to pull that off, and risk looking foolish, then maybe I'm going to be OK.* Perhaps we establish a bit of a safe harbor at a traumatic moment in their life journey, and hopefully an invitation to self-discovery as they embark on a new crossing.

As I look out on the eager but nervous young faces, I often contemplate how one day they will look back on this critical life juncture. As they cross the waters of life, will there be gratitudes or misgivings for the choices made on the journey? Will they have found their inner voice, their self-hood, their life's vocational calling? Parker often recounts the wonderful Hasidic tale about the importance of becoming one's self, of Rabbi Zusya as an old man saying, "In the coming world, they will not ask me: 'Why were you not Moses?' They will ask me: 'Why were you not Zusya?' "[8]

At another time and place, the question asked of Rabbi Zusya was the same basic question that the Cherokee tribal elder was posing to members of the extended tribal family who lost their way. It is the same question that Parker has asked of all of us, through his countless miles and years of pointing us toward our own song and dance of life.

It has been said that when someone dies, a little civilization passes on. Everything that made up his or her essence—the personality, philosophy, voice, esthetics, appearance, accomplishments, style, language, tears and laughter—dies as well. What remains are the gifts to others that have emanated from deep within the wellspring of our being and that have blossomed somewhere along our life pathway, whether in the spring or autumn of our years. As the opening epigraph from George Eliot said, "It's never too late to be what you might have been." The old Appalachian fiddlers put it another way: "You'd better resin up your bow." Surely they are quoting a song that we frequently draw on when welcoming our summer music workshop aspirants:

If the fiddle strings felt no bow strokes
If the concertina bellows broke
If no one sang a single note
Then where's the song of living.

When all you've earned is lost or pawned
And all your money's spent and gone

You'd find out what you've been living on
And never even knew.

And all of life plays like a tune
It sounds so sweet but ends too soon
You'd better resin up your bow
Before it's time to go.[9]

NOTES

1. Palmer, P. J. *Let Your Life Speak*. San Francisco: Jossey-Bass, 2000, p. 4.

2. Parker J. Palmer, Warren Wilson College commencement address, May 19, 2001.

3. Palmer (2000), p. 8.

4. Palmer, P. J. *The Active Life: Wisdom for Work, Creativity, and Caring.* San Francisco: Harper San Francisco, 1990, pp. 15–34.

5. Paul Hawken, in a speech at a Regional Sustainability Conference involving government, business, educational, and nonprofit leaders in Asheville, N.C., Apr. 1999.

6. Palmer (2000), p. 12.

7. The Susanna Clark and Richard Leigh song, "Come from the Heart," was recorded by Guy Clark ("Guy Clark: Old Friends," 1988, Sugar Hill Records). 5 BK April Music Inc./GSC Music/Lion-Hearted Music (ASCAP), 1987.

8. Palmer (2000), p. 11.

9. The "Song of Living" was recorded by Ann Dotson, initially titled: "Joy of Living," on "Its Own Sweet Time," 1990, Beech Hill Music, BMI. Revised title and lyrics by Doug Orr.

True Self
Unleashed

IN MY WORK WITH teachers and educational leaders, there is an excerpt that I quote from Parker's work that is a sure-fire applause line.

> In our rush to reform education, we have forgotten a simple truth: reform will never be achieved by renewing appropriations, restructuring schools, rewriting curricula, and revising texts if we continue to demean and dishearten the human resource called the teacher on whom so much depends. Teachers must be better compensated, freed from bureaucratic harassment, given a role in academic governance, and provided with the best possible methods and materials. But none of that will transform education if we fail to cherish—and challenge—the human heart that is the source of good teaching.[1]

Why do people respond so enthusiastically to this excerpt? Why do heads nod with such conviction when I share this excerpt from *The Courage to Teach*? I suspect two reasons. First, most of the people I know and work with, whether they are in education or other professions, harbor deep cynicism for the status quo process of change. Parker reminds us that merely importing a new technique, a new method, a new process, a new incentive system at best only tinkers with the margins and at worst snarls up preexisting circumstances so badly that the effort to make things better ends up making things worse.

Second, no matter what our work is, we realize that our capacity to do it well depends on the quality and condition of who we are. Parker's refrain is that our work in any human activity emerges from who we are. It depends on our heart—not a mawkish Hallmark heart, but *"heart* in its ancient sense, as the place where intellect and emotion and spirit and will converge in the human self."[2] This heart, this capacity for being fully present, emotionally connected, and purposeful, is the source for good work. When people encounter Parker's words, they find themselves facing questions that challenge practices they have long experienced: How can my institution cherish and challenge the human heart? What practices and ways of working do we subscribe to that ignore or deform those who work, learn, and lead in our community? What would it take to alter our technical calculus and adopt practices that animate the heart and selfhood of the individuals in our community?

We are institutional creatures. Our lives and trajectories are inexorably bound up in the logic of those institutions, whether a school, firm, hospital, or nonprofit organization. As Parker tells us, "We inhabit institutional settings, including school and work and civil society, because they harbor opportunities that we value. But the claims those institutions make on us are sometimes at odd with our hearts—for example, the demand for loyalty to the corporation, right or wrong, versus the inward imperative to speak truth."[3] When locked in conflict between our inner beliefs and outward lives, we experience the diminishment, the paralysis, that is the "divided life." The alternative is "true self unleashed."

The essays in this section, "True Self Unleashed," have been written by leaders who ask what it takes to lead an institution that honors the human heart as the source of good work. Chapter Five, "Leading from Within," features essays by experienced leaders reflecting on the personal challenges of leadership. To lead from within means to lead from a place of true self and wholeness.

Imagining and opening spaces hospitable to the inner life is hard and lonely work. The forces at work in our institutional settings tend to honor compliance and repel creativity. The logic of the status quo is a powerful operating system that rewards careful maneuvering—yet our institutions and communities cry out for innovation and bold action. In this gap, real leaders work to create schools, hospitals, and businesses where real people can show up and express their genuine selves, seek creative answers to our problems, and live and work in ways congruent to their true beliefs.

This kind of leadership takes conviction and courage. Leaders who seek to create opportunity for students, fellow workers, and neighbors to feel safe enough to share their inner selves with each other must be willing to fight back against cynicism and an ethos that honors thin and shallow forms of interaction. The authors in this chapter describe their efforts to imagine new and genuine ways to learn and work together. They describe inspired visions and the cold and isolating turbulence that comes when leaders seek to move forward against long-held practices.

The authors in Chapter Six, "Rescuing the Sacred," explore what it takes to lead organizations that support the inner work and self-exploration of those working within them. They recognize that they have the power to create light or shadow within their organizations, and they struggle to discern the impact their presence has on those they have been appointed to lead. They describe trying to lift up the value of inner work and help those they work with appreciate the value of the human heart; they work to create practices that understand that although the path toward self-development often travels through private terrain it can be nurtured within community; they recognize that nothing diminishes the human potential of people more than fear, and they work to confront fear both in themselves and within the community.

These are not easy tasks, and the authors describe the wrenching challenge of facing down their own desire to flee or turn away from conflict. Instead of walling themselves off, these leaders call others into partnership, reach out to mend broken relationships, and persist in calling for healing. They do so because they recognize that leadership means holding a community together when its impulse is to fracture and disconnect.

NOTES

1. Palmer, P. J. *The Courage to Teach*. San Francisco: Jossey-Bass, 1998, p. 3.

2. Palmer (1998), p. 11.

3. Palmer (1998), p. 167.

Chapter Five

LEADING
FROM WITHIN

THE STARTING POINT OF A MOVEMENT, though silent and barely visible, can be described with some precision. It happens when isolated individuals who suffer from a situation that needs changing decide to live "divided no more."

Many of us know from personal experience how it feels to live a divided life. Inwardly we experience one imperative for our lives, but outwardly we respond to quite another. This is the human condition, of course—our inner and outer worlds are never in perfect harmony. But there are extremes of dividedness that become intolerable, when one can no longer live without bringing one's actions into harmony with one's inner life. When that happens inside of one person, then another, and another, in relation to a significant social issue, a movement may be conceived.

—Parker J. Palmer

REFLECTIONS

o

Jay Casbon
CEO of the
Oregon State University–Cascades University

Whenever I am with Parker Palmer, whether it is in a board meeting of the Center for Teacher Formation or on a walk along a winding mountain stream in the Cascade Mountains of Oregon, it feels as if I am in the company of an explorer. The questions asked, the running commentary of possibility, or the unexpected—but welcomed—insertion of a huge laugh just when things become a bit too intellectual, fills me with an awareness of a gift received. This is why I have commented to friends and colleagues that Parker is my "psychological Magellan." His life has explored the wildest places of human experience. When I read Mary Oliver's poem "Magellan," I felt I knew the person she wrote about: Parker Palmer. The lines "let us risk the wildest places, lest we go down in comfort and despair" capture the life I have witnessed being lived by my friend and mentor.

When I first accepted my position at Oregon State University–Cascades, Parker e-mailed to invite me into conversation so as to consider rethinking the university. He wondered aloud of the "labored common roads of academe," of a possible new form for a university—a university that could be "formational" by design. The conversation helped to later frame a dramatically new design for student life, the Center for Life Direction. What I have come to understand is that hundreds of people share similar stories about Parker. As a result, my gratitude for him only deepens during each and every encounter.

TURNING TOWARD
A NEW LEADERSHIP

Jay Casbon

*Is it possible to become more intentional about creating spaces—
in relationship, in community—where our fearful shadows can
emerge into the light to be seen for what they are, where the truth
and love within us can appear and make a claim on our lives?*
—Parker J. Palmer

WE LIVE IN A WORLD where the "self" is the center of our time and attention. We live in a world that increasingly inflates emotions through self-hype and an unrelenting hunger for materialistic ways of defining ourselves. We have traded real friends and family for celebrity friends and television families. We have delegated our personal identity to a consumer persona. Our culture seems to say to all of us, if we want success, we must mimic the attention-grabbing celebrities. We must always try to achieve and acquire more, to push forever outward. I grew up with leadership models that mirrored this inflated hype and disconnection.

Recently I had a long conversation with a leader in the Nez Perce tribe here in Oregon. She shared with me the trouble her tradition has with the concept of leadership—as defined by modern Western culture:

> Our people are more focused upon the past and the present. We experience America as a country that places an inordinate emphasis upon the future. Our people have trouble with this concept, and that is why your notion of leadership does not work for my people. Our people count upon present and historical relationships, we always consider the truth in a situation, and how that truth speaks to present action and the well-being of our tribe. Living always in the future is a role we give fools in our mythical tribal stories—roles that always elicit laughter and comic relief. To actually base a psychology, community values, public policy, and even spiritual beliefs in the future—to us—feels like a child's fantasy. And like children, your culture wants silly questions and happy answers, a life without struggle, and easy gratification. In recent years we have become frightened by what we see!

Our discussion turned to the summer movie blockbuster of 2004, *The Day After Tomorrow,* a B disaster movie that showed—with incredible visual effects—a sudden new ice age with enough power to tear down the world as we currently know it. The obvious story is about environmental negligence, planetary destruction, and possible rebirth. Primarily, however, the story line was one of alienation—from the natural world, family relationships, and mostly from ourselves. Dennis Quaid, the leading actor, portrayed a character so preoccupied with his career—something to do with natural science—that he neglected his son, his marriage fell apart, and he lived in a one-dimensional world singularly focused on his own needs and interests. The new ice age gave him the opportunity to take a hero's journey to "right" the wrongs in his life.

My Nez Perce friend pointed out that *The Day After Tomorrow* was the perfect example of a culture that has a limited insight into its "blindness" but can only talk about it in some future-oriented fantasy. "God help us all. . . . Maybe some good will come of it," she said.

When I accepted a leadership role to develop a new university in Bend, Oregon, I had an opportunity to move toward a new kind of model that would embrace working from inside out. I desired to be formational in my values and actions—to create a leadership paradigm where I would not be divided, I would not be cut off from my inner life as I faced the challenges of starting this university. This is a daunting task, for it is difficult to be true to myself and true to the expectations of those I serve. In this very visible, public role, I struggle to integrate my soulful expression with what others demand of me as a leader. I am expected to always be strong, and have all the right answers at my fingertips; given this, it is difficult to see my self-doubt as an asset, as a teacher that can bring clarity and alignment to my inner guidance.

In the past, I have found my leadership roles to be somewhat mysterious and foreign to my self-concept. The conventional leadership styles that I observed were focused mostly on personality, a mentality of winners and losers, and the latest high-performance leadership theory being peddled by the popular press. I yearned for a leadership that developed from a deeper place within myself and others. In my heart, I believed leadership was a direct reflection of our inner values and wholeness. Not experiencing any organization that welcomed my needs and ideas, I settled for an identity that could survive at the margins of organizational life. I lived a divided leadership life and fashioned an identity as an educator who happened to be serving in leadership roles. It was only in the last five years, after I began to experience the principles and practices of "courage work" and the writings of Parker, that I claimed leadership as a role that

I could embrace. The breakthrough came as a result of seeing leadership within the context of real community.

Parker wrote: "But if it is true that we are made for community, then leadership is everyone's vocation, and it can be an evasion to insist that it is not."[1]

Claiming leadership, within a community, rekindled my innovative spirit. The community connection revelation helped me understand, in spite of my title as CEO, that I did not have to count on myself to be the sole creative force for success. The opportunity was also a tall order in the present economic and political climate of Oregon. Dealing with constant funding challenges, creating needed academic partnerships with other institutions, building a faculty of scholars who loved to teach and work with students, creating a different kind of student life paradigm, and integrating the university into the rich fabric of the environment and culture of the high Cascades country of Oregon was a worthy challenge for all involved.

Learning to Lead Formationally: Resisting Disappointment

In my office over my computer, I have a quote from Thomas Merton that has served as a touchstone for me: "The humble person receives praise the way a clean window takes the light of the sun. The truer and more intense the light is, the less you see of the glass."

On my first day on the job, I was informed that our new campus would suffer a 20 percent budget cut. I also discovered that our new campus had inherited a bevy of personnel challenges from the initial startup efforts a year before. I remember sitting down in my office and reading the Merton quote, asking myself, *Where is the light in this situation?* Having reassured myself that at least there is a flickering light, I asked, "Can I transcend this disappointment in such a manner as not to cloud the 'glass' of my leadership?"

The bad news did trigger within me some old feelings of past leadership battles, some successes and also a fair amount of mistakes. From my courage work in the last few years, I knew that I needed to safeguard myself from deeply buried shadows, lest I resort to fear and scarcity. I knew that I had to point myself in the direction of wholeness, especially when the heaviness of uncertainty could so easily cloud my vision.

The concepts I have learned to incorporate from the influence of Parker are, notably, formulating open and honest questions and facing challenges with wonder. If I began my quest of facing the challenge with questions, within a community context of leadership, I would not be alone. I knew that the temptation to fix and to save the organization, tempting as that might be, is but an inflated egoic illusion. The real goal is to be found in human hearts, mine and those of the team I was beginning to assemble.

I could see clearly the paradox of building a new university without having the funds required to do the job. But a key point of Parker's writings has always been to embrace paradox. I learned that befriending paradox would help to keep me open to creative solutions. I knew limits often served to enhance creativity, that less can lead to more. Attempting to manage a shrinking budget, while at the same time growing enrollment and faculty, appeared on the surface to be paradoxical, just as the understanding that limited resources can also lead to new ways of thinking, to new ways of considering sustainability.

When Scarcity Opens Up Community

Parker has written about the mysterious and powerful concept of abundance: "In the human world, abundance does not happen automatically. It is created when we have the sense to choose community, to come together to celebrate and share our common store. Whether the 'scarce resource' is money or love or power or words, the true law of life is that we generate more of whatever seems scarce by trusting its supply and passing it around."[2]

One university administrator I know discovered that her business model for her department was no longer sustainable. State support had been cut by 30 percent while her fixed costs were increasing every year. After many meetings with her faculty, meetings that focused on finding new solutions, a group consensus emerged and the college was able to shift some programmatic offerings to an improved delivery model. She openly discussed a range of personnel options that could improve the financial picture of the college, and as a result of those conversations she persuaded a small number of faculty to take early retirement through a gradual phase-out plan that included part-time instruction. Additionally, she worked with her provost to reduce some institutional costs, and she was able to land several research projects that were directly tied to the instructional mission of her department. Two of the grants resulted in creation of one new major and two new minors. The results spurred a wave of pent-up creativity within her faculty that enhanced the reputation of the college, dramatically improved enrollment, and balanced the budget.

"Passing it around" was the key for success in this situation. This leader's courage to lead with honest and open discussions with faculty eventually led to a consensus to embrace the outcomes and claim ownership of their college. The budget was balanced, and everything about the college improved, but most important the faculty now understood and embraced their own "common store" of assets and gifts. Her faculty realized that a vibrant college had little to do with the conventional metrics that too many colleges embrace as the holy grail of effectiveness: flush budgets, impeccable credentials endorsement by accreditation groups, scholarship production by the faculty, and strong student enrollment. Yes, these elements of credibility are important—even very important—but true greatness lies more with lived ideals. The faculty in this case realized it takes courage and vision to undergo serious soul searching, to choose community as the means to excellence.

Embracing Shared Leadership

When I accepted my new position at Oregon State University–Cascades, I knew I had a unique opportunity to create a culture of shared leadership. I wanted to create psychological space for my faculty and leadership team to deeply explore the many questions I knew were coming. I wanted us to learn to slow down and listen, not be reactive to each new crisis, and allow the wisdom of our team to emerge. I had participated in a shared leadership model as a board member and facilitator in Courage to Teach. I had seen how shared leadership builds the leadership capacity of the group. I knew that, over time, we would learn to understand and appreciate the critical nature of process, that process determines the outcome, that the right process builds a community with integrity—another valued principle of courage work.

I did not have to wait long before an opportunity to test my ideas on process and leadership developed. Early last year, one of my most talented faculty talked to me about a salary issue. My first inner response was to think, *This is not the time to talk to me about a salary increase when the university is reeling with budget cuts!* But I knew, from the Courage to Teach work, to listen and withhold judgment and advice, take the listening to a deeper level within myself, and give my colleague all the time necessary to share her frustration and disappointment. I remembered something that many of the Courage facilitators talk about in our meetings together: "When you don't know what to do, turn to wonder."

I wondered what a bigger solution would look like. Could a "little" salary issue handled in a creative and generative manner help to build a community with integrity and purpose? Do seemingly small things sometimes have a large impact? My colleague told me that her salary was considerably below every other faculty person of her rank and experience. She told me that she had attempted to receive some satisfaction on this issue and that she was losing faith in a system that never acknowledged her contributions. I listened. The conversation ended, and I promised I would "look into the situation" and get back to her in a couple of weeks. I sensed she didn't believe me at all.

I met with my faculty leadership team and presented the issues. Everyone knew the situation needed to be corrected, and they all also knew there was no money; to make matters worse, our governor had also issued a statewide salary freeze. Our hands appeared tied. No solution! As we were about to end our conversation, one of the team said that he now felt "tainted" by somehow knowing about the situation—having a deep respect for the faculty person in question—and being part of "a bureaucratic conundrum that allowed no flexibility; and in a sense, being codependent with a mindless governance system devoid of soul and compassion."

The group did not leave the room but sat in silence. I had learned from my work with Parker to trust and honor silence. Courage work had also taught me to address conflict honestly and directly; communication and goodwill are antidotes for policy violence that is often well established, and mostly hidden, within an organization. I asked the group to invite the faculty person into the discussion so that we could all hold a space for our dilemma, that we commit ourselves to explore the challenge fully and see what might emerge.

After about three weeks of revisiting the situation, the group—along with the full participation of the faculty person—did find an innovative way to reclassify the position (thereby sidestepping the state salary freeze) and securing enough funds to create a remedy by delaying a scheduled faculty hiring by a few months. The decision had an immediate positive impact for all involved. All knew that this "little" problem helped the group to develop community muscle and the much-needed capacity for navigating the uncharted waters that lie ahead.

Confronting Organizational Violence

The uncharted waters also included our own capacity to do harm. Organizations that are disrespectful, demeaning, and arrogant do cause pain and harm. I wanted this new culture to be grounded in nonviolence; free from physical violence and from psychological violence. Parker wrote: "By violence I mean more than physical savagery that gets much of the press. Far more common are the assaults on the human spirit so endemic to our lives that we may not even recognize them as acts of violence."[3]

Recently I overheard a heated conversation from down the hallway. I decided to get involved and walked into the outer office of our financial aid operation. The student was upset at the manner in which her financial aid had been "mishandled" by the university. The student repeatedly said, "This is not about the money; it's about the demeaning way that I've been treated. I've talked to five different people, received five different answers, and not one real human contact was established. No one listened to me and no one would even hint that maybe there is a problem here. What does a student have to do to be seen? I'm not attacking anyone here personally, but I feel this bureaucracy is so numbing that I cannot be heard or seen!"

I listened, looked straight at her, and apologized. Our financial aid director entered into the conversation by saying, "I see you and feel terrible that your frustration was not handled in a respectful manner." A minute or two passed in silence, and I asked that all of us find a way to change whatever needed to be changed so no student feels violated and harmed. I thanked the student for insisting that we hear her story. The exchange turned into a conversation, and a solution to her specific financial aid problem was found and immediately resolved. I asked the student if she would be willing to serve on a student committee working in the area of enrollment service and financial aid. She was eager to get involved.

I knew about organizational violence firsthand. I had once worked as a dean at a university that used violence as a regular means to gain and sustain power. The university had a beautiful campus, a prestigious faculty, a solid endowment, respectable national rankings, and brilliant leadership. At least that was the story most people thought was accurate, even within the institution.

There were other indicators that were mostly hidden from public view. Many students chose not to return after their freshman year because there was a lack of "community spirit." The faculty was disconnected from the university and themselves; a beloved professor, who was courageous enough to ask the questions everyone else wanted to ask but did not ask, refused to attend his own retirement party. The prescription rate for tranquilizers of the faculty were "off the charts" compared to other universities of similar size. There was also an alarmingly high rate of cancer fatalities within the faculty community. The university president stopped having real discussions with his deans and the board of trustees, and finally, largely owing to no counterbalance to this president's leadership, he made a terrible financial decision on his own that cost the university more than $10 million. It was not until a local newspaper published the story that the president was eventually fired and the university began the slow, but very needed, healing process.

I mourned the tragedy of this situation and grieved for my own culpability. I also felt hope that this university, with new leadership, would eventually turn to wholeness.

Honoring Parker Palmer

For a real community to appear, the leader does not have to disappear. The leader does have to be able to hold a conscious space, a place that can see into the gap of possibility—and at the same time clearly observe the often tragic circumstances blocking and resisting organizational wholeness. I owe a debt of gratitude to Parker for helping me see what he calls the "tragic gap" that is present in all human activity. His mentorship, his courage to formulate the hard questions, his unfailing ability to see and feel deeply into the darkest of human experiences as well as the possibilities and victories has affected how I now live with leadership, and how I could come to claim my life as part of a larger community of many leaders. The university that I now call my home is, like my leadership, an imperfect work in progress. The leadership team continues to ask hard questions, and we are thankful that we have each other to share and create the journey.

My formation as a leader has taught me to keep things as simple as possible. Formation has a vitality, a life force, an energy, and an intention of wholeness that is translated through leadership. I have five elements in my journal that I consult each and every day. I do so in my quest to ask myself, to the degree that I am able, to reflect on open and honest questions concerning my leadership at the university:

1. Am I truthful with myself and my colleagues?
2. What open and honest questions do I have for today?
3. Am I able to listen to my own source of truth?
4. Am I able to trust the truths that my colleagues may offer?
5. Do the "results" of today's work honor the values of our community and mission?

If I can remain true to this work and commit myself to a formational approach to leadership, just maybe I can be like the clear glass Thomas Merton wrote about: "The humble person receives praise the way a clean window takes the light of the sun. The truer and more intense the light is, the less you see of the glass."

NOTES

1. Palmer, P. J. *Let Your Life Speak.* San Francisco: Jossey-Bass, 2000, p. 74.
2. Palmer (2000), p. 107.
3. Palmer, P. J. *A Hidden Wholeness.* San Francisco: Jossey-Bass, 2004, p. 168.

REFLECTIONS

○
_____

Michael Lerner
president and cofounder of Commonweal

I first met Parker Palmer at the Fetzer Institute, where I participated in his workshop. His work reminded me of the work of Rachel Naomi Remen, my close friend and colleague at Commonweal, the health and environmental research institute where I have worked for the past thirty years. Both Parker and Rachel have found similar ways of using texts or comparable materials as the starting point to reconnect us with the larger order of things.

What I appreciated most about Parker is that he came to this work through community organizing. He was also open about his wound, depression. I appreciate people whose life experience and teaching methods include but are not limited to what they have learned both from a life of direct service and from their wounds.

Like Parker, I have learned a great deal from community organizing work. I had a heart attack a year ago that added to my experience of wounds. I am more inclined to trust teachers whose lives have been devoted to practical service, and who have been humbled by their wounds, because both service and wounds are helpful antidotes to the inflationary tendency of being a teacher who connects people to spirit.

The essay that the editors asked me to contribute to this volume emerges from another one of my own wounds: my struggle to work in philanthropy in a way that does not destroy me or the people whose lives I connect with in this most curious and difficult craft. Fortunately, philanthropy is not my primary work; I stay balanced and nourished by work in healing and in environmental health. But even part-time work in philanthropy is psychologically perilous. The Fetzer-sponsored seminars using Parker's methods have proved deeply useful to those of us who toil in the seductive but treacherous field of organized philanthropy. I can attest to that.

ON PHILANTHROPY
AND THE INNER LIFE

Michael Lerner

AT THE DEEPEST LEVEL, philanthropy and spirituality are intimately related. Both stem originally from a compassionate concern for humanity, and indeed for all life. Yet organized professional philanthropy is as fundamentally different from true philanthropy, which is spontaneous and innate compassion for all life, as organized religion is from the original spontaneous and innate spiritual impulse. So when we consider the relationship between spirituality and philanthropy, we must begin by asking what we are talking about: original spirituality and its correlate, spontaneous philanthropy, or organized spirituality and its correlate, organized philanthropy?

Let me start by defining spirituality as I understand it in this essay. My experience of spirituality has a distinct historical and geocultural context. I have lived my first six decades in the space between the end of World War II and the new so-called War on Terrorism that is evolving into a new lethal chapter in human history. My experience has been shaped by what I regard as four critical cluster developments of this period: (1) the emergence of an Age of Extinctions in which the basic conditions of all life are being degraded at a rate not seen for sixty-five million years; (2) the acceleration of the new technologies (information technology, biotechnology, nanotechnology, and robotics) that Bill Joy has rightly described as taking us from an age of weapons of mass destruction to an age of technologies of mass destruction; (3) the whole "global problematique" as it

---

This essay is a revision of an earlier one written for a conference in November 2000 on philanthropy and the inner life. The original essay was dedicated to three friends who have thought very deeply on this subject: Charles Halpern, Charles Terry, and Rob Lehman. Like these three friends, I have spent the past three decades at the interface of progressive philanthropy and the nonprofit community it serves. Revising excerpts from that longer essay for this volume in honor of Parker Palmer, I found myself reconsidering and rewriting much of what I had written before.

affects not only ecological conditions but distribution of wealth, rate of social change, and patterns of social conflict; and (4) the spiritual event that Arnold Toynbee thought would be remembered as the greatest development of the twentieth century: the arrival of the Dharma in the West.

Any discussion of philanthropy and spirituality that is removed from these developments seems to me to be doomed from the start.

My definition of spirituality is that it is the shared essence of all the great religions and spiritual traditions. It is what Leibniz and Huxley called "the perennial philosophy," the one truth at the heart of all great wisdom teachings. If my version of spirituality connotes the essential heart of all the great spiritual traditions, I can also say what it is *not*. It is *not* the religious certainty of those who are willing to dehumanize others, especially those of fundamentally opposed social, political, and religious beliefs, because they view themselves as the instruments of a higher power. I understand the religious fundamentalists, and I honor the fact that their life experience has guided them into these rigid certainties. But I stand with the ecumenical movement that unites us as human beings, not with the religious rigidities that give us the right to kill each other.

Many practitioners of progressive philanthropy in our time are drawn toward spiritual practices at the interface of the Dharma teachings of the East and the Western Judeo-Christian traditions that are often their common heritage. Many would also acknowledge the influence of American Indian traditions in their spiritual life, and indeed of other traditions from around the world as well. Ecological consciousness, the honoring of the feminine and the indigenous, and a commitment to social justice deeply color their understanding of spirituality. It is useful to be explicit about this experience because it is so different from the life experience of such other authentic and honorable spiritual seekers as a Southern Baptist Christian, an Orthodox Jew, a Hindu traditionalist, or a New Islamist.

If commitments to health, the environment, and justice are some of the common lineaments of the inner life as experienced by those engaged in progressive philanthropy, we can then ask the more specific question, How do those engaged in progressive philanthropy seek to *live* their spirituality? At the daily level at which organized philanthropy is practiced, there are profound tensions between personal spiritual lives and work. We should not, of course, be engaged in organized philanthropy if we are not acting to the very best of our limited abilities to invest the resources we are given so as to serve life as effectively as possible. But the fact that we seek to serve life does not mean that the whole process on which most organized philanthropy depends—the increasingly efficient and destructive extraction of resources from all life on earth; the monetization of these resources and their concentration in the hands of a very few by the global corporate system; and then the return of an infinitesimal fraction of this surplus, at the discretion of a favored few, to causes they favor—is spiritually unproblematic.

For these and other reasons, the practice of organized philanthropy is, for many of us, an ethically deeply contested activity. There is a great psychological difference between the Samaritan act of giving of one's substance to another in need, when one's substance is modest and a true sacrifice is involved, and the philanthropic act of giving from either a large personal fiscal surplus or a fiscal surplus accumulated by someone else when one has been hired to help perform that task. The act of the Samaritan and of the professional philanthropoid are in no way spiritually equivalent. The philanthropy of the wealthy individual who gives generously of his substance can, with the right intent, be close to that of the Samaritan. But the history of the great foundations demonstrates that more often than not the intent of the donor was not in the Samaritan tradition.

Contemplation as a Common Thread in the Inner Life

Contemplation is a common thread in the inner lives of many in progressive philanthropy. Contemplation is distinct from the ethical content with which we surround it. There is a difference between access to the inner life through contemplation and the moral codes that accompany every religious or spiritual tradition. Moral codes, though they have a shared core, clearly differ according to the tradition. Contemplation can doubtless help some of us cope better with some of the tensions surrounding organized and monetized philanthropy. But contemplation cannot resolve these tensions, many of which are structural.

Most of us would not reflect on spirit and philanthropy if we did not find meditation or some other spiritual practice useful in our own personal lives. But beyond this point of agreement, we may see the significance of contemplative practice quite differently. Some people doubtless believe that if more people adopted contemplative practices, the world would be a better place. Others believe that people with spiritual practices are in some way more evolved than people without spiritual practices. Many may further believe that some spiritual practices are demonstrably better than other spiritual practices.

Perhaps one thing about contemplation that can be asserted with confidence is that throughout human history sitting in silence has been praised by those who are drawn to its practice. All the other assertions in the previous paragraph are, to me, more problematic.

Would the world be a better place if more people meditated? I would hope so, but I am not certain, given the terrible things that have been done and are being done today in the name of religion.

Are people with spiritual practices more evolved than others? I wish this were true, but it would be difficult to assert this on the basis of my life experience. Some of the most truly "spiritual" people I know are people for whom the language of spirituality has no attraction whatsoever. Some of the most dedicated spiritual practitioners I know have a great deal of psychological work left to do. An important recent article in *Tricycle,* "Spiritual Bypass," eloquently describes a reality familiar to many of us. The author, a psychologist, points out that in the West many seekers believe they can "bypass" their psychological problems with spiritual practices.

Are some spiritual practices better than others? That is, again, a very complicated question. If we deny that some practices are better than others, we have no defense against practices that are at best unskillful and at worst depraved, deeply unwise, or simply unkind. But if we prefer some practices to others (to be intellectually honest, at some level we must), we may be on the path to those particularisms in the name of which religious wars have been fought endlessly. The best response to the assessment of spiritual practice to be found in scripture for me is "By their fruits shall ye know them."

One of the fruits of contemplative practice in all great traditions is said to be the development of wisdom and compassion. I have not found that the development of either wisdom or compassion is reliably proportional to the esotericism or intensity of a seeker's spiritual practice. Some of the wisest and most compassionate people I know have no interest in or need for a spiritual practice. This is why I have always been grateful that the Dalai Lama called one of his books simply *A Policy of Kindness.* He could have chosen a title having to do with Love or Compassion, both exalted words, but instead he chose the simple and straightforward word *kindness.* We may puzzle over how loving and compassionate we are, but we all know very directly what kindness is. A policy of kindness can be adopted by anyone, whether she meditates or not.

The Eye of the Needle

With respect to the nexus of philanthropy and spirituality, we cannot forget that many of the religious traditions have warned their adherents about the traps that wealth and power set for the seeker. Jesus said to render unto Caesar that which is Caesar's. The Beatitudes bless the poor and the meek but not the rich and the powerful. There is a Hindu teaching that the goddesses of wealth and wisdom do not live happily together in the same house. I recall a Buddhist text cautioning against accepting the hospitality of the wealthy. But the injunction against association with wealth is not universal in all traditions. The Lord of the Old Testament had no compunctions about showing his favor with riches. All major religious traditions forge some alliance with power and wealth, no matter what their founders said about the subject.

What happens to original spirituality when it enters the house of wealth and power? What happens to spirituality in our day, more specifically, when grant applicants discover that a funder has an interest in matters spiritual and contemplative? This is not an easy question for any of us, despite the fact that some progressive philanthropists have done skillful and important work incorporating spiritual and contemplative values in their funding. Yet the fundamental power asymmetry between funder and applicant requires that we ask these questions.

Dominant social classes at all times have some religious or spiritual preferences. One of the recognized avenues for advancement for those seeking their fortunes has always been to emulate the beliefs of the class to which they aspire. Whether the robe is black or orange makes little difference. Once those who seek to make what they can of themselves in the world recognize that a particular religious or spiritual practice is an avenue to proximity to power and wealth, the consequences both for the use of this avenue and the corruption of the spiritual tradition involved are equally self-evident.

Instrumentalism in Religious and Spiritual Practice

What happens when spirituality and wealth come together is that those seeking access to resources may adopt the spiritual practices in question for at least partially *instrumental* rather than *intrinsic* reasons.

Instrumental thinking has always been part of the context of religious and spiritual experience. From the earliest days in human history, when agricultural surpluses first enabled a priestly class to emerge, organized religion has always been closely associated with worldly power.

We should distinguish clearly between the instrumentality that leads an individual toward a spiritual path for reasons other than self-realization and the instrumentality that leads funders and nonprofit activists to think strategically about spirit, philanthropy, and the environment. The latter form of instrumentality raises a far more subtle set of questions.

For example, the National Religious Partnership for the Environment, directed by Paul Gorman, one of the remarkable men of our time in this field, is the best example we have of a conscious philanthropic effort to make ecological consciousness what it should be: an essential dimension of religious and spiritual life in our time.

Similarly, the goal of some very thoughtful funders of contemplative practice, to support the restoration of spiritual experience in the progressive community and not leave the religious dimension of life primarily in the hands of conservatives, was a substantial strategic notion.

Likewise, the experiment in teaching the leaders of the major environmental groups contemplative practice, in the hopes both that they could find deeper sources of energy for their work and that they might collaborate more effectively together, was an interesting initiative.

It does not belittle any of these efforts to point out that the motivation in all three cases was both intrinsically related to core values and also in some sense strategic or instrumental. Paul Gorman, who was kind enough to read an earlier version of this text, offered an enlightening example of how the work of the National Religious Partnership for the Environment may be seen to transcend the intrinsic-instrumental dichotomy I have used in this discussion. Paul wrote

> In the case of the Religious Partnership, there really was a different relationship between religious and spiritual vision as goals in themselves and whatever instrumental benefits these might yield. The goal of the Partnership really was/is faithfulness to God's love and creation; thus, renewal of religious life in itself; in fresh relationship to God's handicraft.
>
> Not as an *alternative* but rather as a *natural consequence* of renewed faithfulness would whatever "instrumental" benefits be forthcoming. The message to Congress, say, would not simply be "environmental protection" but a quality of devotion that could reach hearts and be transformative beyond partisanship.

Conversely, of course, conservatives have made remarkably successful instrumental use of the alliance between conservative Christians and corporate interests for many years. Doubtless, for some of those involved, these efforts also had a deep spiritual basis that transcended their instrumental value.

The basic point I want to make is not that instrumental approaches to religion and spirituality are either good or bad. They are inevitable. The point is that when we think instrumentally about the human spirit, our relationship to that spirit changes. It is like thinking instrumentally about love, or art, or any deeply creative act. But it is also possible, as Paul points out, to undertake social or environmental acts fully as spiritual acts, in which instrumental outcomes are only expressions of our spiritual commitment.

Yet it remains true that when we draw on our connections to what is deepest about being human to achieve political goals, no matter how extraordinarily vital to planetary survival those instrumental goals may be, we enter an arena in which we must proceed with great care. The religious community has been forever divided on this issue, with some recognizing the dangers of faith-based social strategies and proposing complete detachment from the political world, while others, such as Gandhi and King, see political action as essential to the spiritual life. Gandhi once observed that if God came to India "he would have to come as a loaf of bread."

Suffering, Spirituality, and Philosophy

Many people who work in progressive philanthropy find the work, especially if they stay in philanthropy for an extended period of time, personally challenging. Work in philanthropy often looks easy from the outside. Certainly it has more than its share of benefits, both financial and experiential. Yet many thoughtful practitioners in progressive philanthropy suffer.

There are many sources of suffering in progressive philanthropy. Three common ones are (1) constant exposure to the science-based "bad news" of how humanity is destroying the basis of healthy life on earth in this Age of Extinctions, (2) recognition that philanthropy has thus far done little to change the major trend lines of this Age of Extinctions, and (3) frustration that conservative philanthropy has been able to have such a powerful impact on American social policy over the past decades while progressive philanthropy has never achieved the unity and focus of its conservative counterpart. In addition to these policy-based sources of suffering, there are the common personal and institutional sources of suffering: (1) guilt at occupying a position of privilege and power in a progressive subculture that views privilege and power with great suspicion; (2) sadness at the destructive impact of the power imbalance in philanthropy on human relationships; (3) frustration at being removed from the direct action that makes nonprofit work satisfying; (4) frustration at the dysfunctionality that is endemic in the relations among the board of directors, the CEO, and the staff of many foundations; and (5) conflict between the wish to return to direct nonprofit action and the comforts of a secure position with a foundation.

The suffering that results from these conditions is real. The recognition that most other people in the world suffer from infinitely more dire problems only compounds the guilt philanthropoids feel at their common and (in the greater scheme of things) trivial sources of discontent. The question is what to do with this suffering. Obviously, the first concern is to act with as much skill as possible to achieve better outcomes in the real world.

But there are many sources of suffering in philanthropy on both the policy side and the personal and institutional side that are unlikely to change. So the question of how to live with these and other sources of suffering, both personal and professional, is a compelling one.

Thus far I have described the sources of suffering of professional progressive philanthropoids. The sources of suffering of family board members of many of these foundations should also be noted. People who inherit great wealth often suffer agony as difficult as what afflicts those who struggle with the more common conditions of life. The pain is particularly exquisite in our culture because those who suffer from wealth can find almost no sympathy outside the direct circle of their peers. "I wish I had that problem" or "Poor little rich kid," the world sneers. The problem is often compounded in progressive family foundations for three reasons: (1) bringing the family together around philanthropy can exacerbate (as well as heal) family issues about money; (2) growing up wealthy frequently saps the experience of competence and self-confidence, often leading to a sense of inadequacy in foundation roles; and (3) the progressive culture that inverts conservative value structures regarding wealth and power adds a further layer of guilt about playing the role of the donor.

It is not uncommon, then, to find a progressive foundation with fine progressive values in which family board members are uncomfortable in their roles; the president is stressed as he tries to cope with complex family dynamics; and the program directors, who often believe they could do a better job at managing the foundation than the president, are caught between these inner foundation dynamics and the equally vexing problems of trying to design and implement a funding strategy that will do more good than harm in the real world. Yet for all this—paradoxically—one finds some of the most effective progressive philanthropy achieved by the large mid-sized family foundations. (The very large foundations have a set of pathologies of their own, but space does not allow me to address them here.)

These, then, are some of the sources of discontent that drive many in progressive philanthropy toward the contemplative experience. In all the religious and spiritual traditions, suffering is seen as one of the great paths of the inner life. The observation of suffering is what brought the Buddha to spiritual life. The existence of suffering is indeed the first noble truth of Buddhism. Likewise, the Christ was called a man of sorrows and acquainted with grief. Christianity certainly sees suffering as one of the great paths to Christ consciousness. Patanjali, who wrote the first text on yoga, said in the *Yoga Sutras* that acceptance of suffering as an aid to purification, study of great wisdom teachings, and complete surrender to the divine force in each of us constitute yoga in practice. Jung said that consciousness begins in suffering.

There are, of course, some grant makers who do not find the role of funder psychologically challenging. Some simply enjoy the power asymmetry. Some pragmatically see themselves in the role for a limited period of time to contribute to causes they worked for over decades on the nonprofit side and now have a responsibility to put in some years in the funder role. Some say that the power asymmetry that troubles some progressive philanthropoids is true in any relationship of power. But what distinguishes philanthropy from other forms of power is its fungibility. The funder could in principle fund almost anything. Thus, although a corporate or nonprofit CEO has power in a defined structure, the funder is perceived as having potential power of almost unlimited range, even if the foundation guidelines are narrowly defined. As a result, the circle of those with whom the funder is in a potentially toxic power relationship is much larger.

My way of dealing with the psychic toxicity of philanthropy is not, sadly, available to most funders. I made a clear and early choice to keep my primary identity with my work at Commonweal, the nonprofit center where I have worked for thirty years. It is a blessing to me that most of those who I come into contact with through the Commonweal Cancer Help Program, which offers weeklong residential retreats for people with cancer, know nothing of my other life as a funder. The personal transactions between us are clean and clear. To those who come to the Cancer Help Program, I can offer something of myself—a much more wonderful experience of giving than any grant I have ever made. This is similar to the strategy many wealthy people adopt. They cultivate a defined professional life in which they can make a contribution, keeping their work as funders completely separate. One major foundation president took regular summer sabbaticals to do anonymous manual labor in restaurants, construction sites, and the like.

Suffering is, fortunately, not the only path to the spiritual life. One spiritual aphorism has it that the wise learn by observation, the rest by experience. If we can observe the choices in life that tend to cause suffering, sometimes we can learn to make better choices. Some wise people choose the life of the spirit because they can see its benefits without having been driven to it by suffering. Some people are simply born with an affinity for spiritual life and take to it without suffering out of a lifelong sense of vocation.

If Philanthropy Serves Civil Society, Why Is America So Unjust?

I have spent more than a decade writing about philanthropy as part of a conscious effort to survive psychologically and spiritually while continuing to participate in this curious institution. Despite this decade of effort, I must admit that real clarity about philanthropy has continued to escape me. I have had four other commitments over the past forty years: to social theory, to at-risk children, to people with cancer, and to environmental health. In each of these four arenas I usually came to some real clarity in my own understanding of the field in the first five years of my engagement with the subject. So I am intrigued by the fact that organized philanthropy has resisted my efforts to come to understand it in a comparable way.

If philanthropy is as wonderful for civil society as the foundation trade publications claim, why does the country with the most developed philanthropic sector tolerate the greatest social inequities of any Western democracy? I can well imagine that without philanthropy America would be in far more dire straits. For all their faults, foundations remain one of the few independent power bases left in the country. I have come to believe that philanthropy reflects some of the best and worst qualities of America. It is part and parcel of our distinctly entrepreneurial, free-market, winner-take-most culture. It does some great things, and it exacts great costs. It is part of who we are as Americans, both for better and for worse.

Philanthropy in America has, I believe, a deeply paradoxical relationship with social justice. On the one hand, philanthropy is widely recognized by real scholars of the field to serve the social class that owns or controls most of the surplus wealth in the country. Likewise, philanthropy is properly seen by many scholars as a "buffer for capitalism." Yet why do so many foundations, founded by conservative captains of industry, tend to become more progressive with the passage of generations and time? The answer may have something to do with Abraham Maslow's hierarchy of needs. Maslow famously posited that our most basic needs are for survival, food, and shelter, and as we satisfy these needs we are liberated to consider higher needs. The descendants of these conservative captains of industry, endowed with the deeply double-edged gift of inherited wealth, frequently come over time to a compassion for the earth and its creatures that is rarely the focus of a forebear sufficiently single-minded to focus on the accumulation of great wealth.

Likewise, spiritual concerns are at the top of Maslow's hierarchy of needs. It is true that many poor people are deeply religious and often spiritual. It is true that spirituality is found among people of all social classes. But it is also true that those who have solved the more pressing survival issues in life have, as Maslow recognized, greater opportunity to immerse themselves in questions of life meaning and purpose.

In fact, inherited wealth and the absence of a need to make a living and to solve practical problems of life often bring a veritable crisis of meaning in life, and a need for psychological and spiritual inquiry. Wealth thus provides space for both creative and destructive responses to the higher questions posed by Maslow's hierarchy of human needs. The opportunity to explore the meaning of life can result either in psychopathology or in psychospiritual creativity. The philanthropoid, living in the outer circles of the culture of wealth, may face the same set of dilemmas.

Between the Apollonian and the Dionysian

Standing as my life experience and nature have led me to stand, between the Apollonian and the Dionysian, the scientific and the intuitive, the skeptical and the mystical, the philosophical and the spiritual, I am always slightly uncomfortable whenever one world seems to exclude the truth contained in the other. My particular need is to live simultaneously in both worlds in order to feel whole. It is the quintessential experience of the exile.

The deepest questions about the nature of the universe remain opaque to me. Does the soul survive death? I hope so, and I am increasingly inclined to believe it may, but I do not know. Are contemplative experiences, in which some deep aspect of the nature of the universe seems to reveal itself, reflections only of the coherence of the collective unconscious, or do they also reflect organizing principles of the universe? I am inclined toward the latter view, but again, I do not know.

But even if I only see through the glass darkly into the world of spirit, at the end of the day one is forced to act, forced to choose a side. I choose a side each morning when I sit down to meditate. I have found very gradually, over thirty years of practice, that the truth of contemplation is a more powerful and congenial one for me than the truth that regards spirituality as a secondary aspect of being human.

The collective unconscious into which we move in a practice of silence is an unquestionable psychological reality for me. I suspect, but do not know, that the mysteries of the collective unconscious are also mysteries of the universe—that the inner universe reflects something of the outer universe. In Boehm's formulation, the universe consists of not only energy and matter but also of mind, and therefore there appears to be an implicate as well as an explicate order. In the practice of silence, my body relaxes, my mind clears, and sometimes I can move behind my thoughts into a wordless place that feels spacious, full of light, and true. In that place, the psychic knots that I face present themselves to me for reflection, and whatever wisdom and kindness I have been given to find in this lifetime seems to be nourished.

I choose the fruit of contemplation over that of skepticism for the same reasons I chose hope over despair in this Age of Extinctions, sincerity over irony in the ironic world of postmodernism, and engagement over apathy in the face of the enormous tasks before us. My friend Ted Schettler, a physician and environmental health activist, once said to me that he does the work as an act of witness.

My personal spirituality is above all one that trusts acts over beliefs. I trust the kindness of my wife playing with our newly adopted dog over the profession of great skill of some esoteric meditation practice. I trust those who engage in good work, who care for family and friends, and who navigate through their lives with as little harm as possible far more than I trust intimations of spiritual accomplishment. I like Ted's formulation, seeing the work we do for health, for the environment, and for justice as a form of witness. It is the work, above all, that I trust. My spiritual community is the community of those, wherever they are found, who do the work to save what we can of life. I do not care much what the private beliefs are that bring us to the work. I know my community by the fruit of our work, not by the words we each murmur to ourselves as we do the work. The practice of silence helps me in the work. That is all I ask.

REFLECTIONS

○
_____

Russ S. Moxley
director of the Center for Leadership and Ethics
at Greensboro College

I first met Parker Palmer through the reading of one of his books. My good friend and former colleague Dan Pryor gave me a copy of *The Active Life*, with clear instructions that I read it. I read it, then reread it. I wrote voluminous notes in the margins. In my head, I dialogued with Parker about his ideas. I was moved by what he wrote. After this book, I read every other book by Parker that I could find. His writing is a light that illuminates my journey.

When I completed the manuscript for *Leadership and Spirit* and was told by my editor from Jossey-Bass that it was time to get endorsements for the back cover, I gulped deeply and then decided that I would ask those to write an endorsement whose work and ideas I most valued. Parker was one of those people. In a gracious and generous way that I later came to understand is a reflection of who he is, Parker agreed. Who he is—an individual who lives an undivided life—has given me hope for what's possible for me and others on this journey we call life.

Then the opportunity presented itself for me to meet Parker in person. The place was Marble Collegiate Church in New York City, and the purpose was a daylong retreat. Jean, my wife, accompanied me to New York and participated in the retreat with me. This retreat, and opportunities that followed to be with Parker in other retreats, started me on a different leg of my journey. My sense of myself—my true self—has deepened, and my understanding of right work has changed.

In the essay that follows, I write about some of the experiences in life and work that distort and disfigure organizational leaders, and in fact all of us. We become dismembered. In my relationship to Parker, and through my experience in Courage to Teach and other formation programs like it, I am finding an opportunity to remember myself, to reclaim my wholeness, to become "the person I started out to be."

IT ALSO TAKES
COURAGE TO LEAD

Russ S. Moxley

*The point is not to become a leader. The point is to
become yourself, and to use yourself completely—all your gifts,
skills, and energies—to make your vision manifest. You must
withhold nothing. You must, in sum, become the person you
started out to be, and to enjoy the process of becoming.*
—Warren Bennis, *On Becoming a Leader*

IT WAS IN 1998 THAT I FOUND this quote from Warren Bennis, one of the
most creative thinkers and prolific writers about leadership in our time. I
was a Senior Fellow at the Center for Creative Leadership (CCL), a nonprofit research and educational organization headquartered in Greensboro,
North Carolina. At that point, I had worked for almost thirty years in leadership education and development. For twenty of those thirty years, I had
been involved in various leadership roles at work and in the communities
in which I lived. I was well versed in the leadership literature and had written about management and leadership issues. I had taught hundreds of
seminars and workshops on management and leadership skills and perspectives. I had learned about leadership from my own engagement in it—
from my successes and failures, from challenging job assignments, from
the good bosses I enjoyed and the bad bosses I endured. That same year—
1998—I was writing a book, *Leadership and Spirit,* which was later published by Jossey-Bass. The very process of writing was a rich developmental
experience for me. I had always assumed that when I learned enough I
might write; what I found was that it was in writing that I learned. One of
the most important things I learned—or perhaps, realized—as I reflected
on my years of being involved in leadership activities and doing leadership
development work is that Warren Bennis had it right: becoming a leader
is becoming oneself. It is learning to engage in leadership roles and activities out of a deep sense of one's identity and integrity. Leadership development, properly understood, is helping individuals become the persons they
started out to be.

But this is not how we have understood or practiced leadership or leadership development. For years, the public discourse about leadership—the research, the plethora of books, the multitude of workshops and courses, and even my own professional work—focused on helping individuals bring what is outside in. The critical assumption that underlies most of the work in leadership development is that there are ideas, theories, and understandings of leadership as well as skills and behaviors that individuals must *acquire* if they are to be effective leaders. Literally millions of dollars are spent each year in one leadership development program or another helping individuals develop the competencies—the tools, the techniques, the methods, the skills—they need to accomplish leadership tasks. Through the years, I have facilitated or trained in hundreds of these skill-building workshops.

To be sure, ideas about leadership are important. Theorists and practitioners have learned a lot about the *what* of leadership, including what distinguishes leadership from management. We know that the *what* of leadership includes creating a vision or sense of direction, building and maintaining alignment with that direction, and effecting and managing change. These tasks are important; absent them, we will say our company or community lacks leadership.

There has been as much focus, if not more, on the *how* of leadership. The *how* of leadership is also important; there are skills and abilities individuals need so they can build and maintain important work relationships and accomplish leadership tasks. I started my career teaching *how* courses: how to actively listen, how to be assertive and give helpful feedback, how to manage conflict in a win-win way—behaviors I believed individuals needed to enhance their effectiveness.

The problem is not with what has been done; the problem is that the focus has been too narrow. It has focused on the externals, on bringing what's outside in. It has concentrated on acquiring what one does not have. It has emphasized the *what* and *how* to the exclusion of the *who*. But in reality, effective leadership comes from the *who*. It comes from within. It is just that simple. And just that hard.

Let me tell a story to illustrate this point. For five years, I served on the management and organization development staff at a major oil company. One of my first assignments with the company was to develop a training program to help managers and executives develop the skills to give effective feedback during annual performance appraisals. The president of the oil company argued persuasively that everyone deserved to know how they were doing. I think he was right. But it wasn't happening. The company had data showing that only a small percentage of people were getting any

performance appraisal at all, much less an effective one. My first performance appraisal, for example, happened on my way out of the office on a
Friday afternoon when my boss, a training manager, handed me a sheet
showing my merit increase and told me I was doing a good job.

When we analyzed the data, we assumed that the reason managers were
not giving performance appraisals was that they did not know how. It was
a skill deficit, we thought. Provide them skill training in giving effective feedback—skills in describing positive and negative behavior, in communicat-
ing the impact of that behavior, and in listening to defensive responses—and
surely the percentage of performance appraisals would go up.

At the request of the company, I spent countless hours and many thousands of dollars designing and delivering a performance appraisal training program. The program was, as workshops go, a good one. It was
experiential education as its best. Some theory, but mostly behavior modeling and skill-practice exercises. Hundreds of managers were required to
participate.

What did I learn? I learned that as important as it is to develop these
skills, it isn't sufficient. You can provide managers and executives, even the
most seasoned ones, with the best possible skill-development experience
and the vast majority will still not give candid, straight feedback to others.

The problem is not a lack of skill; it is a lack of courage. Managers and
executives at all levels (and again, I am one of them) know the truth they
want to communicate in performance reviews, and most know how to do
it, but still they hesitate and put it off as long as possible, and then when
push comes to shove they deliver feedback in an ineffective way. They fear
being candid; they fear that shooting straight will have more negative than
positive consequences.

Let me say this another way. The problem in giving honest feedback
and telling the truth is not with the *what* or *how* of leadership; it is with
the *who*. It is not so much a matter of skill as it is a matter of identity and
integrity. One definition of integrity is telling the truth, speaking openly
and honestly, being forthright. It is hard to do. It takes courage to tell the
truth in performance appraisals. It takes courage to act with integrity.

This important truth that the *who* of leadership is just as important as the
what or *how* is something I was able to articulate after reading Parker J.
Palmer's book about teaching. When I first read *The Courage to Teach*, I
told colleagues that it was the best book about leadership I had read that
year, that almost every time he used the word *teacher* in the book I could
substitute the word *leader*. In the book, Parker asserts that good teaching
comes from the identity and integrity of the person, and that we do not ask

about the self who shows up to teach as often as we ask about the *what* and *how* of their work in the classroom. This is, obviously, similar to the claim I am making about leadership.

Performance appraisals are not the only time we find it hard to tell the truth and operate with deep integrity. Too often we feel it necessary to hide our voice, keep dissenting opinions to ourselves, toe the company line, and represent management's position. We go along with decisions with which we don't agree, with wrong directions taken, with organizational policies and practices that wither the human spirit. It is the only sane and safe way to live, we argue, or at least the only way to survive in an organization.

But saying we agree when we don't, and supporting policies and practices that we secretly oppose, is collusion, and today collusion is happening on a massive scale. More than any other single factor, collusion is undermining the productivity and health of individuals, teams, groups, communities, and companies.

Jerry Harvey, a professor at George Washington University, has written beautifully about the problems of collusion, our tendency to say yes when we want to say no, our tendency to go along with decisions with which we do not agree. Perhaps Harvey's best known writing is a parable called *The Abilene Paradox,* about a decision made in his wife's family, with Harvey as a participant, to drive from Coleman, Texas, to Abilene on a sweltering August day to eat lunch in a cafeteria, only to learn on the return trip that no one really wanted to go. Each had agreed to go to please the others. "Going to Abilene" has entered our lexicon as a way of describing the collusion that happens in relationships, workgroups, and whole organizations when we say yes while wanting to say no.

Collusion comes in many guises. Collusion happens when we remain silent, knowing our opinion will not be well received. Collusion happens when we voice our opinion but do it with so many caveats that we undercut our argument. It is collusion when we talk *about* a person but not *to* the person. It is collusion when we excuse or reward behaviors we say we don't like.

For several years, I facilitated a public school redistricting steering committee in the city in which I live. Early on, we agreed that we would express disagreements openly and honestly, that we would put our differences on the table. We committed to working through conflict, or at least acknowledging it, rather than ignoring it. But it did not take long to realize that conversations in the parking lot after the meetings were different from what was said during the meetings; it was in the parking lot that men and women were speaking their heartfelt opinion. It was not surprising, but it was still collusion. I suggested a new norm: we would say nothing after a meeting that was not said during it. As you might guess, that was difficult, almost impossible, to do.

One name given to collusive behavior is groupthink. The dynamic is as understandable as it is simple: one or more individuals understand that the group supports a different position. Because the individuals want to be seen as team players, they don't own or express their opinion, at least not as strongly as they feel it. They succumb to peer pressure. They go along to get along.

In *Reframing Organizations,* authors Lee Bolman and Terry Deal report that this is exactly what happened in the *Challenger* disaster. At least one engineer at Morton Thiokol, the company that provided the now infamous O-ring, suggested postponing the flight because the company had no data on how the O-ring would perform at the temperatures that were expected at the time of the launch. But others at Thiokol and NASA felt pressure to proceed with a liftoff, and the reluctant Thiokol engineer relented. He said yes after first saying no; he said yes when he still wanted to say no.

There is a lot in organizations and groups that encourage people to collude: use of coercive power, encouragement to be a good team player, the unwritten norms that suggest conflict or disagreement is wrong. But at some level it is always a choice we make. The problem is that collusion tears at the fabric of our individual identity and undermines organizational effectiveness.

Parker describes collusion as "hiding behind the wall." We are born whole and integral, but early in life we learn to "wall off" ideas and truths most precious to us. We are unwittingly encouraged to do this by parents and parent-figures, by teachers, by friends, and later by bosses.

Parker suggests, and I think he's right, that we tend to speak our truth only when we realize that the pain of living a divided life—the pain that comes when we realize we are diminishing ourselves as persons—is worse than any consequence we might suffer from coming out from behind the wall. When we decide we will not wall off our truth but instead let it make an on-stage appearance, then we decide to live "divided no more." Living divided no more is living and leading with transparency, with deep integrity; it is allowing others to know what's going on inside us.

Living "divided no more" is the antidote to collusion. But it takes courage to come out from behind the wall, to speak the truth as we know it, to say no when we want to say no. It takes courage to live with integrity. It takes courage to lead.

Embracing Light and Shadow

There is yet another way in which it takes courage to become oneself and to lead with integrity or wholeness. In *Leadership and Spirit,* I wrote

> Of all the soft stuff that executives and managers, and all the rest of us try to avoid, inner consciousness may be the softest of all. Inner consciousness cannot be quantified. It cannot be studied empirically. It cannot be experienced by any of the senses. It is not part of the curriculum of the Harvard Business School. It is hard to understand, much less appreciate. Managers and executives have enough problems with which to wrestle; they see no need to go on an inner journey to find more. . . . It is easier to operate on a belief that what you see is what you get.[1]

Parker says it this way: "Leaders, in the very way they become leaders, tend to screen out their inner consciousness."[2]

What makes the issue more problematic is that most executives—indeed, most of us—are only dimly aware of how what goes on deep inside of them affects their leadership for good or bad. Individual leaders often do not realize how the fears, anxieties, and insecurities they carry internally affect themselves or how they project them onto relationships and organizations. Yet, all of my experience, as a manager, leader, and as a coach to managers and executives, convinces me that our inner life and outer work are inextricably linked. What you see is not all that you get. What is not seen—what we project—is not always benign. We project both light and shadow.

Recently I had an opportunity to again experience the costs of an unexamined inner life. I was serving as an executive coach to two of the top executives of a national organization. To prepare for the coaching, I gathered extensive data through one-on-one interviews with the executives, the peers and direct reports who worked closely with the executives, members of the organization's board, and people outside the organization. Data from a multirater feedback instrument was used to round out the picture of each executive. To get to the bottom line—what I learned about these two leaders was that one had lots of insecurity and fear lurking inside himself and the other had lots of anger inside herself.

The fear and anxiety of the male COO showed itself in many ways: in his unwillingness to deal with even the simplest of conflicts, with his discomfort and hesitancy in relating to board members and business leaders in the community, in his unwillingness to make decisions even after all the data were in. For instance, he sent performance appraisals through the mail; face-to-face conversations were not to be.

The insecurity and fear was toxic to the executive; it kept him from using his good gifts and all his energy in his leadership role. But it wasn't just the executive who carried the insecurity. Individuals in the organization carried it as well; it was projected onto them by the executive. The executive's fears were also toxic to the organization; too much energy was spent dealing with the shared sense of insecurity that they were carrying for the executive.

For her part, the woman executive could turn even the smallest incident into a major brouhaha. But she didn't always, and this was part of the problem. At one moment, she was warm and charming; the next she was demeaning and demanding. On several occasions, she got so angry that she threw things in meetings, not hitting anyone but scaring everyone. In describing this executive's tendency to go from warm to warmongering, one of her direct reports said she could and would "turn on a dime." Her anger, I believe, was based on some deep-down fears: maybe fear of the chaos of organization life, or perhaps fear that she wasn't enough, or fear that she had only herself to count on (she was fond of quoting the old bromide, "If it is going to be, it is up to me").

None of those who worked with her thought of her as fearful. It was not evident to them. The anger was, but the fear wasn't. But the fear was evident in the individuals who reported to her, the peers who worked with her, and in the organization; this is where the executive had projected it. People "walked on eggshells around her," they never knew "which person would show up for a meeting," and "lived in fear of setting her off." The fear was toxic.

Neither of these executives was all that self-aware. To use language that has become popularized in recent years, they did not have a high level of emotional intelligence, neither intrapersonal nor interpersonal. They did not know, at least not consciously, how their inner life affected their outer work. They did not know that employees breathed a sigh of relief when they left town on a business trip or on vacation. Even I noticed a difference when they were not around; it was a more relaxed, more energized workplace.

There is much that could have been gained if these two executives had traveled down and in and confronted their fears. They probably would have been more comfortable with themselves, more who they were meant to be, and less angry and fearful. Their shadows would not have held them in such a tight grip, and it would have been less likely that they would project it onto others. Their colleagues and staff, in turn, would have been relieved from living with and carrying the executives' fear and anger. If the costs are so real and so great, why do we screen out our inner consciousness? Why don't we take the journey in and down to examine our inner life?

From what I have learned, on my own journey and as an executive coach, the decision to take an inner journey down and in toward those parts of ourselves that we have worked long and hard to dismiss or deny requires enormous courage. Carl Jung said it this way: "This confrontation [with self] is the first test of courage on the inner way, a test sufficient to frighten off most people, for the meeting with ourselves belongs to the more unpleasant things that can be avoided so long as we can project everything negative onto the environment."[3]

For sure, confronting my own shadow took courage. For many years, the idea never occurred to me. No boss ever suggested it. No leadership development course or program ever had it as part of the curriculum. Nothing in my formal education process suggested a need for it. It took two difficult experiences, one professional and one deeply personal, to nudge me into an inner journey. The personal experience was a divorce. Like no other experience, the divorce and the counseling I engaged in at the time brought me face to face with my insecurities, my fears, my dependencies. The therapist with whom I worked was the first person in my life to encourage me to embrace my shadow rather than deny or project it. At first, I resisted the idea; I wanted to get rid of these unwanted parts of me.

What I eventually learned is that understanding my shadow, and learning to dance with it, if not embrace it, is a critical step to becoming a whole, true self. And it takes courage to become whole. It especially takes courage to take an inner journey toward those parts of ourselves we try so hard to deny. This is an ongoing piece of work for me. But I have learned that if I, and the other leaders with whom I have been privileged to work, don't take this journey, we continue to project our shadow—our fears, our insecurities, our deep-seated anger—on others with whom we work. We (you and I) cannot engage in leadership with a deep sense of identity and integrity unless we take this journey. It takes courage to lead.

I have heard Parker speak to this same reality when he says: "A new leadership is needed for new times, but it will not come from finding new and more wily ways to manipulate the external world. It will come as we who lead find the courage to take an inner journey toward both our shadows and our light—a journey that, faithfully pursued, will take us beyond ourselves to become healers of a wounded world."[4]

This journey is critical for leadership, but it is also critical for each of us as individuals. Living without a deep sense of integrity and identity slowly deforms us. Hiding our truth and denying our shadow are but two of the ways this happens. There are many other cultural expectations and organizational practices that contribute to our deformation, and there are decisions we make that lead us down detours and wrong directions. Here are a few of them:

- Rather than engaging in leadership with a deep sense of identity, individuals try to be the kind of leader others expect. They attempt to live up to some mythical ideal—always strong, never weak, sometimes heroic, bold and self-confident, always steady in the eye of the storm, charismatic.
- The use of coercive power in leadership roles is dismembering. It deforms those who employ it and deforms those on whom it is used. It takes courage to give up sources of coercive power—systems of rewards and punishments—and rely only on personal power, power grounded in self-worth and self-confidence. It also takes courage to refuse to be coerced.
- Typical practices of top-down, command-and-control leadership are dispiriting. We can and must do better. We need to learn new ways to conceptualize and engage in leadership, ways that use the birthright gifts of many people in a shared process, but giving up old ways of leadership to try new and uncertain ones takes courage.
- The suggestion that there are formulas an individual can use to become a leader—some ten easy steps to CEO effectiveness—rather than telling the truth about the hard journey down and in that is required to become a whole, integral person, distorts reality.
- The climb up the organizational ladder can be deforming; individuals often lose a sense of their own terra firma as they climb one rung after another. The evidence of recent years is staggering; corporate perks and executive power too often corrupt and deform.
- Men and women are convinced that their birthright gifts are not enough—and that consequently they are not enough. Individuals (again, read this as all of us) need to develop new competencies *and* remember and use birthright gifts.
- Even the leadership development programs and practices we have used for many years (this is an area where I am culpable) can steer us away from true self. One example: the most widely used instrument in the world is the Myers-Briggs Type Indicator. When used well, the MBTI helps individuals understand and embrace important personal and leadership preferences, and it helps them understand and honor differences between and among people. But too often the MBTI is used in a way that puts people in boxes ("No wonder you rushed to closure on that decision; you're a J"), or as an excuse for behavior ("What did you expect from me? After all, I'm an extrovert"). When used in these ways, the MBTI does violence to an individual's identity.

When we live and lead in these ways, we become caricatures of ourselves. In the evocative words of May Sarton, if and when we wake up, we learn that that we have "worn other people's faces." Sometimes we wear other people's faces for so long we forget our own. We lose our sense of who we are. It takes courage to become oneself, to become the person we started out to be. It also takes courage to lead.

To Become and Lead as the Person We Started Out to Be

If the first task is to become yourself, how do you go about it? If so many of the forces you encounter deform, how can you be intentional about becoming the person you started out to be? Bennis points the way, as we saw in the opening epigraph: you "use yourself completely—all your gifts, skills, and energies—to make your vision manifest. You must withhold nothing."

Use All Your Gifts

Through the years, I have learned that using our gifts is not the hard part; what is hard is discerning and embracing them. "We arrive in this world with birthright gifts," Parker says, "then we spend the first half of our lives abandoning them or letting others disabuse us of them." Part of remembering ourselves and reclaiming our identity is discerning and using our gifts.

Career counselor John Crystal offers the best way I have found to remember our gifts: "Think about those things you have always found it easy to do and don't remember learning how." We tend to value the knowledge and skills we have worked hard to acquire; if we earned it from the sweat of our brow it must be important, or so we tell ourselves. But when aspects of work or life come easy, we think they must not be all that important. Crystal asks us to consider the reverse, that the "things we have always found it easy to do" might point us toward our gifts.

At other times it is the insights and encouragement from others that help us discern our gifts. I was in my early fifties when a development editor from a major publisher told me I was a "gifted writer." She told me this on the basis of a chapter I was writing for an edited book. Before then, I would have never considered using the word *writer* to describe myself. It is still hard. In this and other ways, I continue to discern my gifts.

Gifts, when properly discerned and claimed, provide individuals with knowledge of the distinctive contribution they can make to the practice of leadership. When the activity of leadership uses the gifts of many ordinary people, rather than relying on the gifts of the extraordinary few, it is immeasurably strengthened.

Equally important to discerning and using gifts is to understand that there is a flip side, a limit, to every gift. Acknowledging limits can be equally as difficult as embracing gifts. During my childhood, my father, with the best of intentions, told me I could be and do anything I set my mind to do. The sky's the limit, he said. The question, simply put, was whether I had the discipline and will to fulfill this unlimited potential.

It was after several years of being a manager in a major corporation and after ten years of being a manager at the Center for Creative Leadership (and a reasonably good one) that I realized my aspirations of one day being a vice president really didn't make sense because of limits that were truly part of my nature. But the temptation, as writer, teacher, and leadership practitioner Charles Handy reminded me, is to "go with the conventions of the time, measuring success in terms of money and position, climbing ladders others placed in my way, collecting things and contacts rather than giving expression to my own beliefs and personality."[5] I wanted to climb those ladders, I wanted the position and the prestige, and it was with reluctance that I admitted that being an executive was not a good fit with my true nature. It was, I was later to learn, freeing to come to this realization. I have found that as I live more fully into my gifts and limits I become more myself, engage more authentically in leadership activities, and do more work that is right work for me.

Use All Your Skills

As important as birthright gifts are, they are not always enough. There are, as I have previously noted, important leadership and life skills that we learn along the way. We learn them from a variety of experiences: from challenging jobs, from other people, from the hardships we experience in life and work, and from training events and retreats. The skills we develop are important, especially as we use them to better express who we are, use them to speak our truth rather than collude, use them in ways that complement our birthright gifts, and use them to make our vision manifest.

For example, in Courage to Teach and Courage to Lead retreats participants learn the skill of asking simple, open, honest questions. It is a new skill for many. They often have to unlearn the old habit of giving advice. At first, using open, honest questions seems unnatural and awkward. It takes intentionality and practice to do it well. But over time, individuals begin to integrate the skills, and they become part of their way of being, on retreat and elsewhere.

Here's the key: we want and need to develop skills that help us express— not hide—our true self. We want and need to develop skills that help us live in authentic relationship with others, not "manipulate them in more wily ways." Again, it takes courage to use our skills in ways that express our truths and birthright gifts. Without this courage, all the skills in the world will not help us lead from a deep sense of identity and integrity.

Use All Your Energies

There is an old Indian proverb that we are all houses with four rooms: the mental, the physical, the emotional, and the spiritual. For too long, too many of us have limited ourselves to just a few of these rooms. We have not used all the available energies in our work and in the practice of leadership. Our organizations haven't encouraged it, and we haven't done it.

At the turn of the century, organizations wanted our brawn, not our brain. During this time, Frederick Taylor, the father of scientific management, said workers would be dangerous if they were allowed to think. Today organizations know that intellectual capital is perhaps their most important asset. Slowly, organizations have begun to recognize and give sideways acknowledgment of the importance of emotional energy. They have learned that emotion and motivation come from the same root word, and that it was the way individuals felt about their work and the organization that was motivating or demotivating.

But what about spiritual energy? Too often organizations expect individuals to leave their spiritual longing—the need for meaning, connectedness, and significance—at home, or at least locked securely in their car in the company parking lot.

The notion that we can use our mental, physical, and emotional energy at work and leave our spiritual energy at home is grounded in an assumption that we can compartmentalize life. We have tried, and sometimes we think we have succeeded. But we have paid a price; we have contributed to our own diminishment. This is at obvious cost not only to ourselves but also to our work. Organizations are not going to get the best we have within us, are not going to get full-headed and full-hearted commitment, unless we bring our whole selves to our work and our leadership activities.

It takes courage to use all our gifts, skills, and energies to make our vision manifest.

It takes courage to choose to live out of a deep sense of identity and integrity.

It also takes courage to lead.

NOTES

1. Moxley, R. *Leadership and Spirit*. San Francisco: Jossey-Bass, 1999, p. 129.

2. Palmer, P. J. "Leading from Within." In L. Spears (ed.), *Insights on Leadership*. New York: Wiley, 1998, p. 6.

3. De Laszlo, V. S. (ed.). *The Basic Writings of C. G. Jung*. New York: Modern Library, 1993, p. 381.

4. Palmer, P. J. "Leading from Within." *Noetic Sciences Review,* Winter 1996, 40, 37.

5. Handy, C. B. *The Hungry Spirit: Beyond Capitalism: A Quest for Purpose in the Modern World*. New York: Broadway Books, 1999, p. 79.

REFLECTIONS

o

L. J. Rittenhouse
president of andBEYOND Communications

When I met Parker Palmer at a church seminar in 2000, I was struck immediately by his manner of speaking. He talked about the value of listening, and he listened. He talked about the importance of doing honest work, and he spoke honestly about his work struggles. During a break, I told him about my friendship with May Sarton, whose poems he used for teaching. I described my mission to expose sloppy, dishonest CEO communication. After the meeting, we began a correspondence that inspired me to write articles on Parker's work.

One of these was published in a magazine for executive recruiters, *Executive Talent*. It appeared in 2001, just months before September 11. Against the aftermath of those attacks, Parker's description of unsafe situations sounds prophetic:

> I know from my experience inside corporations and large-scale organizations that everybody is busy sizing up the leader and asking, "Is this a person divided or a person of integrity? Is what we see what we get? Are they the same on the inside as they are on the outside?" Students ask it about teachers in the classroom. Employees ask it about their bosses. Citizens ask it about their politicians. When the answer is, "No, what we're seeing on the outside is not the same as who they are on the inside," then everything starts to fall apart.
>
> When leaders with the power to call the tune and shape the dance are perceived as lacking congruence or integrity, they create unsafe situations. And what do people do in unsafe situations? They start hiding out. They start faking it. They start giving less than what they have to give.[1]

When I decided to leave a safe career to pursue a vocation that promised greater wholeness between my life and work, I also expected to find great surprises. Meeting Parker is one of these. In the words of poet Annie Dillard, I am "still spending the power" of our live and brief encounter.

IF WE PAY ATTENTION

L. J. Rittenhouse

NINE YEARS BEFORE I MET Parker Palmer, in 1991, I started a financial communications business. After a decade of Wall Street deal making, I needed a change. I wanted to explore the connection between communication and financial performance. As an investment banker, I had helped corporate executives increase their companies' earnings through acquisitions and financings. Too often, however, CEOs described these strategies to investors without providing key assumptions to back them up. They provided fluff when investors wanted substance. I began advising CEOs who chose to communicate forthrightly. These leaders wanted help in uncovering corporate blind spots.

In 1994, a colleague sent me a copy of the Berkshire Hathaway annual report. Reading the CEO's letter to shareholders was like discovering the New World. Author and CEO Warren Buffett's straight talk revealed his conviction that candid communication is a moral act. His ranking as the second richest man in the world (with 99 percent of his wealth tied up in the company stock) proved that candor, along with intelligence and principles, could be a winning strategy. Inspired by his example, I took my business in a new direction. Just as debt-rating agencies judge the creditworthiness of a company, I decided to analyze CEO communication as a measure of the candor-worthiness of a company.

After reading hundreds and hundreds of letters to shareholders, I began to see patterns. Some leaders used words efficiently. For example, one paragraph in Buffett's letter contained numerous ideas frequently seasoned with humor. Other CEOs needed one paragraph to communicate one idea. I found business topics that were cited over and over again. When I organized these topics into a model, the measure of candor and the gaps in the CEOs' communication became readily apparent.

Each year I use this model to rank roughly 20 percent of the CEO annual report letters from a representative sampling of *Fortune 500* companies. Over the years, I have found that companies scoring high in candor outperform companies that rank low. From 2001 through 2003, people who invested in the twenty-five companies that scored highest for candor got wealthier. Each investor would have gained a fourteen-percentage-point advantage in added stock appreciation.

People who consider CEO letters to be boring and muddled public relations documents are skeptical. They wouldn't read them to find truth telling or to help make investing decisions. They ask me, "Why waste my time?" Indeed, about two-thirds of the CEO letters in my annual survey are chock full of jargon and lack context. They fail to meet basic standards of candor and efficiency. But some letters *are* worth reading. This other third of the letters in my survey are authored by CEOs who show respect for the power of words and of keeping one's word. The continuity in their communication mirrors consistent superior financial performance.

Anyone can study communication to evaluate a CEO's integrity. The first thing to look for is clarity. Is the CEO skilled in language arts? Can he or she use simple words to convey complex ideas? Can the CEO organize thoughts and credibly advance arguments?

The second thing to examine is whether the leader offers a full and balanced report. Managers who neglect to describe how their actions increase profits and cash flow are not likely to be good stewards of investors' money. Candor strengthens competitive advantage. It allows CEOs to clearly anticipate both dangers and opportunities. Such leaders win investor trust. The following four strategic principles reveal the strength or weakness of a CEO's candor rating.

1. *If you can't understand what a CEO is writing about in a shareholder letter, then one of two possibilities is likely to be true: either he doesn't want you to understand what the business is doing, or he too does not understand the business.* Too often, people believe that their lack of knowledge is the reason they don't understand a shareholder letter. However, my research shows that 25 to 30 percent of the CEO letters in my survey qualifies as "fog." This includes jargon, as well as contradictory and awkward sentences that lack vital context. Imagine how employees, customers, and investors would be confused after reading this paragraph from a shareholder letter:

> Looking forward to 2003, we intend to leverage our relationships . . .
> to invigorate our performance categories and help further strengthen
> our business in all the primary channels of distribution we service. In
> 2003, we will be introducing new fashionable and technologically advanced
> product tied to new integrated marketing programs that leverage
> our on-field authenticity.

Some CEOs "spin" information. It's easy to spot this when leaders compare past and current financial results. For example, a well-known investment bank reported in 2002 that their stock price was up 39 percent over two years. Such an atypical comparison—two years—suggested that the more common year-to-year result might not have been as "robust." Sure enough, a little digging in the financial statements showed that the stock increased only 11 percent from the prior year.

However, when leaders communicate honestly, and deliver on their promises, stakeholders take notice. Employees work harder when they get unambiguous direction from the top. Freed from the burden of second-guessing management or, even worse, covering their backsides, employees can more effectively increase customer loyalty and sales. Similarly, investors are more likely to hold onto the stock through market volatility, thus shoring up the company's financial foundation.

2. *Leaders who report about what went wrong during the year are more likely to do what's right for their businesses.* CEOs who act as stewards of their businesses will give a balanced report of both their wins and losses. This should give investors comfort. After all, leaders who discuss their failures are less likely to repeat mistakes. Yet, while most everyone knows that things seldom go according to plan, about two-thirds of the companies in my annual surveys report problem-free performance. This feat is nothing short of miraculous—and highly suspect.

Companies that describe "what went wrong" in their letters will report on declining earnings, revenues, and stock prices and how they failed to meet previously stated goals. Only a handful of leaders go deeper to describe what they learned from these failures. One of these, CEO Roger Enrico, offered a unique post-mortem of PepsiCo's problems in his 1996 shareholder letter:

> When you chart our growth over all that time, you see it isn't exactly a straight line. Every once in a while, like last year, we seem to stumble.
>
> As a 25-year veteran of PepsiCo, very much in the action most of that time, I've tried over the last year to figure out what exactly accounts for our unevenness. . . .
>
> So what did we conclude? Well, odd as it might sound, we think we simply tried too hard sometimes, overreached, got out in front of our headlights, if you will, in our quest for growth.
>
> Over 30 years, our mistakes have been relatively few, thank goodness, but they've almost always been caused by investing too much money too fast, trying to achieve heroic overnight success where, in retrospect, the odds were tougher than they seemed.

Since 1996, PepsiCo's stock has consistently outperformed the S&P 500 index. The same cannot be said of its archrival, Coca-Cola. Despite well-documented media coverage of Coke's problems in employee relations, marketing, and sales, Coca-Cola's shareholder letters have skirted around their problems. Since 1996, that company's stock has underperformed the S&P 500.

It's even harder to find CEOs who take personal responsibility for corporate missteps. To date, Warren Buffett is among a small number of CEOs who, like President Harry Truman, remember where the buck should stop. In 2001 Buffett wrote

> Last year I enthusiastically told you that we would step up our expenditures on advertising in 2000 and that the added dollars were the best investment that GEICO could make. *I was wrong* [emphasis added]. The extra money we spent did not produce a commensurate increase in inquiries.

3. *CEOs who tell you how they are paid are more likely to steward the resources of the business.* Stewardship is another term for good corporate governance. It embodies the principle of making business decisions based on attitudes of entrustment, not entitlement. Compensation practices can reveal how committed boards and executives are to stewarding investor capital. It shows whether the leadership is out to *make money* for shareholders or to *take money* from them.

Practically all investors believe that compensation is a leading indicator of CEO stewardship. Nevertheless, fewer than 15 percent of the CEOs in my letter surveys describe their companies' compensation practices and principles. One of these was CEO John Gifford of Maxim, a computer parts manufacturing company. He reported in his 2002 shareholder letter, "Management did not get any bonuses because they did not meet their targets." Sadly, the chance of spotting this kind of candid talk about compensation is about as rare as sighting peregrine falcons in Manhattan.

In 2003, CEOs Jeff Immelt of GE and Paul Anderson of Duke Energy won special recognition for detailed reporting of incentive compensation in their shareholder letters. Instead of burying the details of their compensation in proxy reports, these leaders described in plain English what they could earn if they meet precisely defined goals aligned with investor interests. Both leaders rank high in independent surveys for implementing sound governance practices that promote capital discipline.

The amount of CEO pay has become a stewardship issue. In 2003, the gap in compensation between large company CEOs and average workers surpassed 900-to-1.[2] Charlie Munger, the vice chairman of Berkshire Hathaway and CEO of Wesco, observed back in 1998 that such inequity would have negative consequences:

> I do think it will have pernicious effects on the country in its entirety as management pay keeps escalating because I think you're getting a widespread perception that the very top corporate salaries in America are obscene. And it is not a good thing for a civilization when the leaders are regarded as not dealing fairly with those for whom they are stewards.[3]

4. *The values of the corporate culture determine the reliability of accounting numbers.* Enron's 2000 annual report was published in early 2001. Even though the company continued to rank at the top of *Fortune* magazine's lists of "Most Admired" and "Innovative" companies, the shareholder letter signed by executives Kenneth Lay and Jeff Skilling offered clues that trouble was brewing.

For example, the letter reported that Enron earned $1.3 billion for the year, but the income statement in the same report showed earnings of only $978 million. This difference raised obvious questions: Did the gap result from careless proofreading? Was management trying to "spin" the earnings? Or had they lost touch with reality? In the spring when this letter was released, Enron's stock was trading at around $60.00 a share. By the end of the year, numerous investigations of accounting fraud and nonexistent earnings caused the stock to fall to $0.60 a share.

In 2002, a reporter from *Barron's* called just after the HealthSouth scandal broke. She wanted to know if CEO Richard Scrushy's recent shareholder letter offered clues to possible accounting irregularities. I didn't have to read far to find "smoking guns." A boast about consistently meeting analysts' earnings expectations indicated management's preference for creative, rather than conservative, accounting. This was demonstrated by the facts that (1) the earnings number in the letter didn't match the number in the audited income statement, and (2) the letter contained a claim that the balance sheet was strengthened by extending debt rather than by reducing it. Both practices should have raised doubts about the company's capital stewardship.

Scrushy's letter was thick with humbug. Even if someone else had penned it, he had signed his name. This would have prompted me to undertake extensive due diligence to test the company's true investment merits. Later, I listened to experts at a public meeting, including a respected journalist, cry, "Foul! How could anyone have known this duplicitous behavior was going on at HealthSouth?" I replied, "Read the shareholder letter."

Most investors distrust this approach to valuing companies based on CEO communication. They complain, "It's too subjective, too soft." They prefer to rely only on financial accounting numbers, comforted by an illusion that the precision of numbers will ensure objectivity and reliability. They forget that accounting numbers are approximations of value. In order to come up with their figures, accountants make important judgments about the timing of results to estimate the cash coming in and going out. They must decide whether to treat losses and gains as part of continuing earnings or as one-time events. The ethics practiced and communicated by the CEOs will determine if their accountants interpret these numbers conservatively or aggressively.

CEOs at Enron, HealthSouth, Tyco, Adelphia, and WorldCom fostered corporate cultures based on deception. Investors learned in hindsight that the accounting in these companies could not be trusted. Indeed, the fallout from the recent stock market bubble showed how widely investor trust was abused. Business journalists more intent on selling copy than on upholding integrity failed to print hard-hitting investigative articles. Brokers and analysts recommended companies that met "earnings guidance" without understanding how these companies met their targets. By paying more attention to corporate lobbyists than to its own Securities and Exchange Commission, the government failed both investors and the public.

My response to corporate corruption was to write a book about the ethics of CEO communication, *Do Business with People You Can Tru$t: Balancing Profits and Principles,* which was released in 2002. I argued that if rank-and-file investors had trusted their own good common sense they could have spotted problems in high-flying companies that experts ignored. Instead, greed and an inability to trust their own judgment undid plain folks' confidence. In the end, if blame must be placed, there is plenty to go around.

At the peak of the bubble market in 2000, I met Parker Palmer. We began a dialogue that helped me to see a new dimension in my CEO research—the degree to which leaders are open to introspection, reflection, and learning. I wondered if the spiritual truths that Parker championed with educational leaders could be applied to business leaders. Our talk grew into an article, "Leadership and the Inner Journey." In it, Parker invited leaders to journey to wholeness. This desired state is achieved by integrating our deepest aspirations with the circumstances of our lives. As with all quests, the steps taken on this journey are as important as the destination. Leaders who wish to succeed must confront a paradox: to become whole, they must come to terms with their brokenness, their fears and failures. Observing that personal qualities needed for such self-discovery are dangerously deficient in CEOs, Parker warned:

Today's leaders have the potential to make decisions that affect the course of history, but seldom are they invited to examine what animates them inwardly. History is full of tragedies created when leaders act from a place of inner darkness. When I speak with leaders, I sometimes expand on Socrates: If you must live an unexamined life, please don't inflict it on others.[4]

This idea of choosing CEOs whose greatness comes from their curiosity and caring about things outside of themselves, as well as their strategic and execution skills, seems laughable today. That's not the image projected on CNBC or in the business press. *Fortune Magazine* is not likely to publish its rankings of "Most Vulnerable, Spiritual CEO." Yet my research shows that executives increasingly use nonfinancial words such as *soul, spirit, faith, belief,* and *love* to describe their business practices.

Just as Parker advocates a networked model of learning based on community, CEOs are transforming their hierarchical organizations into communities of fast-moving global networks. As corporations span the globe, CEOs are learning about the colored mosaic of human experience. They are discovering the usefulness of Parker's definition of truth: "an eternal conversation about things that matter, conducted with passion and discipline."[5]

This notion of finding strength in vulnerability is not some New Age paradigm. Parker reminds us that history is a long story about people with few material resources who have sought wholeness and inspired profound change. In our lifetimes, we have the examples of Rosa Parks, Vaclav Havel, and Nelson Mandela. At moments of extreme personal challenge, these leaders overcame their fears and found the power of their inner voices.

Parker knows that vulnerability is not a condition we seek. We prefer the illusion of certainty to the discomfort of the unknown. Yet in my life, external events have often disarmed my defenses and forced me to confront my own inner darkness. At the point when despair was all-encompassing, I found courage and hopefulness. These journeys taught me that real, not illusory, security comes only when I detach myself from what I most fear to lose—not in grasping at it.

I still recall how frightened I was about leaving my job as a successful Wall Street banking executive. After over a decade of financial deal making, I knew I needed more than a prestigious job that consumed all my time. I had to choose between staying in a job that lacked fulfillment but brought a comfortable income and starting a business that had no definition and no income. I picked the latter. It was ridiculously impractical and quixotic.

I called a friend the night before I was to resign and spoke confidently about my exciting future. Then I burst into tears. She invited me to dinner.

In between courses, I talked about my fear of leaping into the unknown. She listened straight through as we ordered coffee. Then, reaching out across the table she uttered words I will never forget. "Take my hand," she said, "We'll jump together."

Friends and colleagues helped me chart this unknown territory by describing my gifts. Unlike the knowledge and skills I acquired from work experience, this required them to name my spiritual talents. They had to assess my character, passions, and vocation. One colleague scribbled this: "(1) you can see further than the nearby details of life; (2) you have a big brain, which is capable of unconventional thinking; putting together information and ideas that are ordinarily compartmentalized; and (3) you have big energy, which makes things you care about happen."

Her words helped me to find a path marked by these gifts. Whenever I used my gifts, I felt fulfilled and satisfied. This deepened my understanding of who I was and who I could become.

This journey of self-discovery requires constant learning. It is the link that joins Parker's work with that of CEOs who choose to build corporate cultures that inspire learning. These leaders invest in programs to "empower employees" with new skills and knowledge so they can improve bottom-line performance. However, my annual surveys show that few CEOs embody the principles of learning. They almost never describe what *they* are learning. This was especially true in the letters written after the 9/11 terrorist attacks.

The majority of CEOs—eighty out of one hundred—described something that related to the attacks—how they weakened the economy, how people responded, and even how the attacks brought them new business. Eighteen percent neglected to mention them at all. It was as if they had been asleep on 9/11 and ever afterwards. Of the one hundred, only two CEOs looked inward in their letters and tried to reflect on the personal significance of these catastrophic events. One of these was Phil Knight, the CEO of Nike, who wrote

> We entered FY '02 with a 1% decline in U.S. futures orders. We had our work cut out for us. Then came September 11, and with it a bow wave of uncertainty. Restaurants, stadiums, theme parks, malls, all thinner of crowd, showed the wan face of anxiety. We were at a threshold, one of those defining moments that pop up out of nowhere in every life, both individual and corporate. You can cross that threshold with courage or turn away in fear. Either way, you change forever.

Knight reminds us that not making a choice is also a choice. The decision to turn away and deny what happened is as much of a choice as deciding to act to prevent future terror attacks.

CEO Dave O'Reilly of ChevronTexaco wrote

> Last October's creation of ChevronTexaco Corporation, on time and
> as planned, was a major achievement that we're proud of. The tragic
> events of September 11, however, overshadowed the merger and tem-
> pered our sense of celebration. The terrorist attacks were a reminder—
> a terrible one—of how interconnected the world has become. . . . This
> interdependence can and should be a force for positive change—all the
> more reason for those of us in the global energy industry to work with
> renewed intensity.

O'Reilly describes what seems inescapable—we are all interconnected.
Since this can be a force for evil or for good, he urges his industry to work
even harder to achieve positive change.

Both leaders circle around a paradox. Security doesn't come from ex-
cluding others, it results when people act knowing that if anyone is left
out—we are all left out. Security will come when both CEOs and boards
of directors develop strategies based on another paradox—investors are
best served when corporations balance their duties to shareholders with
their responsibilities as global citizens. An exclusive focus on short-term
profit growth is simply not sustainable. Mr. Knight, whose company has
been criticized for labor practices, and Mr. O'Reilly, whose investors ques-
tioned some of his company's environmental decisions, each have marked
new trails. If they act on their insights, they can lead others in promoting
sustainable planetary change.

The events and aftermath of that deceptively sunny day in September
have forever changed how I look at the world. For over a decade, I worked
at the World Trade Center, which stood only five miles from my home. I
still recall the smell of burned bodies and smoldering debris that seeped
through my closed windows during the warm nights after the attack. For
me, any monument that rises on the site of "Ground Zero" will forever
memorialize the explosive power of unexamined inner darkness—fear,
avarice, self-loathing, prejudice, and hate.

My interview with Parker was published in *Leader to Leader* magazine
only days after September 11. Since then, the United States and the business community appear no closer to appreciating the powerful connection
between candid, authentic communication and sustainable business performance. Words continue to be misused and distrusted. Our political
lives are shaped by a culture of deception that presumes leaders are lying
unless proven to tell the truth. Even worse, citizens seem to have grown
weary of trying to tell the difference and appear not to care.

People accustomed to deception often question why I would evaluate CEOs' integrity by analyzing their communications. They suspect that some CEOs will learn my methodology in order to earn high marks. They will create letters that do not fairly represent their businesses. I have seen some CEOs attempt this. They never succeed. It's like trying to become an artist through painting by numbers. Authenticity in writing cannot be faked any more than can authentic living. A CEO's heart cannot be manufactured. As Charlie Parker, the acclaimed jazz saxophonist, observed, "If it ain't in your heart, it ain't in your horn."

Parker reminds us that, for much of human history, the word "heart" didn't just refer to emotions as it does today. Instead, it encompassed "the center of the human self, where everything comes together—where will and intellect and feeling and intuition and the capacity to hold a vision all converge. It's about the integrity of the human self."[6] The words chosen by a CEO will reveal, if we pay attention, whether a leader chooses to journey closer to this place of integrity.

NOTES

1. Rittenhouse, L. J. "Leading from the Heart." *Executive Talent,* Spring 2001, p. 83.

2. "Executive Compensation Scoreboard." *BusinessWeek,* Apr. 19, 2004.

3. "Berkshire Hathaway's Warren Buffett and Charlie Munger." *Outstanding Investor Digest,* Sept. 1998, 24, 55.

4. Rittenhouse, L. J. "Leadership and the Inner Journey." *Leader to Leader,* Fall 2001, p. 27.

5. Parker, P. J. *The Courage to Teach: Exploring the Inner Landscape of a Teacher's Life,* San Francisco: Jossey-Bass, 1998, p. 104.

6. Rittenhouse (2001), p. 27.

REFLECTIONS

○
_____

David Dodson
president of Make a Difference in Communities

In the late 1980s, just as I was making the transition from "funder" to "doer," the Lilly Endowment invited me to join a circle of colleagues engaged in searching for fresh and challenging approaches to leadership development. In contrast to the bottom-line, make-it-happen view of leadership development so prevalent in our culture, Lilly had the courageous foresight to emphasize soul more than strategic brilliance as a defining measure of powerful leadership. I soon learned that Parker Palmer stood at the center of this effort to restore attention to the "inner work of the leader." I began to read whatever Parker wrote, and when we finally met in the early 1990s I knew I had found a mentor.

INSPIRING COMMUNITIES
OF CARING AND CONSCIENCE

David Dodson

MY LIFE'S WORK HAS FOCUSED on helping people change their communities and institutions from within in order to produce conditions where equity can prevail and all people have a fairer chance to thrive. For six years, I worked at a philanthropic foundation, investing in the efforts of grassroots leaders to change self-limiting community circumstances. For over a dozen years, I have been based in a nonprofit organization that works hand-in-hand with the communities themselves. Always the purpose of my work has been the same: to help communities work as well for the people living in the shadows as they do for the rest of us.

Whether or not he set out to do it intentionally, Parker Palmer has become an indispensable resource for legions of people working for community change. Whether the goal is better schools, safer neighborhoods, or more transparent government, Parker's ideas have an uncanny ability to make us better advocates and leaders. He calls us to our conscience, pricks our hypocrisy, and stiffens our spines. By transforming those who would lead, his ideas help leaders transform their settings. As a teacher and encourager of community leaders, I don't leave home without him.

My work to increase opportunity, reduce poverty, and strengthen communities takes me deep into places that time and the economy have forgotten: the Mississippi Delta, the cane fields of South Central Florida, Indian reservations, the Rio Grande Valley, the threadbare towns of the Appalachian coal fields, even Southern Africa. To the outside observer, these places seem to be on the receiving end of social progress. They are poor, their young are fleeing to brighter opportunities elsewhere, their traditional leaders are worn out, they lack the political connections to muster outside aid or powerful allies. Yet in every one of these places there is a core of people who are predisposed to hope rather than despair—people who read reality through different lenses, who dare to dream of transformation. These are the leaders who are not content for the people and places they love to be left behind. It is my role as an activist to help provide organizing and conceptual tools that can help these unlikely visionaries validate their visions of leadership.

Divided No More:
A Movement Approach to Educational Change

Over a dozen years ago, a major foundation asked our organization to create a cadre of school-based leaders—counselors, teachers, and principals—who would transform the practice of academic guidance so that more students, and not just the "gifted," would be directed toward college and promising careers. We canvassed the state to find educators who were restless for change and convened them for a yearlong program of education and development. The educators examined data about academic tracking and ability grouping. They explored whether their schools were giving equal encouragement to all students, or whether some groups were more favored than others. They read about schools where high expectations were the norm for every child. Most significantly, they were encouraged to examine the belief system that shaped the expectations and guidance practices in their own schools.

A few months into the program, we held a session where each participating school looked at the patterns of student achievement and course placement by race, gender, and income. The results showed a clear tendency of schools to encourage some groups toward college while steering others toward lesser goals. All at once, a rather quiet school counselor stood up, his brow tight with pain. "I'm overwhelmed by the immorality of what we're doing. We're putting kids into tracks that lead nowhere. Nowhere." The room went dead as people looked anxiously at one another. Then a buzz began. "He's right. He's right." From that moment on, the dynamic of the program was forever changed. Truth had been spoken, shared, recognized, embraced. Only later, after reading Parker's article, was I able to name what took place that day: we had experienced, serendipitously, a "divided no more" moment.

"Divided No More" is a deceptively simple and profoundly powerful little article that captures the power of what Parker so usefully terms "the movement approach to educational change."[1] Movements, he says, unfold in four stages. They begin when people decide to "stop living divided lives," when the burden of thinking one way and acting another becomes intolerable and we are forced to bring our values and our actions into congruence. "Most of us know from experience what a divided life is. Inwardly we feel one sort of imperative for our lives, but outwardly we respond to quite another." When the tension of being divided becomes too much to bear, it "snaps inside this person, then that person, and then another . . . a movement may be under way."

The movement reaches a second stage, when the people who have decided to live divided no more "discover each other and enter into relation of mutual encouragement and support." When the school counselor stood up and proclaimed that he could no longer preside over an immoral system that tracked some students away from opportunity, his outburst caused others to recognize their own "dividedness." From that epiphanic moment forward, our leadership program was transformed into a community of mutual support and truth telling, a place of intellectual and spiritual solidarity where, in Parker's words, people realized that "even though they are out of step, they are not crazy."

At the third stage of the movement, "people start to translate their private concerns into public issues." Such was the case with our leadership program. A few months after the counselor's confession, we took our participants to Harlem to show how exemplary schools could help students secure a future even amid the most challenging circumstances. The trip overturned the world of an elementary school counselor from an all-white school in a blue-collar town. "I have no excuse, no excuse" we heard her mutter to herself repeatedly as she walked the halls of a Harlem middle school. "Our problems are nothing compared to these kids'. There's no excuse for me not to do better." Two weeks later, this counselor, who had never before attended a meeting of her school board, much less addressed the board in public, testified on the inadequacy of her district's approach to guidance and left the school board transfixed. Her private concern became a public issue.

At the fourth and final stage, "movements return to intersect with organizations." This, at least, was the hope of our program: that our newly aware leaders would return to their schools and districts to leverage changes in the daily practice of academic guidance and college preparation. Many did, with profound and encouraging results. More significantly, twelve years after the work began the movement still thrives, led by alumni who are helping others close the gap between the values they hold as educators and the practices their schools employ to sift and sort students.

As one of the people responsible for shepherding this learning community, I am forever grateful for the serendipitous discovery of Parker's "Divided No More." It helped me become aware of the dynamics that our leadership program was unleashing. Later, when we shared the idea of divided no more with the participants, it helped them name the miraculous transformation that was happening to them, individually and collectively.

"Divided-no-more" moments are rare in my work. Whole-scale movements are rarer still. They probably elude deliberate manufacture. They

are accidents of grace. Yet even if we struggle in vain to engineer movements for change, we can create spaces and opportunities that are the
seedbed of these movements. Consciousness and conviction can emerge
when people face reality and speak the truth in the safety of each other's
company. This is a profoundly valuable gift.

Leading from Within: The Power of Light

Anger and frustration with the status quo are often the key motivation for
people to change their communities. "We're sick and tired of being sick
and tired. Things have got to change," people repeatedly tell us. Much of
my work with distressed communities involves helping people to develop
skills of critical analysis, understand the dynamics of community development, generate resources and relationships to give life to their ideas, and
learn to influence the politics of change. Perhaps invariably, this work invites people to think that leadership involves manipulating the world,
changing things "out there." Under such circumstances, leadership becomes an external act, which isn't altogether inappropriate since so much
needs changing in distressed communities.

But the more I work in distressed communities, the more I understand
that leadership is equally about interior and exterior work. Many of the
places in America that most need to change have very limited models of
what good leadership can be. Across the rural South, for instance, powerful,
extractive economic interests have held communities in sway for decades.
Assets and opportunities are tightly controlled, imagination is discouraged,
and power is wielded hierarchically, often for the benefit of a privileged few.
This history and experience have produced limited notions of leadership
and followership: leaders control and direct; the rest obey and follow. Even
when the disenfranchised come into some power, they revert to these same
old models, the only kind they've ever known. So, when the coal miner's
daughter is elected to office she assumes the leadership style of the mine
owner who kept her ancestors down. Or the newly minted African American leader becomes as hierarchical as the plantation overseer because experience tells him "that's how you get things done."

Parker's disarming definition of a leader as "a person who has an unusual degree of power to project on other people his or her shadow, his
or her light" is an indispensable tool for helping people in such circumstances broaden their notions of leadership. The idea that leaders are
called to exude a spirit of "inner confidence, wholeness, and integration,"
and to project a spirit of "light" and "hope," inspires community leaders
to transform their approach to leadership and the work at hand.

Several years ago, we worked to develop leadership among citizens in a deeply impoverished community in rural Florida. The group was heterogeneous in every way: race, gender, ethnicity, education level, leadership experience. More than a few were self-anointed leaders with docile or terrified constituents—a teaching opportunity if ever one existed! We took a risk in asking the group to read and discuss Parker's article "Leading from Within." The effect was electric and powerful. No sooner had the discussion begun than Parker's words began to sail around the group as the participants praised and cajoled each other:

> "Don't be showing me your shadow, now. I need to see your light."
>
> "Oooh. There goes your shadow again!"
>
> "Who I am does not depend on what I do." (My identity doesn't depend on my title.)
>
> "Be not afraid. Let your light shine."

In many years of community work in many settings, I have never seen a grassroots group adopt a set of ideas so spontaneously. Why, I still wonder, did "Leading from Within" have this impact? For certain, these leaders had intimate experience with the "shadow side" of leadership. Most were in daily contact with institutions that deprived many people of their identity so a few could enhance theirs. Many had stood in the shadows that others had cast on them and knew they wanted—needed—to lead differently. They knew who they did *not* want to be like.

At a deeper level, I think "Leading from Within" invited them to look inside to authenticate and act on their best impulses and values. In a community setting, which devalued "ordinary" people like them, "Leading from Within" invited them to move "downward and inward" to find the wellsprings of leadership in their own souls. No "training" had ever done this before. Finally, it gave them permission to share with others the heavy burden of community transformation:

> One of the great gifts we receive on the inner journey is the knowledge that ours is not the only act in town. Not only are there other acts in town, but some of them from time to time are even better than ours. On this inner journey we learn that we do not have to carry the whole load, that we can be empowered by sharing the load with others, and that sometimes we are even free to lay down our part of the load. On the inner journey we learn that co-creating with others leaves us free to do only what we are called and able to do, and to trust the rest to other hands. With that learning, we become leaders who cast less shadow and more light.[2]

Ever since that remarkable experience in Florida, "Leading from Within" has been part of the core curriculum of our work with community leaders, and "light and shadow" has remained part of our behavioral definition of a leader. Even if our discussions of the article don't always invoke such group call-and-response as it did in Florida, it still retains the power to lead people to rethink the balance between the inner and the outer work of leadership.

Not long ago, on the Skeleton Coast of Namibia, we held a retreat to debrief a five-year project that involved community members in creating a new campus of the national university hard on the Angolan border. The project had inspired the community to see themselves as cocreators of a new form of higher education, one more responsive to community interests than the traditional models of African higher education. Predictably, this new expression of community power evoked a negative reaction from the educational traditionalists who held power in the university. The champions of the new campus were becoming despondent at the thought of a prolonged bureaucratic fight to preserve their educational vision. Suddenly, someone spoke up, "We can't be gloomy. The community expects us to shed light." "Yes," echoed another, "we must shed light. Light." Soon the whole group had taken up the motto, "Let us shed a strong light." On the coast of Southern Africa, many miles from the cane fields of Florida and even further from the author himself, Parker's image of leadership had sprung to life spontaneously, reminding us once again that "we are here to shed light."

Welcoming the Stranger: The Challenge of Community

Every so often, I am inspired to reread *The Company of Strangers,* Parker's wonderful book about the role of the congregation as an agent of community building. Not only does the book challenge the church to be the church in profound ways but it reminds me, in my work with communities, that one of the toughest tests of a community is how hospitable it is to the stranger. Indeed, the ability to welcome the stranger may be the litmus test of real community, a litmus test that leads the community builder to confront work we often undervalue or ignore:

> Even though they are the antithesis of the gated communities that epitomize exclusion in affluent, modern America, distressed communities also struggle with welcoming the stranger. Scarcity can be as much the enemy of community as exclusivism and affluence: "Having struggled so long to get power for ourselves, why should we share it with you?" is the unspoken watchword in many hard-pressed places. "Why share

with those who aren't like us when there isn't enough to go around in the first place? Let the others wait."

Parker's disarming response is to remind us that abundance, not scarcity, is the ultimate reality in a world created in love and that hospitality is a paradox that enriches us as we give to others. These are wild, even disorienting ideas in a society where forces of greed and frantic self-centeredness often seem to prevail. Yet they are indispensable ideas for those of us who work to build community. If we believe in abundance, we have no reason to fear sharing ourselves and our communities with "the other." If we embrace the paradox of hospitality, we will find ourselves enriched.

Our work in the impoverished sugar growing communities of Central Florida offers a powerful example of how the suspicion of the stranger, once overcome, can yield to abundant new life in community. Our leadership work in Florida was structured to build trust and relationships across the fault lines of race, ethnicity, and class as people learned, worked, ate, and lived together over the course of the six-month program. The sleepover component of the program created strange bedfellows indeed. Plantation owners became roommates with former sharecroppers, business owners with grassroots organizers, Haitians with Latinos. As the program evolved, strangers gradually became neighbors. But the true flowering of communal abundance emerged when the forty participants in our leadership program were asked to plan their entertainment. What could a resource-poor community possibly muster to delight and entertain?

Then it dawned on the group. "We have dozens of ethnic groups represented in our midst. We each have our distinctive traditions, music, and food. Let's create our own entertainment by sharing who we are with one another." These entertainments proved so inspiring and enjoyable that they led to another idea: "What if we used all these wonderful homegrown cultural assets to draw tourists to our community?" Suddenly, a community that had viewed itself as deprived was advertising newly discovered abundance, abundance uncovered because one-time strangers had begun to behave as neighbors.

Soul and Role: Seeing Ourselves, Saving Ourselves

Like teaching, ministry, or any work that requires practitioners to model leading from within, the work of helping communities renew themselves can test our own capacity for renewal. A few years ago, drawing on his own youthful experience as a community organizer, Parker convened a small group of community activists and change agents to explore the inner dimensions of community work. Activists rarely pause to reflect; somehow the very act reeks of ideologically incorrect self-indulgence. So the convening was a rare, countercultural event.

For the opening session the first evening, Parker arranged the meeting room with an altar table with a lighted candle and a simple circle of chairs. Once we were comfortable—as comfortable as action-oriented people can be in a self-consciously reflective setting—Parker invited us to consider a simple question: "What parts of your role nourish your soul, and what parts stifle your soul?"

"Everything about my role nourishes my soul. Isn't that the right response for a wholly dedicated person?"

"But wait, there's the constant travel. The disappointment when communities follow the low road of politics as usual. The constant scrambling for resources."

"Hmm, the question's not so simple after all, is it?"

Characteristically, Parker had launched us on a journey of inquiry that continues to this day. For Parker is right: this is what vocation comes down to—a lively dance of "soul and role," the ever-engaging quest to find the right balance between being and doing, between action and reflection, so that we can serve joyfully without depleting ourselves, without exhausting our gifts before we can share them with others. Not all of us may be fortunate enough to strike a lively and fitting balance between soul and role as we move through this world. But in his writing and his bright example, Parker has equipped us generously for the passage. It is up to us to continually ask the questions and be open to the answers.

NOTE

1. Palmer, P. J. "Divided No More: A Movement Approach to Educational Reform." *Change,* 1992, 24(2), 10–17.

2. Parker, P. J. *Let Your Life Speak: Listening for the Voice of Vocation.* San Francisco: Jossey-Bass, 2000, pp. 73–93.

Chapter Six

RESCUING
THE SACRED

WE WILL FIND the common ground of public life not by destroying our particularity but by pursuing it, pursuing it to the depths where we encounter the ground of being which gave rise to and sustains us all.

—Parker J. Palmer

○

REFLECTIONS

○
———————

Zalman M. Schachter-Shalomi
professor of religious studies
at Naropa University

Parker Palmer and I have not spent a lot of time together. I wish we could have invested more time in fellowship. Very seldom have I had such a high-content connection with another person. I felt that we were—for all the differences in background—if not twin souls—at least soul cousins. It was not only that we could finish each other's sentences, we did not even have to say much; there was a look I got from him that told me that he *knew.*

I have met enough educators to know which ones are creating educational protocols and which ones communicate. Parker brings an open heart with deep listening to what is being said, and he also hears below the surface. His compassion is the carrier wave for his words.

The last time I was with him in physical space was when I held a dialogue with Houston Smith. Parker remarked to me that it was what Martin Buber meant by I-Thou meeting. I believe that no one is better suited than he to show us how to educate and form the future bodhisattvas, the ones who can help heal our planet.

Parker: at eighty, I don't travel much these days, but I will cherish time shared with you. Come and visit if you can.

TAKE THIS TO HEART

Graduation Address at
Naropa University, May 8, 2004

Zalman M. Schachter-Shalomi

THIS IS NOT ONLY a commencement address beamed at you. It is also my own valedictory at my retirement and becoming an emeritus. So I am speaking to you and including myself.

What can I say that you do not know? I offer reminders of what you already know in your innermost.

The psalms have a hope for us as we find ourselves in a dark tunnel. There are many sore places on the planet. Our mother the earth needs healing from her ecological wounds. From clear cutting, strip mining, deforestation, damage to the ozone layer, monoculture of crops to the polluting of soil, air, and water.

The social fabric of our culture is brittle and short fibered.

Intimate relationships are sustainable only with intensive and serious maintenance.

Our government has turned against the poor while lining the pockets of the rich. Lavish budgets are invested in what they euphemistically call "national defense," investing more than any nation in building armaments of mass destruction while education, health, and welfare are languishing. The tax burdens are being shifted onto the shoulders of nearly bankrupt states. The road ahead is not smooth.

And still we are now celebrating a graduation. Some of you I have taught—but what I have to offer is really for me as well as for you. I talk to you and your colleagues. I wish I had those optimistic words usually offered that send you off into a world where all is waiting for your advancement and success; a world where the graduate scholarships are waiting for you to develop further and live the good life. Instead I see immense burdens of student loans in a sparse job market.

It is not encouraging.

There are some good things awaiting you, but they are not pleasant and you and your cohort will have to prepare yourself for the tasks ahead.

Here I have only one counsel to offer: kindness to each other, to your own self, and to those with whom you will interact.

There are examples of countless unsung people who daily practice random acts of kindness, who are gentle even with those with whom they have differences.

There are people who advocate and practice compassionate listening, there are those who embrace voluntary simplicity, who remove the calluses from their hearts and keep them open to feel the pains of others.

Seek them out, I urge you, and join them in their compassion.

This is not the worst of all times, but it certainly is not the best.

Keep up your practice. Some of you have taken refuge—a good place to enter and restore your vows from time to time.

When I grew up in Austria I heard the Nazi boast after the Anschluss: *Heut' gehoert uns Deutschland—morgen die ganze Welt*. Other nations perceive in our financial-corporate capitalistic oligarchy a plan to dominate the globe. We are not welcomed by them to do this.

The Founding Fathers of this country had a different vision. Many were Free Masons who had spiritual insight in "nation building"—look at the emblems on the dollar bill.

E Pluribus Unum: the hope that we will work in concert and become "Out of Many, One." The hope that a good Providence would favor our endeavor.

Annuit Coeptis: "Providence Has Favored Our Undertakings." And beneath the unfinished Pyramid, pointing to the constant effort to bring about under God's seeing eye "A New Order of the Ages," Novus Ordo Seclorum.

They worked to create a social template that would maximize individual freedom and the pursuit of happiness, and they did not mean the possession of ever more obsolescent goods that deplete our material and natural irreplaceable resources and become toxic landfills.

You will need to do the almost impossible—gradually changing the tires of this country while the car is running. Not by violent revolutions but in patiently working on the matrix of our society.

You will need to do your healing work while still more poisonous stuff is released into air, water, and soil.

You will need to earn a living and at the same time become engaged in recovering the silenced voice of the people, for the people in the midst of the din of the dissembling media.

You will have to hold a clear, unsullied awareness despite the ever-entrancing attack of the aggressive marketing forces.

You are the ones who with others will have to heal America.

Precious America! I, who came here as a sixteen-year-old refugee fleeing from Hitler, have each year devoutly celebrated the Fourth of July.

What a haven it was and still is for the "tired and the poor." What hopes were kindled in us when we first saw the Statue of Liberty, and this wonderful land.

Instead of what they have called the Patriot Act, a measure repressive of our vaunted liberties—let us act as patriots who love this land and want to heal it as the great nation it can be.

"America, America, God mend thine every flaw; confirm thy soul in self-control, thy liberty in law."

So we hope and pray for our country, but don't forget to also be Matriots, of our mother the Earth, people dedicated to prevent a planeticide.

Look from time to time at that image of the planet taken from outer space, one blue living world in the cosmos.

As our liturgy has it, Sustain the world which Thou hast founded, yea, save our Earth suspended in space—Amen.

We are a diverse group, with different denominational labels, commitments, and creeds. But we are also aware of a caring Providence, the God beyond triumphalism.

No longer do we each claim that at the end of days only our own religion will be vindicated while the others are infidels who are eternally damned. We all share our world and our core values. We are aware that the heart of our commitment is to be good, to cherish the sacred and the truth, and to work for the good of all sentient beings.

I suppose the good of all sentient beings is what they at one time called "salvation."

In our emerging reality map, we see not a mechanistic Cartesian clockwork but Gaia, our planet as a living biosphere, an organism of which we all are cells making up organs. Each religious tradition and community is like an indispensable organ within the greater organism of the world life.

No longer can any tradition claim to be the sole source of truth. We each are cells in a vital organ of the planet. The liver cannot lord it over the kidneys, nor can the brain over the heart. We are all integral and essential for the planet, organically interdependent and connected. This we can all affirm and create cohorts of helpers.

In each of the traditions you will find committed and concerned coworkers who will share the burden of working for healing, motivated by their sense of being deployed by God.

Make friends with them in all their diversity. Grieve with them over what afflicts us—get to feel it and to own it as well and then celebrate together the privilege of being alive and of serving in the sacred task to restore our ailing planet to health.

You and your friends are, alas, on your own. Those who are entranced by the media and are content to remain parasitical consumers will resent you.

You will need to make your coalitions with likeminded people. You cannot rely on the public arena to urge you to do this work. Your spiritual get-go has to be energized by yourself and on your own.

In an almost desperate plea to you, I urge you to take this to heart. It is your world and that of your children. When some day you will be in the place of your parents at the graduation of your children, may you see more light and joy as you send them on their way.

Alumni and parents! Be available to share of your life experience with the graduates! Make your insight accessible to them, but do not force it. With open hearts and ears, be present to them as they wrestle in their souls with what is worthwhile and what is pressing, what is mere indulging and what is worthy of exertion, what makes for complacency and what makes for heroic virtue, what is expedient and what is valuable, what is trivial and what is significant.

Your heart-full witness will make you good and appreciated mentors, and neither you nor your young friends will feel lonely and abandoned.

Honored colleagues! You installed mind operating systems in your students. You did well—I plead with you to be available and answer the help lines to upgrade these systems when the students write, call, or visit. You are alive in them when you remember them; offer a little prayer on their behalf, and send blessings their way.

Graduates, keep in contact with the teachers who led you to light, truth, and discernment, whose values you have installed in your own ideals.

Call or send them a note when you become aware that you appreciate what in your life connects you to your Naropa Experience. Let them hear from you.

I am a teacher—I know how much this means when someone from my past appears and shows gratitude. I pray every day, and I urge you to spend some time and to consult your values and ideals.

This is one of the best daily meditations. Sit and allow action directives to come down from the Greater Intelligence and bring them into your lives. To maintain your own inner health, you need to become stewards of your own time.

While you have to work and earn a living and need to interact with the engine that drives commodity time, don't take up your residence in that pressure tank.

Your home and soul time is organic, regulated by heartbeat, breath, sun, moon, the seasons, and the tides.

Remember the Sabbath—time out, and keep it sacred to pamper your souls on it, to cherish love and friendship, to access the Original Blessings of a caring creation. Take a quiet walk in what is left of unspoiled nature; it will recalibrate your reality expectations and open your heart.

As our Native American elders have taught us, remember our connection with all our relations, the two- and four-leggeds, the flyers, the swimmers, the trees, and the water.

I do not ask you to spend your spiritual practice time in passive contemplation. But be receptive to what you can download from the web of life. God is accessible on the inner-net; keep logging on. And keep the hope that it will be better—when you work for it.

May the blessings of God rest upon you. May God's peace abide with you. May God's presence illuminate your heart, now and forever more.

REFLECTIONS

o

Sharon Daloz Parks
associate director of the Whidbey Institute

I first met Parker when I was teaching at Harvard Divinity School, and
he and his family were living at Pendle Hill. Parker and I share a commitment to the recovery of a recognition of spirit in the intellectual life,
especially in American higher education. I particularly remember a significant conversation we shared when he was writing *To Know as We
Are Known.*

In my current work at the Whidbey Institute, I lead a seasonal leadership retreat cycle for professionals from across sectors that is inspired, in part, by the seasonal retreat model developed by Parker. This
essay originated in a presentation at Trinity Church Wall Street, in
New York City, where Parker and I shared the platform at a national
conference held just seven months after the collapse of the Twin Towers of the World Trade Center, only a few blocks away.

HOW THEN SHALL WE LIVE?

Suffering and Wonder in the New Commons

———————

Sharon Daloz Parks

> A child sobs
> An eagle soars
> My soul grows larger

We are asked to live and work at one of those hinge points in history—a time when our cosmology and in turn our social covenants are being profoundly reordered. A passage from Christopher Fry's *Sleep of Prisoners* captures the moment:

> The human heart can go the lengths of God.
> Dark and cold we may be, but this
> Is no winter now. The frozen misery
> Of centuries breaks, cracks, begins to move,
> The thunder is the thunder of the floes,
> The thaw, the flood, the upstart Spring.
> Thank God our time is now when wrong
> Comes up to face us everywhere,
> Never to leave us till we take
> The longest stride of soul men ever took.
> Affairs are now soul size.
> The enterprise
> Is exploration into God,
> Where no nation's foot has ever trodden yet.
> Where are you making for? . . .
> It takes
> So many thousand years to wake.[1]

"The human heart can go the lengths of God." "Events are now soul-size." Increasingly, it seems that you and I are being asked to live in an enlarged, soul-size world.

In the wake of September 11, 2001, the place we have come to know as Ground Zero has become a holy pilgrimage site. It has also become a micro manifestation of the larger world to which we all belong—our new global commons—the context in which we now ask the question, "How then must we live?"

There are two primary responses to this question. One is to fortify ourselves in every possible way to protect ourselves (physically, emotionally, economically, politically) at all costs (politically, economically, emotionally, physically, spiritually). This is an understandable response that spawns gated communities and tries to create a gated nation. An alternative response is to open our hearts and minds to the new realities that are upon us—including new and big questions: What constitutes safety? Who are "we"? How big is my world? Why do they hate us? What is now asked of us? Can we all dwell together—and flourish—in this small planet home we share? What do we mean, now, by the "common good?"

As we consider these questions, it is helpful to look at the image behind the concept of the common good—the image of *the commons*. The commons has always been an integral feature of the human landscape. Because we are social creatures, we meet and disperse to meet again, whether at the crossroads of a village, in the great plazas of Europe or Latin America, on Main Street, or at the ballpark. Classically in American society, the commons was the village green, surrounded by an ecology of institutions—the school house, a house of worship, the bank, the general store, the town meeting house, doc's house, the sheriff's office, the jail, the post office, a flock of households, and the farmlands beyond. The life of the commons was and is composed in commerce and communication, celebration and memorial, play and protest. The commons is always both a place and a possibility—a reality and an aspiration. The commons is not a nostalgic, romantic notion. The commons has always held a mix of sins and tragedies as well as graces. Slaves were bought and sold on the commons in the South, and Quakers and Jesuits were hanged on the Boston Common in the North. In more recent times we witnessed the tragedy of Tiananmen Square. Though imperfectly realized, the practice of the commons does, however, press toward inclusion and justice. "The commons" conveys a sense of an irreducibly shared life within a manageable frame.

Travel and communications technologies, an international economy, and an emerging ecological consciousness have swept us into a new commons that is global in scope and personal in impact. If not before, then surely after the events of September 11, 2001, we have awakened to a much less manageable world. We, in the United States, have discovered that the towers of the World Trade Center belonged in more ways than we had imagined to this new planetary commons. Those who led the attacks believed that the activity in those towers influenced their lives a world away. Those who died in the towers included citizens from home places all over our planet, and their deaths evoked a great outpouring of common grief and broad recognition that something of deep significance had occurred within the shared, interdependent reality of the whole human family.

We are now being invited to become responsive and responsible citizens in the life of this new commons—a place that is complex, diverse, and vast. We are discovering that the formation of citizenship for this new commons requires transforming encounters with "otherness."[2] When we encounter those other than our own "tribe" in a manner that awakens our empathy and compassion and enlarges our sense of belonging, power, and hope, then "us versus them" is transformed into "we." We become more committed to the *common* good—the good of all, rather than just to me and mine. The boundaries of our souls are revised outward. We begin to become at home in a larger "here."

For many, encounters of this kind have taken the form of a particular set of images and stories from the events of September 11 that have become alive in our imagination. They are working in us, and we are undergoing re-formation. One of the images that has taken up residence in my soul comes from Joanne Martindale. She is an Army National Guard chaplain and director of chaplaincy at a psychiatric hospital in Ancora, New Jersey. For forty-four days immediately following the attacks, she served at Ground Zero and Staten Island. She tells this story:

> Along with other chaplains, I provided pastoral care for the New York Police Department, fire fighters, and other workers who were going through the debris from the terrorist attacks. One day I saw a police officer welding open a car crushed at Ground Zero. When the officer opened the car he found a man's body and the body of a child in a fastened car seat. He saw the stuffed animal and the small shoes next to the car seat. The man lost his ability to cope, and in desperation threw the welding tool several feet in the air. He saw me walking by at that moment, and this tall, big-boned police officer said to me, "If you are very strong, can handle a grown man's anger, and can walk at least three miles around this God-forsaken dump, then walk with me, Chaplain." We walked for two and a half miles around the dump before he said, in a broken voice, which led to nonstop crying for almost an hour, "I accidentally dropped my four-month-old baby seven months ago, and our baby died from broken neck injuries. When I saw that child in the car seat earlier it reminded me of my only son, who's now gone. Why is there so much pain in the world, Chaplain? Why did this happen to me? Why does God want me sorting through the bodies and the debris at this site? What can I do with my grief?"[3]

The new commons is global in scope but personal in impact, and it asks big questions. In today's world, any one of us already has or is vulnerable to experiencing profound suffering similar to the policeman welder. We are asking if our souls have been prepared—formed—for that depth of personal suffering. At the same time, whether our own suffering is large or small, we want to be capable of walking in the shoes of the chaplain, able to go the distance and be a holy presence for others in a world of big questions. Why did this happen to me? Why is there so much pain in the world?

I became acutely attuned to the vital importance of engaging these big questions when I was a senior research fellow and visiting professor for six years at Harvard Business School. I had the privilege of interviewing entering MBA students. I discovered that although some of these twentysomething young adults had come to business school with thoughtful purpose and meaningful commitments that they expected to live out in the world of our commercial institutions, the majority of these bright, talented young adults had been fundamentally cheated. They were already held hostage to assumed lifestyle choices. No one had initiated them into the great questions of calling and purpose, their lives and their time. No one had asked them to consider: What do I really want the future to look like, for me, for others, for my planet? Why is there a growing gap between the haves and the have-nots? In this society, why do gross patterns of injustice continue to be legitimated by skin color? Why are antidepressants being prescribed for an increasing number of children? Why is the prison population growing in our society? What are the reasons for climate change? How will we heal the rupture between science and religion? How shall we practice commerce and design governance in the life of the new commons?[4]

They had not been offered the gift of encounters with otherness that could awaken them to beckoning questions stretching us and prompting formation of the capacity to reach for more than a job, a career, or a lifestyle. Only live encounters that evoke big enough questions give rise to worthy dreams. Yet whether in the upper class or the underclass, too many young adults are being offered dreams of their future that are not worthy of the promise of their lives.

What are the hallmarks of the encounters that evoke big questions and the stretch of soul that is now needed? Conversations with two colleagues inform my response. Betsy Taylor is the executive director of the Center for a New American Dream, an organization in Washington, D.C., that works to help individuals and institutions shift our patterns of consumption in order to enhance our shared quality of life. Betsy is a woman of deep spirituality, a prophetic and faithful voice. She and I were talking on the phone coast to coast when she remarked that she had just come from a high-level meeting where a number of significant leaders in our society were present. As she shared with them her perceptions about what our patterns of consumerism are doing to us and to our world, she said their response was respectful and sober-minded, and they acknowledged that she was right. But they also revealed their preoccupation with other matters, leaving no time for what was recognized as a critical concern. Betsy said quietly, "Sharon, it really is up to us." Then she continued: "I don't know what to do. I really don't know what to do. But I do find that it is important *to stay in touch with the suffering.*"

Later, reflecting on my conversation with Betsy, I recalled conversations with another colleague, Jerry Millhon, a turnaround manager who was then the executive director of Fossil Rim in Glenrose, Texas, a place that stewards two thousand acres of land and works to preserve endangered species (prairie chickens, rhinos, cheetahs, and many others). When Jerry coaches other managers across a range of organizations, he advises them *to stay in touch with the wonder.* "When you stay alive to the wonder of what is happening in your organization," he says, "you stay in touch with the essence of what you are trying to do."

As I have reflected further on the work of these dedicated and effective colleagues, what has become clear is that even though Betsy is tracking the suffering, I know she is consistently alive to wonder, delight, and awe— whether it is in her relationship with her own children, or in another context. On the other hand, although Jerry insists that we stay in touch with wonder, I have noticed that when he enters a new organization, one of the first questions he always asks is, "Where is the pain located—where is there suffering?" Both Betsy and Jerry live and work in the paradox that to be human is to suffer and to know that we create suffering. To be human is to dwell also in awe, reverence, and joy—alive to the fact that we are an integral part of a single, vast, and luminous tissue of life. We experience inexplicable grace; we are blessed with conscience and consciousness. We can ponder, "Who are we, under and among these stars?" Consciousness and conscience are best schooled at the crossroads of suffering and wonder. Suffering and wonder pose the biggest questions.

In my own contemplation, I attempt then, for my own soul's sake, to pay attention to encounters with suffering and wonder in the life of our new commons. I remain, for example, haunted by "Trapped," the account in the *New York Times Magazine* of February 17, 2002, about fifty-five villages in the hills of northern Afghanistan. There the Hazara people have lived for a thousand years. Their supply routes were cut off by war, and several thousand of them began dying of starvation and disease—diseases known and diseases no one can name. They were thrilled when American planes began to fly over their villages. They had heard rumors that we were dropping food packets. But the planes flew on, loaded with bombs to be dropped elsewhere, and the food never arrived. Meanwhile, as the winter snows approached, they remained cut off from their traditional supply routes. The healthy among them made a hard, difficult choice. Finally, forty families, two hundred people, decided that they would flee and go to Iran. They were inadequately prepared, many of them had either plastic shoes or open-toed sandals, and yet they had to walk four hundred miles on foot, through some of the roughest terrain in the world. It was cold. They slept in a single mound, with the ones on the inside rotating to the outside through the night—rotating so that in the morning they would all still be alive. It took them twenty days and twenty nights to reach the boarder—with everyone alive.

But those who might have taken them across demanded money, and they had no money. Thus they were forced to try to return—and then they began to die. A few did make it back to their villages, and some time later the International Rescue Committee, looking for those who were suffering that others might have missed, did find them and stemmed the tide of starvation. But for several thousand people living in fifty-five villages that have never appeared on anyone's map, the rescue came too late.

Receiving such accounts through print or electronic media can serve merely to inform me, or it can serve the formation of my soul, my vocation, my life. I have a choice. I can read and deflect the new knowledge into a mental bin of "interesting information." Or, in contrast, I can take it in and allow it to become alive in me. If I do so, I become connected with a people, a region, and dimensions of suffering and courage different from my own. If I meditate on the implicit connections between their experience and mine, I become aware of my direct and indirect complicity in their suffering. The significance of allowing my self to be touched by their suffering is that, as Parker has described it, "it can burn through to compassion,"— creating a conviction of possibility. I find myself saying "There has to be a way," which gives rise to the courage to risk. My imagination opens into alternative possibilities in response to the question, How, then, must we live? I am moved to new frontiers of prayer and into new behaviors. I find myself compelled to ask deeper and bigger questions about war, and especially about this war—and I am led to places I did not plan to go.

As I keep in touch with suffering in these and other ways, I try also to be alive to wonder and to what is wonder-full. Just as suffering appears in multiple forms and dimensions, wonder also is evoked through many forms.

During a recent Christmas season, our friends Bill Graves and Frances Wood went to Mexico and visited a region where the monarch butterflies roost during our winter. Led by a trained guide, they were part of a small group on horseback who slipped into an open pocket in the forest where just ahead they beheld great, tall trees, totally covered with monarch butterflies. The group fell silent. Everyone quietly wept.

The mystery of the monarch butterflies' long migration has begun to arrest our attention. Monarch butterflies are becoming our teachers as we begin to learn both spiritually and scientifically the wonder of the intricate web of life on which we depend, while discovering how much of it depends on us. We are the first generations to know that we affect the fate of the monarchs and most other species. We are also beginning to recognize that we do not have a theology of creation, a philosophy of science, an economic imagination, or a social ethic to greet that fact. Thus we discover that in the encounter with the wonderful, as in the encounter with suffering, we are invited to see ourselves in right proportion—who we are, who we are not, and who we might become. We have the opportunity to get a better grip on what is precious and what is peripheral.

Suffering and wonder are often intimately related. Many saw on national television the account of the firehouse in New York City, where on September 11, 2001, everyone returned alive. We watched them, one by one, come into the firehouse, meet, fall silent, weep, and embrace each other in the wonder of being alive—in the face of so much suffering and death. Similarly, we can imagine that the women who lost their husbands in the events of September 11 and who subsequently gave birth to a child they had conceived with the father now dead know intimately as they hold that new life in their arms what it is to live at the crossroads of suffering and wonder.

Suffering and wonder are the twin poles that can reliably orient our souls as we learn to navigate in the life of the new commons. What is at stake is the formation of values and ethics, souls and societies.

In the consciousness of authentic suffering and authentic wonder we all become contemplatives. As Parker has written, "Contemplation is not the special skill of a disciplined few who have mastered some esoteric set of techniques. Contemplation is any way of penetrating illusion and touching reality. We arrive in this world with an inborn contemplative capacity—the soul, the inner teacher, the God in every person—that helps us survive and thrive by keeping us grounded in reality, if we will let it."[5]

If we will let it. Indeed, a primary challenge to spiritual formation in our time is that the critically needed grounding in reality is easily sidestepped. There are so many temptations to bypass the suffering of others and escape the encounters that awaken us to wonder. So much in contemporary society distracts us, distances us, numbs us—and thereby cheats us out of the life-transforming encounters with both suffering and wonder that can enable the wise and shy soul to be formed in a larger citizenship, a deeper patriotism, and the greater faithfulness for which we have been created.

In a world running on cybernetic time, we skim the surface of things, unable to pause, go deep, and let wonder and suffering take hold of us. In a media-rich world, we are systematically distracted from the suffering of others and numbed to our own. In a world where news is increasingly "spin" and multiple pieces of information on a single screen vie for our attention, we are insulated from the complex but clear-eyed truth that would call us to rigorous discernment between what hurts and what sustains the flourishing of life. In a society where an escalating level of violence is pawned as entertainment, it is more and more difficult to be either astonished or reverent before the daily reality of authentic, piercing, devastating, avoidable suffering that riddles the fabric of the whole earth community. In an economy that places most of us in the anxious class, it is easy to lose touch with what is precious and become confused about what we truly long for. In a society where abuse of alcohol and drugs—both legal and illegal—has become normative among large segments of our population (including and especially our young), we fail to initiate our young into the natural high of genuine aliveness, and we blunt the edge of our own. In a culture in which the individual ego is placed at the center of our conventional notions of success, we are unable to transcend the sense of false self-importance that suffering and wonder alike yield and require.

In contrast, David James Duncan, a noted author living in the Northwest, describes another way of being. He has tried to absorb the consequences of sanctions against Iraq—the deaths of thousands of children—because of our destruction of water systems and subsequent unwillingness to allow importation of either plumbing or chlorine. He tells us that a trusted mentor once said, "If you don't know how to take something, take it on the physical level." Then Duncan continues,

> The closest I can come to following this advice, with regard to Iraq's children, is to rely on the physical senses, eyes, and heart of a woman named Gerri Haynes. Gerri, a nurse from Woodinville, Washington, heads a group called Washington Physicians for Social Responsibility. She had been on three missions of mercy to Iraq and ten months before the most recent war in Iraq she returned yet again.
>
> Before this recent trip—amid all the flag-waving and war-rumblings— Gerri's oldest daughter tried to persuade her to stay home. Gerri didn't describe their discussion, but she did say that after finally accepting Gerri's sense of mission, daughter offered mother an old-souled piece

of advice. "If you do go," she said, "be completely present, wherever you go."

These words returned to Gerri in an Iraqi hospital virtually bereft of medicine and hope. While her group moved from bed to bed, Gerri approached a woman sitting next to her dying child. Gerri speaks no Arabic. The woman spoke no English. Trying to be "present" anyway, Gerri looked at the child, then at the woman, and placed her right hand over her own heart.

The Iraqi mother immediately placed her right hand over her own heart.

Gerri's eyes and the mother's eyes simultaneously filled with tears.

The hospital was crowded. Gerri's visitation time was short. She started to move to the next bed, but then remembered her daughter's words: "*completely present . . .*" She and the mother were already crying, their hands over their hearts. There was nothing Gerri could do, despite all her medical training, for the child. "How much more present," she wondered, "is it possible to be?"

She stepped forward anyway. With no plan but vague allegiance to the commandment "*completely present,*" the nurse without medicine stepped toward the bed of the dying child and inconsolable mother. She then put both of her hands out, palms up.

The Iraqi mother fell into her arms.

"If only this experience were unique!" Gerri told me. "But I can't tell you, any longer, how many mothers I've now held in this same way."

Her voice grew faint over the phone. I heard: ". . . *diseases that children would almost never die from in the U.S. . . .*"

I heard: "*Medicine so basic . . .*"

Then her voice faded, or maybe I drowned it out. I've never taken interview notes while sobbing before.[6]

This set of reflections suggests that, as theologian Margaret Miles has shown, we are being invited to reclaim the ancient prayer at the heart of Christian asceticism: "God, make us truly alive." If spiritual formation is grounded in practices, ways of life, things that people do with and for each other to make and keep life human, then we are invited to practice being fully present to our own suffering and especially to the suffering of all those we regard as "other." We are invited to practice being fully present to wonder, opening ourselves to what Dorothy Day called "the duty to delight," placing ourselves in the presence of awe and joy. In so doing, we will be compelled to engage the big question, How do we together transform the patterns of life that distract and numb—and oppress?

"The human heart can go the lengths of God." "Affairs are now soul size." Spiritual formation for citizenship in the life of the new commons invites us to a stretch of soul that can embrace the suffering and wonder of our shared life—across oceans and continents, and across the desk and the neighborhood. In the confidence that it is this stretch of soul for which we were created and for which we pray, I borrow from and modify the words of the poet Rilke: "Take your well disciplined strengths, and stretch them between the two great opposing poles of suffering and wonder, because inside human beings is where God learns."[7]

> A child sobs
> An eagle soars
> My soul grows larger

NOTES

1. Fry, C. *Sleep of Prisoners*. New York: Oxford University Press, 1951, pp. 47–48.

2. Daloz, L. A., Keen, C. H., Keen, J. P., and Parks, S. D. *Common Fire: Leading Lives of Commitment in a Complex World*. Boston: Beacon, 1996.

3. See *Inspire* (Princeton Theological Seminary News), Winter 2002, p. 23.

4. See Sharon Daloz Parks, *Big Questions, Worthy Dreams: Mentoring Young Adults in Their Search for Meaning, Purpose, and Faith*. San Francisco: Jossey-Bass, 2000.

5. Palmer, P. J. "Contemplatives by Catastrophe." *Spirituality and Health*, Spring 2002, p. 49.

6. Duncan, David James. "When Compassion Becomes Dissent." *Orion*, Jan.–Feb. 2001, pp. 22–24.

7. "Just as the Winged Energy of Delight." In *Selected Poems of Rainer Maria Rilke: A Translation from the German and Commentary by Robert Bly*. New York: HarperCollins, 1981, p. 175.

REFLECTIONS

○

Diana Chapman Walsh
president of Wellesley College

I first encountered Parker in March 1990 in Taos, New Mexico. Rick Jackson enlisted him to lead a community retreat of Kellogg Fellows. We gathered each morning with one or more poems and explored questions they stirred in us about work, love, life, death. I was deeply affected by the haunting questions Parker excavated from these interchanges. In the reverent, expansive, and playful holding environment he so masterfully shaped, Parker's questions awoke in me an astonishing outpouring of creativity. I left Taos with a sheaf of original poems that came to me and (so it seemed) through me in torrents of words all week, day and night. I left, too, with a new "inner teacher" who has since become my constant companion.

Parker and I have participated in each other's conferences, served on panels together, and made a point of staying in touch. We share Quaker roots, a love of language and word play, doctorates in sociology, and a soul connection beyond description. When he spoke at my inauguration, Parker said, "The world needs presidents who are also poets; keep your poetry alive." If my presidency has become my poetry, it reflects Parker Palmer and his work.

ON BEYOND REVENGE

Leadership for Peace

Diana Chapman Walsh

OVER THE PAST ELEVEN YEARS I have been leading one of the nation's leading liberal arts colleges, my alma mater, Wellesley College. That work has called on every resource I have, and more. I have grown in the role in ways I'm sure I myself can hardly recognize. I've aged in it (that I do see), and I have lost many of my illusions while gaining fresh sources of hope. I have experienced moments of exquisite joy and periods of deep despair. I've lost and found myself many times over—my confidence, my equilibrium, my commitment, my heart.

I have spent time in the company of extraordinary people, many iconic celebrities and many others contentedly anonymous. I have learned much in communion—and in struggle—with hundreds of students and faculty as we have tried our best to guide an institution we treasure through confusing moments of conflict, challenge, and change.

At the same time, I have watched with agony as my country has come under attack by forces that seem incomprehensibly frightening and filled with hate. I have watched my government react to that terrifying new reality in ways that I fear are putting us in greater peril. I am no expert in international relations, in the art of statecraft or political leadership. I know I lack information, knowledge, and resources that our national leaders have at their constant command. I do trust that they are good and well-meaning people doing their best to walk a tightrope that will leave their children and ours a world worth having.

But I am increasingly worried that they are making grievous mistakes, both here and abroad: meeting violence with violence, feeding the fires of hatred, acting in isolation with arrogance and hubris, hardening themselves to the suffering and pain their actions are causing. I believe there are other, different ways to lead. In the days after September 11, 2001, some of us had dared hope that an act so incomprehensibly horrific might finally call forth "the great sea change on the far side of revenge" imagined by Seamus Heaney in his poem "The Cure at Troy."[1]

Unfortunately, as we now know, quite the opposite has occurred. The United States has become a "rogue nation," according to Clyde Prestowitz,[2] enmeshed in the "millennial war" eloquently described by James Carroll.[3] The book you are holding in your hands is about the awesome choice we are facing now—all of us—between leading from our humanity and what we know to be right and true, or leading from our fears and our inability to summon the empathy to engage worlds and worldviews we aren't ready to comprehend. So we call them evil.

I worry that seeing the world in this way, as a binary world of good and evil, is itself the problem; I wonder if there might be a radically different kind of leadership that would reframe it. Can one be a militant pacifist without being driven or drawn into the dualism of a world of war and not-war? How can we erect boundaries around the suicide bombers, symbolic and real, those people in a system who are so attached to negativity that they can imagine only sabotage and mayhem? How can we recognize and refuse the provocation to ratchet up cycles of violence? Is there another form of leadership that would draw on the tradition of nonviolent resistance, but transform it for our time? Are there other strategies, tactics, and rules that leaders could be developing and invoking if their ultimate goal were peaceful means for peaceful ends?

These are monumental questions to which I do not pretend to have answers. Nor would I presume to invoke a feminist or women's perspective as a simplistic alternative to the world order that informs national foreign policy. But the experience of leading, on a far more modest scale, a women's college through its own local moments of conflict, confusion, and fear has brought into focus what it might mean to make a commitment to a leadership of peace.[4]

The part of the story that is mine to tell is of women's leadership. The fact that the college I am leading is one of a dwindling number of single-sex institutions is a fundamental and complicated aspect of that story. Our students like to proclaim that we are "not a girls' school without men but a women's college without boys." There's a depth in that defensive joke that hints at some possibilities I want to raise about what women might bring to leadership in these troubled and troubling times. I offer sincere questions, not settled opinion; I bring more aspiration and yearning than prescription or conviction.

I want to be careful and clear in the way I talk about gender. It's so easy to fall into traps and stereotypes that muddy the picture and drive us into our corners, to tape on our boxing gloves. We all know the gender scripts, and we see many exceptions: men who are listeners, nurturers, emotional virtuosos; women who are decisive, forceful, brilliantly analytical. We know the scripts are changing too, becoming more flexible, slowly but perceptibly.

Among Wellesley's distinctions is the unusual fact that, since opening in 1875, the college has always been headed by a woman president. Lining the walls of the grand entrance hall in the library at the heart of the campus, the imposing portraits of my eleven predecessors always command a moment of reflection. The portrait gallery heralds the college's historic belief in the potential, indeed the necessity, of women's leadership, going back to a period in the United States—not so long ago—when such a belief was eccentric, risky, even radical. It remains so, still, in many parts of the world.

By the time I was tapped in 1992 to become the college's twelfth president, the revolution in women's life options had progressed sufficiently far that the case I had to make—first to myself and then to others—was that an all-women's education remained a compelling cause. I had spent most of my adult life developing my leadership skills in an evolving series of partnerships with men, most in medicine, science, and social science. This pattern began two weeks after I graduated from college, when I married my husband (now of thirty-seven years), who soon became a distinguished biomedical researcher. It continued through at least a dozen significant professional partnerships with powerful men. Parker Palmer was one of them, a transitional figure for me in important respects, a man who helped me unlock what he would call an "inner teacher" of my own.

The discovery and development of an inner teacher that I could reliably use as a touchstone for my work in the world was a gradual, and painful, process. I wish I were a person of deep and abiding faith—in myself, in others, in an ordered and just world, in a transcendent God or gods of any type or description. My father, a good and emotionally wounded man, had little apparent access to his inner life and had a conviction (so our mother once told us) that no god could have been so cruel as to have taken both his parents from him by the time he was twelve. The logic seemed convincing enough to me as a child, and it helped me to comprehend, if not entirely to forgive, the nights when my father's drinking loosened his temper and spiraled out of control. Our family always maintained a studious and stoic silence around Dad's bouts with alcohol, and I suppose it was our effort to keep that huge ache under wraps that stifled honest talk of pain, uncertainty, and fear, and with it tender talk of joy, hope, and love. In his eightieth year, without any warning, my father's heart stopped while he slept, as if to avoid in his dying the strain of finally having to find words for the feelings of love and self-compassion he found so impossible to express.

I could easily have lived a similar life: honorable, dutiful, and flattened by unspeakable pain. So many lives are lived that way. I watched my father's anger wrestle with his fear, like a frantic animal writhing in a trap. Now I see that the same volatile mix of pent-up rage and panic is threatening to destroy our fragile planet. The world itself is in danger of dying in its sleep; by not attending to these conflicts, we fall victim to this unresolved panic and rage.

This book is a wake-up call, and the hour is late. My fellow contributors are people of utterly profound and sophisticated faith in the resilience of the human spirit, even through the depths of despair and darkness. I want to speak to the readers, like me, who have not been so sure that they belong in the company of the fortunate ones whose birthright religious faith is deep and unshakable—but who also need to find a way to have faith in the human spirit and what we still can do.

A crucial part of my gradual awakening was a three-year Kellogg Fellowship that exposed me, incrementally, to spiritual disciplines and possibilities well beyond my comfort zone. They heightened my sensitivity to inner understandings and insights that, with practice and guidance, I was able to learn to consult and trust in new ways. At first, I kept those discoveries under wraps, as private, personal, and quite distinct from—indeed, at odds with—my scholarly pursuits and commitments in the world of objectively testable theories and propositions I had worked so hard to master.

But the move into a major institutional leadership role was such a dramatic leap away from my contained, private world of contemplation and my public, but more limited, professional world of academics to the chaotic, public world of unrelenting action that I had to find new ways to integrate head and heart. I had to bring myself completely to my new work; gone were borders and boundaries between work and life. I had to rely on my intuition as one input into the many new and tough decisions that came at me through every portal. I also needed to scramble rapidly up a learning curve, which meant I needed to be sure to extract from each experience the lessons that would enable me to sharpen and hone my instincts over time, as I made inevitable mistakes and tried to convert them to learning. Defining myself as a learner helped lighten the burden of perfectionism that weighs heavily in the history of my college, and my life.

The pressures and projections were unnerving at first, and I knew I would have to be firmly grounded in order to remain true to myself. I sensed that being true to myself was the most important commitment I could make, and the only outcome I could hope to control. I had to learn, somehow, to operate mindfully from an inner center as an essential part of the everyday work of leading in a hectic, demanding job. The necessity of doing that work on the fly and in the heat of the moment turns out to be among the great growth opportunities inherent in a complex management job.

Looking back over this particular journey of mine, I am coming to understand that something called me to dedicate three decades of my adult life to an extended and intensive immersion in the patriarchal world of male power, and to master the epistemological and methodological tools of academic social science research. Then, as I approached my fiftieth year, and having stared down the worst of my demons, something else called me back to this special women's space to see if I could apply what I had learned to the pressing task of finding new ways to lead in a world gone awry.

The fault lines in current conceptions of effective leadership are visible everywhere: in corporations, the professions, athletics, the church, and politics on a national and a global scale. Can women bring something fresh to confront structures and cultures still operating according to a logic of centralized authority, competition, and isolation? Is this a realistic hope? Do we have the courage? Can we muster the skill? These are some of the questions I have been living this past decade.

As people break out of slavery, too often they yearn to be masters themselves, instead of daring to imagine what it would mean to escape to true freedom. What if women were to emerge, now, into our full leadership, bringing the memory of centuries of disempowerment and invisibility to bear on the problem of how to move beyond tolerance to true and deep engagement with what is other and alien? Is there something particular and real we might discover?

My experience at Wellesley College—encouraging our students in their four years of remarkable learning and growth—persuades me that there is at least the potential for women to develop and model an alternative philosophy about how to lead peacefully and well. From my front-row study of my own trials and errors as an institutional leader, and from my institution's successes and disappointments, I believe that such a philosophy would have at least five basic elements.

Leading from an Inner Core

First, it would include a consistent and disciplined effort to stay anchored in an inner center and to lead from that core, basing decisions and actions insofar as possible on a reliable foundation of personal identity and integrity. The summer after my first year on the job, I engaged an organizational consultant to conduct what is known as a "360 degree assessment" of my performance, confidentially interviewing a cross-section of people at the college about strengths and weaknesses they were observing in the way the new president was doing her job. I commissioned a follow-up review two years after that.

It was hard to hear the findings that confirmed my worst suspicions about bad habits I had privately hoped others might not be noticing. But opening myself to this candid review signaled that I wanted to approach my work with curiosity, and in an analytic spirit. The academy is such a hypercritical and judgmental place. It can be unforgiving, punishing, sometimes even cruel and contemptuous. I wanted to confront these tendencies right away, partly because I recognized from my student days how demoralizing such a culture can be and how antithetical it is to the goal of learning, partly because I knew instinctively that I wouldn't be a successful president if I were on the defensive, avoiding risks and being afraid to fail. At the same time, I knew it would be crucial to preserve the dignity of the office even while shaking free of some of the suffocating formality and rigidity that were built into the president's role.

Becoming "presidential" took time and conscious effort. I had to learn to set boundaries so that I could guard my identity and integrity amid all the projections that were coming at me from every direction; it was amazing how many people had quite specific ideas about what the president should (or should not) be, and do, and say (even what she should wear). I had to work at being explicit about my role and my expectations, and at being organized and purposeful so that I could be more responsive than reactive. After a while, I realized that holding my initial reactions until I could move with firmness and conviction helped me be trustworthy and keep my commitments.

I worked at listening (to be real), rather than promising (to be liked), and at asking myself whenever someone made a request of me, Do I have this to give? I wanted to be a leader who was patient, calm, analytical, fair, someone who instilled confidence in others. That meant being circumspect in every interaction and mindful of those not present. I wanted to be able to reframe reality for people in living ways when they were stuck or confused, and I wanted to have the ability to enter into scarcity and find abundance, purpose, and hope.

That was a lot to want, and I'm working at it still. I contracted with an organizational consultant, Richard S. Nodell, to support me in the ongoing process of inventing an approach to leadership that combines my values and preoccupations with the challenges my leadership team and I have been facing at Wellesley. He is teaching me, too, to notice the fruitful intersections between my unfolding story and that of the college, under the larger arc of women's leadership in the world.

I try to listen well and to speak from my own truth, rather than speaking to correct or affirm someone else. I try to know my own truth. One thing I do know is that my effectiveness depends, more than anything else, on my ability to engage in an ongoing and caring discernment of the condition of individuals and groups within the extended college community, and the condition of the college as a whole. This in turn requires that I endeavor to create respectful, attentive, and quiet spaces within which I (and others) can find ourselves at our best, most honest, and most alive.

Leading in Partnership

Second, the leadership I am envisioning would employ working partnerships formed around tasks and explicit delineations of roles and mutual responsibilities, expectations, and aspirations. These partnerships are the basic units for conducting meaningful work, and they need to be negotiated carefully, attended to regularly, and integrated into a unified vision for the whole organization. Central to those discussions is an ongoing exploration of the largest meaning of the work. It took me some time to understand that the time and energy spent on these partnerships was a necessary part of accomplishing our goals and a crucial investment in a vital managerial resource. There is a strong tendency to dismiss this kind of work as interpersonal and diversionary. But now I see the effort spent on the critical partnerships through which we guide the college—partnerships with the deans and vice presidents as well as key trustee and faculty leaders—as an indispensable part of my job and theirs, not a question of choice or preference. We often call in our consultant to hold the environment for this work; the presence of a third party creates a more expansive space for an exploration involving two or more interested parties. Particularly when we are leading a process of institutional change, the pressure on these partnerships can become intense.

My most bruising experience of this intensity was in a four-year partnership with a member of my senior staff, an African American dean I had recruited to join my team, through an excruciating backlash against her leadership. Repeatedly, she and I had to break away and explore an incident or incidents in which one or both of us was led to believe that the other was violating a basic trust or understanding we thought was clear between us. More often than not, the information was distorted in some way, or one of us was managing exigencies of which the other was unaware. Once we were able to sort out what had actually happened, we could resume our work, our confidence in one another and in our partnership restored. This experience was a roller coaster ride for us both, but we remained faithful to our mutual commitment to stay in partnership, no matter what else occurred. As a result, we were able to accomplish most of the goals we had set, against daunting odds.

Rejecting the Use of Force

As part of the commitment I make to these partnerships, I refuse categorically to resort to force. This is the third principle, and I apply it even (perhaps especially) when it is least clear to me what I can offer as an alternative. For a while I set the password on my e-mail account as "no war," as a subliminal reminder of a resolution I was constantly being provoked to forget. Simply holding that boundary can have a powerful effect when people are picking fights with each other and looking for someone to blame; "the administration" and "the boss" are (like Mom) convenient candidates for displaced rage.

The invitation to be drawn into someone else's conflict generally indicates that the principals are weary of engaging it themselves, or unwilling to do so from the start. Avoiding the conflict is a form of avoiding work. Sometimes it's a situation in which two senior managers have reached an impasse and want to invoke the boss's authority to sidestep the conflict. Another frequent structure, in these litigious times, is when person X alleges that person Y is creating a "hostile work environment" and claims that the institution is legally responsible for punishing person Y. The setup is that person Y is equally certain that person X is the bad actor in need of correction and will strike back with a vengeance if criticized by someone in authority. If the situation deteriorates so badly that lawyers are called in to plow through the mountain of charges and countercharges, what they generally find are smart people spending an inordinate amount of time baiting and aggravating one another.

Refusing to resort to force is more than a personal preference; it reflects a conception of the role of the leader as a teacher and therefore a nonpartisan—that is, not merely neutral but standing outside the realm of partisan politics. In taking this stance, the leader can transcend partisan arguments by ensuring that they take place at the appropriate level and in the appropriate manner. When people in an organization bring their conflicts to the leader, sending them back with a clear charge to define their own process for working them out increases the likelihood that they will own and accept the solution, using their own expertise, ingenuity, and any extra resources they may need if they are really stuck. The intent is not to abandon them, but to create a structure within which they can rediscover their own resourcefulness.

Honoring Differences

Fourth, this leadership of peace requires respect for differences and will-ingness to engage them creatively as a resource for learning. At Wellesley, holding gender constant has the paradoxical effect of bringing other dif-ferences into sharp relief. The financial strength of a large endowment en-ables the college to underwrite a need-blind admission policy and enroll a generation of students as accomplished and highly motivated as ever, and far more diverse, culturally, ethnically, socially, geographically. With fewer than half of our students today drawn from the white, native-born citizens of the United States who used to define and shape the institution, student diversity is a great source of institutional vitality and pride. Wellesley sees itself (and sells itself) as a global learning community in which women from a spectrum of backgrounds and experiences challenge and teach one another to question their assumptions and expand their perspectives.

At the same time, of course, we have our tensions, and we try to under-stand conflict as a necessary, productive force. Differences of opinion and experience—polar positions and contradictions—are a critical part of life and learning. Education involves first mastering new categories and then integrating the new into a larger, more organic whole. The differentiation stage—apprehending what is different from what is already known—re-quires heightening and sharpening differences, intellectually and experien-tially; widening the gap between two opposing poles; and really seeing, feeling, and understanding what is different. The integration stage involves finding a new position that can incorporate the two conflicting realities in a third, more complex, and more comprehensive whole, an important step in any creative process.

But even though one learns from differences that are heightened and am-plified, not muted and papered over, this sometimes leads to personal at-tack and personalized response, which turn differences of viewpoint, fact, or interpretation into individual wounds. When this happens, it threatens relationships and shifts the focus quickly from the intellectual work of un-derstanding and learning about a substantive difference to the emotional work of mending or compensating for damaged identity or pride. We need to learn to engage in conflict, serious and sometimes painful, sometimes even irreconcilable, as an ordinary and inevitable part of social life. Only when conflict is understood in its inevitability and its productivity will we begin to develop capacities and skills to manage it well.

On college campuses in this era of multiculturalism, issues of power, re-source allocation, and political organization intermingle with questions of identity and representation: who can speak for "us" and to whom does that *we* extend? How do we know we are valued? Where is the evidence that we belong? These questions lie at the heart of struggles over free speech, debates about affirmative action, incessant and shrill culture wars. At the most fundamental level, these struggles for the soul of the institution reflect social and spiritual estrangement from mainstream culture more than they reflect mere competition for resources and power. Meeting them as power struggles produces solutions that promote consumerism (more resources for my marginalized group so that I can feel valued and seen) rather than the need for spiritual regeneration, which lies at the root of the problem.[5] There is much in our culture to which rejection is the healthy and appropriate response; the voices from the margins are bringing us wisdom we need to hear. We need a new grammar, and a new leadership, for engaging these existential crises in the context of community.

Supporting Community

This brings us to the fifth and final element I would invoke as an ingredient of the leadership of peace I am hoping women can help catalyze. We know that women have tended to place special value on investing personal energy in maintaining supportive communities that can hold their members through difficult phases of learning and growth; this has been their assigned role for centuries, and many contemporary women bring those organizing and group process skills to families, neighborhoods, voluntary associations, and places of work. Joyce Fletcher's ethnographic study in an engineering firm describes in vivid detail what she calls "relational practice" in the workplace: a set of behaviors and values that put a premium on empathy, honest exchange, mutual support, and sensitivity to emotional nuance.[6] The women engineers in her study consciously employ these relational behaviors as pragmatic strategies for getting the job done. The behaviors are not defaults, not simply natural, and they are definitely not symptoms of weakness or deficiency. They require special skills and an expanded "logic of effectiveness," Fletcher argues, and she shows how these valuable team-building skills (ones that all corporations say they want in this era of interdependence and diversity[7]) are trivialized and suppressed by the male-dominated corporate culture. These women engineers are enacting what I think I see our students trying valiantly to develop and articulate: a resolute leadership of and toward peace.

Not that it is easy. An environment in which women can develop their authentic individuality has to take into account centuries of disempowerment and self-doubt that have been built into the culture. It has to counter tendencies toward passivity and isolation, and address the inevitable pressure on women to make all relationships interpersonal at the expense of staying focused on work tasks, roles, and responsibilities. At Wellesley we worry, at times, that our tightly knit community can stifle disagreement, coddle students more than it challenges them, and fuel their sense of entitlement. We worry that the wealth enabling us to provide such an excellent education may be heightening rampant consumerism and undermining community values. We worry that our conversations can become circular and tedious. And we worry, at the other end of the spectrum, that maybe we are simply promoting a traditional, male model of success. All of those worries are grounded in realities we face.

Yet a residential learning community whose sole purpose is the liberal education of women has distinctive strengths. It offers a laboratory in which values of cooperation, collaboration, and mutual concern are underscored, taken for granted, encoded in the DNA of the institution. As a result, almost instinctively, another kind of leadership emerges. It draws on the wisdom women carry for the culture. We know that a recognizably feminine worldview—a product of historical conditions that have shaped women's experiences as "the other"—has for many years embodied those aspects of human striving (by women and men) that are more contextual, more holistic, and more attuned to the environment, to connections, and to sustaining relationships than is the patriarchal male model within which this feminine prototype has had to make an uneasy peace. We know, further, that the conventional gender order has denied the feminine; dominated women; and advanced competition, militarism, and imperialism.

These are the lineaments of a feminist moral vision. It posits a consciousness, an epistemology, an ethic, and an aesthetic that are prototypically female—a "morality of responsibility," in Carol Gilligan's words, that stands in contrast to the masculine "morality of rights."[8] There's a danger, though, in claims like this; they can lay an essentialist trap for women and men, and heighten sex stereotypes if they characterize the feminine or the masculine as immutable and inevitably deterministic. Extrapolating from broad cultural constructions of gender to individual attributes is the essentialist mistake, but if we remember that everyone has elements of the masculine and the feminine and that it is the experience of living in a particular gender world (it's actually not a world order; *gender order* is the technical term) order (one that can be changed) that produces distinct ("gendered") perspectives, then we stand on firmer ground.

As fascism was engulfing Europe in 1938, Virginia Woolf wrote a fiery essay, *Three Guineas*, addressing the primary question still facing the world today: "How, in your opinion, are we to prevent war?"[9] The question was put to Woolf in a letter she left unanswered for three years. *Three Guineas*, her delayed response, begins with a rumination on a second letter sitting on her desk, a fundraising appeal for support of an effort to rebuild a women's college. Maybe she'll direct her gift, she muses, toward "rags and petrol and . . . matches" to burn the college down. But, Woolf continues, *if* the college will teach a women's ethic, *if* it will take up its role as custodian of a uniquely feminine value system, *if* it will do its part to prevent fascism and war, then perhaps it will merit one of her three guineas.

European fascism came and went, at a horrendous cost, and now we face a threat of another kind. Addressing the current crisis is going to require all the wisdom and patience we as an educated and privileged democratic society can muster. We are going to have to develop the ability to collaborate and communicate with fluency across a range of cultures, races, religions, and socioeconomic groups. We are going to have to learn to appreciate and skillfully use conflict as a creative intellectual force for mining what we can know from our disagreements and differences, across the country and around the world. We are going to need the grace to design and sustain communities of meaning and hope, communities that will offer all their members the opportunity to learn and grow, to make a contribution and to be seen and recognized for who they are and what they bring. We are going to need men and women of good will, and of subtle skill, to build such communities, here and around the world, with all deliberate speed. The hour is late, the work is hard, and the stakes are high. We must hasten to build a new world order, and we must take our time.

NOTES

1. Heaney, S. *The Cure at Troy*. London: Farrar, Straus and Giroux, 1990, p. 77.

2. Prestowitz, C. *Rogue Nation: American Unilateralism and the Failure of Good Intentions*. New York: Basic Books, 2003.

3. Carroll, J. "Millennial War." *Boston Globe*, June 17, 2003, p. A17.

4. Walsh, D. C. "Toward a Leadership of Peace for the Twenty-First Century Academy." In S. M. Intrator (ed.), *Stories of the Courage to Teach*. San Francisco: Jossey-Bass, 2002.

5. Fogel, R. W. *The Fourth Great Awakening and the Future of Egalitarianism*. Chicago: University of Chicago Press, 2000.

6. Fletcher, J. K. *Disappearing Acts: Gender, Power, and Relational Practice at Work*. Cambridge, Mass.: MIT Press, 1999.

7. Lipman-Blumen, J. *The Connective Edge*. San Francisco: Jossey-Bass, 1996.

8. Gilligan, C. *In A Different Voice: Psychological Theory and Women's Development*. Cambridge, Mass.: Harvard University Press, 1982.

9. Woolf, V. *Three Guineas*. Orlando: Harcourt, Brace, 1938.

REFLECTIONS

○
———————

Peter M. Senge
founding chair of SoL (the Society
for Organizational Learning) Council

Although he and I have never met, I have long been struck by how many
close colleagues have worked with Parker Palmer and been deeply moved
by his work. In my own writing and work, I've been focused on understanding how we create organizations and larger systems that often fail
to realize our higher aspirations or embody our deeper values. I believe
one key is for change leaders at all levels to understand the nature of
wholes and what it requires to add to the service of the whole. I believe
these questions sit at the heart of Parker Palmer's work as well.

A WORLD
SHAPED BY CHOICE

Peter M. Senge

WE LIVE IN A TIME OF PARADOX. Arguably, at no time have humans had greater power in the sense of greater ability to shape the world around us. Yet we experience utter and complete powerlessness to shape the course of change.

Recently, I was part of a small three-day meeting that included many highly successful entrepreneurs, authors, and similar "thought leaders," as the meeting organizers had dubbed us. Many of the participants had founded companies, created new technologies, or contributed to important intellectual movements. Needless to say, this was not a group lacking in self-confidence. Yet as the meeting progressed, I sensed a deep undercurrent of disease. All had much to say about the future, our ostensible subject, yet all seemed to me to express a common fatalism. Finally, I drew a simple curve on the board during one of our conversations. "Is this not the future that all of us assume, that none of us believe can be influenced?" I asked. Everyone agreed. "Does this future not raise deep, perhaps troubling questions for us all?" Again, there was common assent. "What does this say about our plight?" No one seemed to know how to respond.

The simple picture I drew was an exponentially rising curve, one of those curves that continually bend upwards, ever accelerating. I labeled it "technological advance." But I think I could have just as easily labeled it "anxiety," or "uncertainty," or "powerlessness." It is, I believe, the icon of our age. It is the background that we all assume and yet rarely talk about directly. The irony of this curve is that it is a human artifact. It is created by us. Relentless technological progress is not written into the cosmos. It is not one of the laws of physics. It is a product of the way our present modern society is organized and functions. It brings new wondrous devices. But it also brings ever-increasing frenzy, disorientation, and dependence—or at least it has throughout the Industrial Age.

This essay was published as "Systems," in *Imagine What America Could Be in the 21st Century,* edited by Marianne Williamson, Rodale Press, 2000.

The Industrial Age has been an epoch of harvesting natural and social capital to produce productive and financial capital. We have destroyed forests, topsoil, and farmland, and with that the habitat for many species. The loss of biological diversity has been matched by the loss of cultural diversity. Not only have one quarter of all species vanished in the past century, so too have over half of the two thousand or more human language systems, with them the diversity of thought and expression that the humans have developed over tens of thousands of years. The waste of natural capital (about a ton per American per week) is matched by waste of human capital, vast numbers of underemployed, and over a billion of us today severely malnourished, many starving.

And the real changes may be just around the corner.

Writing in a recent issue of *Wired* magazine, Bill Joy, chief scientist and cofounder of Sun Microsystems, describes "why the future doesn't need us."[1] He speculates in harrowing terms about a convergence of robotics, genetic engineering, and nanotechnology (making things smaller and smaller—especially the onset of "molecular electronics" and molecular computing) that is making self-replicating, "sentient machines" no longer a science fiction fantasy. "The age of spiritual machines," in the words of inventor Ray Kurzweil, is upon us. Joy quotes several technology leaders who not only think about this but accept it as virtually inevitable. Some find the prospect of humans merging with robots unthreatening. He paraphrases one famous inventor: "The changes will happen gradually and we will get used to them." Others are less sanguine, including several who see sentient robots succeeding humans as the earth's dominant species. Just when we thought that ecological disaster might be the ultimate unintended consequence of technological advance, welcome to the Matrix. Indeed, the two—ecological deterioration and the age of spiritual machines—may go hand in hand. If we continue to foul the environmental conditions required for many previously successful species and perhaps our own biology, might we be setting the table for a species that are more symbiotic with such an environment?

So, it is not as if technological advance has been an undiluted benefit. This, of course, is not news. Such concerns run through a large number of the essays in this volume. Yet we continue to act as if there is no possibility of exerting any influence over it—as if uncontrolled technological advance of the sort that characterized the past two hundred years, and appears to be accelerating still, is some immutable law of nature.

I think this suggests a particular problem, and perhaps a particular key to a future we could be proud to leave for our grandchildren. The problem is not technology per se. The problem lies with the creators of technology—that is, us. The problem is that we have lost our capacity to make choices, especially on a scale commensurate with the scope of our impact. What sort of future lies ahead may hinge on discovering that capacity.

The Age of Machine Systems

Ironically, individual technologists rarely feel that they have no control over their own efforts. Indeed, many exhibit a kind of technological hubris. Yet these very same individuals feel that they have little or no influence over the larger patterns of technological advance, over whether or not genetic engineering is good for humans, or even particular applications of genetic engineering. The reason for this larger fatalism lies in the systems that control these patterns, or appear to.

What do I mean by "the systems?" I mean what most of us mean when we use this term. For example, there is the system of global financial markets, which interacts with the system of capital ownership, which interacts with the system of corporate management and in particular the system of executive management, including the system of developing, guiding, and rewarding corporate executives. Taken together, these multiple interacting systems, in concert with labor markets, consumer demand patterns, and governmental legislation and regulation make up what people often call "global capitalism" or the "global corporate order," or whatever current term is in favor, to point toward that which we cannot control but which controls us. Often, such terms are actually a mask for a type of conspiracy theory, that some small group of people "behind the curtains" are really in control. But, having been behind many of these curtains, I have not found any such people. I have only found more people who feel that they must keep running like crazy, who also assume that someone or something else is in control.

Donella Meadows, a noted environmental researcher and writer, put it eloquently many years ago: "No one wants or works to generate hunger, poverty, pollution, or the elimination of species. Very few people favor arms races or terrorism or alcoholism. . . . Yet these results are consistently produced by the system-as-a-whole, despite many policies and much effort directed against them."[2]

This is what I mean by *the system*.

In fact, most of us have a particular industrial age understanding of "system," the machine system. From 1750 to 1820, labor productivity in England increased two hundredfold, driven by the prototype industrial age machine, the steam engine. This, of course, was the birth of the prototypical industrial age organization, the assembly line. The assembly line also gave birth to the image of the human organization as mechanical system. The assembly line became such a transformative social construct that it became the model for school as well as work. The modern urban school system, a product of the midnineteenth century, was overtly copied from the assembly lines that educators so admired, complete with discrete stages, rigid time schedules, and bells on the walls. Eventually this machine-age systems thinking produced the modern corporation, which though much more complex than a single assembly line, still exists in our collective social consciousness as "a machine for making money."

The irony is that *we* created the machines, and the machine systems. We then convinced ourselves that someone else was the culprit. This is how powerful the image of the machine has become in this age of technological advance. We have learned to see everything in our world as if it is a machine. Biologists contrast living systems from machine systems by the terms *autopoeitic* versus *alopoetic*—literally, self-created versus other-created. Machine-age thinking has led us, logically and relentlessly, to see more and more of our world, including ourselves and the larger systems we create in the image of the machine—as if they are created by someone else.

So, it really is no surprise that we experience powerlessness despite our technological prowess. The powerlessness is a by-product of the same thinking that produced the prowess.

Unless this changes, I hold little hope for fundamental change.

The Age of Living Systems

But our machine-age way of seeing is just that: a way of seeing. There is an alternative. We can see "the system" as *patterns of interdependency we enact in our daily ways of living*. Although this may sound abstract, it is actually quite concrete.

Imagine a group of people working together to create a new product. Imagine that they are struggling, falling short of the demanding targets for quality and timeliness. The first question they ask is, "Who set these aims?" They realize that they set them themselves, out of their excitement at creating a truly unique product. As soon as they step back, they discover anew that excitement—creating a totally new product that serves real needs and demonstrates a new possibility for environmental stewardship. You see, the product will be 100 percent remanufacturable. This has never been done before in their industry. Moreover, they are convinced that such a product will be vastly less expensive to produce and will commend a totally different level of loyalty from customers, who will share in the emotional rewards of a product where nothing ever goes into a landfill.

But, despite these inspiring aims, now the team is in trouble. The product is late and everyone is blaming each other. The design engineers believe that the manufacturing engineers are causing delays by adding last-minute requirements for ease of assembly and disassembly. The engineers responsible for the electronics have also added new "functionality" that they believe will excite customers. Other engineers responsible for other engineering subsystems have done likewise. So, they have come together to have it out. First come the complaints, and along with them the frustration. There is little point in disguising the feelings of victimization each engineering group feels vis-à-vis the others, or pretending that each group is on top of their situation and is only waiting for the others to "get their acts together." Everyone senses the frustration and soon realizes that they are all feeling more or less the same.

Then one of the engineers says, "There's only one boat and we're all in it—we can either keep acting as if the hole is in the other group's end or figure out how to sail together." Everyone recognizes the truth of the analogy. And then a young woman engineer asks, "Aren't we creating a tragedy of the commons here?" She proceeds to draw a diagram (the sort that engineers love) that many recognize right away; it reveals a recurring pattern first identified many years ago by biologist Garrett Hardin, who observed that people often get trapped in a pattern where each individual or group, pursuing their own self-interest, expands their activities to the point where some commons upon which they all depend is destroyed, and all lose. "We are like the sheepherders," she continues, "who each want to expand their own flock, until they overgraze the commons and all end up losing. Our 'flock' is our engineering subsystem, and our goal is to make it the hottest, most mind-blowing thing we can imagine. This gets us the praise of our peers and perhaps a promotion as well." "Yes," adds another engineer, "and the commons we are destroying is our good will toward one another." "And," adds another, "our ability to work together to come up with really creative solutions that actually help one another, not just our own specialization." Suddenly, everyone seems to see the same pattern. "My gosh," whispers another, "look what we are doing to ourselves." From that point, the frustration begins to dissolve and a new collective creative capacity emerges. They finish the product several months prior to scheduled release, at record levels of quality.

Actually, we are all born as systems thinkers, able to see the systems we enact. Few children by the age of four have not discovered that if they do not clean their room their mother or father will. They understand perfectly well the pattern of interdependency around keeping their room clean, just as they understand many of the other social systems enacted within their families and networks of friends. Then, unfortunately, they go to school.

But imagine a different kind of school, where our natural love of understanding the world around us and our desire to make a difference are continually nurtured. Children continue to pursue their innate curiosities about why things happen the way they do. Rather than being *instructed* in received wisdom dispensed by all-knowing authority figures, they are guided in becoming more aware of how they make sense of things, how they *construct* their world. They learn through doing rather than listening. They learn in the many ways that suit who they are as unique people. Rather than rebel against adults seeking their obedience, they seek out the adults who can mentor them, who represent role models they respect, who have life experiences they value. And they find these adults everywhere in their lives.

Andrea and Paolo are middle school students, in a science class—although not really like any science class you would recognize. First, their entire yearlong science curriculum revolves around understanding the ecological, cultural, and economic impacts of a new national park being created north of their town. They are consultants in designing the park. They have worked with local farmers to better understand land use consequences and worked with Indian groups whose land abuts that of the park. Now, Andrea and Paolo are back to their "classroom" to sort out different options for trail systems in the park. This is important because, next week, they will go back to the farmers and Indians with their recommendations. If everyone can agree, they will jointly present their proposals at the formal Park Service planning meeting next month.

But now they have a problem because the two of them can't even agree. Andrea favors a trail plan that takes advantage of especially beautiful overlooks, but when she simulated this choice using the system model they had developed with their teacher, she was surprised to see the erosion caused in a delicate wetlands. Paolo had warned her that this was a fragile nesting area and they should completely avoid it. But his preferred route crossed near an old burying ground, which she was convinced would offend the Indians. Moreover, the simulations alerted them to the possibility that, although Paolo's trail system could accommodate more visitors and generate more revenues, the possible political backlash might end up as an economic disaster.

After vigorous debates with the other students, they agree on a plan of attack. They will stop worrying about coming up with *the* answer—in fact, they see that there is no one answer, just different options and trade-offs that require thoughtful choices. The key, they decide, is to get everyone thinking together about these options. Working with the small group of local farmers and Indians, they will try to develop a range of scenarios that embrace the options. They will transform the formal planning meeting next month into a learning laboratory, just like their classroom. In fact, they even think of a way to dry-run the whole plan: they will create a mockup at next week's "community day."

This is no extracurricular project for the science students. This is the way they learn science—incidentally, about twice as fast as in the old classroom instruction mode. In fact, it is also the way they learn English, history, and foreign languages. Their school is now a staging ground for young people working in their community. After all, they are teenagers, not little children. As most of the world's societies have long recognized, they are becoming adults and need to be engaged in responsible activities to make their world a better place. How else can this be done except by turning the school inside out? By the way, Community Day (where they will try out their ideas) is a monthly gathering when everyone throughout the community involved in the students' hundreds of joint learning activities gets together at the school, to talk about how their projects are going. As a researcher from the local university puts it, "on Community Day, people reconnect with the social network that is the school." For Andrea, Paolo, and all the other students, school is no longer a system created by someone else and to which students and teachers alike must become obedient. It is hundreds of colearners throughout their community continually creating a living curriculum, "lifelong kindergarten," as MIT Media Laboratory researcher Mitch Resnick puts it.

Actually, neither of these is an imaginary story. Both are based on ways that people are working and learning together today. I have seen hundreds of such stories, many of which have been instigated and studied through the collaborative efforts of members of a global network called SoL, the Society for Organizational Learning.[3] They do not characterize an ideal utopia. They simply illustrate that it is possible to approach any setting in such a way that we can continually learn how we are enacting the systems that shape our daily lives—and then begin enacting systems more in line with what we truly value.

Such learning is not easy. Indeed, it is full of conflicts. We often enact systems with competing objectives. Moreover, we are unique human beings with unique ways of making sense of things, and the more we are able to be who we are, the more our differences come out. It is also messy. Stepping into a world of seeing how we continually create our own social realities means stepping beyond a world of bosses and teachers in control, people who set the goals and have the answers. But I am convinced that it is a legitimate path toward creating ways of living together with respect and dignity, and to living more in harmony with nature.

Three Ways of Thinking About the Future

There are three fundamentally distinct ways to think about the future. The easiest is extrapolation, to conceive of a future that is an extension of the present and recent past. The second is to imagine what might be independent of what is, or as free of influence from the present as one can become. The third is to cultivate awareness and reflectiveness, to become open to what is arising in the world and in us, and to continually ponder what matters most deeply to us.

The first is the easiest and by far the most common. It is also the most dangerous in a time of deep change. If indeed there are many aspects of our present ways of living that are not sustainable, such as the destruction of living systems upon which social systems depend, there are few things more certain about the future than that it will *not* arise as a mere extrapolation of the past.

The second I believe also holds hidden dangers. It is easy to engage in "reactive imagination," focusing on some facet of the present situation that we dislike and imagining a world that is very different from this. This "negative image" offers actually only a disguised version of the present. It can appear imaginative when in fact it is not. It can be an unintended projection of ego, motivated by fear.

"All great things are created for their own sake," wrote Robert Frost. In these simple words Frost expressed the timeless sensibility of the artist, who looks deeply within and without, who takes responsibility for her or his creation while simultaneously experiencing an overwhelming sense of humility as a mere agent for what is seeking to emerge. This is the fundamental distinction between machine-age planning and the creative process. The former seeks to manifest human intentions. The latter seeks to align human intentions and actions with the course of nature.

Paradoxically, in this aligning lies real freedom and choice. "The free man [*Mensch*] is the one who wills without arbitrary self-will," wrote Martin Buber. "He must sacrifice his puny, unfree will that is controlled by things and instincts for his grand will, which quits defined for destined being. Then, . . . He listens to what is emerging from himself, to the course of being in the world . . . in order to bring it to reality as it desires."[4]

This third way of thinking about the future is also a way of thinking about the present. In fact, the two are inseparable. We become agents of creating a future that is seeking to emerge by becoming more aware of the present. This third way requires deep thinking about not only what exists today but how it came to be this way. This third way replaces blind trust in human ingenuity with trust in life. Imagination, rather than becoming more limited, is actually freed and becomes the servant of awareness, which in turn requires continuous cultivation.

In this third way, human and nature become integrated spontaneously. We become nature's agent. There is no nature outside ourselves, nor ourselves outside of nature. In fact, the very word *nature,* pointing to something outside ourselves, becomes unnecessary, as it is for many indigenous people.

We would do well to heed the admonishment of noted quantum theorist David Bohm: "What folly to think that we can correct the fragmentation of the world via processes that recreate that fragmentation." This fragmentation starts when we see a world of corporations, institutions, and systems outside of and separate from ourselves. Ironically, only by recognizing that these are continually created by our daily acts of living will we start to see that they also are expressions of our current choices.

The domain of making more conscious collective choices is largely a mystery to us today. I do not know what will be needed to cultivate this capacity. I believe that it is the not the work of isolated individuals but of communities. I also think there is a guiding principle for the journey: we produce what we do not intend because we enact systems that we do not see. Learning to see is a life's work of reflection and action. Rudolf Steiner, echoing a sentiment of Goethe's, beautifully articulated the twofold nature of this work: "In searching for your self, look for it in the world; in searching for the world, look for it in your self."

Notes

1. Joy, B. "Why the Future Doesn't Need Us." *Wired,* Apr. 2000, pp. 238–262.

2. Meadows, D. "Whole Earth Models and Systems." *Co-Evolution Quarterly,* Summer 1982, pp. 98–108.

3. See Senge, P., and others. *The Fifth Discipline Fieldbook.* New York: Doubleday, 1994; Roth, G., and Kleiner, A. *Car Launch.* New York: Oxford University Press, 1999; Hotchkiss, M., and others. "The LAKES Story." *Reflections, the SoL Journal,* Summer 2000, *1*(4); and Senge, P., and others. *Schools That Learn.* New York: Doubleday, 2000 (a new Fifth Discipline education fieldbook). To learn more about SoL, see http://www.SoLonline.org.

4. Buber, M. *I and Thou* (R. G. Smith, trans.). New York: Scribner, 1958, p. 130.

Parker J. Palmer
Resources and Bibliography

BOOKS

Livsey, R. C., and Palmer, P. J. *The Courage to Teach: A Guide for Reflection and Renewal*. San Francisco: Jossey-Bass, 1999. (Translated into Chinese, Japanese, and Korean.)

Palmer, P. J. *A Hidden Wholeness: The Journey Toward an Undivided Life*. San Francisco: Jossey-Bass, 2004.

Palmer, P. J. *Let Your Life Speak: Listening for the Voice of Vocation*. San Francisco: Jossey-Bass, 2000. (Translated into Korean.)

Palmer, P. J. *The Courage to Teach: Exploring the Inner Landscape of a Teacher's Life*. San Francisco: Jossey-Bass, 1998.

Palmer, P. J. *Leader's Guide to the Active Life*. New York: HarperCollins, 1992.

Palmer, P. J. *The Active Life: A Spirituality of Work, Creativity, and Caring*. San Francisco: Harper San Francisco; San Francisco, 1990: Jossey-Bass, 1999. (Translated into Korean and Spanish.)

Palmer, P. J. *To Know as We Are Known: Education as a Spiritual Journey*. San Francisco: Harper San Francisco, 1983, 1993. (Translated into Korean and Portuguese.)

Palmer, P. J. *The Company of Strangers: Christians and the Renewal of America's Public Life*. New York: Crossroad, 1981.

Palmer, P. J. *The Promise of Paradox: A Celebration of Contradictions in the Christian Life*. Notre Dame, Ind.: Ave Maria, 1980; Washington, D.C.: Servant Leadership School, 1993.

Palmer, P. J., Wheeler, B., and Fowler, J. (eds.). *Caring for the Commonweal: Education for Religious and Public Life*. Macon, Ga.: Mercer University Press, 1990.

PAMPHLETS (SELECTED)

Palmer, P. J. "Seeking Vocation in Darkness and Light" and "Finding Life in the Company of Strangers" (The G. D. Davidson Lectures). Swannanoa, N.C.: Warren Wilson College, 1998.

Palmer, P. J. "Seasons." Kalamazoo, Mich.: The Fetzer Institute, 1996.

Palmer, P. J. "The Violence of Our Knowledge: Toward a Spirituality of Higher Education" (The Michael Keenan Memorial Lecture). Saskatoon: St. Thomas More College, 1993.

Palmer, P. J. "On Leadership and the Courage to Be Involved." West Long Branch, N.J.: Monmouth College, 1993.

Palmer, P. J. "Faith or Frenzy: Living Contemplation in a World of Action" (The Clampitt Lecture). Wilmette, Ill.: Trinity United Methodist Church, 1992.

Palmer, P. J. "Leading from Within." Indianapolis, Ind.: Indiana Office for Campus Ministries, 1990; Washington, D.C.: Servant Leadership School, 1993.

Palmer, P. J. "Ain't Gonna Study War No More: On Education, Peacemaking, and Having the Mind of Christ." Wallingford, Pa.: Pendle Hill, 1984.

Palmer, P. J. "Lectio Divina: Another Way to Learn." Wallingford, Pa.: Pendle Hill, 1981.

Palmer, P. J. "In the Belly of a Paradox: A Celebration of Contradictions in the Thought of Thomas Merton." Wallingford, Pa.: Pendle Hill, 1979.

Palmer, P. J. "And a Little Child Shall Lead Them." Wallingford, Pa.: Pendle Hill, 1978.

Palmer, P. J. "A Place Called Community." Wallingford, Pa.: Pendle Hill, 1977.

Palmer, P. J. "Meeting for Learning: Education in a Quaker Context." Wallingford, Pa.: Pendle Hill, 1976; Philadelphia: Friends Council on Education, 2000.

Palmer, P. J. "Escape and Engagement: Some Reflections on the Inward and Outward Life." Wallingford, Pa.: Pendle Hill, 1975.

MONOGRAPHS (SELECTED)

Palmer, P. J. *The Art and Craft of Formation*. Kalamazoo, Mich.: Fetzer Institute, 1994.

Palmer, P. J. *Reflections on a Program for the "Formation of Teachers."* Kalamazoo, Mich.: Fetzer Institute, 1992.

Palmer, P. J. *Scarcity, Abundance and the Gift of Community*. Chicago: Community Renewal Press, 1990.

Palmer, P. J. *Going Public*. Washington, D.C.: The Alban Institute, 1980.

Palmer, P. J., and Jacobson, E. *Action-Research: A New Style of Politics, Education and Ministry*. New York: National Council of Churches, Dept. of Higher Education, 1971.

Palmer, P. J., and Jacobson, E. *The Church, the University, and Urban Society: Focus on the Church*. New York: National Council of Churches, Dept. of Higher Education, 1971.

Palmer, P. J., and Jacobson, E. *The Church, the University, and Urban Society: Implications for the University*. New York: National Council of Churches, Dept. of Higher Education, 1971.

Palmer, P. J., and Jacobson, E. *The Church, the University, and Urban Society: A Problem in Power.* New York: National Council of Churches, Dept. of Higher Education, 1971.

Palmer, P. J., and Jacobson, E. *The Power of Development: Some Possibilities We See.* New York: National Council of Churches, Dept. of Higher Education, 1971.

Palmer, P. J., and Jacobson, E. *Urban Curricula and the Liberal Arts College.* New York: National Council of Churches, Dept. of Higher Education, 1971.

CHAPTERS IN BOOKS BY OTHER AUTHORS

Palmer, P. J. "There is a Season." In P. Loeb (ed.), *The Impossible Will Take a Little While.* New York: Basic Books, 2004.

Palmer, P. J. "Toward a Spirituality of Higher Education." In D. Henry and B. Agee (eds.), *Faithful Learning and the Christian Scholarly Vocation.* Grand Rapids, Mich.: William B. Eerdmans, 2003.

Palmer, P. J. "Meeting for Learning Revisited: Trailing Quaker Crumbs through the Wilderness of Higher Education." In M. Birkel (ed.), *The Inward Teacher.* Richmond, Ind.: Earlham College Press, 2002.

Palmer, P. J. "Foreword: Listening to Teachers" and "Afterword: What I Heard Them Say." In S. Intrator (ed.), *Stories of the Courage to Teach: Honoring the Teacher's Heart.* San Francisco: Jossey-Bass, 2002.

Palmer, P. J. "Foreword" and "Afterword: The Quest for Community in Higher Education." In W. McDonald (ed.), *Creating Campus Community.* San Francisco: Jossey-Bass, 2002.

Palmer, P. J. "Foreword." In C. Whitmire, *Plain Living: A Quaker Path to Simplicity.* Notre Dame, Ind.: Sorin, 2001.

Palmer, P. J. "A Vision of Education as Transformation." In V. Kazanjian and P. Laurence (eds.), *Education as Transformation.* New York: Peter Lang, 2000.

Palmer, P. J. "Foreword." In R. Kessler, *The Soul of Education.* Alexandria, Va.: Association for Supervision and Curriculum Development, 2000.

Palmer, P. J. "The Grace of Great Things: Reclaiming the Sacred in Knowing, Teaching and Learning." In S. Glazer (ed.), *The Heart of Learning: Spirituality in Education.* New York: Jeremy P. Tarcher/Putnam, 1999.

Palmer, P. J. "Foreword." In W. Timpson, *Metateaching and the Instructional Map.* Madison, Wis.: Atwood, 1999.

Palmer, P. J. "Foreword." In J. Elkes, *Dr. Elkhanan Elkes of the Kovno Ghetto: A Son's Holocaust Memoir.* Brewster, Mass.: Paraclete, 1999.

Palmer, P. J. "Foreword." In M. O'Reilley, *Radical Presence: Teaching as Contemplative Practice.* Portsmouth, N.H.: Boynton/Cook, 1998.

Palmer, P. J. "Leading from Within." In L. Spears (ed.), *Insights on Leadership*. New York: John Wiley & Sons, 1998.

Palmer, P. J. "Foreword." In D. Markova and A. Powell, *Learning Unlimited*. Berkeley, Calif.: Conari, 1998.

Palmer, P. J. "The Renewal of Community in Higher Education." In W. Campbell and K. Smith (eds.), *New Paradigms for College Teaching*. Edina, Minn.: Interaction Book Co., 1997.

Palmer, P. J. "Foreword." In A. Fraker and L. Spears (eds.), *Seeker and Servant: Reflections on Religious Leadership (The Private Writings of Robert K. Greenleaf)*. San Francisco: Jossey-Bass, 1996.

Palmer, P. J., "Foreword." In H. Johnson, *The Growing Edge*. Amherst, Mass.: Gemini, 1996.

Palmer, P. J. "The Clearness Committee: A Way of Discernment." In J. Mogabgab (ed.), *Communion, Community, Commonweal*. Nashville, Tenn.: The Upper Room, 1995.

Palmer, P. J. "Leading from Within." In J. Conger, *Spirit at Work*. San Francisco: Jossey-Bass, 1994.

Palmer, P. J. "The Nature and Nurture of Public Life." In B. Murchland (ed.), *Higher Education and the Practice of Democratic Politics*. Dayton, Ohio: The Kettering Foundation, 1991.

Palmer, P. J., "Foreword." In D. Kirby, *Ambitious Dreams*. Kansas City, Mo.: Sheed & Ward, 1990.

Palmer, P. J. "All the Way Down: A Spirituality of Public Life." In P. J. Palmer, B. Wheeler, and J. Fowler (eds.), *Caring for the Commonweal: Education for Religious and Public Life*. Macon, Ga.: Mercer University Press, 1990.

Palmer, P. J. "The Spiritual Life: Apocalypse Now." In T. Edwards, *Living with Apocalypse: Spiritual Resources for Social Compassion*. San Francisco: Harper San Francisco, 1984.

Palmer, P. J. "Dorothy and Douglas Steere: More Than the Sum of the Parts." In L. Kenworthy (ed.), *Living in the Light: Some Quaker Pioneers of the 20th Century*. Kennett Square, Pa.: Friends General Conference and Quaker Publications, 1984.

Palmer, P. J. "The Quest for Community in America." In V. Kussrow and R. Baepler (eds.), *Changing American Life Styles*. Valparaiso, Ind.: Valparaiso University, 1977.

Palmer, P. J. "A Typology of World Views." In K. Underwood (ed.), *The Church, the University, and Social Policy*, Vol. II. Middletown, Conn.: Wesleyan University Press, 1969.

Palmer, P. J., and Vander Ark, T. "Introduction." In S. Intrator and M. Scribner (eds.), *Teaching with Fire: Poetry That Sustains the Courage to Teach*. San Francisco: Jossey-Bass, 2003.

Palmer, P. J., Jackson, M., Jackson, R., and Sluyter, D. "The Courage to Teach: A Program for Teacher Renewal." In L. Lantieri (ed.), *Schools with Spirit.* Boston: Beacon, 2001.

PERIODICALS (SELECTED)

Palmer, P. J. "Finding Your Soul." *Spirituality and Health,* Oct. 2004, 7(5), 38–43.

Palmer, P. J. "Teaching with Heart and Soul." *Journal of Teacher Education,* Nov.–Dec. 2003, 54(5), 376–385.

Palmer, P. J. "Springing Toward the Heart of Healing." *Agora,* Spring 2003, 15(3), 71–72.

Palmer, P. J. "Contemplative by Catastrophe." *Spirituality and Health,* Spring 2002, 5(1), 48–51.

Palmer, P. J. "Now I Become Myself." *Yes! A Journal of Positive Futures,* Spring 2001, pp. 18–20.

Palmer, P. J. "Are You Listening to Your Life?" *O (The Oprah Magazine),* Jan. 2001, pp. 128–130.

Palmer, P. J. "Life on the Möbius Strip." *The InnerEdge,* Aug.–Sept. 2000, 3(4), 23–24.

Palmer, P. J. "Evoking the Spirit in Public Education." *Educational Leadership,* Dec.–Jan. 1998–99, 56(4), 6–11.

Palmer, P. J. "All the Way Down: Depression and the Spiritual Journey." *Weavings,* Sept.–Oct. 1998, XII(5), 31–41.

Palmer, P. J. "The Grace of Great Things: Reclaiming the Sacred in Knowing, Teaching and Learning." *The Sun,* September 1998, 273, 24–28.

Palmer, P. J. "Thirteen Ways of Looking at Community (With a Fourteenth Thrown in For Free)." *The InnerEdge,* Aug.–Sept. 1998, 1(3), 5–7.

Palmer, P. J. "The Heart of a Teacher: Identity and Integrity in Teaching." *Change,* Nov.–Dec. 1997, 29(6), 14–21.

Palmer, P. J. "Teaching & Learning in Community." *About Campus,* Nov.–Dec. 1997, 2(5), 4–13.

Palmer, P. J. "The Grace of Great Things: Reclaiming the Sacred in Knowing, Teaching and Learning." *Holistic Education Review,* Autumn 1997, 10(3), 8–16.

Palmer, P. J. "Spirituality in Education." *Shambala Sun,* Sept. 1997, 6(1), 50–52.

Palmer, P. J. "Community and Ways of Knowing." *Wingspread Journal,* Summer 1997, 19(3), 12–14.

Palmer, P. J. "Seeking a New Leadership—From Within." *The Witness,* May 1997, 80(5), 8–13.

Palmer, P. J. "The Hidden Wholeness: Paradox in Teaching and Learning." *The National Teaching and Learning Forum,* 1997, 6(5), 1–5.

Palmer, P. J. "On Minding Your Call—When No One is Calling." *Weavings,* May–June 1996, *XI*(3), 15–22.

Palmer, P. J. "Leading from Within." *Noetic Sciences Review,* Winter 1996, *40,* 32–37.

Palmer, P. J. "Contemplation Reconsidered: The Human Way In." *The Merton Annual,* 1995, *8,* 22–37.

Palmer, P. J. "The Violence of Our Knowledge: Toward a Spirituality of Higher Education." *Grail: An Ecumenical Journal,* Sept. 1995, *II*(3), 93–113.

Palmer, P. J. "The Loom of Teaching: A Letter from Parker Palmer." *The National Teaching and Learning Forum,* 1994, *3*(3), 1–3.

Palmer, P. J. "Good Talk About Good Teaching: Improving Teaching Through Conversation and Community." *Change,* Nov.–Dec. 1993, *25*(6), 8–13.

Palmer, P. J. "The Violence of Our Knowledge: Toward a Spirituality of Higher Education (The Hester Lecture, Part II)." *The Southern Baptist Educator,* Sept. 1993, pp. 3–10.

Palmer, P. J. "The Violence of Our Knowledge: Toward a Spirituality of Higher Education (The Hester Lecture, Part I)." *The Southern Baptist Educator,* Aug. 1993, pp. 7–13.

Palmer, P. J. "Divided No More: A Movement Approach to Educational Reform." *Change,* Mar.–Apr. 1992, *24*(2), 10–17.

Palmer, P. J. "The Stations of the Cross: A Meditation." *Weavings,* Mar.–Apr. 1991, *VI*(2), 15–25.

Palmer, P. J. "The Courage to Teach." *The National Teaching and Learning Forum,* 1991, *1*(2), 1–3.

Palmer, P. J. "Good Teaching: A Matter of Living the Mystery." *Change,* Jan.–Feb. 1990, *22*(1), pp. 10–16.

Palmer, P. J. "Called to the Academic Life." *Plumbline: A Journal of Ministry in Higher Education,* Oct. 1989, *17*(3), 8–15.

Palmer, P. J. " 'Learning Is the Thing for You': Renewing the Vitality of Religious Education." *Weavings,* Sept.–Oct. 1989, *IV*(5), 6–19.

Palmer, P. J. "The Way We Know and the Way We Live." *Noetic Sciences Review,* Spring 1989, *10,* 16.

Palmer, P. J. "All the Way Down: A Spirituality of Public Life: Part II." *Action Information* (The Alban Institute), 1989, *XVI*(1), 6–11.

Palmer, P. J. "All the Way Down: A Spirituality of Public Life: Part I." *Action Information* (The Alban Institute), 1989, *XV*(6), 1–6.

Palmer, P. J. "The Clearness Committee: A Way of Discernment." *Weavings,* July–Aug. 1988, *III*(4), 37–40.

Palmer, P. J. "Community, Conflict and Ways of Knowing: Ways to Deepen Our Educational Agenda." *Change,* Sept.–Oct. 1987, *19*(5), 20–25.

Palmer, P. J. "Borne Again: The Monastic Way to Church Renewal." *Weavings,* Sept.–Oct. 1986, *1,* 12–21.

Palmer, P. J. "A Place Called Community." *Christian Living,* July 1984, *31*(7), 1–9, 20–26.

Palmer, P. J. "Comments on 'Spiritual Life in a Secular Age.'" *The NICM Journal* (National Institute for Campus Ministries), Summer 1982, 7(3).

Palmer, P. J. "Truth is Personal: A Deeply Christian Education." *The Christian Century,* Oct. 1981, *XCVIII*(33), 1051–1054.

Palmer, P. J. "New Teaching for a New Age." *Warm Wind,* Spring 1981, *5,* 17–21.

Palmer, P. J. "Tribute to an Unreasonable Man." *NICM Journal* (National Institute for Campus Ministries), Winter 1981, 6(1), 91–97.

Palmer, P. J. "Quakers and the Way of the Cross." *Friends Journal,* July 1980, 26(11), 3–8.

Palmer, P. J. "The Conversion of Knowledge." *Religious Education,* Nov.–Dec. 1979, 74(6), 629–640.

Palmer, P. J. "Community: The Gift and the Disciplines." *NICM Journal* (National Institute for Campus Ministries), Summer 1978, *3*(3), 42–49.

Palmer, P. J. "How We Teach Is More Important Than What We Teach." *Religion Teacher's Journal,* Apr. 1977, *11*(3), 42–44.

Palmer, P. J. "Pastoral and Political Community: A Ministry to Higher Education." *NICM Journal* (National Institute for Campus Ministries), Winter 1977, 2(1), 59–72.

Palmer, P. J. "Turnings: Some Notes on Conversion." *NICM Journal* (National Institute for Campus Ministries), Summer 1976, *1*(3), 16–28.

Palmer, P. J. "Challenge to Objectivity from the Prophets of Advocacy." Liberal Education, May 1972, *LVIII*(2), 150–156.

Palmer, P. J. "Objectivism and Pragmatism in Religion, Science, and Society." *The Christian Scholar,* Spring 1966, *XLIX*(1), 17–23.

Palmer, P. J., and Jacobson, E. "The Institution and the City." *Liberal Education,* Mar. 1970, *LVI*(1), 97–105.

Palmer, P. J., and Palmer, S. "Paradoxes of Community." *Friends Journal,* April 1976, 22(8), 230–232.

Palmer, P. J., and Palmer, S. "Paradoxes of Community." *NICM Journal* (National Institute for Campus Ministries), Winter 1976, *1*(1), pp. 62–69.

INTERVIEWS IN PRINT

Breeze, A. "Spirituality and Leadership: A Conversation with Parker Palmer." *Concepts & Connections: Newsletter of the National Clearinghouse for Leadership Programs,* 1996, *4*(3), 1–4.

Brummel, M. "Getting Out Would Do Your Faith a World of Good: The Editors' Interview Parker Palmer." *U.S. Catholic,* February 1991, *56*(2), 6–13.

Claxton, C. "Teaching, Learning and Community: An Interview with Parker J. Palmer." *Journal of Developmental Education,* Winter 1991, *15*(2), 22–25, 33.

Dougherty, K. "Seeking Creative Solitude and Community: An Interview with Parker Palmer." *The Active Learner: A Foxfire Journal for Teachers,* Fall 1998, *3*(3), 28–31.

Hatton, S. "The Teacher as Moral and Philosophical Guide: An Interview with Parker Palmer." *Teaching By Heart: The Foxfire Interviews.* New York: Teachers College Press, 2004.

Newby, J. "The Power of Healthy Community: An Interview with Parker J. Palmer." *Quaker Life,* Sept. 1993, *XXXIV*(7), 5–7.

Powell, W. "On Creating a Space: An Interview with Parker Palmer." *Families in Society,* Jan.–Feb. 2001, *82*(1), 13–22.

Rittenhouse, L. J. "Leadership and the Inner Journey: An Interview with Parker Palmer." *Leader to Leader,* Fall 2001, *22*, 26–33.

Rittenhouse, L. J. "Leading from the Heart: An Interview with Parker Palmer." *Executive Talent,* Spring 2001, *2*(1), 82–88.

Scott, M. A. "Parker Palmer on Active Living." *The Symposium,* Aug. 2001, *IV*(1), 11–13.

Seymour, Mike. "Authentic Living and Teaching: Rejoining Soul and Role (An Interview with Parker J. Palmer)" and "Making Space for the Mystery: Reawakening Life and Spirit in Teaching and Learning (An Interview with Parker J. Palmer)." *Educating for Humanity: Rethinking the Purposes of Education.* Boulder, Colo.: Paradigm, 2004.

Sparks, D. "Honor the Human Heart: An Interview with Parker Palmer." *Journal of the National Staff Development Council,* Summer 2003, *24*(3), 49–53.

van Gelder, S. "Integral Life, Integral Teacher." *Yes! A Journal of Positive Futures,* Winter 1998–1999, pp. 44–47.

Wall, J. "Action and Insight: An Interview with Parker Palmer." *The Christian Century,* Mar. 1995, *112*(10), 326–329.

Webb, B. "Spiritual Formation and Social Change: An Interview with Parker Palmer." *Fugitive Faith.* Maryknoll, N.Y.: Orbis Books, 1998.

Weithe, G. "The Courage to Teach: Rejoining Soul and Role." *Wisconsin Academy Review,* Winter 2003, *49*(1), 21–24.

AUDIOVISUAL MEDIA FEATURING PARKER J. PALMER (SELECTED)

Courage to Teach: An Interview with Parker Palmer [DVD Recording]. Bainbridge Island, Wash.: Center for Teacher Formation, 2004.

Courage to Teach: Journeys of the Heart [Video Recording]. New York: Carousel Film and Video, 2000.

An Interview with Parker Palmer [Cassette Recording]. San Francisco: New Dimensions Foundation, 1996.

The Learning Curve: Teacher Development and Training [Video Recording]. Seattle: KCTS Public Television, Sept. 2002.

Mentor's Gallery: An Interview with Parker Palmer [DVD Recording]. Spokane, Wash.: Gonzaga University, School of Professional Studies, 2004.

A Movement Model of Social Change [DVD Recording]. Boston: Institute for Healthcare Improvement, 1998.

Teaching from the Heart: Seasons of Renewal in a Teacher's Life [Video Recording]. San Francisco: Jossey-Bass, 1999.

PUBLISHED POEMS

Palmer, P. J. "The Monastery Cows." *Weavings,* Nov.–Dec. 1994, *IX*(6), 32.

Palmer, P. J. "Promised Land." *Weavings,* Sept.–Oct. 1992, *VII*(5), 26.

Palmer, P. J. "Grand Canyon." *Weavings,* Nov.–Dec. 1989, *IV*(6), 42.

Palmer, P. J. "The Winter Woods." *Friends Journal,* Jan. 1982, 28(1), 7.

Palmer, P. J. "Writing." *Friends Journal,* Nov. 1980, 26(16), 8.

Palmer, P. J. "Dictionary." *Friends Journal,* Nov. 1980, 26(16), 9.

Palmer, P. J. "Two Toasts." *Friends Journal,* Nov. 1980, 26(16), 9.

Palmer, P. J. "The World Once Green Again." *Friends Journal,* Nov. 1980, 26(16), 9.

Palmer, P. J. "The View from Findhorn." *Warm Wind,* Spring 1980, *II*(2), 20–21.

THE EDITOR

SAM M. INTRATOR is an assistant professor of education and child study at Smith College. He received his Ph.D. from Stanford University and an M.A. in English literature from the Bread Loaf School of English at Middlebury College. A former high school teacher and administrator, his books and research inquire into what it takes for teachers and students to cocreate intellectually vibrant and genuinely meaningful experiences in the classroom. Intrator has received a number of awards for his teaching and public service including a Kellogg Fellowship and the Distinguished Teacher Award from the White House Commission of Presidential Scholars.

Intrator teaches courses on urban education, teenagers in American culture, and the teaching of writing. He also founded and codirects the Smith College Urban Education Initiative, an educational outreach program that seeks to deepen students' understanding of the theoretical, practical, and human issues facing urban educators by engaging students in intensive service learning experience in urban school settings.

He is the author of *Tuned In and Fired Up: How Teaching Can Inspire Genuine Learning in the Classroom,* which in 2004 was a finalist for the $200,000 Grawemeyer Award in Education (Yale University Press); the editor of *Stories of the Courage to Teach: Honoring the Teacher's Heart* (Jossey-Bass); and the coeditor of *Teaching with Fire: Poetry That Sustains the Courage to Teach* (Jossey-Bass), which was a finalist for the 2004 Distinguished Achievement Award by the Association of Educational Publishers.

He lives in Florence, Massachusetts, with his wife, Jo-Anne, and his three children: Jake, Kaleigh, and Casey.

The Contributors

IAN G. BARBOUR holds graduate degrees in both physics and theology. He is professor emeritus of science, technology, and society at Carleton College and winner of the 1999 Templeton Prize for Progress in Religion. Among the books he has written are *Ethics in an Age of Technology, Religion and Science: Historical and Contemporary Issues,* and *When Science Meets Religion.*

PAUL BATALDEN, M.D., is a graduate of Augsburg College, University of Minnesota Medical School, and the University of Minnesota pediatric residency program. He currently teaches in the Center for the Evaluative Clinical Sciences at Dartmouth Medical School, directs a combined graduate medical education program in leadership, leads the health professional development efforts of the Institute for Healthcare Improvement, and works with the Accreditation Council for Graduate Medical Education.

THOMAS F. BEECH is president and CEO of the Fetzer Institute whose mission is "to foster awareness of the power of love and forgiveness in the emerging global community." Previously he served as executive vice president of the Burnett Foundation in Fort Worth, Texas, and as executive director of the Minneapolis Foundation. He has served on the boards of the Council on Foundations and Independent Sector.

JAY CASBON is the CEO of the Oregon State University-Cascades University campus and a professor of education. He is the board chair of the National Center for Teacher Formation, a senior adviser for the Oregon Small School Initiative, and an adviser to Oregon's Chalkboard Project, a project funded by five Oregon foundations that have dedicated resources to improving Oregon's public schools through statewide dialogue and discussion.

DAVID DODSON is president of MDC, Inc., a nonprofit organization based in Chapel Hill, North Carolina, that seeks to Make a Difference in Communities by expanding opportunity, reducing poverty, and promoting inclusive leadership.

343

JOEL ELKES, M.D., is senior scholar in residence at the Fetzer Institute, distinguished service professor emeritus at Johns Hopkins University, distinguished university professor emeritus at the University of Louisville, a founder of the science of psychopharmacology, and author of *Dr. Elkhanan Elkes of the Kovno Ghetto: A Son's Holocaust Memoir.*

HENRY EMMONS, M.D., has a holistic psychiatric practice in the Twin Cities of Minnesota, and serves as a consultant to many colleges and other organizations. Inspired by Parker's work, he started the Inner Life of Healers program at the University of Minnesota's Center for Spirituality and Healing, which has reached out to hundreds of health practitioners who wish to renew their spirit and sustain their vocation.

JEAN FERACA is Wisconsin Public Radio's distinguished senior broadcaster, host and executive producer of the international cultural affairs call-in program "Here on Earth," and a poet whose published collections include *South from Rome* and *Crossing the Great Divide,* both nominated for Pushcart Prizes, and *Rendered into Paradise.*

SALLY Z. HARE has taught in public schools for more than thirty years and taught preservice and in-service teachers in undergraduate and graduate education. She currently holds the Singleton Endowed Professorship in Teacher Education at Coastal Carolina University in Myrtle Beach, South Carolina, and is director of the Center for Education and Community. She is a senior adviser to the Center for Teacher Formation and facilitates Courage to Teach programs across the country.

MARIANNE NOVAK HOUSTON is a retired middle-school teacher who is a leader in the Courage to Teach retreat program. She lives in Kalamazoo, Michigan, and from that base facilitates Courage to Teach retreats across the United States and abroad. Among the many honors she received for her work in classrooms at all levels was the National Educator Award from the Milken Foundation in 1994.

MARCY JACKSON codirects the Center for Teacher Formation and is a formation facilitator in Washington State. She has been facilitating Courage to Teach retreat programs for teachers and educational leaders since 1996. For the past twenty-five years, she has worked extensively with individuals, groups, and families as a child and family therapist. She has led retreats in a variety of settings: hospitals and health care, educational and retreat centers, community mental health, and tribal communities.

RICK JACKSON codirects the Center for Teacher Formation, established to develop Courage to Teach programs and deepen and expand the work of formation. He cofacilitates Courage to Teach programs as well as formation retreats in philanthropy and other nonprofit settings. He also teaches and consults to nonprofits, schools, and foundations on the role of youth in culture, ethics, leadership, and community development. He was an executive with the YMCA for more than twenty-five years.

DAVID C. LEACH, M.D., is an endocrinologist and teacher who is the executive director of the Accreditation Council for Graduate Medical Education. Dr. Leach was awarded the "Good Samaritan Award" by Governor John Engler for twenty-five years of work at a free clinic in Detroit. He lives in Chicago with his wife, Jackie, and enjoys walking to work.

MICHAEL LERNER is president and cofounder of Commonweal, a health and environmental research institute; the Smith Farm Center for the Healing Arts; the Jenifer Altman Foundation; and the Barbara Smith Fund. He is the author of *Choices in Healing: Integrating the Best of Conventional and Complementary Approaches to Cancer.* He was awarded a MacArthur Prize Fellowship for contributions to public health in 1983.

DAVID J. MAITLAND is chaplain and professor of religion emeritus at Carleton College, and the author of *Aging as Counterculture: A Vocation for the Later Years* and *Against the Grain: One Man Remembers.*

DAWNA MARKOVA is currently a codirector of SmartWired.Org, a foundation that exists to create an asset-focused global evolution centered on fostering the capacity of young people. She is the author of *I Will Not Die an Unlived Life: Reclaiming Purpose and Passion; The Open Mind; The Smartwired Revolution: Positive Parenting That Makes a Difference;* and *How Your Child Is Smart;* and is the coeditor of *Random Acts of Kindness* and *Kids' Random Acts of Kindness.*

RUSS S. MOXLEY is local coordinator for Courage to Teach in North Carolina, an independent trainer and consultant who focuses on executive coaching and leadership development workshops, and the director of the Center for Leadership and Ethics at Greensboro College. Previously, he was a senior fellow at the Center for Creative Leadership. He is the author of *Leadership and Spirit* and coeditor and contributing author of the *Center for Creative Leadership Handbook on Leadership Development.*

MARK NEPO is a poet and philosopher who has taught in the fields of poetry and spirituality for thirty years. He has written several books, including *The Book of Awakening, Acre of Light,* and his most recent books of poetry, *Suite for the Living* and *Inhabiting Wonder,* both available from Bread for the Journey. Mark serves as a program officer and poet-in-residence for the Fetzer Institute in Kalamazoo, Michigan.

MARY ROSE O'REILLEY is professor of English at the University of St. Thomas in St. Paul, Minnesota, a poet, and author of *The Peaceable Classroom; Radical Presence: Teaching as a Contemplative Practice;* and *The Barn at the End of the World: The Apprenticeship of a Quaker, Buddhist Shepherd.*

DOUGLAS ORR is president of Warren Wilson College, having served as vice-chancellor for development and public service and professor of geography at the University of North Carolina–Charlotte. His books include *Land of the South* and the *North Carolina Atlas: Portrait for a New Century.*

SHARON DALOZ PARKS is an associate director of the Whidbey Institute and director of Leadership for the New Commons. Formerly she held faculty and research positions at Harvard University in the divinity and business schools and the Kennedy School of Government. She is author of *Big Questions, Worthy Dreams: Mentoring Young Adults in Their Search for Meaning, Purpose, and Faith* and coauthor of *Common Fire: Leading Lives of Commitment in a Complex World.*

L. J. RITTENHOUSE is president of andBEYOND Communications, a New York-based investor relations firm that advises executives on the financial impact of candid communication. Her holistic model of business success shows that honest, balanced, and comprehensive disclosure is linked to superior financial performance. An investment banker and corporate finance specialist, Rittenhouse is the author of *Do Business with People You Can Trust.* She is a founding member of Families with Children from China.

ZALMAN M. SCHACHTER-SHALOMI is professor of religious studies at Naropa University, where he held Naropa's World Wisdom Chair. He serves as the Rabbinic Chair of Aleph: Alliance for Jewish Renewal and is the founder and president of the Spiritual Eldering Institute. Zalman was born in Poland in 1924. When the Nazis threatened Europe, his family journeyed to New York. He is the author of many books, including

Spiritual Intimacy and *From Age-ing to Sage-ing*. His forthcoming book is *Hello God, It's Me: A Guide to Meaningful Jewish Practice*.

PETER M. SENGE is a senior lecturer at the Massachusetts Institute of Technology and founding chair of the SoL (the Society for Organizational Learning) Council. He is the author *of The Fifth Discipline: The Art and Practice of the Learning Organization* and *Presence: Human Purpose and the Field of the Future*. He lectures throughout the world about decentralizing the role of leadership in organizations to enhance the capacity of all people to work toward healthier human systems.

SHIRLEY H. SHOWALTER was president of Goshen College when she wrote this essay. She joined the Fetzer Institute as vice president of programs in November 2004. She has published many essays on higher education, spirituality, and the intersection of the two. In 1999 she was awarded the John S. and James L. Knight Foundation Presidential Leadership Award.

BARDWELL SMITH taught at Carleton College from 1960 to 1995 in religion and Asian studies with a special research interest in Buddhism and the social order in Sri Lanka and Japan. He served as dean of the college at Carleton and helped to establish consortial undergraduate overseas programs: Associated Kyoto Program; Associated Colleges of the Midwest Program in Indian Studies in Pune, India; and the Intercollegiate Sri Lanka Education (ISLE) program.

W. DOUGLAS TANNER JR. is cofounder and president of the Faith and Politics Institute, an interfaith organization in Washington, D.C. An ordained United Methodist minister and a former campaign manager and congressional aide, he works with members of Congress, their staffs, and others closely connected to Capitol Hill.

JANE TOMPKINS is a teacher, author, lecturer, workshop leader, and administrator who brings a holistic perspective to issues of teaching and learning. She has been a leader in curricular reform and innovative pedagogy in literature and is currently a professor of English and education at the University of Illinois at Chicago. She has recently begun to create lounge and café spaces and renovate classrooms as a way of making the university a friendlier environment for commuter students.

DIANA CHAPMAN WALSH is president of Wellesley College, and previously a professor at the Harvard School of Public Health and chair of Harvard's

Department of Health and Social Behavior. She has written, edited, and coedited many articles and books, among them *Corporate Physicians: Between Medicine and Management.*

MARGARET J. WHEATLEY is president of the Berkana Institute and author of *Leadership and the New Science; A Simpler Way; Turning to One Another: Simple Conversations to Restore Hope to the Future;* and most recently, *Finding Our Way: Leadership for an Uncertain Time.*

ROBERT "CHIP" WOOD is currently the principal of Sheffield Elementary School, Turners Falls, Massachusetts. He has been a teacher of children and teachers for more than thirty years. He is author of *Yardsticks: Children in the Classroom, Ages 4–14; Time to Teach, Time to Learn: Changing the Pace of School,* and other works. He is a cocreator of the Responsive Classroom approach to education, a Courage to Teach facilitator, and a cofounder of the Northeast Foundation for Children.